TO "TURTLE" MARSHA
FLAKE UHL, THE
DAUGHTER OF THE
MARINE I ADMIRED
THE MOST B GEN BILL
FLAKE MARINE RAIDER
HERO.

Jim (Doc) Gleason
SEMPER FIDELIS

REAL BLOOD!
REAL GUTS!

REAL BLOOD!
REAL GUTS!

U.S. MARINE RAIDERS
AND THEIR
CORPSMEN
IN WORLD WAR II

BY

JAMES GLEASON
RAIDER CORPSMAN

JOHN McCARTHY
CONSULTING EDITOR

Raider Publishing First Edition May 2003

10 9 8 7 6 5 4 3 2 1 0

Library of Congress Control Number: 2003092054

        Gleason, James
Real Blood! Real Guts! : U.S. Marine Raiders And Their
Corpsmen In W W II / James Gleason
     ISBN 0-9740496-0-3
1 World War II 1939-45 - United States.
2 World War II 1939-45 - Japan - Campaigns - Pacific Area
3 United States History - 1939-1945
4 U.S. Marines - Marines - Marine Raiders - Campaigns

Photographs Courtesy of
     U.S. Marine Corps
     U.S. Navy
     Frank Cannistraci

DEDICATION

IN MEMORY OF OUR FALLEN RAIDER COMRADES
WHO GAVE THEIR LIVES IN THE FAR OFF ISLANDS
OF THE PACIFIC SO THAT OTHERS MIGHT LIVE, IN
HONOR OF THOSE RAIDERS WHO HAVE SINCE
LEFT US, AND IN TRIBUTE FOR ALL RAIDERS STILL
LIVING.

THE BONDS FORGED IN COMBAT MADE US
COMRADES AND FRIENDS FOR LIFE,
ONES WHO WATCHED OVER EACH OTHER
BOTH THEN AND NOW

AS WE TRAVEL DOWN THAT LONG ROAD
TOWARD THE INEVITABLE,
WE ARE ASSURED THAT IN THE NOT TOO
DISTANT FUTURE

ALL RAIDERS AND THEIR LOVED ONES WILL
COME TOGETHER IN BROTHERLY LOVE,
TO ONCE AGAIN MARCH ARM IN ARM FOR...
ALL ETERNITY.

JAMES D. GLEASON
U.S. MARINE RAIDER CORPSMAN

In memory of my adoptive parents Minnie and Lyman Gleason, may they rest in peace!

To my wife Nancy, for her love, patience and encouragement these many years.

For my daughters Barbara, Connie, and Marsha; their husbands, Roman, Tim, and Stan, grandchildren Joe, Donn Lee, Crystal, Amber, Jennifer, Michelle and Her husband Jerry, and my great grandson Jeremiah III.

Never forget the men who gave their lives so that this great country might remain free!

This book could not have been written without the dedication of the U.S. Marine Raider Association, official historian Major J.C, Beau and his deceased wife, Grace. His book, THOSE WHO SERVED, is the primary source for those researching the history of the Marine Raiders.

For his tireless efforts to record the history of the 1st Marine Raider Regiment, Major Beau in April 2002, was the recipient of the Marine Heritage Foundation's, General Oliver P. Smith Award and the Commandant of the Marine Corps, General James L. Jones Gold Medallion Award, both were presented to him by the Commandant.

Raiders have spent countless hours in gathering vital information to assure the Raider legacy lives on. Raider Lowell Bulger literally held the Association together for many years. My thanks to Raider Photographer Frank Cannistraci, Stormy Sexton, Archie Rackerby; Frank Guidone, Rudy Rosenquist, John Dragon, Ed Frederick at Kinko's, Jerry Courtier, Bobby Walden of the V.A., and others too numerous to mention, for their help over the years.

I express my gratitude to the present and past Editors of the Raider Association's, Raider Patch magazine that has been in circulation for over 40 years. Raiders have written hundreds of letters telling of their war time experiences to both the Patch and myself. Those letters, along with oral discussions, and Marine Corps and Medical Corps historical material are the basis for this book.

To Consulting Editor John McCarthy; Your advice and guidance is much appreciated.

To Nancy Kilgore, daughter of Raider Charles Kilgore and wife Barbara, who spent countless hours in proof reading and correcting my drafts; I am indebted to you.

To Pat Almond and his wife Gloria; thank you for your encouragement and support.

I wish also to pay tribute to those that fought alongside the Raiders or gave us support. Our fellow Marines, Corpsmen, Doctors, Dentists, and Chaplains of other Marine units, Army, Army Medics, Air Force, our loyal Solomon Island Natives, in particular Sgt Maj Jacob Vouza. The Navy sailors of the APD 4 stack Destroyers, who were with us from start to finish. The submariners of the USS Argonaut and USS Nautilus, our Marine Navajo Indian Code Talkers and War Dog Platoon, UDT's, the men of the close combat support Air Squadrons, Navy Ships, Navy and Coast Guard Amphtracks & Higgins boat coxswains, all our Seabee " Pops and Grand Pa's", the brave Coast Watcher's. Australian, New Zealand, Fiji and Samoan Native troops, all Marine units, artillery, tanks and others who followed us along the same tortuous jungle trails.

And a very deserved special recognition to our never to be forgotten friends, the men and women of the Central Identification Laboratory, Hawaii, who brought back to their homeland 19 of our Makin Island Raiders in 1999. CILHI earned our respect and gratitude and will always remain a part of our Raider family.

It took the combined power of the Army, Air Force, Coast Guard, Marine Corps and the Navy, not only of the United States, but also of all our Allies, to assure victory in World War II.
To all Raider Widows and families..."You remain special in our love for you, in honor of your departed loved ones."

WE SALUTE YOU ONE AND ALL!
SEMPER FIDELIS AND GUNG HO!

FOREWORD

"I am looking forward to your book about Corpsmen. Fleet Marine Force (FMF) Corpsmen have established a unique brotherhood with Marines, a relationship bonded in blood. FMF Corpsmen were the most highly decorated sailors in the Navy.
GENERAL AL GRAY 29th Commandant of the U.S. Marine Corps

"Good luck with your book about Corpsmen Jim. Raider Corpsmen and Doctors were always at the ready whenever called upon to aid their Marine comrades. Whether we were suffering from an illness or wounded by enemy fire, they always responded immediately. While constantly facing death on the battlefield they proved themselves to be worthy of the title Marine Raiders."
BRIG GEN JAMES ROOSEVELT, C0 4th Marine Raider Battalion
Son of President Franklin D. Roosevelt.

"I'm happy to see a book written about Raider Corpsmen! When I was wounded on Vangunu I was totally in the hands of my Corpsmen. They stood by me when they could have easily dropped me and left while under fire."
BRIG GEN WILLIAM FLAKE, CO 4th Raider Battalion D,Q Company.

"God Bless the Corpsmen, without them neither myself nor thousands of other Marines, would be walking the Earth today. They are the finest thing that ever happened to the Marine Corps."
COL MARTIN J. (STORMY) SEXTON 3K, Legendary Marine Raider

AUTHOR'S NOTE

REAL BLOOD! REAL GUTS! The U.S. Marine Raiders and their CORPSMEN OF WW II, is written with the Raider and his family in mind. I have attempted to include all battles in which Raiders and former Raiders fought, the Medals each Raider received, and a roster of those killed in action during each battle.

Corpsman, Doctor and Chaplain rosters are included for each Battalion and the H&S Company.

Unlike books written by historical 'revisionist' authors, the stories and facts herein are largely those written or related verbally over the years, by the men who actually participated in the many Raider battles of WW II. Many were recorded shortly after the war, when memories were still sharp and clear. No effort has been taken to make them politically correct.

I am not a writer by profession however; it is my hope that in some small way, my book will add to the legacy and memory of the Marine Raiders, and their attached Raider Navy Personnel about whom very little has been written.

I am very proud to be able to say. "I was a Marine Raider," as were all Marine Raiders and Marine Raider Corpsmen, Doctors and Chaplains,

Without the bravery of all Raiders there would be no story to tell.

"Thank all of you for your friendship over these many, many years!"

James Gleason
Tampa, Florida
May, 2003

CONTENTS

*Rosters for Corpsmen, Chaplains, Doctors, and
Dentists include Name, Battalion/Company, Rate/
Rank, Date, Where KIA or WIA, and Citations

THE U.S. MARINE RAIDER
BULLETIN

Volume 1   Hollywood, California   April 15, 1953   Number 1

MEET SET FOR VISALIA

These Raiders Recently Reveled in Roast at The Nikabob in Hollywood

The First "Raider Patch"

UNITED STATES MARINE RAIDERS ASS'N.   October 1956

REUNION ISSUE

WASHINGTON REUNION

We will depart from our regular "Patch" this issue and bring you a resume of the Washington Reunion. (Editor)

Friday, 24 August.

Registration of the members and wives at the Congressional Hotel. (See figure 1) Right from the start this had all the ear marks of a bang-up time.

Sunset Parade

Friday evening the group meet at the Marine Barracks for the very impressive Sunset Parade, (see figures 2 and 3), which brought a lump to our throats once again and our minds slipped

back into the years gone-by when we stood the same ceremony when the Raider Battalions were active. To see the new Marine Corps executing the very precise Marching Manual of Arms was reassuring to these old Marines that the Esprit de Corps forever will live on.

The association cannot find words enough to express its appreciation to the Marine Corps for making this reunion the most memorable in our history.

Following the Sunset Parade the members returned to the Presidental Room of the Congressional Hotel for a reception and cocktail party. (See figures 4 and 5) During the party old acquaintances were renewed and a

REGISTRATION CONGRESSIONAL HOTEL (Figure - 1)

The First Color "Raider Patch"

1ST MARINE RAIDER REGIMENT
1ST MARINE RAIDER BATTALION DOCTORS

NAME	BN/CO	RANK	YR	BATTLE	MEDAL
CABELL, CHARLES	1HQ	LT	44	Guam	Bronze Star
CHRISTENSON,C.H.	1HQ	LT	44	Guam	Bronze Star
KLEIN, HAROLD T.	1HQ	LT			
KNOX, STUART C.	1HQ	LtCdr	43	New Georgia	Silver Star
McLARNEY,EDWARD	1HQ	LtCdr	42	Guadalcanal	Navy Cross
			42	Guadalcanal WIA	
McLENNAN,PHILLIP	1HQ	LtCdr			
MILES, SAMUEL S.	1HQ	LTJG	42	Tulagi KIA	Silver Star
REGAN, JAMES F.	1HQ	LT	43	Enogai	Silver Star
SKINNER,R, W.III	1HQ	LT	42	Guadalcanal WIA	Navy Cross

1ST MARINE RAIDER BATTALION CORPSMEN

NAME	BN/CO	RANK	YR	BATTLE	MEDAL
ALDRICH, LEWIS JR.	1D	PHM2			
ARNETT, FRANK H.	1HQ	PHM3			
BANNON, RUSSELL	1HQ	PHM3			
BECKLEY, CLIFFORD	1HQ	PHM3			
BEEBE, CLEVELAND	1HQ	HA2	44	Guam WIA	
BLACKBURN,ROBERT	1HQ	PHM3			
BLACKWELL,STERLING	1HQ	PHM2			
BOONE, GEORGE A.	1HQ	PHM2			
BOREN, JAMES E.	1B	PHM3			
BOSWORTH, PERRY	1C	PHM3			
BOUCHER, RALPH J.	1HQ	PHM3			
BREESE, WILLIAM W.	1HQ	PHM3			
BROWN, CLAUDE K.	1C	PHM2			
BROWN, JAY A.	1HQ	PHM2	42	Guadalcanal WIA	Silver Star
BROWN, RICHARD L.	1HQ	HA1	43	Bairoko WIA	Silver Star
BROWN, ROBERT J.	1HQ	PHM3			
BURCH, E.J.	1D	PHM3			
CARR, JOHN H.	1HQ	PHM2	43	Bairoko WIA	
CHRISTMAN, L. M.	1HQ	PHM2	44	Guam WIA	
CLEVELAND,ALFRED	1HQ	PHM3	42	Guadalcanal	Silver Star
CLIFFORD, FRED W.	1HQ	PHM3			
CLUBB, ROBERT W.	1B	PHM3	43	Enogai	Silver Star
COE, ROBERT E.	1HQ	HA2	44	Guam WIA	
COLEMAN, CHARLES	1B	PHM2			
COLEMAN, KARL B.	1HQ	PHM2	42	Guadalcanal	Navy Cross
CORBETT, JAMES J.	1DC	PHM3	43	Enogai KIA	Silver Star
CORUM, JOHN W.	1A	PHM3			
CROSS, STERLING	1D	PHM1			
CRUZ, JOE G.	1HQ	PHM3	43	Bairoko WIA	
DROZ, RUSSELL S.	1HQ	PHM1			
DUKETT, MARSHALL	1HQ	PHM1			

NAME	BN/CO	RANK	YR	BATTLE	MEDAL
EILERS, DELBERT D.	1HQ	PHM2	42	Guadalcanal	Navy Cross
			42	Guadalcanal	Silver Star
ELLER, BYRON H.	1C	PHM2	43	Enogai	Silver Star
FAIRCHILD, JOHN R.	1HQ	HA1			
FECHTER, JOHN W.	1HQ	CPHM	42	Guadalcanal	Silver Star
FRANKLIN, V. V. JR.	1HQ	CPHM			
FREEMAN, JOHN	1HQ	PHM2	44	Guam WIA	
GALLAGHER, JOHN	1HQ	PHM1	42	Tulagi	Bronze Star
			42	Guadalcanal WIA	
GORDON, FINLEY A.	1HQ	HA1	44	New Britain KIA	Navy Cross
GREEN, WILLIAM L.	1HQ	HA1			
GRIFFITH, HERMAN	1HQ	HA1			
HURT, ROBERT J.JR.	1D	PHM1			
ISBELL, WILLIAM JR.	1A	PHM3	44	Guam WIA	
JOHNS, NELSON A.	1HQ	HA1			
JOHNSON, HOMER	1HQ	HA1			
KERPER, GRIFFIN H.	1HS	PHM1	42	Guadalcanal	Silver Star
KINCANNON, WM. B.	1HQ	PHM3	42	Guadalcanal	Navy Cross
KOENING, WILLIAM	1 B	HA1			
LABOUTELY, ROGER	1BC	PHM3	44	Guam	Bronze Star
LAW, ROBERT D. JR.	1 B	PHM3	44	Guam	Silver Star
LELAND, GAROLD R.	1HQ	HA1			
LEWIS, OSCAR G.	1A	PHM3			
LINDER, DAVID B.	1HQ	PHM1			
LORANGER, LEO L.	1HQ	HA1	45	Okinawa KIA	
LOWE, ROBERT J.	1C	PHM3	45	Okinawa WIA	
MANTYLA, UNO A.	1HQ	CPHM			
MARSH, WILBUR L.	1HQ	PHM1	42	Guadalcanal	Navy Cross
MARSHALL, CHARLES	1HQ	PHM2			
MATHIS, LLOYD T.	1HQ	PHM2	42	Guadalcanal	Navy Cross
MATTOX, ROY E.	1HQ	HA1			
McFANN, HAROLD	1HQ	PHM2	42	Tulagi	Silver Star
McGILLICUDDY,JOHN	1HQ	HA1			
METZGER, GEORGE	1HQ	HA1	44	Guam WIA	Navy Cross
MITCHELL,OLIVER C.	1HQ	PHM3			
MOLLOY, WILBUR V.	1HQ	PHM2	42	Guadalcanal WIA	
MORGAN,VINCENT A.	1HQ	HA1			
NEWBERRY, LYLE W.	1B	PHM1	44	Palau WIA	
NICHOLS, BILLY F.	1B	PHM2			
OLIVAS, RICHARD A.	1D	CPHM			
PARKER,THADDEUS	1HQ	PHM2	42	Guadalcanal	Navy Cross
			42	Tulagi	Ltr Comm
			43	Bairoko KIA	Silver Star
PERRY, FRANK J.	1HQ	CPHM	44	Guam	Bronze Star
PICOS, BERNARD JR	1HQ	HA1			
POTTER, ALBERN JR	1HQ	PHM2	42	Guadalcanal	Navy Cross
POWERS, ROBERTJR	1HQ	HA1			

NAME	BN/CO	RANK	YR	BATTLE	MEDAL
ROEBUCK,GERALD	1B	PHM2	42	Guadalcanal WIA	Navy Cross
			42	Guadalcanal WIA	Ltr Comm
SEAGER,CHESTER	1HQ	PHM2			
SHIRLEY,LAWRENCE	1HQ	HA1			
SMITH, ROBERT L.	1A	HA1	42	Guadalcanal KIA	Silver Star
SPRINGER, JACK	1B	PHM3			
TOEBUCK, GERALD	1HQ	HA1			
VANDERVEER,C.L.	1B	PHM3			
VAN SANDT, WM.S.	1HQ	HA1			
WALKER, GEORGE .	1HQ	HA1			
WINTERBOTTOM,A.W.	1HQ	HA2			
WYLIE, DAVID K.	1HQ	PHM3			
YOUNG, JOHN W.	1HQ	HA2			

1ST RAIDER BATTALION HEADQUARTERS AND SERVICE COMPANY
DOCTORS, PHARMACISTS AND AIR OFFICER

NAME	BN/CO	RANK	YR	BATTLE	MEDAL
COLE, HAROLD H.	1H&S	LTJG			
KINDER, JAMES W.	1H&S	WO			
KROPIDLOWSKI, A.	1H&S	LTJG			
MILLER, HARRY A.	1H&S	LT			
ROBBINS, HOWARD	1H&S	LtCdr			
ROUNDS, GEORGE	1H&S	LTJG			
VAN COTT, WESLEY	1H&S	LtCdr			

1ST AND 2ND RAIDER REGIMENT
HEADQUARTERS AND SERVICE COMPANY

NAME	BN/CO	RANK	YR	BATTLE	MEDAL
ANGUS, ROBERT M.	1H&S	PHM3			
BAKER, CLARENCE	1H&S	HA1			
BASKIEWICZ,WALTER	1H&S	HA1			
BECKER, WILLIAM V.	1H&S	PHM3			
BORNSTEIN, JOSEPH	1H&S	PHM2			
BUFTON, RICHARD	1H&S	HA1			
CLARK, JACK M.	1H&S	PHM3			
COOPER, CLEO E.	1H&S	PHM3			
DIXON, LESTER F.	1H&S	PHM3			
ENDRESS,THEODORE	1H&S	PHM3			
ERWIN, JOE D.	1H&S	PHM1			
ESPINOZA, MIKE E.	1H&S	HA1			
ESTERLINE,WAYNE	1H&S	PHM2			
FAMILARO, JOHN E.	1H&S	HA1			
FESHOH,WILLIAM	1H&S	HA1	44	Guam KIA	
FOSTER, KENNETH	1H&S	HA1			
FRATUS, WILLIAM H.	1H&S	HA1	44	Guam WIA	
FRAZIER, ARVEL G.	1H&S	HA1	45	Okinawa WIA	
GEORGE, CHESTER	1H&S	HA1			

NAME	BN/CO	RANK	YR	BATTLE	MEDAL
GIBSON, WILLIAM	1H&S	PHM2			
GLEASON, PHILIIP J.	1H&S	PHM3			
GLENNEY, WILLIAM	1H&S	PHM3			
GROOMS, CLARENCE	1H&S	HA1	44	Guam	Bronze Star
HAKALSKI, STANLEY	1H&S	HA1			
HAVELKA, JOSEPH	1H&S	HA1			
HAY, ROGER T.	1H&S	HA1	44	Guam WIA	
HELSEL, BENAMIN	1H&S	HA1			
HORD, ERVIN L.	1H&S	HA1	44	Guam	Bronze Star
HUSSMAN, GEORGE	1H&S	PHM2			
JACOBS, EDWARD	1H&S	HA1			
JONES, THOMPSON	1H&S	HA1			
JORDAN, RAY D.	1H&S	PHM2			
JOSLIN, DWIGHT	1H&S	HA1			
KADZIEL, JOSEPH	1H&S	HA1			
KEOGH, WILLIAM	1H&S	HA1			
KLAUSE, OSCAR	1H&S	HA1	44	Guam KIA	
KNIGHT, HOWARD P.	1H&S	HA1			
KUFFNER, FRANK	1H&S	HA1			
LAWTON, RONALD	1H&S	PHM3			
LEVY, LEOPOLD	1H&S	PHM3			
MANSFIELD, DON L.	1H&S	PHM3			
MCDONALD, JOSEPH	1H&S	HA1			
MILLER, EARL F.	1H&S	HA1	45	Okinawa WIA	Bronze Star
MYERS, PETER J.	1H&S	PHM3	45	Okinawa KIA	
PRIDGEN, WILLIAM	1H&S	PHM1			
RIDDLE, WILLIE P.	1H&S	PHM2			
RUNCK, THOMAS D.	1H&S	PHM3	44	Guam	Bronze Star
SERRA, JOSEPH H.	1H&S	PHM3			
SPEER, RICHARD D.	1H&S	PHM3			
STARK, RAYMOND	1H&S	PHM2			
STOTTS, CLAYTON E	1H&S	PHM2			
STUTZ, ROBERT J.	1H&S	PHM2			
WHITEHURST,THOMAS	1H&S	PHM2			

Marine Raider Navy Personnel Roster courtesy Major Jerome
J.C.Beau, USMC (Ret), Historian, U.S. Marine Raider Association.

2ND MARINE RAIDER REGIMENT
2ND MARINE RAIDER BATTALION DOCTORS

NAME	BN/CO	RANK	YR	BATTLE	MEDAL
ELERDING, GEORGE	2HQ	LT			
FOSTER, RALPH A.	2HQ	LT		Bougainvile WIA	
GLEYSTEEN, RODNEY	2HQ	LT			
HEDGECOCK, LEWIS	2HQ	LT			
HENRY, DAVID M.	2 D	LTJG			
HOOT, PAUL M.	2HQ	LCDR			
MacCRACKEN,WM.B.	2HQ	LT	42	Makin	Navy Cross
McGOWEN, MARVIN	2HQ	LTJG	42	Guadalcaal WIA	
ROBINSON, CHARLES	2HQ	LTJG	42	Guadalcaal	Silver Star
RODGERS, TERRY C.	2C	LT			
STIGLER, STEPHEN L.	2HQ	LT	42	Makin	Navy Cross
			45	Iwo Jima	Bronze Star
WARE, DRUE E.	2HQ	LT	43	New Georgia	Silver Star

2ND MARINE RAIDER BATTALION CHAPLAIN

NAME	BN/CO	RANK	YR	BATTLE	MEDAL
McCORKLE, WILLIAM	2HQ	LT	43	Bougainville WIA	Silver Star

2ND MARINE RAIDER BOMB DISPOSAL OFFICER

NAME	BN/CO	RANK	YR	BATTLE	MEDAL
DE WINDT, ADRIAN	2HQ	ENS			

2ND MARINE RAIDER BATTALION CORPSMEN

NAME	BN/CO	RANK	YR	BATTLE	MEDAL
ASH, JAMES R.	2HQ	PHM2			
BENNETT,CHARLESJ	2HQ	PHM3			
BLAKE, HOWARD P.	2HQ	PHM2			
BULLOCK, LESTER D.	2B	PHM3			
BURRESS, ARTHUR	2HQ	PHM2			
CANTRALL, ARTHUR	2A	PHM2	43	Bougainvile	Ltr Comm
CASEY, JAMES M.	2B	PHM1	43	Bougainvile	Bronze Star
CHANEY, NEIL G.	2H	CPHM			
CURLEY, ALLEN L.	2C	PHM2			
CURTIS, ROLAND P.	2HQ	PHM3	44	Guam WIA	
DESMARTEAU,ED. M.	2D	PHM2			
DIRICKSON, HOWARD	2C	PHM2			
DOWSON, WARREN S.	2C	PHM3			
EASTMAN, GEORGE	2HQ	PHM2			
ELTERMAN, W. J. JR.	2AH	CPHM			
FARBER, BERTRAM W.	2HQ	PHM2	43	Bougainville WIA	
FASANA, JOHN W.	2EF	PHM1			
FAVINGER, RICHARD	2HQ	PHM2			
FISHBERG, SAM (WALKER)	2HQ	PHM3			
GALANO, LESLIE A.	2F	PHM2			
GEIS, FLOYD C.	2A	PHM1			

NAME	BN/CO	RANK	YR	BATTLE	MEDAL
GILLHAM, INGRAM JR.	2HQ	PHM3	43	Bougainville WIA	
GORMAN, WILLIAM L.	2HQ	PHM3	43	Bougainville WIA	
GORTON, RICHARD L.	2HQ	PHM2			
GROTHMAN, OSCAR	2HQ	PHM3			
HARBERT, JACK L	2HQ	PHM3			
HART, CHARLES E.	2A	PHM1	43	Bougainville	Ltr Comm
HOGAN, REED B.	2C	CPHM	43	Bougainville WIA	
HOLLAND, RAYMOND	2F	PHM3			
HOWARD, JOHN G.	2F	PHM3	43	Bougainville KIA	
HOWE, LAWRENCE	2HQ	PHM2			
JACKMAN, WILLIAM	2HQ	HA1			
KISTLER, RALPH B.	2F	PHM2			
KLOCK, EDWARD J.	2HQ	PHM3			
KNOTTS, JOSEPH R.	2HQ	PHM2	43	Bougainville WIA	
KRAUSE, ROBERT B.	2F	PHM3			
LANIER, RUPERT	2HQ	PHM1			
LEMON, HOWARD E.	2D	CPHM			
MILLER, CLARENCE	2HQ	PHM3			
MOLD, NEIL W.	2CF	PHM1			
MOORE, JAMES L.	2HQ	PHM3			
OLSON, WALTER G.	2HQ	PHM1			
PELLETIER, GEORGE	2HQ	PHM3	43	Bougainville	Ltr Comm
PROCTOR, WESTLEY	2BE	PHM1	43	Bougainville	Bronze Star
REITE, HARRY E.	2F	PHM3	43	Bougainville	Bronze Star
SCHAAP, WARNE N.	2DE	PHM2			
SCHILLER, JOSEPH P.	2HQ	PHM2			
SPARKMAN, CULLEN	2HQ	CPHM			
THOMPSON, GEORGE	2BE	PHM2			
TIEMAN, LARRY W. W.	2HQ	PHM2			
TOSCH, JOSEPH M.	2HQ	PHM3			
WINCHELL, ELMER	2E	PHM2			

Marine Raider Navy Personnel Roster courtesy Major Jerome J.C. Beau, USMC (Ret), Historian U.S. Marine Raider Association.

2ND MARINE RAIDER REGIMENT

3RD MARINE RAIDER BATTALION DOCTORS

NAME	BN/CO	RANK	YR	BATTLE	MEDAL
HUMBERT, JOSEPH	3HQ				
MILLIGAN, BRUCE	3HQ	LT			
PAINTER, ROBERT	3HQ	LT			
PAQUETTE, LOUIS J.	3HQ	LTJG			

3RD MARINE RAIDER BATTALION CHAPLAIN

NAME	BN/CO	RANK	YR	BATTLE	MEDAL
CRONIN, ROBERT J.	3HQ	LTJG	43	Puruata	Silver Star
			44	Guam WIA	Bronze Star

3RD MARINE RAIDER BATTALION CORPSMEN

NAME	BN/CO	RANK	YR	BATTLE	MEDAL
ALMOND, LLOYD H.	3HQ	HA1	44	Guam WIA	
ACCARDO, JOSEPH	3HQ	HA1			
BARBOSA,BENJAMIN	3HQ	HA1	44	Guam WIA	
BARROWCLOUGH, G	3HQ	HA1			
BENNETT,SHELDON	3HQ	PH2	44	Guam WIA	
BLACK, JAMES JR.	3HQ	PHM2			
BOONE, CHARLES	3HQ	HA1	45	Okinawa KIA	
BOYER,WILLIAM T.	3HQ	HA1			
BRUNSON,NATHAN	3HQ	CPhM			
BUMCORT, RALPH	3HQ	PHM3			
BUNTEN, H. C.	3HQ	PHM3			
CAMPBELL, TOM	3E	PHM3	43	Tarawa WIA	
			44	Saipan	Bronze Star
CUNNINGHAM, J.	3HQ	PHM3			
DEERING, FRANK.	3HQ	PHM3			
DONNELLY,EUGENE	3HQ	HA1			
DOSS, JOHN M.	3HQ	PHM3	44	Guam KIA	
DOWLER, WILLIAM	3BK	PHm2			
FEARN, JOHN A.	3HQ	PHM2			
GALLEGOES,ORLANO	3HQ	PHM3			
GAULDEN, CLYDE	3M	PHM3			
GORDY, VEARL R.	3D	PHM2			
GUSTAFSON,ALVIN	3HQ	PHM2			
HADWELL,TRUMAN	3HQ	HA1			
HAYWARD,GORDON	3HQ	PHM2			
JANSSEN, WM. W.	3K	PHM3	44	Guam WIA	
JEFFCOAT, SIDNEY	3HQ	PHM2			
JOHNSON,ANDREW	3DQ	PHM2			
JONES, BILLY L.	3HQ	PHM2			
KELLY, RICHARD	3DC	PHM1			
KOLB, EDWIN JR.	3HQ	PHM2			

NAME	BN/CO	RANK	YR	BATTLE	MEDAL
LADYMAN, EDDY	3HQ	HA2			
LANCASTER,DON	3HQ	PhM2			
LEAR, HAROLD V.	3HQ	PhM3			
LIEN, ROBERT	3C	PhM3	44	Guam WIA	
MALINOWSKI,CHESTER	3HQ	PhM2	45	Okinawa WIA	
MANGUM,CECIL L.	3K	PhM2	43	Bougainville KIA	
MARTIN, BRYCE T.	3HQ	PhM2	45	Okinawa	Bronze Star
MAYA, MANUEL M.	3K	PhM2	43	Bougainville WIA	Silver Star
McCAULEY, JAS E.	3HQ	PhM2			
McCONNEL,HUGH	3HQ	PhM3			
McWALTERS,P. W.	3HQ	PhM2			
MEYER, HENRY L.	3HQ	PhM2			
MOSEBRUCKER, J.	3Q	HA1	43	Bougainville KIA	
NASON,CLARENCE	3HQ	PhM2			
NEAL, WILLIAM F.	3HQ	HA1			
NEFZGER, RAY	3HQ	PhM3			
OAKLEY, AMOS C.	3HQ	PhM2			
O'DONNELL, FRANK	3M	PhM2			
PAGE, GLEN D.	3B	PhM1			
PETERSON, DON	3HQ	PhM1			
PRINGLE, ROY P.	3HQ	PhM2			
RABITO, SAL A.	3HQ	PhM3			
ROBERTS,ROBERT	3HQ	PhM3	43	Bougainville WIA	
ROBINSON,BERNAD	3E	PhM2			
SAN MIGUEL,PETER	3A	PhM1			
SKEES, CHARLES	3A	PhM2	44	Guam	Bronze Star
SLATER, ROBERT	3HQ	PhM3	43	Bougainville WIA	
SMITH, HAROLD L.	3E	PhM2	44	Guam	Bronze Star
SMITH, JOHN JR.	3HQ	PhM1			
SOMMERS,MELVIN	3D	PhM3	43	Bougainville KIA	
SWANSON, JOYCE	3HQ	PhM1			
TARVER, GEORGE	3C	PhM2			
THOMPSON,CHARLES	3HQ	CPhM			
TUTOR, FRED H.	3HQ	PhM1			
WARD, GERALD W.	3K	PhM2	43	Bougainville WIA	Silver Star
WARE, ROBERT M.	3C	PhM1			
WEBSTER, DANIEL	3HQ	PhM2	43	Bougainville WIA	Silver Star
WOOLDRIDGE,JOS	3L	PhM3	43	Bougainville	Silver Star
YOUNG, FOREST	3HQ	PhM2			
ZINK, HAROLD R.	3HQ	PhM1			

Marine Raider Navy Personnel Roster courtesy Major Jerome J.C.
Beau, USMC (Ret), Historian U.S. Marine Raider Ass'n.

1ST MARINE RAIDER REGIMENT
4TH MARINE RAIDER BATTALION DOCTORS

NAME	BN/CO	RANK	YR	BATTLE	MEDAL
BUTLER, FRANCIS	4Q	LTJG			
LOCKHART, JESSE	4HQ	LT			
MARSH, CHARLES	4HQ	LT			
NOURIE, RAYMOND	4HQ	LTJG	43	Bairoko	
			50	Korea	
				KIA	Bronze Star
TESSMAN, C. C.	4HQ	LT			

4TH MARINE RAIDER BATTALION CHAPLAINS

NAME	BN/CO	RANK	YR	BATTLE	MEDAL
MURPHY, JOHN P.	4HQ	LtCdr			
REDMOND, PAUL J.	4HQ	LT	43	New Georgia	Army Legion Merit
			44	Guam	Bronze Star
			45	Okinawa	Bronze Star

4TH MARINE RAIDER BATTALION CORPSMEN

NAME	BN/CO	RANK	YR	BATTLE	MEDAL
AMIS, GLENN L.	4HQ	HA1			
AUSLEY, JAMES D.	4HQ	HA2	44	Guam	Bronze Star
BAILEY, FRANK W.	4HQ	HA2	44	Guam WIA	
BENDER, SHELDON	4HQ	PHM1	43	Bairoko WIA	Ltr Comm
BRADY, DONALD S.	4HQ	HA1	44	Guam	Bronze Star
BROWN, JACK R.	4HQ	PHM2	43	Bairoko WIA	
BUNN, JASPER L.	4HQ	HA1			
BURUSS, JOHN T. JR.	4Q	HA1			
CARSON, JAMES L.	4HQ	PHM2			
CLIFFORD, PAUL	4HQ	PhM2			
COLIP, RALPH F.	4HQ	PhM3			
COY, THOMAS J.	4HQ	CPHM			
DORSEY, EDWARD	4HQ	HA1			
ELLINGTON, EDWARD.	4HQ	PHM2	43	Bairoko	Silver Star
FERRIN, HAROLD G.	4P	PHM2	43	Bairoko	Silver Star
FISHER, DAVID H.	4HQ	PHM3			
FITZPATRICK, DENNIS	4HQ	HA1			
FORD, KENNETH E.	4AN	PHM3	44	Guam WIA	
FORRY, JOHN A.	4C	PHM2			
GLEASON, JAMES D.	4D	HA1			
GOLDSTEIN, MORRIS	4E	HA1			
GRANT, LONSON S.	4B	PHM2			
HAGUE, EUGENE L.	4HQ	PHM3	44	Guam WIA	
HAZELTON, DONALD	4HQ	HA1			
HENLEY, MILES C	4HQ	HA1	44	Guam	Bronze Star
HILL, HERMAN O.	4HQ	HA2			
HORNE, PAUL K.	4HQ	HA1			
HUDSON, OTTO G.	4E	PHM2	43	Bairoko	Ltr Comm
HURWITZ, CHARLES	4DQ	HA1			

NAME	BN/CO	RANK	YR	BATTLE	MEDAL
KJELLAND, GEORGE	4HQ	CPHM	43	Bairoko	Ltr Comm
KRAEMER,THOMAS	4HQ	HA1	45	Okinawa KIA	
LACY, WILLIAM G.	4HQ	PHM1			
LEGG, LAURENCE	4DQ	PHM2			
LOWNSBURY, ORIN J.	4HQ	HA1			
MALCOM, WM.J.JR.	4HQ	HA1			
MAYFIELD, JAMES G.	4Q	PHM3	43	Bairoko	Silver Star
MCDERMOTT, LYLE C.	4BD	PHM2	43	Bairoko	Ltr Comm
MEEKS,BARTHOLOMEW	4HQ	HA1	45	Okinawa WIA	
MILLS, RAYMOND V.	4HQ	PHM2			
NELLIGAN, JOHN J.	4HQ	HA1	44	Guam KIA	
NELSON, CHARLEY	4HQ	HA1	45	Okinawa WIA	
PELTON, LEONARD	4BN	HA1	43	Vangunu	Silver Star
PHILLIPS JOHNNIE	4B	PHM2			
PIGG,DAVID (ADAMS)	4C	PHM1			
RENZI, ADOLPH P.	4O	PHM2			
ROLLINS, ODIE C.	4HQ	PHM1			
RUSK, ARCHIE, H.	4D	HA1			
RYAN, EDWIN F.	4BO	HA1			
RYAN, EDWIN F.	4BO	HA1			
SCHILLING, FRED	4AN	PHM2			
SANDEFUR, WM.T.	4HQ	PHM3	45	Okinawa WIA	
SHELLENBERGER, W.	4E	PHM3	43	Bairoko	Ltr Comm
SITTON, LEWIS W.	4HQ	PHM1	43	Bairoko WIA	Silver Star
SPARLIN, STONEWALL	4HQ	PHM3	43	New Georgia	Ltr Comm
STULLER, LEROY N.	4HQ	HA1			
THOMPSON,STANLEY	4HQ	PHM1	43	Bairoko	
			44	Guam WIA	Silver Star
THRAPP,WOODROW	4HQ	PHM3			
WOOD, SAMUEL D.	4P	PHM2	43	New Georgia	Silver Star

Marine Raider Navy Personnel Roster courtesy Major Jerome J.C.
Beau, USMC (Ret), Historian U.S. Marine Raider Association.

INTRODUCTION

In late 1941 and early 1942, following the Japanese attack on Pearl Harbor, the United States declared war on Japan and the Axis powers.

Nazi Germany had swept through Europe and parts of Asia defeating and conquering everyone that stood in their way. France, Poland, Austria, Denmark, Norway, the Netherlands, Czechoslovakia, Belgium and Hungary were occupied and the Soviet Union had been invaded.

During the same time period, Japan was equally successful in defeating the Armed forces of Britain, Australia, New Zealand, United States, Portugal and the Netherlands, throughout Asia and the South Pacific while continuing their long war with China.

Seemingly, the only good news to come out of the war at the time was Army Air Force Gen. Jimmy Doolittle's, surprise bombing of Tokyo in April 1942. Loss after loss to the rampaging armed forces of Nazi Germany and Japan seemed to be an every day occurrence during this period and American morale was extremely low.

On 7 August 1942, U.S. Marines launched a surprise invasion of Japanese held positions on Tulagi, Florida and Guadalcanal in the British Solomon Islands.

The unit chosen to spearhead the first amphibious attack on Japanese defended territory in World War II, was the 1st Marine Raider Battalion at Tulagi, British Solomon Islands. It was here; the Raiders inflicted the first defeat of the war on Japan's seemingly invincible Imperial Forces. Ten days later on 17 August 1942, the 2nd Marine Raider Battalion made the first submarine launched raid in the history of the Navy, upon Japanese held Makin (Butaritari) Island.

Thus began the battle history of the previously top secret 1st and 2nd Marine Raider Regiments, the Marine Suicide Battalions of World War II, in the Pacific. They were the first in and the last out of the War, fighting in every major island battle and being chosen to spearhead the invasion of the Japanese homeland as 4th Marines. Instead of becoming invaders they instead became occupiers, when the first Marine to set foot on the mainland of Japan in 1945 was a Raider.

The "hush, hush", all volunteer Elite Marine Raiders were a small band of heroes of less than 4,000 men including, their Raider Combat Corpsmen, Doctors and Chaplains. The four Raider Battalions fought on 7 islands during 1942-43, before reforming the famous 4th Marine Regiment early in 1944.

To an American public starved for good news of any nature, the initial Raider assaults resulted in an outpouring of publicity and admiration for this intrepid band of Marines. They were instant heroes worldwide, and engraved the name "Raider", in the famed battle history of the United States Marine Corps. All of this came as a surprise to the Raiders and was all out of proportion to their size and status at the time.

Due to deaths, wounded in action, and the ravages of tropical diseases another 4,000 replacements were added to their muster rolls in order for the Raiders to stay operational during their short two-year existence.

The Marines of the Raider Battalions were trained as a lightly armed hit and run force patterned after the British Commando. They also trained as guerrilla's able to operate behind enemy lines while living off the land, much as Chinese Communist forces who had fought against the Japanese with success.

Raiders and former Raiders were awarded 8 Medals of Honor, 158 Navy Cross and Army Distinguished Service Cross Medals, and 18 Legion of Merit Medals. 30 Navy ships were named for Marine and Navy Raider Heroes. Two Raiders participated in each of the historic IWO JIMA Flag raising's on MT. SURIBACHI.

The Raiders added another first to their illustrious history when Marine Sgt. Clyde Thomason became the first enlisted Marine in WW II to become a recipient of the Medal of Honor

As battle hardened veterans, Raiders participated in 19 battles prior to there being designated, as the new 4th Marine Regiment. As 4th Marines they participated in the invasion of Guam and Okinawa, and were training to be the initial attack force in the invasion of the Japanese mainland prior to the Japanese surrender.

Many wounded Raiders discharged from hospitals in the United States and overseas were re-assigned to other Marine Divisions where they became leaders in the training of those green troops, readying them for future battles against the Japanese.

Raiders, and former Raiders fought in every major island invasion against the Japanese in WW II. Many spent the entire war without every having returned home until they boarded transports after the occupation of Japan and China.

One need only note the events of World War II that are still remembered today; over half a century later, to realize the important part, a small band of 8,000 Raiders, played in the history of their country and the Marine Corps.

Familiar names such as the SOLOMON ISLANDS, OKINAWA, IWO JIMA and JAPAN; are invoked daily in our two Raider Museums; written of in our quarterly Raider Patch Magazine, and discussed and displayed on our two Marine Raider Web Sites.

ALTHOUGH FEW IN NUMBER, THEY PROUDLY STAND AMONG THE BEST AND BRAVEST THE MARINE CORPS HAS EVER PRODUCED. THEIR ACCOMPLISHMENTS HAVE SURVIVED THE TEST OF TIME AND THE RAIDER LEGACY LIVES ON!

NAVY AND MARINE TERMS AND ABBREVIATIONS

AA -Antiaircraft
ADJ -Adjutant
ADM- Admiral
AMPHTRACK -Amphibian Tractor (LVT)
APA-Troop Ship
APD-Destroyer Transport
BAR-Browning Automatic Rifle
BN-Battalion
Brig- Military Jail
CAP-Captain
CC- Chaplain Corps, Navy
CPHM-Chief Pharmacist Mate
C in C-Commander in Chief
Co-Company
CO-Commanding Officer
COL-Colonel
CP- Command Post
CPL,CORP- Corporal
C Rations- Food, canned
DC-Dental Corps,Navy
DD-Destroyer
DE- Destroyer Escort
DECK- Floor of a ship
DI- Drill instructor
DOW- Amphibious Truck
DOC- Hospital Corpsman
Ens- Ensign
FMF -Fleet Marine Force
Gung Ho- Work Together
HA1-Hospitalman First
HA2-Hospital Man Second
HA3-Hospital Man Third
Hatch- Door fitted with watertight cover
    aboard ship
HEAD-Toilet, bath aboard ship
H.Q.-Headquarters
HQMC -Headquarters, Marine Corps
H&S -Headquarters & Service HIGGINS
    BOAT-Landing Craft
IN A SHIP-Aboard Ship
INF -Infantry US Army
Joe- Coffee
K Bar-
KIA-Killed in Action
LC-Landing Craft
K Rations- Food rations, boxed
Ladder-Steps aboard ship
LCDR-Lt Commander
LCI-Landing Craft, Infantry
LC-Landing craft
LCT-Landing Craft, Tank
LCVP -Landing Craft, Vehicles and
    Personnel
LST-Landing Ship, Tank
LSV-Landing Ship, Vehicle
LT-Lieutenant
LTJG-Lieutenant Junior Grade
LTCOL-Lieutenant Colonel
1LT- 1st Lieutenant
2LT- 2nd Lieutenant
LVT-Landing Vehicle, Tracked Amphtrac

M1- 30 caliber automatic rifle
MAC-Marine Amphibious Corp
AG-Marine Aircraft Group
Maj - Major
Mar-Marine(s)
MarCor-Marine Corps
MAJ- Major
MC- Medical Corps, Navy
MG-Machine Gun
MG -Marine Gunner; Machine Gun
MIA-Missing in Action
MSgt-Master Sergeant
MIA- Missing in Action
MOH-Medal of Honor
Mustang- Enlisted man promoted to
    rank of officer
PHM3-Pharmacist Mate First
PHM2-Pharmacist Mate Second
PHM1-Pharmacist Mate Third
PLT-Platoon
Poncho-
P.O.W. Prisoner of War
Porthole- Window aboard ship
PT-Motor Torpedo Boat
PBY-Navy Seaplane
QM-Quartermaster
QM-Quartermaster
RDR-US Marine Raider
RECON-Reconaissance
Runner-Marine assigned to deliver
    messages for an officer
Sand Spit - visible sandbar
Semper Fi- Always faithful
782 Gear- all field equipment
Scuttlebut-Drinking fountain aboard
    ship, rumor,gossip
Seabee (CB)- Naval Construction
    Battalion
Sgt-Sergeant
Shelter Half-slang for Marine wife
Skivvies- Underwear
Slit Trench- trench body waste
SNLF-Japanese Special Naval
    Landing Force ("Marines")
SS-Submarine or Silver Star Medal
    SSgt-Staff Sergeant
TBF-Radios used by FMF Marines
TSgt-Technical Sergeant
    UDTUnderwater Demolition Team
USA-United States Army
USMC-U.S. Marine Corps
USN-United States Navy
VAdm-Vice Admiral
WIA-Wounded In Action
WO-Warrant Officer
WW-World War
XO-Executive Officer, Second in
    command
YP-Patrol Vessel
ZEKE-called
Zero-Japanese Fighter Plane

Rubber Boat Training

*4th Marines abard transport prior to the occupation of Japan
in August 1945. War's end was announced on board.*

Prologue

'Til We Meet Again"

Missing Makin Island Raider KIA's Return Home

Thirteen flag-draped caskets containing the mortal remains of Raider's killed during the Makin Island raid laid out at Arlington National Cemetery.

IN HONORED GLORY!
THE NEVER FORGOTTEN CLASS OF '42
COME HOME TO REST FOR ETERNITY
17 AUGUST 2001

A line of several busses wound their way between rows of white crosses as far as one could see. Slowly coming to a halt, they were met by U.S. Marines, both male and female, in their full dress blue uniform of the day. Acting as escorts, these Marines guided those coming off the bus toward a roped off grassy area in an open field.

      The visitors were a mostly elderly group of men and women, and a sprinkling of the middle aged with a few children among them. As they began their walk, many were using canes or a walker for support. Here and there could be seen someone struggling to push a wheel chair through the grass, while many of the men walked with noticeable limps.

When they arrived, the elderly stood behind the ropes, while the others were ushered to seats beneath a long green canopy. Resting in front of them in an evenly spaced row were thirteen flag draped caskets with a vacant space for the symbolic 14th casket to be placed upon arrival at the grave site.

Each coffin held the remains of one of the thirteen Marine Raiders who lost their lives in combat with Japanese troops on Makin Island (now Butaritari) in August 1942. One of the Raiders was Sgt Clyde Thomason, the first enlisted Marine to be awarded the Medal of Honor in World War II. The remaining six Raider families chose to have their loved ones buried in their hometowns.

Off in the distance on this overcast, muggy August day, the sound of band music could be faintly heard and an occasional glimpse of a group of marching men seen moving slowly in the distance. The music grew louder and suddenly from behind a cover of trees appeared the U.S. Marine Corps Band followed by six black horses, with mounted members of the U.S Army's Full Honors Funeral Team, pulling a black caisson with a flag draped casket.

Next in line were two companies of Marines resplendent in their full dress blue uniforms. They were followed by the Commandant of the Marine Corps, the Chief Chaplain of the Navy, and a group of several Raiders and other mourners marching to pay a final tribute to those about to be buried within the hallowed grounds of Arlington National Cemetery.

The coffin was removed from the caisson by six stalwart members of the U.S. Marine Corps body bearers who, with precision drill movements, step by step in unison and seemingly gliding across the grass they lifted the casket overhead and placed it upon the empty stand between the other caskets.

Following a brief prayer by the Chaplain, three rifle volleys resonated over the rolling hills followed by the playing of taps. The folded flags ceremoniously placed on each casket were retrieved by the Marine Honor Guards and carried toward each designated next of kin. Here they knelt and presented the flag to that person, saying the following:

"On behalf of the President of the United States, a grateful nation, and a proud Marine Corps, this flag is presented as a token of our appreciation for the honorable and faithful service rendered by your loved one to his country and Marine Corps."

The Marines and the Marine Band then marched off the

field, thus ending the 17 August 2001 full honors burial ceremony of those Second Battalion Marine Raiders killed in combat exactly 59 years before on 17 August 1942.

With few dry eyes, the mourners slowly boarded their busses to return to their hotel. It had been a long day, with earlier religious services held in the Fort Myers Chapel.

Earlier in the day, upon the arrival of the casket, followed into the Chapel by the Honorary Raider pallbearers, the service began with a Call to Worship by the Chief of the Chaplain Corps and a prayer by Raider Chaplain Shirl Butler. Next was a scripture reading by a Navy Chaplain, followed by a moving eulogy by General James L. Jones 32nd Commandant of the Marine Corps and a final message by Melvin D. Heckt, President of the U.S. Marine Raider Association.

There were no surviving parents attending, only brothers, sisters, aunts, uncles, cousins and friends. Most had never known the heroes interred this day. It was now time for the mourning family members of those laid to rest to return to their hotel and search for any Raider survivors who might have known there loved ones.

In an amazing display of love for a friend they did know, ten alumni of Beverly Hills High School who were classmates of Raider Corporal R.B. Maulding, were in attendance to pay him honor.

It seemed only fitting these long lost American heroes had now returned home to their final resting place because of the efforts of their Raider comrades who had never forgotten them.

The Raiders had once again added to Marine Corps lore, as the Makin burial ceremony is said to have been the second largest full honors burial ever to take place in the glorious confines of Arlington National Cemetery. Only the burial of President John F. Kennedy was larger!

Corpsman Administering Blood Plasma on Beach Head

Wounded Pushed over Reef on Rubber Boat To
Reach Higgins Boat to be Evacuated

Marine Raider Combat Corpsmen
Who were they? What did they do?

General Al Gray, U. S. Marine Corps
29th Commandant of the USMC

"Wherever you find the Marine Corps or the Navy, you will find Navy Corpsmen. In times of peace, they provide quality health care to our Marines and their families. In times of war Corpsmen are employed in amphibious operations, on the beaches, and on the battlefield with our Marines. In fact, 21 Navy Corpsmen have received the Medal of Honor, 18 of them while serving in the Fleet Marine Force. (Many of the Medals were awarded posthumously, often for shielding wounded Marines with their own bodies).

Whenever medical service is required, the Hospital Corpsman is there, willing and prepared to serve our Marines and our country. I salute our Corpsmen for their courage, valor and willingness to serve above and beyond the call of duty."
— Gen. Al Gray, 29th Commandant of the USMC

Fleet Marine Force (FMF) Corpsmen have established a unique brotherhood with Marines – a brotherhood bonded in blood. FMF Corpsmen are the most highly decorated sailors in the Navy.

CORPSMEN VOLUNTEERED TO BECOME MARINE RAIDERS

During World War II there was nothing more confusing to civilians and even to Army, Sailors and Marines, than to see a young man dressed in Navy Blues one day and in Marine Greens the next. There were many near battles; with both the Army Military Police and the Navy Shore Patrols, who wanted to nab him for being out of uniform, or even worse for pretending to be a swabbie or a leatherneck.

Few people knew then; including the newly minted Doctors and Hospital Corpsmen, that the Marine Corps was too small to provide medical service for their men. By Congressional Order on 17 June 1898 the Hospital Corps was established, and since that time the U.S. Navy Medical, Hospital, Nurse and Chaplain Corps have been assigned to provide for the care and well being of all Marine Corps personnel.

It wasn't until 1916 however, that Combat Hospital Corpsmen, Doctors and Navy Chaplains were detached to serve with what would become the amphibious Fleet Marine Force in 1935. While on duty, they were required to wear Marine khaki or Marine Green uniforms, but on liberty or leave they were allowed to wear either uniform. They trained with, and became an integral part of all Marine amphibious assaults against enemy forces.

A large number of Navy Corpsmen served with the Marine Corps during World War I, World War II, Korea and Vietnam. Always in awe of the Marine esprit de corps and individual bravery, some Corpsmen even switched to the Corps following their initial enlistment period.

Navy Corpsman Harold C. Roberts served with the Marines in France in World War I, and received both the Navy Cross and the Army Distinguished Service Cross for his bravery in battle. Roberts switched to the Marine Corps and served as the Executive Officer of the 3rd Defense BN, on Tulagi during WW II. Serving as Executive Officer with the 22nd Marine Regiment, Col Roberts was killed in action during the battle for Okinawa, where he received his second Navy Cross posthumously.

PHARMACIST MATE HAROLD McFANN; was the first Raider Corpsman in WW II to be awarded a medal. He received a Silver Star for his heroism in action at Tulagi. He then asked to be assigned to the Pensacola Naval Air Station for training to become a pilot. Upon his graduation he chose to become a Marine Aviator. Marine 1LT McFANN was unfortunately killed in a training accident in 1943.

PHARMACIST MATE THADDEUS PARKER received the Navy Cross on Guadalcanal, as well as a Letter of Commendation, on Tulagi. Tragically, he was killed in action on New Georgia and was posthumously awarded the Silver Star. He became the only Raider Corpsman to have a ship named after him in WW II.

PHARMACIST MATE DELBERT EILERS was awarded the Navy Cross and the Silver Star in two different battles on Guadalcanal.

John Bradley was a Navy Corpsman who "just jumped in to lend a hand," during the historic raising of the flag at Iwo Jima on Mt Suribachi. He won the Navy Cross for heroism and was wounded in both legs. A quiet, private man, he gave just one interview in his life. In it he said. "People refer to us as heroes. I personally don't look at it that way. I just think that I happened to be at a certain place at a certain time and anybody on that island could have been there, and we certainly weren't heroes, and I speak for the rest of them as well. That's the way they thought of themselves also."

Hospital Apprentice Joseph Beno served as a dental technician during WW II and aboard a Hospital Ship in the Korean War. He then requested admission to Naval Flight Training School. Upon graduation he chose to become a Marine Aviator and served three tours of duty in Vietnam. Upon his retirement, LtCol Beno had received the Distinguished Flying Cross twice, the Air Medal 26 times, was qualified to fly 27 types of military aircraft and became only the second aviator in the history of the Marine Corps, to amass more than 6,500 hours of flight time.

Each of these Corpsmen, imbued with the fighting spirit of the Marine Corps, exemplify their respect for both the Corps and the Navy.

The fearlessness and bravery in caring for their Marine comrades during WW II didn't come to an end with the defeat of Japan in 1945. Many Fleet Marine Force Corpsmen, including your author, either stayed in service or were recalled to serve with their Marines once again during the Korean War.

Upon being assigned to the Fleet Marine Force, Corpsmen experienced their first exposure to the Corps and what a shock it was! They suffered through Marine combat training with the units they were assigned to, such as the Raiders. It was a rude awakening as they not only had to play catch up from a physical standpoint but also were required to attended additional medical training classes taught by the Battalion Doctors, Dentists and Chief Pharmacist Mates.

No more jaunty white hats and adoring girls! Forgotten were clean sheets, pogey bait and ice cream. The grim reality was living in tents while struggling with bugs, insects, mud, dirt and physical exhaustion, for you were now a MARINE! The Marines and Raiders had found "A Few More Good Men, " who were to become their "Angels of Mercy". For a Corpsman and his Raider buddies, the familiar words "In sickness and in health, Until death do us part", was a very prophetic refrain.

Although medical personnel assigned to the Raiders had to be volunteers, the Raider Commanding Officer's were usually not given the opportunity to pick and chose, as they did with each Marine volunteer. The Senior Medical Officer was in charge of all things medical. When the Combat Company Corpsmen were assigned to a Battalion, a Company and then a Platoon they were then primarily under control of the Battalion Commanding Officer.

At first the cocky Marines rubbed the Corpsmen wrong. They had to get used to being called pill pushers, swab jockeys, and an even worse choice of words. To the Corpsmen, the Raiders were a swaggering, boisterous, bragging bunch of silly ass jar heads. It was the need to prove themselves with these loudmouths; in spite of their previous easy Navy boot camp training in comparison to that of the Marines, that made each reconsider their views of the other.

While training with the Raiders, the company Corpsmen had to perform their own medical duties and learn the tactics of the Marine infantrymen. Many times during the war, Corpsman relied on their hand to hand fighting techniques and weapons training, when they and their shipmates had clashes with the enemy. One Corpsman went to the extreme, taking over the firing of a machine gun when the gun crew of his Marine platoon was knocked out of action.

How could a Corpsman not be impressed by the physical prowess and fighting spirit of each Raider? What an experience it was during training problems to see the guys of the heavy weapons platoon carrying 100 lb. loads including ammunition, tripods, mortars and BAR'S on 20-30 mile forced hikes. Even more impressive, was the little 5'6" communications man following right behind them, struggling with two radio packs on his back that almost touched the ground.

Every platoon was assigned a Combat Corpsman to accompany the Raiders when they went into action against the enemy. Every Corpsman, had to be in the best physical condition possible in order to complete the same rigorous training required of the Raiders. Corpsman, were well aware they had to shape up and not let their buddies down. It didn't take long for them to learn the importance of the Corps philosophy of taking care of the man on your left and the man on your right. To this, a Raider Corpsman automatically added taking care of the man in front of him, because that is where he usually had to go when the first call for "Corpsman, Corpsman", rang out.

Raiders began to notice it was good old Doc who always seemed to be around to take care of all their ills. Whether in the barracks in camp, while on a 20-30 mile forced march, when practicing knife and bayonet hand to hand combat during a night problem, practicing landings from rubber boats, destroyers or submarines or on the rifle range, their Corpsman was always "on call."

When a march or other activity stopped for a few minutes break, Doc often didn't get a chance to rest at all. There were too many blisters to treat, APC's (aspirin, phenacitin and caffeine) to hand out, ointment to apply for jungle rot and crotch itch, a sore ankle or arm to bandage, or salt tablets to administer and any other first aid needed at that particular time.

It was during this period that both Corpsman and Raider learned to respect and admire each other, and Corpsmen came to really be known as "Doc". The true love of each other experienced only in combat, became a reality when the cry "Corpsman, Corpsman! rang out on the battlefield, on island after island.

As they bled together, and cried together, and died together, while fighting the Japanese they became lifelong friends. This love of comrades in arms has withstood the test of time, for even after sixty one years should you ask a Combat Corpsman what he did in the War his proud reply would be, " I was a Marine Raider."

Doctors, Dentists and Corpsmen with the Marine Raiders, other than Company Corpsmen, were considered rear echelon for the purpose of operating first aid stations that were supposed to be 500 or so feet from the front lines. However, that was rarely the case, as they often found themselves within 25 to 50 feet of the front lines out of sheer necessity. It wasn't at all unusual for the Doctors and their Corpsmen assistants to be seen calmly performing surgery on the most seriously wounded Raiders with bullets flying all over the place.

Headquarters Corpsmen maintained and operated the sick bay and held sick calls, assisted during operations, extracted and filled teeth. They tried their best to see that adequate safe drinking water, showers and heads (toilets) were available, garbage and body wastes were safely disposed of and preventive measure's taken to lessen the exposure to the many tropical illnesses of the South Pacific.

Our battalion Doctors taught us as much as possible in the short period prior to our initial combat. The trouble was, they were just as uncertain as the Corpsmen, about how to treat the myriad of illnesses beginning to show up at sick call. No one realized then, more men would be lost to sickness than enemy bullets, but that became a reality within a very short period of time.

Thrust into the shooting war; with Japanese troops that chose to ignore the Geneva Convention concerning non-combatants, it was no longer safe for Corpsman to wear Red Cross armbands so they were usually armed with a .45 caliber pistol or a .30 caliber carbine rifle. It was very infrequent that a Combat Corpsman had time to fire their weapon, but if necessary they could and did use their weapon, bayonet, knife or bare hands in the way they were instructed, in order to save their life or that of their Raider buddies.

When a Raider was wounded and the call went out for, "Corpsman", here came Doc with his medical kit flopping as he was running (sometimes just crawling) while trying not to lose his weapon. The injured man frequently had to be treated where he fell with Jap bullets aimed at both him and the Corpsman who was trying to apply first aid, while the other Raiders tried to use covering fire to protect them. Japanese philosophy was that to kill or wound Corpsmen, Doctors or Marine Officers would cause instant disruption within the attacking force.

If a Corpsman was unable to roll or carry the wounded man out of the line of fire they had no other choice but to face the fire. It was then when Corpsmen were shielding a Marine's body from more bullets or perhaps holding up a blood plasma unit attached to a rifle, that they were most likely to be killed or wounded.

The Japs enjoyed wounding a Corpsmen second only to an Officer, but Doc continued to run from man to man giving morphine, stopping the flow of blood from a head wound, applying battle dressings to gaping chest wounds or using tourniquets for blood spurting from a missing arm or leg.

Just as a Raider would sacrifice his own life for a comrade in arms, so too would a Corpsman. Thus mutual admiration grew between a Raider and his Doc, with the Corpsman being well

6

aware of the bravery displayed by every Raider.

This didn't mean the Raider still wasn't called a jarhead or a sea-going bellhop. Or that the Corpsmen escaped being called a pecker checker or a chancre mechanic. However, it was mostly in jest for there was a love of each for the other, between all the survivors, that will live on into eternity.

When the word "Corpsman up", or "Corpsman, Corpsman" rang out, the Doc rushed to the side of the wounded Raider. Their first concern was the need to stop the flow of blood to prevent shock and almost certain death. Sulfanilimide powder was sprinkled in the wound, and a sterile pressure dressing was applied after the clothing was cut away to determine if there was more than one wound. NO ATTEMPT TO CLEAN THE WOUND WAS MADE AT THAT TIME! This procedure was left to those at the Battalion aid station.

BRAVERY WHILE UNDER FIRE

The Medal of Honor is the highest award a grateful nation bestows for valor on the battlefield.

Five Medals of Honor were bestowed upon Navy Hospital Corpsmen in World War II, all of whom served with the Fleet Marine Force as Combat Corpsmen.

During the Korean War, seven Navy Medals of Honor were awarded; four were awarded Navy Corpsmen, all serving with the Fleet Marine Force as Combat Corpsmen.

Of the fifteen Medals of Honor received by Navy personnel during the Vietnam War, four were awarded to Naval Personnel serving with the Fleet Marine Force, one was for a Navy Chaplain and three were for Navy Combat Corpsmen.

The Navy Cross is the second highest Navy medal that is awarded for bravery in combat.

Sixty-seven Navy Corpsmen were awarded the Navy Cross in World War II. Fifty-five of those Corpsmen were attached to the Fleet Marine Force (FMF). Eleven of those fifty-five were Marine Raider Combat Corpsmen.

Of the twenty-nine Navy Crosses awarded to Navy Medical Corps Doctors in WW II, fourteen were given to those attached to the Fleet Marine Force (FMF) while four of those fourteen were Raider Doctors.

Included in the Raider roster of 8,054 men were 365 Corpsmen, Doctor's and Chaplains. While representing only (4.5%) of the Raiders complement, Corpsmen, Doctors and Chaplains received 17% of the medals awarded Raiders for bravery.

Thirty Navy ships were named after Raider heroes, including one for Cpl Mitchell Red Cloud Jr. (KIA Korea 1950),

Two of these ships were named after Raider Medical personnel. One for Raider Corpsman Thaddeus Parker PhM2, KIA on New Georgia and the other for Raider Doctor Samuel S. Miles, Lt Jg KIA on Tulagi.

The Combat Corpsmen and Doctor casualties in the Pacific Theater in World War II were far out of proportion to their numbers. Those men and boys attached to the Fleet Marine Force were to lose more men in combat proportionately than the Marines themselves.

COMBAT CORPSMAN

With little medical training or a college degree, the Combat Corpsman has been required to function with the versatility or no other enlisted man. The Corpsman has been the Marine's physician, and their nursemaid. When they are engaged in combat, the ever present Corpsman - dirty, unshaven and tired with sweat running down his cheeks, blood and bits of tissue splattered across his shirts and pants is more often than not exposed to enemy fire. Amid screaming and shouting, surrounded by death, he hurriedly tends to the wounded and the dying, even with bullets flying by he covers the wounded with his own body. As the Marines around him fight on, the Corpsman, his throat swollen dry, gently cradles yet another dying man in his arms. When the battle has passed and the battlefield becomes a graveyard solemn and quiet, the platoon is at rest, while the ragged and dusty Corpsman, his clothes damp with blood and sweat, continues his treatments, cleaning gaping wounds, bandaging sore feet, treating ugly ulcers and dispensing all manner of pills. Unlike a movie or television, the blood never leaves a Corpsman's boots; the stench never leaves his nose, the piercing screams never leave his ears, and the memory of war never leaves his mind..... Anonymous

Brigadier General James Roosevelt USMC (Ret), served as Executive Officer of the 2nd Raider Battalion and as Commanding Officer of the 4th Raider Battalion when it was formed in 1942 at Camp Pendleton, CA. It is doubtful that anyone: other than the son of the President, Franklin D. Roosevelt, would have been accepted by the Corps suffering with so many physical disabilities. Jimmy had poor eyesight, serious stomach problems and feet so bad he had to wear civilian shoes until new boots were issued to the Raiders. Despite his medical problems, he served with honor and was one of the founding members of the U.S. Marine Raider Association.

During a conversation prior to his death, Jimmy repeated an observation both he and other Raider Officers often noted. "Raider Corpsmen and Doctors were always at the ready whenever called upon to aid their Marine comrades. Whether we were suffering from an illness or wounded by enemy fire, they always responded immediately."

While constantly facing death on the battlefield Corpsmen, proved themselves to be worthy of the title "Marine Raider". They marched where the Raiders marched. Ate what they ate. Dug foxholes where they dug foxholes, Slept where they slept. Got wet when they got wet. Were killed as they were killed. Were wounded as they were wounded. Cried when they cried. Bitched like they bitched and at the same time, they LOVED EVERY DAMN ONE OF THOSE CRUDDY JARHEADS!

While in combat, morphine was dispensed to relieve pain when a Raider was wounded. Packaged in a small tube with a needle attached, it had a stylette inside the needle that had to first be pushed forward into the tube in order to break the seal and then removed before the morphine could be administered.

Blood plasma was given to the wounded to help prevent shock. The vinyl bag containing the plasma, had to be raised in the air by the Corpsman or fastened to the butt of the Raiders rifle after the weapon had been driven into the ground.

It was sometimes necessary to apply more than one pressure dressing to stop the flow of blood. As a last resort to stop the bleeding a tourniquet would be used, with the time it was applied marked on the Raiders forehead. Splints were applied as needed, but they were not always available on the front line. Often a wounded man's rifle or a tree limb was used as a substitute splint.

How and when a wounded Raider was moved back to the Battalion aid station was strictly determined by the flow of the fire fight. If other casualties had to be treated the Corpsman would rush to the closest one. When not under fire the Corpsmen or the stretcher-bearer's would carry or help a wounded Raider to the rear. Both Corpsmen and stretcher bearer's often placed their own lives in grave danger when attempting to remove an injured comrade from the battlefield.

In the Marine Corps everyone is trained as an infantryman no matter what his specialty. Thus, when a Command Post or hospital was in danger of being over run, cooks, bakers, bandsmen and other special ratings were right there to reinforce their buddies on the firing line or to act as stretcher bearers.

One of the great hazards of fighting in the Solomon Island

jungles was the high incidence of tropical diseases. Such diseases could almost completely decimate a fighting unit within two or three weeks of exposure under battle conditions. Parasites, fungi, infections, disease carrying insects and the illnesses resulting from dengue, filariasis, gastro-enteritis, dysentery and others proved to be more of a threat than ever imagined. The islands had the highest malarial infection rate in the world and malaria became the most prevalent disease during the campaign for the Solomons. Over 5,414 cases of malaria were diagnosed, of almost 8,000 Marines placed on the sick list on Guadalcanal from August until the end of September 1942.

Casualty lists of the killed and wounded in action are often the highlight of media stories of combat. What isn't stressed however, is the debilitating effect on under strength units in battle because of those that are unable to continue due to illness. Although prompt and professional medical treatment saved the lives of 97% of the men wounded during the war, few know that illness was responsible for more than half of the casualties overall.

Of grave concern was a shortage of quinine to treat malaria attacks, so the anti-malarial drug atabrine was prescribed and fluids forced as a means of treatment. Getting Marines to voluntarily take atabrine was something else because of rumors the drug had a negative affect on sexual desire and performance. Raiders became experts at PRETENDING to swallow the atabrine when they were dispensed in the chow line. The ground was soon colored yellow as they faked taking them while at the same time dropping them on the ground. It soon became necessary to place a Corpsman in line to throw the pills into their open mouth while an Officer stood by making certain that neither Corpsman nor their Marine buddies shirked their duty. It was a pleasant surprise to everyone that in a short period of time, atabrine proved more effective in controlling recurring malaria attacks than quinine.

Ringworm, boils, open body ulcers, insect bites, cuts, bruises, sprains, crotch itch, jock itch and any other kind of itch imaginable, vied with jungle rot (feet), dengue fever, catarrhal (cat) fever, elephantiasis (mumu), jaundice, diarrhea and dysentery, to challenge malaria as the most debilitating non-combat problem among the troops. Nothing affected more men than foot infections, as Raiders walked not rode into battle.

Next to a canteen filled with water and a few sheets of toilet paper, the most valued item to a Raider other than his weapon, was a clean, dry pair of socks. Fungus infections (jungle rot), blisters, broken skin and swollen feet can be caused by heat, moisture and friction, which will take a man out of action as effectively as a bullet. Attacking the enemy through swamps and during the rainy season meant continually wading in mud and water up to and beyond your knees while sleeping in foxholes filled with water. Drying your feet, wearing dry socks, using foot powder and applying fungicidal ointment became the accepted treatment for this problem.

Perhaps the most irritable of all the illnesses faced was diarrhea or dysentery. Because of poor sanitary conditions and lack of bathing almost all Raiders suffered from this malady at one time or another. A stinking muddy path, made almost impassable by the men who couldn't control their bowels along the way, mandated the use of slit trenches for the men to straddle while in camp.

The poor Raider on the front lines sharing a foxhole with his buddy had to defecate in his pants or take his life in his own hands with a mad dash to the nearest tree or bush which would shield him from the enemy. Few in their right mind would attempt this in fear of becoming the target of their own buddies who might mistake him for a Jap infiltrator. This affliction often took all the energy a Raider had left as he was really "weak in the poop!"

Burial services were conducted by one of the four Raider Chaplains when at all possible and also attended by their comrades whenever possible. The most distasteful part of this detail was to collect the large numbers of the Japanese dead, as there were much larger numbers of them. Japs seldom had time to bury their own dead, and many bodies had become bloated or almost devoured by jungle insects. In attempting to remove bodies following a Jap banzai attack, extremities such as arms and legs were often separated from the body. The sweet, sickening smell of death, of bowels emptying and the stench of flesh decaying never seemed to go away and will never be forgotten by anyone who has been through that obnoxious experience.

It is impossible to describe the near animal existence of the Raiders involved in an assault. Once ashore they moved forward silently often through driving rain and slipping into a humid foul smelling jungle. Slipping and falling over muddy, half hidden tree roots, struggling through creeping cutting vines, struggling up, over, and down mountains and hills, into valleys teeming with insects and wild animals for days on end without a change of clothes, bathing or shaving. They fought off hunger with meager food rations and little or no water. A helmet could be used as a wash basin, a food container, and even as a potty, while in extreme circumstances it served as a pillow.

When their objective was reached they were dirty, muddy and totally exhausted. Following a battle Raiders resembled the living dead, emaciated, weak, hungry, and disheveled, with horror written on their faces. No longer young boys, they were now men who stared death in the face and won, for now at least! They didn't smell they STANK! There is no other way to describe some one who has been forced to go through living hell with no means to bathe or wash his clothes. However in an amazingly short time behind the front lines, they were again laughing, joking and insulting each other after shaving, bathing, donning clean clothes and eating a hot meal.

NAVY SECRETARY JAMES FORRESTAL
1953 COMMENDATION

The achievements of military medicine in World War II were numerous and remarkable, and results were equally remarkable. Out of every 100 wounded men, 97 recovered.

The chief reason why so many more lives were saved in World War II was the high standard of professional skill and training of the physician, dentist, and the bravery and dedication of the Combat Corpsmen.

Many Corpsmen that became Prisoners of War of the Japanese, used their skill and strength to save lives and instill hope in their fellow captives through the many years of forced labor and deprivation. The performance of their duty has "Been in keeping with the highest traditions of the Naval Service."

A MARINE'S BEST FRIEND

Courtesy Frank Cannistraci 2HQ "ask anyone, who is and what is a Corpsman? You may be told he's just another swabbie in the U.S. Navy. But when serving with the Marines, he didn't wear his bell-bottom trousers or his jaunty white sailor hat. Instead, he wore a helmet, carried side arms, hauled ass trudging through the jungles in his wet mud covered boots, lugging a heavy canvas bag loaded with first aid medical supplies. Like us, he slept in muddied foxholes, ate cold C-rations, faced enemy bullets and mortar fire. He exposed himself to answer any frantic call for help to render first aid to the wounded on the battlefield. Countless lives were saved by these few dedicated men. Numbering in the tens of thousands

Not enough can be said or written about our Corpsmen. They did not seek publicity or acknowledgment nor did they ever exploit their deeds and efforts through the news media for all to know. They truly performed a SILENT SERVICE. We Marines are proud and eternally grateful!

YES, they may look like, live like and act like Marines, in truth - THEY ARE MARINES! We salute you!

NO GREATER LOVE
By: LTCDR JAMES F. REGAN, USNR. 1HQ

AUTHOR: Doctor REGAN was awarded the Silver Star for his bravery at Enogai, New Georgia on 8 Jul 1943. His professionalism and devotion to duty was indicative of all Navy medical personnel who served with the Raiders).

"Leaves from the diary of a RAIDER NAVY DOCTOR who found comradeship, tolerance, and inspiring self—sacrifice in the hell of jungle battles at Triri, Enogai Inlet, and Bairoko Harbor, New Georgia, British Solomon Islands."

"You'd never think of JIM CORBETT as a spiritual kid. He was blond and skinny, with mischievous eyes and an impish grin. He was always ready for a fight or a frolic and he was perhaps 19 years old. He was one of our medical corpsmen with the 1st Marine Raider Battalion in the South Pacific. In the jungle one grim afternoon, under intense enemy fire, JIMMY unhesitatingly crawled out in front of the lines to help another Raider who had been wounded. A Nip sniper shot him in the spine.

It was sundown when we got him back to the palm shack we used as a sick bay. He was paralyzed but conscious, and able to talk in a labored fashion. He knew a little about medicine and I think he realized he was beyond hope. Yet, as I worked over him, he didn't think of himself. He asked, with difficulty, 'How are the boys? Many hurt? I told him it wasn't too bad. He was glad to hear it and tried to grin. Then he said hesitantly, 'Did I do all right' I said, 'Swell job. You did fine.' He murmured, 'Thanks' and closed his eyes. Suddenly and strongly he said, 'Don't mind me. Help the boys.' He never spoke again.

I am a NAVY DOCTOR, a surgeon trained to deal with the material things of life. Yet I learned a reassuring spiritual lesson in the jungle. I learned that the perils of war are developing in our fighting men a quality no one could have foreseen, a comradeship, a selflessness, akin to spirituality. This doesn't mean that our men are sprouting wings, it means that the very stoicism of their existence is giving them a fresh, realistic, comforting perspective. Their lives are reduced to the essentials LIVING, EATING, SLEEPING and DYING. They know that if one man fails, many may die. They don't want to fail, and they don't want to die

We shove off on our New Georgia operation tomorrow (Codeflame TOENAILS).

Today there are 13 men in the soggy gloom of sick bay, a tent under the dripping trees of Guadalcanal where it always rains. We have been training here. One of the patients is a stocky, good-natured, mid-western farm boy called RICK. He has a painful knee injury. Yet today I found RICK up and dressed, surrounded by his gear, sharpening his knife. When I ordered him back into the sack, he gave me a slow, ingratiating, lopsided grin. "I feel swell Doc honest. It don't hurt a bit. I bet I could kick a goal with it." Perspiration popped out on his face. He went ashen. I felt his knee. It was acutely swollen I said, "Okay. I'll make you a deal. If you can hike to the beach and back with full equipment you can go with the outfit tomorrow." It was two miles to the beach; I would have bet anything he couldn't make it. Yet he came limping back in 55 minutes, I said sternly, "You're a fool HICK. You'll never be able to keep up. If you drop out, I'll have to shoot you myself to keep the Nips from getting you. Why do you want to try it?"

He found words difficult, but his mouth set to a stubborn line. "I just gotta go Doc that's all." I been 15 months with this gang. I gotta go along." Well he's going, but I wonder, what is the word for the blind doggedness that drives an injured man to accompany his pals on a mission he knows may cost his life? Patriotism? That's one word. But certainly it is a very personal kind of patriotism, a determination to carry his share of the load, no matter how tough the going. America's future is safe in the hands of men like that.

5 July 1943: We hit the beach at Rice Anchorage. New Georgia When I returned RICK to duty, there were 12 men in sick bay back at our training base on Guadalcanal today there are none. They're all here, AWOL from the hospital. One by one, some sheepishly, some cockily, they came out of their hiding places as the APD Destroyer transports DENT, TALBOT, WATERS, McKEAN, and the USS KILTY, CROSBY, SCHLEY and McCALLA carried us deep into enemy territory. Several are burning with fever, but it's too late to send them back. Besides

THEY WOULDN'T GO!

We landed shortly after midnight. I stepped out of the boat into knee deep mud. The COLONEL'S voice said, 'Grab something Doc.' The muddy beach was littered with crates. I found one by falling over it. As I got it to my shoulder, somebody said, This way Doc. It was one of my erstwhile patients, loaded like a mule. We followed LTCOL SAMUEL B. GRIFFITH, who had a crate on each shoulder. All hands have worked all night getting supplies inland. Now we are flaked out in the mud, 300 yards into the jungle, waiting for daylight. The Nips' artillery is firing over our heads, long on range. One of the Raiders smashed his foot. As I treated him in the pitch darkness, I manufactured conversation to keep his mind off the pain. The only thing I could think of to talk about was how Congressmen back home were competing to see which could promise returned veterans the most money. Between groans, the kid raged, 'Great God Doc, do they think we're fighting this war for money?'

Our 1st Raider Battalion medical staff included 3 Doctors and 32 Corpsmen. The Doctors are: LT STUART C. KNOX a jolly, rugged man who weighs more than 200 pounds, LT CHARLES L. CABELL slender, bald, matter-of-fact and myself LT JAMES F. REGAN. We are to stay near the points of advance as we move inland. We have one Corpsman for each platoon. Their job is to administer daily doses of salt and atabrine (An anti-malarial synthetic which the men try to avoid because of a rumor that it induces sterility, which would be unbecoming to a Raider) and to handle casualties. Before the week is out, a dozen of these lads will have won decorations and citations; some of them will be dead. As we stand in the jungle mud, we make a final check to be certain none of us is wearing insignia or brassards, we know Nip snipers can't resist our RED CROSS ARMBANDS!

7 July 1943: Our first casualties at Triri, New Georgia: Yesterday was like the day before all swamp and coral hills and swamp, with a nine foot deep river (Tamakau river) that we crossed on a single fallen tree, slippery with moss. We slept on a muddy island in a swamp that seemed limitless. One of our Corpsmen, THADDEUS PARKER, a self-confident little chap, came down with malaria, and someone called me. I found PARKER'S pal an enormous Platoon Sergeant we called BIG STOOP, ANTHONY J. PALONIS, lying beside the little fellow in the mud, wrapped around him to keep him from shivering. BIG STOOP said, 'I'll take care of him. Doc! (PATCH EDITOR: THADDEUS PARKER had served with BIG STOOP at Tulagi

and Guadalcanal when PARKER won the Navy Cross at Edsons Ridge and a Letter of Commendation at Tulagi.)

It rained hard in the night, and we drained the jungle leaves in the morning to get drinking water. That was our breakfast. The columns formed in the early light and moved on. At midmorning, just ahead, firing broke out, then subsided. We crept forward into a village. I set up sick bay in a shack, which means I took off my kit, found a rough bench for an operating table, swabbed it with disinfectant, and waited for casualties. The first was a youngster I knew. A tall gangling towhead that always said he wanted to be a farmer so he could drink a gallon of milk every day. He was shot through the hand and was sobbing convulsively, I said reprovingly, "Even broken legs don't cry like that. He wailed furiously, "I'm not crying. I'm just so damned mad. Get me out of here." I dressed his hand and told him to rest; when I looked again he was gone.

10 July l943: We advanced 2,000 yards at Enogai Inlet, New Georgia. We lost PhM3 JIM CORBETT two days ago in the action at Triri. I was walking toward the sound of the firing, when a voice rasped, "Damnit Doc get down." I dodged, dropped into the muck, and wriggled forward. Presently, I saw LT JOE M. BRODERICK 1DB, under a clump of ferns. Blood was dripping from his arm and knee. I started for him but he whispered. "Sheer off Doc I'm hot." After a time I made out the form of LT TOMMY D. POLLARD, 1ABD, just ahead. I saw him as he fired. BRODERICK fired at the same instant. The top of a big tree ahead trembled, swayed, and two bodies toppled out. BRODERICK called softly, "Watch that tree to the left. TOMMY." BRODERICK said calmly, "Okay now Doc." I started toward him but he pointed ahead. "I'm all right. Go get the others.

We were mystified that night by the disappearance of a lad named POWERS, (THOMA.S F."JINX" POWERS 1ED), a stocky, witty chap we all liked. He had been wounded in the abdomen and had started for my dressing station, but never arrived. We were afraid he was dying or had died in the jungle but we couldn't find him.

CHRIS, (PhM3 LAURENCE M. CHRISTMAN, 1HQ), one of my Corpsman, crept up to me in the night, He was shivering violently; his teeth chattered so he could hardly talk. He whispered, "It ain't fever Doc. I'm, I'm scared. I'm scared as hell. Am I different from the other guys Doc?" I tried to comfort him.

A pitched battle began at dawn not more than a block and a half from the coral ledge where the casualties lay. Yet we had to leave them for a while to bury four of our dead. We found a place under a tree. DR. STUART C. KNOX, read a Psalm and recited the Recessional; God of our fathers. Lord of our far-flung battle line, bullets cracked through the foliage and bits of leaves fluttered down.

As I hurried back to the wounded I met young JINX POWERS. He was ragged and bloody but cheerful. He had lost his way, followed sounds, and wandered into the Jap camp after dark. He shot two Japs who challenged him and then climbed a tree where he had been ever since. I sure was glad to see our boys coming," he remarked casually. It struck me as a pretty fine understatement. His wound is not serious; the bullet missed vital organs and is lodged under the skin of his stomach, He wants it left there as a souvenir.

The Nips were wiped out by mid-afternoon and we moved forward. One of the first men I met was Christman, the corpsman who had been afraid. He was fairly swaggering with confidence. He said, "You know what happened. Doc? I come around a tree and there was a Nip with a bayonet. He flung it up to kill me. I dodged and hit him in the gut and rubbed him out with his own knife. Hell, them Nips ain't so tough." He won't be afraid again!

Our casualties have been heavy. One of the wounded is "KILLER" CAIN, (CORPORAL WILLIAM F. CAIN Jr,) a sober, popular chap. He is delirious. Just before we left our training base he learned he was a new father. He had been excited and deeply moved. Now, in his delirium, it is the one thing on his mind. Some men die quietly but CAIN fights furiously for life. He shouts over and over, "I don't want to die. I want to see my baby." Morphine has little effect. His WILL keeps him alive. Men crowd around the doorway. "Hey Doc can I help?" "Hey Doc need some blood hunh? I got plenty." We do what we can, but WILLIAM F. CAIN will die tonight, screaming defiance to his last sobbing breath.

One boy's hand is blown to shreds. A Jap grenade fell at his feet. He tried to throw it back, but wasn't fast enough. He came walking in, and asked easily, "Can you fix me up O.K. Doc?" As I worked on him he said, "I guess I'll get me a tin can and some pencils. '" I said sharply, "Stow that kind of talk '" He said quickly, "Oh. I didn't mean it. I know what I'm going to do. Let's see; this is July. Maybe I can get home in time to go back to High School this fall. "

PhM1 DELBERT D. EILERS 1Hq, is a short, chunky, even-tempered lad who always volunteers for everything. He won the Navy Cross on Guadalcanal at Edson's Ridge. Later, at a smoker on New Caledonia, he got out of line, was given a

17

deck court martial, and was put on probation. A little later he won the SILVER STAR. Today he did another incredibly brave thing: He accompanied a patrol which rescued two of our men trapped behind the enemy lines. Tonight, very diffidently, he sidled up to me and asked, "Doc do you think the Colonel (LTCOL SAMUEL L B. GRIFFITH) would let me off probation if I asked him?" I said I thought he would.

18 July 43, Slight respite after Enogai Inlet and before Bairoko Harbor. This has been a busy week. The Nips at Enogai left a vast supply of material, cases of heavy white blankets, clean sheets; bedsprings, cans of roast beef, salmon, beans, vegetables, parts of tractors and searchlights. They had fresh water wells, bomb shelters in coral cliffs, neat paths through the woods, a shower bath. The Raiders have been living high. The wounded have been evacuated by PBY Catalina flying boats. Although the Japs have been overhead almost daily, and always nightly, they've been more annoying than dangerous. We've had our share of grim comedy. One day we were loading wounded into a PBY alongside the reef. A Nip plane came over and dropped a bomb beside the PBY. One of our boys, naked as a jay bird, was standing on the reef to hold the PBY off the coral. When the geyser of mud and water subsided, the Raider had vanished. We never saw him again. Long afterward, we learned that he had been partly blown, partly hauled into the departing plane and carried back to the distant base hospital at Tulagi, where he disembarked, unhurt but still stark naked, a discomfited young Marine.

One night when Washing Machine Charlie came over to bomb us as usual, DOCTOR CHARLES L. CABELL 1HQ clapped on his helmet and dived for a dugout. I have mentioned that DR CABELL is bald. I heard him threshing wildly in the dugout and was afraid he had been injured, but discovered he was only having a ferocious hand-to-claw battle with a land crab that had been roosting in his helmet. Another night, two officers dived for the same slit trench and met head on in mid-air. They will recover.

20 July 1943: Back in the jungle at Bairoko Harbor, New Georgia. Yesterday morning we marched against the last Nip base on the Dragon's Peninsula. We didn't get far. A few hundred yards along the trail we contacted the enemy Japanese in force in pillboxes of logs and coral, camouflaged with vines and hemmed in with barbed wire. The battle still continues. Wounded came in so fast we had no chance to get them back to the sick bay at Enogai. I found a level place in the jungle protected by a low coral wall, and set up my aid station. By nightfall we had

about 200 casualties crowded into that little space, fully a fourth of them were stretcher cases: We have recovered the bodies of our dead Raiders. One of these is the little Corpsman THADDEUS PARKER.

PARKER was not far from his enormous: Sergeant pal, BIG STOOP PALONIS when he was hit. A hail of Nip fire was raking the ground, but BIG STOOP leaped to his feet and went to PARKER'S assistance. PALONIS was hit, too. Nevertheless, he pulled PARKER out of the line of fire and carried him back to safety, cradled in his arms. Tears were streaming down his face. When I told him PARKER was beyond hope, his face contorted and he wheeled to go back to the front. As he turned, his legs gave way. That was the first I knew he had been wounded.

We were pinned down under heavy fire at nightfall, at midnight the Japanese staged one of their celebrated suicide bayonet charges, screaming like madmen. A false rumor started that we were going to withdraw and leave the wounded. My Chief Pharmacist's Mate BROWNIE. (JAY A. BROWN 1Hq), a stubby easy going chap, bald, with fringes, of curly hair over his ears crept over to me. "If we are ordered back Doc: " he said quietly. "I'll stay here with the wounded." I said. "Do you realize what might happen to you?" He said soberly. "Yeah. I know all that, but if the boys can take it. I can take it." Of course we were not ordered back. The wounded men had neither food nor water during the night. We started them back to sick bay at Enogai at daybreak today. Having no litters, we improvised them by rolling ponchos on limbs of trees. they were unsatisfactory, the ponchos would slip and let the wounded fall. Their stoicism is incredible; even half-conscious, they are thinking of the other fellows. I knelt beside one man who had fallen. He thought I was his stretcher bearer, and muttered through clenched teeth, "That's okay Mac you couldn't help it."

21 July 1943: The end of the line: Evacuation at Enogai Inlet. I had to be evacuated with the casualty's two days later. I was at Guadalcanal late in August when the remnants of the Raiders came back. As those dirty, ragged, hard, gallant men filed ashore a soft wind was whipping the flag and a band was playing the Marine Corps Hymn. I had to turn away!

MARINE RAIDER ACCOLADES FOR THEIR COMBAT CORPSMEN AND DOCTORS

Father Paul J Redmond wrote in a letter to the author concerning this book, "It is about time the Corpsmen were memorialized, they were outstanding. You know that my first assignment as a Priest was in 1930 posted to Quantico with the Marines."

COL MICHAEL S. CURRIN 3HQ, 4HQ wrote, "I have always had the highest respect for our Corpsmen. They delivered for us in WW II when they were most needed."
AUTHOR: LTCOL CURRIN succeeded LTCOL JAMES ROOSEVELT as the Commanding Officer of the 4th RAIDER BATTALION for the New Georgia campaign.

COL ANTHONY WALKER wrote, "Although many Corpsmen have been decorated for heroism, many others are unsung heroes who all have the undying gratitude of the Marine Combat Infantry Man."

Legendary Raider, COL MARTIN J. (STORMY) SEXTON 3K a survivor of WW II, Korea and Vietnam wrote, "God Bless the Corpsmen, without them neither myself nor thousands of other Marines would be walking the earth today. They are the finest thing that ever happened to the Marine Corps.

When giving his keynote address at a California Veteran's Day service, BGEN JAY W. HUBBARD ended his speech by saying, " I would like to recognize one special breed, our Marine medical service. They serve through the full spectrum of War and it's consequences. They are on the line with troop units performing incredible acts of sheer courage. They and the Chaplain's are about the only place a guy can get a little TLC on the battlefield."

4DQ JOHN "MOE" McCORMICK, Raider author of " The Right Kind of War ", says" Every guy has one or two Corpsmen stories to tell. Much was expected of our Corpsmen and they responded nobly."

ROBERT BUERLEIN, President of the American Historical Association that houses our Raider Museum in Richmond, VA and is an Honorary Raider has this to say about Raider Corpsmen. "Because of the front line objectives of the Raiders their Corpsmen often saw as much as or more combat duty than did many Marines in the Pacific Theater of Operations. When Raiders visit the museum we often notice they still bear signs of their wartime injuries. They are living testaments of the treatment they received from their Corpsmen and Doctors in the battles they fought, and they always make it a point to complement their Corpsmen "Doc's". In a recent History Channel show it was said the Corpsmen had "the most dangerous job on the battlefield!"

ALBERT J. "BO" BOCASH writes, "I was an ammunition carrier for the .30 caliber machine gun of CPL CARL BERKSTRAND 1B'S squad during the battle of Bloody "Edson's" Ridge on Guadalcanal. At daybreak on 13 Sep 1942 we could hear Japs. They spotted our machine gun and opened fire killing Berkstrand and another Raider. I quickly dismantled the gun and threw away the bolt. This is when I was wounded in the hand. I scrambled up the ridge that was very steep and was having difficulty. When I was near the top, VINCENT CASSIDY reached down and pulled me up to the top. I was then treated by COLEMAN (1 HQ CARL B. COLEMAN PhM2, awarded the Navy Cross for bravery) and was later taken aboard a hospital ship and sent to Auckland, New Zealand to recuperate.

BEN CARSON 2BC wrote, "On Makin I was a member of the beach perimeter as the Raiders were attempting to shoot the surf with the wounded. It was really dark but the phosphorescence of the churning surf still permitted some background for the events that unfolded there that night. The rubber boats would have one wounded who could sit up and another wounded draped over the center of the inflated seats. As the boats approached the curl in the biggest surf, the boat would be swept up and completely turn over dumping the wounded and the rest of the crew into that churning surf. As the Raiders were swept back to shore each wounded had at least one and most often two people guiding that wounded person back to the beach. There the wounded would be carried to the tree line to await another try at the surf. The doctors were still on the beach to check for shock and bleeding as each patient returned to the beach. This attempt to shoot the surf continued until near daylight and the wounded were as eager to try again as were the boat crews.

While keeping watch for any Japs that might decide to attack the beach scene I heard something stirring among the darkened coconut grove. All of a sudden there was a burst of fire from Jessie Hawkins and return fire from the Jap recon party. Jessie was hit pretty badly in the chest and as I crawled over to him I could hear his chest making a sucking sound as he tried to breathe. Directly Dr. MacCRACKEN crawled over to Jessie and checked him over. I offered to help carry Jessie to the beach but was told to stay in position since there were now only 7 of us left to man the whole beach defense. Some of the Raiders who were resting on the beach from their surf penetration duties came and lugged Jessie to the beach where Dr. MacCracken bandaged him up and prepared him for the trip to the subs. When the initial attempt to shoot the surf took place, each of the severely wounded heading back for the subs, had a Corpsman or Doctor in the rubber boat with them. As the boats upset and the wounded were dumped in the surf much of the medical supplies and related necessities went overboard and was lost.

AUTHOR, JAMES GLEASON, 4th Raider Battalion Corpsman: "When Raider R.C. HALL read an article I wrote for the Marine Corps League Magazine about the Raiders 50th Reunion in which I referred to myself as "only a Corpsman." He took issue to that and wrote the following to the Raider Patch Editor. 'I will always have a special admiration and respect for our Doctors, Chaplains and above all, the Corpsmen of the Raider Battalions. I don't believe any of us will ever forget their dedication and bravery when the chips were down and the bullets were flying. Many of us walking around today are doing so only because of the familiar cry Corpsman, Corpsman! I might well be lying helpless as I was on Mt. Yaetaki, Okinawa in 1945. I object to Jim or any Corpsman saying " I was only a Corpsman!' (Thanks for your kind words L.C. it was a great honor for the Corpsmen to serve with the Raiders, the finest Regiment in the Marine Corps, bar none! Jim Gleason)

Mary Baldwin, widow of 2H COL ROBERT BALDWIN, Spokane, WA shared this story with me at a Raider reunion. "When Bob was returned to a hospital in Washington to recover from his wounds there was a huge blood drive put on by the Red Cross. An Admiral approached Bob's bed and said 'this is what I want you to say when the newspaper and radio people come around. Tell them the Red Cross saved your life.' " Bob said no", 'The Admiral said, maybe you didn't hear what I told you! " Bob said No, I can't say that because it was a CORPSMAN who saved my life!"

2

U. S. Marine Raiders
Who were they?

Marine General H. M. ("Howlin' Mad") Smith

"We formed four Raider battalions, which did extremely useful work under hazardous conditions in the South Pacific. Selected men were specially trained and equipped for landing unobserved on enemy islands and performing all manner of tasks. These ranged from reconnaissance to surprise raids and attacks on enemy positions, demolition of installations and destruction of equipment. The type of man chosen for this job had to be tough. Our four battalions of Marine Raiders, eventually incorporated into the 4th Marines, were the elite of toughness. A 30-mile march with a hundred pounds of equipment on their backs, followed by hand-to-hand combat with a knife, was sometimes their role. They were taught all the tricks of undercover combat; they could out-read a jungle-tracker, climb mountains like billy goats, and out-swim a fish. The Raiders were a nightmare to the Japanese and engraved the name Marine on the memory of many a native islander. By the very nature of their organization, the Raiders were highly expendable." — Gen. H. M. Smith

"During World War II, the Marine Raiders were the "suicide squads" of the Marine Corps as they volunteered, and volunteered again and again, for the most hazardous of missions."

MARINE RAIDER HISTORY

No military unit of their size of 8,000 men, earned more honors or exceeded the accomplishments of the U.S. MARINE RAIDERS in World War II.

Raiders were there from the first assault on Japanese defended territory at Tulagi and at Guadalcanal in 1942, through the last battle of the war on Okinawa. They fought as the 4th Marine Regiment on Guam, as the 4th Marine Regiment, 6th Marine Division on Okinawa, and with the 3rd, 4th, and 5th Marine Divisions on Iwo Jima.

Following the defeat of Japan in 1945, they were chosen to be the initial Marine unit to land on the Japanese mainland as part the Allied Force occupation troops three days before the Japanese signed the surrender treaty aboard the USS Missouri.

MARINE RAIDER FIRSTS
DURING WORLD WAR II IN THE PACIFIC

- First to engage Japanese forces in an amphibious attack in force in WW II,on an enemy defended island, at Tulagi, BSI
- First to launch an amphibious raid from a submarine on an enemy held island in the history of the Navy.
- First to capture a Japanese battle flag in offensive combat in WW II.
- First to use Navaho Code Talkers in WW II.
- First to use War Dog's in the Pacific in WW II.
- A Raider was the first enlisted Marine to receive the Medal of Honor in WW II.
- Raiders were awarded 8 Medals of Honor for Heroism, on Makin Island, on Guadalcanal(2), Bougainville, on Iwo Jima(2), Okinawa and in Korea.
- A Raider was the first Marine to reach the summit of Mount Suribachi as part of a patrol that was led by a fellow Raider.
- Two Raiders participated in each of the flag raising ceremonies on Iwo Jima.
- A Raider was the first Marine to set foot in occupied Japan as part of the Allied Occupation Force, THREE DAYS PRIOR to the signing of the Peace Treaty!
- Raiders were awarded more Medals for bravery than any other comparatively sized American fighting unit in WW II.

Though a small unit in size, the Raiders became giants in the history of the Marine Corps! Of the top three American

Medals awarded for heroism and bravery, Raiders received 7%, although numbering less than 2% of the men in the Marine Corps.

30 NAVY SHIPS WERE NAMED FOR RAIDER AND RAIDER MEDICAL HEROES WHO WERE KILLED IN ACTION DURING AND AFTER WORLD WAR II.

- RAIDERS have endowed RAIDER MUSEUMS in Richmond, VA and San Diego, CA.
- The U.S. MARINE RAIDER ASSOCIATION is the only veteran's organization of the American Armed Services of World War II, to initiate an educational fund to provide tuition to primary schools for the SOLOMON ISLAND native children.
The SGT MAJOR VOUZA Educational Fund was established in 1972 in honor of SIR JACOB VOUZA, their beloved native scout and his fellow native troops for their bravery and loyalty during World War II. For over 31 years it has donated funds annually for room, board and tuition for Native Solomon Island children in the furtherance of their education. The Marine Raider Association recently established an endowment fund with an added gift of $52,000. so that the scholarships may continue in perpetuity.

MARINE RAIDERS

BORN IN WAR!
RAISED IN COMBAT!
DIED WITH BRAVERY!
RETURNED IN GLORY!

SEMPER FIDELIS!

Only four Battalions and a Headquarters and Service Company strong, the Marine Raiders were truly THE FIRST TO FIGHT and also THE LAST TO FIGHT, as they were given the most difficult and hazardous assignments while taking the offensive against the Japanese throughout World War II. The Raider campaigns are legend and have added another glorious page to the annals of Marine Corps history.

It was never "I" in the Marine Corps or the Marine Raiders it was always "We". Raider Officers directed attacks while on the front line. They didn't direct them from the REAR. Sergeants set examples for their Corporals, Corporals for Privates. Corpsmen, Doctors and Chaplains risked their lives for their Raiders, as their Raiders did for them. Teamwork with the man on your left and the man on your right ruled the days and especially the nights.

Early in World War II, there were a few visionaries both inside and outside the military establishment who had visions of the need for specially trained military units on the order of the British Commando. One of those persons, was Winston Churchill who tried to convince President Roosevelt of the value of a small hard hitting force.

The Marine Corps had conducted amphibious type training for years, and Gen. H.M. "Howlin' Mad" Smith recognized the need for units with this type of amphibious capabilities. Originally neither he nor other Marine Corps Brass felt elite units of this nature should be sanctioned by the Corps. They believed ALL Marines were ELITE and capable of any type amphibious attack against the enemy. It is unknown however why Paratroop Battalions were authorized by the Commandant in 1941, while Raider Battalions were deemed to be taboo.

Captain JAMES ROOSEVELT, the son of the President of the United States, had written a letter to the Commandant of the Marines in 1941. It suggested the need for a fast moving lightly armed unit, capable of hit and run raids against the enemy, and the ability to operate behind enemy lines for protracted periods of time while living off the land. Most believed the letter contained the philosophy of LTCOL EVANS F. CARLSON, who served on the Presidential Guard Unit at Hot Springs, Arkansas; CARLSON had served as a Military Observer during the Chinese Communist Long March and was an admirer of Mao's guerrilla tactics. World War I Army hero, and Medal of Honor recipient, Col William (Wild Bill) Donovan also suggested to the President that a similar type unit be formed, and if formed, requested the Corps to commission him a Marine General to command it. The Commandant's antenna went up with the realization of a potential political decision as opposed to a military decision. Second only to the separation of Church and State, was the separation of Marines and the Army as far as the Corps was concerned.

Fearing an imminent move in which they would have no input, the Corps moved rapidly to form what was to become the four Marine Raider Battalion's, patterned after their Provisional Rubber Boat Companies, which were formed in 1941. On 6 January 1942, the 1st Battalion, 5th Marines, was re-assigned as the 1st Separate Battalion and transferred from the 1st Marine

Division to Amphibious Force, Atlantic Fleet.

On 4 February 1942 the Commanding General, Amphibious Force Pacific Fleet, ordered the formation of four company strength Raider units in compliance with a Commander in Chief Pacific Fleet directive. Concurrently, the Commandant of the Marine Corps ordered organization of the 2nd Separate Battalion on the West Coast and assigned it to the then organizing Raider companies.

Thus the Raiders were born of adversity, unwanted and disdained by the top brass of the Corps. It didn't help any that the Marine Corps was hurriedly trying to bring the 1st Marine Division up to combat strength with inexperienced men, only to lose many of their few top ranked non-commissioned officers, who volunteered for the Raiders.

Volunteers were interviewed and if accepted had to qualify as follows in order to become a Raider:
1. Qualify in hand to hand bayonet and knife fighting, with the ability to kill with their bare hands if necessary.
2. Qualify as a 2nd Class swimmer, as a patrol might have to forge rivers or streams too deep to wade, as many as 5 or 6 times a day.
3. Qualify in guerrilla warfare by learning to live off the land and move rapidly on foot patrol through jungles and swamps as many as 20 miles per day.
4. Qualify as a marksman and in the use of demolition's.
5. Qualify as a mountain climber in night problems.

Marine General H.M. Smith was the foremost proponent of Amphibious Warfare within the Marine Corps, He wrote a Military Manual on the subject during the 1930's. It was Smith, who fought battles with both the Navy Admirals and Army Generals as to who would control a Marine assault force once it came ashore. He also fought long and hard to make available the Higgins Boat and the Roebling alligator LVT that saved so many Raider lives during the war.

Raider Battalions were given the first choice of personnel, weapons and gear. This caused resentment not only with other Marine units, but also brought about a long held animosity between the 1st and 2nd Raider Battalions.

One third of the 1st Battalion personnel were transferred to form the nucleus of the 2nd Battalion, only to have CARLSON reject many of them. This and the differing philosophies of EDSON and CARLSON are still debated until this day among the Raiders. There was one common denominator. The men of the 1st Raider Battalion loved and respected EDSON, just as the 2nd Raider Battalion loved CARLSON. Each of the other Raider Battalions were also fiercely loyal to their Commanding Officers.

The 1st Raider Battalion organized under the Command of LTCOL MERRITT A. EDSON, first trained in Quantico then shipped to Samoa and later to New Caledonia for further training. Rubber boat work, long arduous marches, physical fitness and weapons training were high on the list in preparation for battles soon to come. The 1st Raider Battalion made the first amphibious assault in force against enemy occupied territory at Tulagi, followed by the battles of Edson's Ridge, Matanikau, and the Tasimboko Raid on Guadalcanal, at Rice Anchorage, Enogai and Bairoko Harbor, New Georgia.

The 2nd Raider Battalion was organized at Jacques Farm at Camp Elliott,CA, under the Command of LTCOL EVANS F. CARLSON. They trained in guerrilla tactics, living off the land, hit and run landings, and rubber boat landings prior to sailing for Hawaii in May 1942. Almost immediately two of their companies were ordered to reinforce the Marines at Midway Island. Company C moved onto Sand Island and Company D to Eastern Island where they took up defensive positions. Companies A and B were chosen to conduct a raid on Makin Island from the Navy submarines USS ARGONAUT and the USS NAUTILUS, that took place 17 August 1942. This was the first raid launched on enemy territory from submarines in the history of the United States Navy. The 2nd BN, then conducted a highly successful 30 day patrol on Guadalcanal in the Aola Bay, Mt. Austen sectors, prior to their battles on Bougainville as part of the 2nd Marine Raider Regiment.

The 3rd Raider Battalion was organized in American Samoa on 20 September 1942, and was commanded by LTCOL HARRY B. LIVERSEDGE. They trained in Samoa prior to being ordered first to Espiritu Santo and then to Guadalcanal for further training prior to their landings on Emirau in the Russell Islands and Puruata, Torokina, Empress Augusta Bay and the Koiari Raid on Bougainville, BSI.

The Raider Training Center at Camp Pendleton was organized in 1942, where the 4th Raider Battalion came into being on 23 October 1942. Their Commanding Officer was MAJOR JAMES ROOSEVELT, the son of the President of the U.S., followed by LTCOL MICHAEL CURRIN, when Roosevelt was evacuated due to malaria.

At Camp Pendleton, many Raider volunteers fresh from boot camp, were introduced to another training course lasting eight weeks. Rubber boat tactics, hand to hand fighting, long hikes, guerrilla warfare and weapons training were long, hard and dirty.   Upon completion of their training at Camp Pendleton, the 4th Raider Battalion shipped out to Espiritu Santo and Guadalcanal for further training prior to their invasion of Segi Point, Viru Harbor, Vangunu and Bairoko, New Georgia Island.

On 15 March 1943, the 1st Marine Raider Regiment was formed on Espiritu Santos. It was composed of the Headquarters and Service Company, The 1st, 2nd, 3rd AND 4th Raider Battalions. 1st H&S COMPANY participated in the assault on Rice Anchorage, New Georgia on 5 July 1943.

The 2ND Marine Raider Regiment (Provisional) was organized on 12 September 1943. It was composed of H&S Company, and the 2nd and 3rd Raider Battalions that participated in the assault landing on 1 Nov 1943, at Empress Augusta Bay, Bougainville, Cape Torokina, Puruata Island and the Koiari Raid. H&S Company was disbanded and the 2nd, and 3rd Raider Battalons reverted to the 1st Marine Raider Regiment on 26 January 1944.

Only after the Raiders proved themselves in combat at Tulagi, Guadalcanal, Makin, New Georgia, Vangunu and Bougainville were they recognized as making a significant contribution to the battle history of the Marine Corps.

After the battle for Bairoko and Bougainville, it became apparent the war in the Pacific had outgrown the capabilities of small, lightly armed hard hitting, units such as the Raiders. The Corps had promised the reconstitution of the old 4th Marines lost in the Philippines in 1942, with a new unit deserving of the honor, to bear the honors and name of the original 4th Marine Regiment.

This honor was accorded the Raiders on 1 February 1944, when the Headquarters and Service Company, 1st Raider Regiment and the 1st, 3rd and 4th Raider Battalions were designated as Headquarters and Service Company and the1st, 3rd, and 2nd Battalions of the 4th Marine Regiment (4th Marines) respectively. Most of the 2nd Raider Batalion was assigned to the Regimental Weapons Company, 4th Marines. The Raider Battalion, Training Center, Camp Pendleton was disbanded and it's personnel assigned to the 5th Marine Division.

The following is a newspaper story announcing the designation of the Raiders as the NEW 4th Marines.

FROM INTERNATIONAL NEWS SERVICE
CORRESPONDENT JACK MAHON.
(Kansas City Star dated Monday, 10 April 1944).

MARINES REFORM A BATAAN UNIT

FOURTH MARINE RAIDER REGIMENT IS
REFORMED.FAMED LEATHERNECK RAIDER
BATALLIONS OF TULAGI TO BOUGAINVILLE
BATTLES, SEEK TO AVENGE HEROES OF TRAGIC
DAYS IN THE PHILIPPINES

Advanced Solomon Island base, 20 March (Delayed). The bloodstained heritage of the most honored Marine Regiment in World War I and also of World War II, the undying, heroes of the 4th Marine Regiment of Bataan - will be perpetuated by the fiercest fighting leatherneck unit EVER FORMED.

A new 4th Marine Regiment, comprising four of the most bloodied Battalions in Corps History - the famed Marine Raiders whose battle flags have been raised in victory in all corners of the Pacific has been organized to finish the fight launched by the fallen gallants of the Philippines. The new 4th Marines, under the command of Lieutenant Colonel Alan A. Shapley of Detroit, were organized in January, under the new Marine program to do away with specialized units. Their first operation was in the virtually unopposed occupation of Emirau Island in the St. Matthias Group, northwest of the Solomons.

THEY WILL REMEMBER

To these men has fallen the task of avenging America's dead in the Pacific. They have read of the atrocities perpetrated by the Japanese on our war prisoners in the Philippines; and they will remember Marines who fought at Alongapo, Mariveles, Bataan, and Corregidor in the Philippines. At Midway, Guadalcanal, Makin Island, the Russells, who made raids on Vangunu, Segi, and the Dragon Peninsula section Of New Georgia; in the Munda campaign and the landing and securing of Empress Augusta Bay on Bougainville in November, these are the men of the new Fourth Regiment. The Marine Raiders under Colonel (now Brigadier General) Merritt A. Edson first came into national prominence in this war when they landed on the island of Tulagi and opened the Solomon Island offensive.

In some of the bitterest fighting of the war the Raiders wiped out the Jap garrison, and then moved on to Guadalcanal to take a major part in the battle for the now famous Henderson Field, the latter island's principal airstrip. Other Raiders, under the command of Lieutenant Colonel Evans F. Carlson, made a daring raid on Makin Island in the Marshalls in August 1942. The same force was also in action on Guadalcanal, while other Raiders were also involved in battles on New Georgia Island and Bougainville.

AUTHOR: the former Raiders as Fourth Marines, made the Japanese pay dearly on the killing fields of the islands of Guam and Okinawa. Initially chosen to spearhead the invasion of the Japanese homeland, they were instead given the honor of being the first Marines to land, as part of the first occupation force in the history of the Japanese Empire. While there they were able to reunite with the old 4th Marine prisoners of war and parade before them proudly flying both the new and the old Fourth Marines battle colors.

They added to the glory of the Old Fourth again and again by distinguishing themselves in battle after battle. The reputation gained however was at a high cost as over 400 Raiders were killed, including 8 Combat Corpsmen, and over 1300 were wounded in the battles for Guam and Okinawa alone.

Throughout the war in the Pacific, many former Raider Marines along with their Corpsmen and Doctors were rotated home or were returned to the U.S. to recover from their wounds or illness. As they returned they distinguished themselves in battle once again as part of training cadres for the 4th, 5th,and 6th Marine Divisions.

In recognition for their professionalism and bravery in the battles for Guam and Okinawa, the 4th Marine Regiment constituted mostly of Raiders, was chosen to spearhead the initial attack force for the planned invasion of the Japanese homeland. Instead they landed as part of the occupying force prior to the signing of the Japanese surrender which ended the war in the Pacific.

They were aboard ship, when they received the good news, and continued on to become the first Marines to set foot on the Japanese homeland. On 30 August 1945, 3 days before the formal signing of the Peace Treaty with Japan on 2 September 1945, Raider 4CP ROGER C. SPAULDING led elements of the 4th Marines (Former 4th Raider Bn) ashore as part of the Allied Occupation Force. Sgt Spaulding became the first Marine to land on the shores of the Japanese homeland in WW II.

THE RAIDERS BOTH STARTED THE WAR AGAINST THE JAPANESE AND FINISHED THE WAR AGAINST THE JAPANESE. THEY WERE THERE FROM THE START TO THE FINISH!

War Mud - Jungle

Marine Flyer Harold McFann, Jr.
Former Corpsman Awarded Silver Star on Tulagi

3

The Battle of Midway

The Battle of Midway was the Turning Point in the Pacific War

Oil tanks burning after Japanese air raid on Midway Island

DEFENSE OF MIDWAY ISLAND
2nd MARINE RAIDER BATTALION
17-18 AUGUST 1942

Following extensive training in guerrilla warfare, hit and run tactics, long forced marches, amphibious exercises from APD 4 Stack destroyers, and rubber boat landings two companies of the 2nd Marine Raiders were hurriedly shipped to Pearl Harbor, Hawaii aboard the USS J. Franklin Bell (APA-16) on 8 May 42.

Three days after their arrival at Camp Catlin, Hawaii, 2nd Bn C & D Companies embarked for Midway Island aboard the USS Case (DD-379), USS Gwin (DD-433) and USS St. Louis (CL-49). Upon their arrival on 25 May 42, Raider Dr. TERRY C. ROGERS, and his Combat Corpsmen dug in and set up the company aid stations. C Co aided in the defense of Sand Island and D Co was at North Island during the ensuing battles. Casualties at Midway were 13 Killed in Action and 18 wounded.

D Co PltSgt HAROLD G. SCHRIER, Iwo Jima flag raising hero became the first Raider cited for bravery under fire, and was awarded the Navy Commendation Medal at Midway Island.

The 3rd Defense Battalion's 37-mm antiaircraft battery (Captain Ronald K. Miller), together with Companies C and D, 2nd Raider Battalion (CAPT DONALD H. HASTIE and 1LT JOHN APERGIS). The 37-mm guns were promptly emplaced, four on each island, while one Raider company (C) went into bivouac in the woods on Sand Island, and the other (D) was sent to Eastern Island

By now Sand Island was surrounded with two double-apron tactical wire barriers, and all installations on both islands were in turn ringed by protective wire. Anti-boat mines made of sealed sewer pipe, and obstacles fashioned from concertina reinforcing-steel lay offshore. The beaches were sown with home-made mines consisting of ammunition boxes filled with dynamite and 20-penny nails; although electric detonation was planned, every such mine also had a bull's eye painted on an exposed landward side, so that it could be set off locally by rifle fire. Cigar-box antitank mines were filled with dynamite to be fired on pressure by current from flashlight batteries, and whiskey-bottle molotov cocktails of high-octane gasoline and fuel oil stood ready at every position.

A decoy mockup airplane--dubbed a JFU ("Jap fouler-upper", was prominently placed on the seaplane apron. Finally, all the underground fuel storage on Sand Island was prepared for demolition by the adjacent planting of large changes of dynamite.

THE BATTLE, 4-5 JUNE 1942

Admiral Nagumo launched the Midway Attack Force, composed of a first wave of 36 carrier attack planes followed by a second wave of 36 carrier bombers and a third wave of 36 fighters.

Twenty-five Marine fighters of VMF-221 tackled 108 Japanese aircraft in the first attack against the intruders, in which only three of the original 12 Marine pilots of Major Parks' group survived.

Captain Armistead's 13 fighters which were all old F2As but one, launched the second Marine strike against the overwhelming number of enemy planes resulting in similar losses.

Perhaps the outstanding factor in these two courageous onslaughts by VMF-221 was the almost incredible disparity between the enemy Zeros, and these new airplanes of unusually high performance pitted against the old Marine F2As.

The next wave, that struck just as the first sticks of bombs began to hit all the north shores of Sand and Eastern Island, was composed of Aichi 99 dive-bombers, that` had also started out 36 strong.

The Kaga group in the first wave, whose mission was to attack the patrol-plane facilities on Sand Island, dropped nine 242-kg bombs on and about the seaplane hangars, setting them afire and starting a large oil fire in the fuel oil tanks 500 yards to the north.

The Akagi group plastered the north shore of Eastern Island, destroying the Marine mess hall, galley, and post exchange, which the returning enemy pilots described as hangars. Other targets of the dive bombers included the already burning fuel storage at the north end of Sand Island, the Sand Island dispensary, and the Eastern Island powerhouse, which suffered direct hits from two bombs, destroying virtually the entire plant. At the very end of the strike, the 6th Defense Battalion's Eastern Island command post received a direct hit that killed the Marine sector commander, Major William W. Benson, and wounded several other personnel.

The contribution of Marines to the defense of Midway had been considerable. Not only had the 3rd and 6th Defense Battalions aided by the Raiders contributed their share of backbreaking labor, unremitting vigilance and highly effective flak, but the aviation personnel of Marine Air Group 22, at a cost rarely surpassed in the history of United States Naval Aviation unhesitatingly faced an enemy superior in numbers and aircraft and exacted more than a full return for their sacrifice at a cost of 49 Marines killed and 53 wounded. Fortunately the Raiders suffered no casualties at the Battle of Midway.

On 16 June 1942 C and D Companies embarked aboard the USS REGULUS AK-14 at Midway Island. They arrived at Pearl Harbor 0n 21 June and were transported to Camp Catlin for further training. Shortly after their arrival they were joined by the returning, 2nd Battalion Makin Island Raiders.

2HQ RICHARD FAVINGER PHM2C writes that " I was placed

on a draft for assignment to the Fleet and was waiting for transportation to Pearl Harbor on 7 Dec 1941. Since transportation wasn't available after the Jap attack, the draft was broken up an I went to Camp Elliot 2nd Marine Division, 2nd Bn. After 5 or 6 weeks, Dr. ROBINSON assembled the Corpsmen and told us about the formation of Carlsons Raiders. He asked for volunteers. We had to be single, no dependents, in good physical shape and have a GOOD reason for wanting to join. After he made his selection we had to sit for an interview with Carlson and if he accepted us we were in.

AUTHOR: This varied from the policy established for the other Raider Battalions, where Battalion commanders were assigned medical personnel without the option to chose those they wanted. Doctors were also in charge of the volunteers until they were assigned as company Corpsmen, at which time they became the responsibility of the Raider Company Commanding Officer.

We were then transferred to Jaques Farm for training. Our trainers were men who had been on Commando Training in Scotland. We had to train first as Raiders and then as combat corpsmen. In was very rigorous, the toughest part for me was hand to hand combat and knife fighting, and marches at night, but the weaponry came rather easily.

After the action had been completed at Midway. My job was to identify fingerprints and make ready for burial at sea all of the deceased battle casualties. Coupled with the helpless feeling we experienced during the bombing and strafing gave me an insightful knowledge of how the survivors of December 7th felt.

The training we went through preparing us for what we had to face once we engaged the enemy, made a lifelong impact on how we lived the rest of our lives." My most traumatic memories are of Bougainville and the Piva Trail, from the dropping of the ramp on our landing craft to the withdrawal back to Guadalcanal 60 days later. When I dig out my old records and photo's for my grandchildren I get very emotional and I visually shake. I am sure other corpsmen do this as well!"

AUTHOR: Dick Favinger was one of the few brave Corpsmen I could get to talk about his experience with the Raiders. It was like pulling teeth to draw information out of them. Thanks for you letters and Photo's Dick!)

4

First Raider Battalion Invasion of Tulagi

U.S.S. Samuel S. Miles (DE-183)

Samuel S. Miles was the first Raider, FMF, Navy Officer killed in action on Tulagi, who, with one Corpsman, were the only attached Raider medical personnel to have a ship named in their honor.

Dr. Miles was posthumously awarded the Silver Star Medal for his outstanding bravery and valor in going to the aid of two gravely wounded Marine Raiders on 7 August 1942 at Tulagi, British Solomon Islands.

AMPHIBIOUS INVASION OF TULAGI
BRITISH SOLOMON ISLANDS
1st MARINE RAIDER BATTALION
7 AUGUST 1942

The honor of becoming the first large U.S, Naval amphibious force since 1898, and the first unit to launch and amphibious attack against a Japanese occupied island in World War II, was bestowed upon the 1st Marine Raider Battalion. Spearheading Operation Watchtower they were to attack the island of Tulagi Island, approximately one hour before the major attack on Guadalcanal. Tulagi, a short distance from Guadalcanal, was 1000 yards wide by 4000 yards long.

The 1st Raider Battalon, with the 2nd Bn 5th Marines in support landed on Tulagi on 7 Aug 42 at H-hour (0700), with the Raiders spearheading the attack and the 1st Parachute BN landing a short time later on Gavutu to seize it.

The Raiders under the command of LTCOL MERRITT "RED MIKE" EDSON, debarked from the destroyer transports (APD's) USS COLHOUN, GREGORY, LITTLE and Mc KEAN in Higgins Boats without a landing ramp. All the landing boats got hung up on coral formations some 30 to 100 yards from the beach head and the Raiders had to wade ashore in water as high as their necks. Fortunately the landing was unopposed and the Raiders formed their lines to move against the enemy on the beach and spread out to the hilly areas with many ravines and caves across the island.

Although respecting the firepower of the Japanese the Raiders were not yet aware of the fanatical Japanese tactics of fighting to the death and refusing to surrender! Thoroughly trained to expect night attacks and attempted infiltration of their lines, the Raiders were the first enemy troops who stood their ground and didn't panic while facing the repeated night time Banzai attacks, that were designed to break through the their defenses. It was on Tulagi that Japanese troops learned to fear America's hitherto secret, Marines. Raiders gave more than they took in battle and inflicted defeat upon them for the first time.

Victory didn't come easy however. 1LT EUGENE M. KEY became the first Raider Officer casualty, followed by PVT THOMAS NICKEL. When Dr. SAMUEL S. MILES attempted to aid his comrades, he too was immediately killed, becoming the first Raider Navy Officer to be KIA (killed in action). KEY, NICKEL and MILES were also the first of twenty-six 1st Battalion Raiders to have Navy ship's named in honor of them.

DR SAMUEL S. MILES LT (MC) was awarded the Silver Star Medal.

The Citation read in part:

"For conspicuous gallantry and intrepidity while attached to the First Marine Raider Battalion during action against enemy Japanese forces on Tulagi, Solomon Islands, August 7, 1942. LT MILES, knowing that three men of Company D, isolated to his front, had been killed and numerous others wounded, without regard for his own safety, attempted to cross a zone covered by enemy fire in order to administer first aid to the wounded. In this valiant attempt to carry out his duties, LT MILES lost his life."

Three men in SGT FRANK GUIDONE'S platoon, were hit and suffered fatal injuries on an exposed ridge while another RAIDER suffering from a painful wound, was treated by GUIDONE with sulfa powder and a compress to his arm.

AUTHOR: Each Raider was supplied with a small medical

kit containing Sulfa powder, bandages and morphine. That first day two of the officers, MAJ KEN BAILEY and CAPT JUSTICE CHAMBERS (Medal of Honor, Iwo Jima) were also wounded and had to be evacuated.

Japanese snipers were very accurate and it took only three shots to kill the first three Raiders. Snipers killed PLT SGT ALEXANDER LUKE and barely missed MAJ LOU WALT, who later became Commandant of the Marine Corps. The Raiders had excellent shooters also. The Raiders were deadly accurate with there '03 Springfield rifles at up to 500 yards, and their machine gunners were second to none with their accuracy.

As expected during the night the Japanese launched several suicide attacks as well as attempting to infiltrate Raider lines. There was vicious hand to hand bayonet, knife, sword and bare knuckle fighting throughout the night. Raiders used hand grenades freely rather than firing their weapons and giving away their positions. In the morning the area around the Raider front lines were covered with dead Japs.

Corpsman HAROLD McFANN JR. rushed forward to give first aid to two of his wounded comrades and had to protect them from attacking enemy soldiers. For his bravery, he became the first Raider Corpsman to receive the Silver Star Medal. His award read in part: "For conspicuous gallantry and intrepidity while attached to the 1st Marine Raider Battalion during action against enemy Japanese forces on Tulagi, Solomon Islands, August 7, 1942. On his own initiative, and without regard for personal safety, Pharmacist Mate Third Class HAROLD McFANN JR. advanced beyond the line held by his company, located two severely wounded comrades and, although exposed to intense enemy fire, fearlessly administered first aid. While thus engaged, he was forced to defend himself with a rifle he had found beside a wounded Marine. By his undaunted courage and steadfast devotion to duty, he undoubtedly saved the lives of his two injured comrades. His heroic conduct was in keeping with the highest traditions of the United States Naval Service."

Corpsman McFANN later requested permission to enroll in the Navy Pilot training program at Pensacola, FL. Upon graduation in 1944 he chose to become a Marine flyer. Tragically he was killed a short time later in a plane crash.

Corpsman THADDEUS PARKER, Hospital Apprentice 1c was awarded a Letter of Commendation for his heroism in the battle for Tulagi. He was later awarded the Navy Cross in the battle for Edsons Ridge, Guadalcanal and the Silver Star in the Bairoko Harbor battle, on the island of New Georgia where, he tragically gave his life for his country and his comrades.

His citation read in part:

Parker advanced beyond his front lines on several occasions to render first aid and evacuate officers and men of his battalion. While so serving he was subjected to continuous machine gun and rifle fire. His courage and determination served as an example to his comrades."

GYSGT ANGUS GOSS was recommended for the Medal of Honor by LTCOL EDSON and approved by GEN VANDERGRIFT AND ADMIRAL'S GHORMELY and NIMITZ for his heroics on Tulagi. Although Goss received the Conspicuous Gallantry Medal, from the King of England, his recommendation for the Medal of Honor was reduced to the Navy Cross, thus SGT CLYDE THOMASON, 2nd Raider Battalion, became the first enlisted Marine and Raider in World War II to receive that honor. SGT JAMES SMITH who prepared the short fuse explosive charges for GOSS received the first of his two Silver Star Medals for contribution to the defeat of the Japanese.

The Raiders remained on Tulagi until the end of August undergoing some shelling from Japanese surface craft. The Paratroopers suffered over 20% casualties on neighboring Gavutu and Tanambogo but secured these islands by 9 August.

Overall enemy losses, in the area were 1500 killed, 23 captured and about 70 who escaped by swimming to Florida Island. The Raiders assisted in their destruction as they were systematically hunted down and killed. The long road back had begun as the Raiders had launched the first major offensive attack against the Japanese Marines (Special Naval Landing Forces). The Marine Raiders had destroyed the myth of Japanese invincibility and set the pattern for all future island campaigns in the Pacific.

The Raiders buried their dead on Tulagi, and the heretofore hush, hush special 1st Marine Raiders were the men of the hour. Overnight these young Marines became America's most acclaimed and respected jungle fighters. The Raiders on Tulagi suffered a total of 39 deaths and 42 WIA.

The capture of Tulagi gave the Raiders first hand experience in how best to counter night time banzai attacks designed to terrify enemy troops which until then had always been successful for the Japanese troops in battle. Although it was the Raiders first time in combat they disproved the myth of the enemy being unbeatable and inflicted a sobering defeat upon them for the first time in their relentless drive to occupy territory all across the Pacific Ocean for their Emperor.

Although Japanese troops had 12 years in which to perfect their jungle fighting tactics, they soon learned their sniper fire, cave gun emplacements and night attacks did not icreate panic in the Marines attackers; instead, for the first time, they were facing fear and defeat themselves. From that time until the end of the war they feared Marine and Marine Raider attacks, although they often fought to the last man at the urging of their Emperor.

Corpsmen and Doctor's performed with bravery and determination regardless of the Jap troops effots to use them for target practice. There were to be no Red Cross arm bands or unarmed non-combat medical personnel in this war! As usual Corpsmen, had little rest following the battles, as they treated the less seriously walking wounded not in serious enough condition to evacuate, as well as the large number of Raiders coming to sick call with cuts and bruises, dysentery and symptoms of malaria and other tropical diseases.

The bravery of Corpsmen and Doctors of the Fleet Marine Force and the Raider Battalion's throughout World War II in the Pacific is legendary. No one single unit was more revered by the Raiders than their attached Corpsmen and Doctors. They were indispensable and faced the same hardships and danger in battle as the riflemen.

When the mop up was completed, the Defense of Tulagi, Tanambogo and Gavutu became the responsibility of the 2nd Bn, 5th Marines and the 2nd Marines. A Raider reconnaissance patrol on Florida Island was launched on 8 August from a Higgins boat. Coastwatcher HENRY JOSSELYN arranged for native paddlers with 3 war canoes to transport the Raiders to other small islands in search of Jap stragglers.

On the 15-mile trip to Savo Island there were so many sharks in the water, the Raiders had to blast a path through them with hand grenades. Coming closer to shore they found the reason for the shark frenzy, was the bodies, face down of many sailors, who were apparently lost in the Naval Battle of Savo Island, later to be known as Iron Bottom Sound. Finding no stragglers they returned to Tulagi in their Higgins boat through the shark infested waters while saying prayers for the unfortunate sailors.

Following their search of the Islands, the Raiders were transported to Guadalcanal aboard APD'S LITTLE and GREGORY to reinforce the 1st Marine Division on 31 Aug 1942. The Raiders had killed over 450 Japanese troops while losing 39 killed and 42 Wounded in Action.

RAIDERS WHO LOST
THERE LIVES ON TULAGI

AHRENS, EDWARD	ALLAN, JOHN W.
BARCOMB,CHARLES	BARR, WOODROW
BOWERS, KENNETH	BRADLEY, MARION
BUTTS, LEONARD	CARPELLOTTI,LOUIS
CHURCH, THOMAS	CLARKE, JACK
DIOVISALVO,GERARD	DISMUKES, ALVIN
FLANAGAN,ANDRE	FOX, MILES C.
GIFFELS, GORDON	GILLIGAN, JOHN
GYATT, EDWARD	HAMPTON, ARTHUR
HANSEN, EVAN J.	HINKLE, FRED L.
HUBER, FRANK	JOHNSON, GEORGE
KEY, EUGENE M.	LEHMAN, CLIFFORD
LOVIN, LOUIS A.	LUKE, ALEXANDER
MARTINO, JOSEPH	MILES, SAMUEL*
MILLER,CLAUDE	NEE, MICHAEL F.
NICKEL,THOMAS	PAINE, ROBERT I.
RENYE, BUCKLEY	ROZGA, WALTER
SPEICHER, ELMER	STRANDVOLD, WM.
TROWBRIDGE,GEO	WALSH, PATRICK
WILLAMSON, DON	

* NAVY DOCTOR

1ST RAIDERS AWARDED MEDALS ON TULAGI

NAVY CROSS

AHRENS, ROBERT	EDSON, MERRITT A.
FOX, MYLES	GOSS, ANGUS R.
HACKER, ELMER	HILLS, CLIFFORD G.
HUNT, WILFRED A.	KEY, EUGENE M.

SILVER STAR

BAILEY, KENNETH D.	BARR, WOODROW
BLOTTER, MICHAEL	CARPELLOTTI,LOUIS
CASSIDY,VINCENT	CECKA, ETHODIOUS
CHAMBERS,JUSTICE	COFFIN, HERBERT
CONNORS, JOHN	GILLIGAN,JOHN JR
GYATT, EDWARD	HALL, JAMES G.
JOHNSON,GEORGE	KENNEDY, JOHN E.
LUKE, ALEXANDER	NICKLE, THOMAS
PAINE, ROBERT	ROGERS, VIRGIL
ROZGA, WALTER	RUANE, THOMAS
RYDER, ASTLE A.	SMITH, JAMES
WALT, LEWIS W.	WARD, GEORGE

1ST RAIDER DOCTOR AND A CORPSMAN WERE AWARDED THE SILVER STAR MEDAL ON TULAGI

McFANN, HAROLD JR. PHM3   MILES, SAMUEL S. LT

NAVAL APD DESTROYER TRANSPORTS

These gallant little ships were great friends of the Raiders. They were ancient World War I Four Stack Destroyers that were pressed into service as troop transports. Two Stacks and boilers were removed so they could carry 143 troops. USS McKEAN and USS MANLEY were used by Edsons Raiders on the East Coast for training in rubber boat landings. On the West Coast the USS GREGORY, USS LITTLE, and USS COLHOUN were used by Carlsons Raiders in landings at San Clemente.

All Raider Battalions served aboard APD Destroyers for landing exercise training at one time or another. While aboard they were always treated as shipmates, not as intruders, as was the case on many other troop transports during the war. Although terribly overcrowded there was always a hot cup of "Joe" (coffee) available at any hour from the galley.

4HQ DAN MARSH recalls, " We were required to approach the objective in silence, land quickly, hide the rubber boats and then secure the area and await further orders. Such movement by rubber boat is extremely difficult and requires the full concentration of all hands. In conjunction with these landings, we frequently were required to move through the unfamiliar jungle terrain, maintaining contact and arriving at the assigned objective prepared to attack at first light. These movements were continually rehearsed, and would serve us well in the months ahead."

Marine Raiders salute the officers and men of these daring little APD's and destroyer escorts. They were our shipmates and though few in number, none showed more bravery. Our two "orphan" outfits were thrown together in combat against the vastly more experienced Japanese forces during the early days of World War II. Of the original six APD's only two survived the war.

On 7 August 42 the USS GREGORY, LITTLE, COLHOUN and McKEAN landed the 1st Raider Battalion at Tulagi, to launch the first offensive action in WW II by the Raiders. With the destruction of our cruiser force at Savo Island, emergency supply and transport for Guadalcanal fell to these APD's.

On 15 Aug 42, they took CUB-I, l20 man Aviation Ground Force, to Guadalcanal along with 400 drums of Aviation gasoline, 32 drums of lubricant, 282 bombs, and chamois skin that was used to hand strain the gasoline. On 20 Aug 42 these same ships delivered 3 1/2 days supply of food, 40 tons each, to the short rationed Marines and Raiders.

On 30 Aug 42 USS COLHOUN and LITTLE ferried Raiders from Tulagi to the 'Canal. That afternoon at 1512 a flight of 18 enemy p1anes appeared and dropped two sticks of bombs that hit all around the COLHOUN. Near misses hitting only 50 feet away from bridge to fantail were devastating. These thin armored greyhounds had little or no chance against any type of enemy gunfire. Engines, boilers, pumps and piping were torn from their fastenings and the ship began to sink rapidly by the stern. LCDR MADDEN ordered Abandon Ship and within two minutes the USS COLHOUN went down, with a loss of 51 men.

On 2 Sep 42, USS LITTLE and USS GREGORY ferried 2 Companies of the 1st RAIDERS to Savo Island to investigate rumors of Japanese presence on the Island. JOHN ANTONELI 's A Co, led one Company down the Eastern shore while XO MAJ SAM GRIFFITH led the other Company down the western shore. They circled the island, found no Japs and re-embarked on the LITTLE & GREGORY and arrived at GUADALCANAL after dark. They started to debark, when word came from LTCOL MERRITT EDSON to remain aboard as the Tasimboko Raid was scheduled for the next morning. Since the unloading had already commenced, it was decided to complete it and all Raiders went ashore.

Just after midnight, three Japanese Destroyers entered the channel to shell Henderson Field. A PBY dropped 5 flares to illuminate, and the out gunned LITTLE (Division CDR HADLEY), and Skipper (LCDR LOFBERG) opened fire with one one 4" gun and some 20 mm guns. One enemy shot penetrated the steering engine room, one entered the after fuel tanks and another put the gun 4" out of action. Fuel oil burst into brilliant flames and GREGORY now drew the attention of accurate enemy 5" salvos which shredded her bridge, knocked down the after stack, pried open the galley deckhouse, burst a boiler, and killed seamen with jagged hunks of metal. Flames raced from stem to stern GREGORY'S fighting days were over. On the burning USS LITTLE, before Abandon Ship could be carried out both Skipper LOFBERG and DIV CDR HADLEY were killed on the bridge and the USS GREGORY was abandoned.

Clarence C. Justice and Chester N. Ellis helped their badly wounded Skipper, LCDB HARRY F. BAUER over the side. He ordered them to go the aid of a drowning sailor and he was never seen again. With both ships burning and helpless the Japanese steamed between them at high speed firing shells which killed floating survivors.

USS LITTLE lost 22 killed and 44 wounded. USS GREGORY lost 11 killed, 26 wounded. Survivors spent a miserable, night in overturned life rafts and shattered life jackets Admiral Turner said, "The Officers and men serving in these ships have shown great courage. They entered this dangerous area time after time, knowing their ship stood little or no chance if opposed by enemy surface or air attack. On their last trip they performed continuous service for six days."

The Tasimboko Raid was delayed 4 days while the USS McKEAN and USS MANLEY were brought forward. This raid will be described later but McKEAN and MANLEY made a second trip to bring in reinforcements. After the successful battle, with 2 Raiders killed and 6 WIA, the force returned to the Marine perimeter and the ships to Tulagi Harbor for the night.

On 03 November 42, USS McKEAN and USS MANLEY landed Carlsons Raiders at Aola Bay, 40 miles east of the 1st Marine Division lines around Henderson Field. McKEAN and MANLEY made two more trips between Espiritu Santo and Guadalcanal to supply and reinforce the original Raider companies, C and E. After Guadalcanal was fully secured more Destroyer Transports (APD's)' were rushed into the Solomon s area.

They were USS DENT, WATERS, TALBOT, 'WARD, McKEAN, STRINGHAM and MANLEY. Trans Div 22,LCdr R.H. Wilkinson was composed of four ships and the make up varied also with USS KILTY, CROSBY, SCHLEY, McCALLA Destroyer-Minesweepers (DM3) TREVOR, HOPKINS, ZANE and DD GWIN.

USS MANLEY took I Co, 3rd Raiders in on D-Day, 21 Feb and returned them to Guadalcanal on 21 March 43. Other ships involved were USS WARD, DENT, WATERS, TALBOT, McKEAN, ZANE and SCHLEY.

For the 4th Raiders movement from Guadalcanal to Segi Plantation on 20 June 43, LTCOL M.S. CURRIN employed the use of USS DENT and the USS WATERS. The supporting Army troops were landed on 21 June 43 by USS SCHLEY and CROSBY.

In mid May 1942, Cruiser (CL) ST LOUIS, and DD's GWIN

and CASE rushed two companies (C&D) of CARLSON's Raiders to the island of Midway to help defend that thin strip of sand against the huge Japanese Armada approaching for the Battle of Midway on 3- 5 June 1942).

This same gallant little ship, USS GWIN, Cdr John Higgens, was sunk in the Battle off Kolombangara 12-13 July. She was supporting APD'S that had brought supplies to COLONEL LIVERSEDGE at freshly captured Enogai Inlet on 11-12 July. At 0214 the USS GWIN was hit by a torpedo amidships and exploded burning white hot. She sank with a loss of 2 officers and 59 men. The USS RALPH TALBOT saved the balance of the crew.

On 27 June Co O and P and HQ, 4th Raiders at Segi paddled in rubber boats to Regi and launched the four day overland jungle approach to Viru Harbor. The occupation force aboard USS HOPKINS, KILTY, and CROSBY steamed into Viru on 30 June expecting to find it in the hands of the Raiders, instead they were still a day's march away. When the APD' hove into range the enemy opened fire with a 3" gun at Tetamara and CDR LEITH made haste in withdrawing beyond range and steamed back and forth across the Harbor mouth, finally landing the force at Nono. Raiders marched overland and captured the Japanese Base at Wickham Anchorage, Vangunu on 1 July. On 8 July CLARKS 4th Raiders boarded an LCT and landed on neighboring Gatuki Island, but the 2 day search located no Japs, and on 12 July they returned to Guadalcanal.

On 1 July 43 the 1st Raider Battalion under Regimental Commander COL H. B. LIVERSEDGE and Battalion Commander LTCOL SAMUEL B. GRIFFITH; together with 2 Army battalions, 3rd Bn 145th Infantry (LTCOL G. G Freer) 3rd Bn 148th Infantry (LTCOL D.E. Schultz), loaded aboard Eight Destroyers for the fast run to Rice Anchorage, New Georgia, the backdoor to Munda airfield, the prime enemy target in the Central Solomons. The APD's were, USS DENT, TALBOT, WATERS, McKEAN, KILTY, CROSBY, SCHLEY and McCALLA. During the landing 0130, 05 July, the enemy guns (Four 140 mm) at Enogai Inlet opened fire on the heavily laden APD'S. Only the USS WATERS suffered a hit as she had her main truck shot away. The over-land jungle approach was launched that night and Enogai inlet base was captured on 10 July 43. In preparation for the next Raider battle at Bairoko Harbor, COL HARRY "THE HORSE" LIVERSEDGE ordered LTCOL MICKEY CURRIN and the 4th Raider BN to join the 1st Raiders at Enogai. At Guadalcanal on 17 July, CURRIN's Raiders embarked in the USS WARD, KILTY, McKEAN, and

WATERS and arrived at ENOGAI 0100 18 July. After the Bairoko battle the USS MCKEAN and other APD'S brought in supplies and carried out most of the 190 wounded Raiders. Again on 15 August the USS KILTY, WARD, McKEAN, STRINGHAM, DENT, WATERS and TALBOT carried the Assault troops. to VELLA LAVELLA in the wind up of campaining in the Central Solomons. With the securing of Bairoko and the capture of Munda airfield on 29 Aug, the decimated remnants of the 1st Raider Regiment (1st and 4th Raider BN's) were at last evacuated by USS KILTY, CROSBY, SCHLEY and MC CALLA. With the rapid production of newer, faster, modern, Assault Craft the need and use of these old obsolete APD' s disappeared. Almost the last of these brave little ships to be sunk was the oldest friend of all four Raider Battalions, the USS McKEAN (LCDR R.L. RAMEY, Skipper).

Following the invasion of Empress Augusta Bay, Bougainville on 1Nov 43, assault troops of the 2nd and 3rd Raider Battalions, were landed from big ships (APA'S) but on a reinforcing mission, while barely 22 miles from Cape Torokina at 0350, 17 Nov. McKEAN was hit by an air torpedo. Her crew shot down the plane that hit her, The torpedo set off the after magazine, the depth charge storage and ruptured 3 fuel tanks, which splashed flaming oil over the after part of the ship. All lights and power failed. Debris falling on the siren whistle cord added a weird, eerie blast to the confusion. Marine troops began jumping overboard and almost everyone who did so before ABANDON SHIP had been ordered, was burned to death in the floating oil. In 10 minutes, McKEAN began to sink by the stern. Skipper Rainey after final inspection, went over the side at 0412. Of 185 Marines embarked, 52 were lost. Of the ship's 12 Officers and 141 crew, 3 Officers and 6l men perished. The late Naval Historian, Admiral Samuel Eliot Morison, from whom much of this description was taken, adds this epitaph to the APD's. "Old weak and brittle, Any explosion made them "fold Up like a shoe box", but for lack of better transport they were pressed into service and for two years carried the war to the enemy in the famous campaigns of the Marine Raider Battalions." 76 Patch Editor.

APD TRAINING
DAN MARSH 4TH RAIDER BATTALION
The brightest part of our training to me was the practice landings we carried out from APD's. The Company would cram itself into the small troop compartment of the Destroyer, store the rubber boats on deck and try to stay out of the crew's way as we got

underway. Compared to a troop transport the Destroyers were very fast and standing on deck as they sliced through the water was very exhilarating. Day after day we rehearsed speeding up from below, launching our rubber boats, boarding them and then landing in the proper formation on various small islands. Frequently on going ashore, the natives would approach with baskets of breadfruit, papaya, taro root and whatever they thought would please us. These exercises were a breath of fresh air to us all.

TRAINING

NIGHT MOVEMENT

The other main element of our training was less exciting but just as important. It was the movement by night over water while maintaining contact and the proper formation. We were required to approach the objective in silence, land quickly, hide the rubber boats and then secure the area and await further orders. Such movement by rubber boat is extremely difficult and requires the full concentration of all hands. In conjunction with these landings, we frequently were required to move through the unfamiliar jungle terrain, maintaining contact and arriving at the assigned objective prepared to attack at first light. These movements were continually rehearsed, and would serve us well in the months ahead. Near the end of our training schedule we began to think we were being trained for a specific mission. However, this was never officially confirmed.

5

Makin Island Raid

Sgt. Clyde Thomason, MOH
He was first enlisted Raider to receive Medal of Honor

Sgt. Clyde Thomason, USMCR

OFFICIAL MEDAL OF HONOR CITATION

"For conspicuous heroism and intrepidity above and beyond the call of duty during the Marine Raider Expedition against the Japanese-held island of Makin on 17-18 August 1942. Leading the advance element of the assault echelon, Sergeant Thomason deployed his men with keen judgement and discrimination and, by exemplary leadership and great personal valor, exhorted them to like fearless efforts. On one occasion, he dauntlessly walked up to a house which concealed an enemy Japanese sniper, forced in the door and shot the man before he could resist. Later in the action, while leading an assault on an enemy position, he gallantly gave his life in the service of his country. His courage and loyal devotion to duty in the face of grave peril were in keeping with the finest traditions of the United States Naval Service."

MAKIN ISLAND RAID
SECOND MARINE RAIDER BN
17,18 AUGUST 1942

Two hundred twenty one 2nd Raider Battalion Marines of companies A and B plus a partial HQ Company; made the first amphibious assault landing from submarines in the history of the United States Navy. On 17-18 August 1942 they launched a raid on Butaritari Island, Makin Atoll, Gilbert Islands, aboard the submarines USS Argonaut (SS-166) and USS Nautilus (SS-168)

AUTHOR: The following previously classified after action report written by LTCOL CARLSON while aboard the USS NAUTILUS was obtained through the diligence and determination of Mr. Tom Holtom a nephew of Captain Gerald P. Holtom, KIA Makin Island. The report has been abridged with several sub-sections combined for the sole purpose of clarity and conserving space in this publication.

CLASSIFIED
USS NAUTILUS TASK UNIT #7.15.3 HQ AT SEA.
EVANS F. CARLSON, LTCOL, USMCR
21 AUGUST 1942

OPERATIONS ON MAKIN ISLAND, 17-18 AUGUST 1942
1. In compliance with orders proceeded to Makin with landing made at 0500 on 17 August 1942.
2. Approach to debarkation point in strong onshore wind. Heavy swells and need to keep the submarines NAUTILUS and ARGONAUT moving in order to avoid being carried onto the reef made it impossible to assemble boats alongside for the disembarkment as planned. Many rubber boat motor failures resulted in confusion in the darkness requiring a change of plans if we were to land before daylight as planned. I decided to take both companies to the same beach. Fifteen of the eighteen boats landed near GOVERNMENT WHARF, two a mile north and one with LT PEATROSS aboard landed a mile south in the rear of the enemy.

a. Both companies were badly intermingled upon landing due to the serious difficulty in paddling the rubber boats as few boat motors were. LT PLUMLEY, commanding Co A directed to move across the island to seize the road on the lagoon side.

b. Government House taken at 0545, and PLUMLEY directed to advance on the Japanese Trading Station. CAPT COYTE, commanding company B, directed to place his company in reserve.

A few minutes later 1st Plt of A Co made contact with enemy along lagoon road near the native hospital. Enemy reinforcements arrived by truck and were forced to unload 300 yards back by our .55 cal. Boys Gun.

Natives of Butaritari reported bulk of Japanese troops at On Chong's Wharf. I then requested submarine's to fire in the vicinity of the causeway to cut off any reinforcements. Subsequently the submarine's fired on two ships that entered the lagoon. Both of them were set on fire and sunk.

By 0700 the pattern of enemy defense was determined to be built around machine guns, grenade throwers, automatic rifles and a flame thrower (If confirmed this would be this first use of flame throwers against the Raiders). Sniper and machine gun fire had taken a heavy toll on our right flank.

c. At 1130 the first enemy planes appeared. After circling they dropped their bombs. At 1320 a flight of 11 planes including four Zeroes, two Kawanishi flying boats, four Recon bombers and two Type 95 seaplanes arrived. Bombing and straffing continued for an hour and a quarter. One of the Kawanishi bombers and one Type 95 landed in the lagoon off Kings Pier and were engaged by our machine guns and one Boys anti-tank gun and were destroyed. At about 1430, I was informed by the natives the Kawanishi had landed reinforcements. At that time the center of our line was located in an area with thick foliage which provided an advantage to the snipers. I decided to draw these snipers on to ground more advantageous by withdrawing my right and center to a line where there was a good field of fire. The principal gain to us came during the final 1630 air attack on the 17th when the enemy planes bombed their own troops in the area we had recently evacuated,

d. The time agreed upon for our return to the submarines was 1930. At 1840. our line was shortened by pivoting on our left flank then pivoting the right back to the Government House. Boat crews went to prepare the boats. At 1900, with a covering force established closer to the beach, the bulk of the force was withdrawn to the boats. At 1915 the boats entered the water, with the covering squad and myself, embarked at 1930 after all other boats had left.

e. The hour of 1930 had been set because it would be dark and the tide would be high enabling boats to get over the reef. No one was apprehensive of any trouble getting through the surf. It didn't look nearly as tough as other surfs we had worked in. However, I had failed to take into account the speed of the waves and the rapid succession in which they followed each other. The following hour provided a struggle so intense and futile that it will forever remain a ghastly nightmare to those who participated. The experience of those in my own boat was typical. We walked the boat out to deep water and commenced paddling. The motor refused to work. The first three or four rollers were easy to pass, then came the battle. Paddling furiously for all we were worth we would get over one roller only to be hit and thrown back by the next before we could gain momentum. The boat filled to the gun-whales with water. We got out and swam pulling the boat to no avail. We jettisoned the motor. Subsequently the boat turned over. We righted it but lost our equipment. We continued to battle and I thought our boat was the only one having this difficulty, for the others had left ahead of us. However, after nearly an hour of struggle, men swam up to our stern and reported their boat had returned to the beach because the men were exhausted. They would rest, then walk up the beach to try another spot. I ordered our boat to be turned around and returned to the beach, as our men were equally exhausted. On arrival at the beach I found that over half the boats were there. They were all exhausted and most of their gear had been lost in the surf. The wounded of whom there had been four stretcher cases and several ambulatory, were particularly helpless. I directed the boats be pulled well up on the beach and the men rest. Security was established with such arms as could be scraped together. Subsequent attempts by individual boats at other spots along the beached failed.

f. At about 0100 PVT HAWKINS, one of those posted as security above the beach line was challenged by a Japanese patrol of eight men. He opened fire with his automatic weapon and was fired on from both sides, the bullets entering his chest and he was seriously but not mortally wounded. Investigation showed he had killed three of the Japanese before he had been shot. This incident showed that enemy resistance was by no way ended.

g. At this point the situation was extremely grave. Our initial retirement had been orderly, but the battle with the surf had disorganized us and stripped us of our fighting power. Planes would undoubtedly return at daylight and it was probable that a landing force would arrive. My plan was to await daylight, move to the north end of the island and attempt to find sufficient outrigger canoes to take us to the submarines. A check showed that 120 men were still on the beach, and there was no assurance that others had not returned to the beach at points farther away. Rain and the fact that most of the men had stripped themselves of their clothes in the surf added to the general misery.

h. Shortly after daylight one group of men requested permission to make another try through the surf and after a terrific battle they made it. Other groups were then organized and followed. It was useless to send the wounded, especially the stretcher cases, so I directed MAJ ROOSEVELT to return in one of the boats and take charge of our forces on the submarines. My duty was to remain until the last man could be evacuated. A total of four boats got through safely before an air raid put an end to this piecemeal evacuation. Seventy men were now left on the beach.

i. It is necessary to mention the devoted efforts of the Officers and men of the submarines to relieve us. We were in communications with both subs by blinker throughout the night, our radios having been rendered useless. Early on the morning of the 18th they moved close to the beach, remaining there until enemy air forced them to dive. At 0740 one rubber boat with a motor which was operating left the NAUTILUS, with five Raiders who had volunteered to come to our relief. The boat came to a point just outside the reef and shot a line to us. One man swam in with a message from the Commodore that the subs would remain off the island until we were evacuated. Planes came over and the boat headed out to sea where it was straffed and nothing more was seen of it or of the crew. The NAUTILUS signaled just before diving that she would return at 1930.

j. On the 18th a total of four flights of planes came over between 0920 and 1730. It was evident from there actions the enemy was confused as to the situation. Heavy bombers bombed the island north of Butaritari. Natives from the north reported that LITTLE MAKIN which we had originally planned to attack on the 2nd day was also bombed. The heaviest bombing on Butaritari was in the vicinity of On Chong's Wharf and King's Wharves. By this time I had learned the enemy force ashore consisted of only a few men who were widely scattered. I sent out patrols to gather food and to destroy the radio station at On Chong's. A patrol on the north end of the island discovered and shot one Japanese Marine. The patrol which went to On Chong's shot another. I took a patrol and went over the battlefield of the preceding day checking our own dead and inspecting the enemy dead, searching for papers and collecting equipment with which to arm our own men. Total enemy dead on the field was 83. Opposite our right flank our machine gun bullets killed thirty men on the lagoon side of the road. To the east machine guns were surrounded by their dead crews, killed by our grenades and riflemen. Our own dead on this northern front numbered eleven including my intelligence officer, LT HOLTOM. Our other three men killed in action were members of LT PEATROSS' boat crew, which landed behind the enemy lines to the south.

k.   It is necessary to mention the part taken in this action by LT PEATROSS and his eleven men. I was unaware of his whereabouts until about 1400 on the 17th when one of his men joined our force having penetrated the enemy lines. When the surf had carried his boat to the south, when he landed firing began to his north and he moved inland. Near the trading station he engaged the enemy troops killing eight, while losing three of his own men. During the balance of the day he continued to harass the enemy from the rear, searched houses, destroyed a small radio station, picked off messengers and burned a truck. At 1930 he re-embarked and after a difficult struggle with the surf, succeeded in regaining the Nautilus. The presence of mind, judgement, skill, courage and devotion to duty displayed by this young officer, who was under fire for the first time, are considered outstanding.

l.   Food in the form of canned meats, fish and biscuits had been found at the Japanses Trading Station. During the afternoon of the 18th I had moved our force back to the vicinity of

Government House, where water and cover were available and where the form of an old defense position provided added protection. Patrols were operated from here. It was decided to evacuate the remaining force at 1930 by way of the south lagoon. A small sloop with an auxiliary motor was anchored off the Japanese Trading Station. LT LAMB and two men volunteered to row out to the sloop and explore the possibility of using her for the evacuation. I had a patrol in the vicinity of the Trading Station destroying stores. We covered LT LAMB'S approach to the sloop. As his boat arrived alongside shots were heard. The party boarded but departed a few minutes later. LAMB reported hat when they arrived he was fired at by a pistol thrust through a porthole, the bullet going wild. After tossing a hand grenade on board they finished the Japanese Marine who was guarding the ship. As the ship was half full of water and in a dilapidated condition it was unusable.

m. The patrol I took to the south late in the afternoon was for the purpose of destroying as many stores as possible in the time remaining. The most important job proved to be a quantity of aviation gasoline, estimated to aggregate from 700 to 1,000 barrels. This was accomplished by shooting into the barrels and using TNT for ignition. On this trip the office of the Japanese Commandant, who had been killed in battle, was searched and all available papers, plus a chart were, were secured. AUTHOR: Prior to leaving the island LTCOL CARLSON had given the native chief gold coins to assure the proper burial of all RAIDERS killed.

n. The evacuation was executed from the lagoon side by carrying four boats (all of our remaining boats serviceable) across from the sea side. Natives provided one outrigger, thus affording space for our 70 men, including the stretcher wounded. The evacuation was supervised by CAPT COYTE and LT LAMB the latter, twice wounded and nearly drowned on the 17th, and nearly missing death on the sloop on the 18th. All five boats were lashed abeam of each other. Two boats had motors although only one worked throughout as we set off across the lagoon at 2030. The Nautilus had been previously informed that she meet us off Flink Point. Off Flink Point we flashed a signal and received an immediate response. At 2308 we arrived alongside.

o. The natives reported the enemy had three days advance warning of our arrival. The defending force had held maneuvers up and down Butaritari between On Chong's and Government House and the snipers were located in the tree tops between Government House and Stone Pier for three days.

AUTHOR: LT PEATROSS AND Doctor MacCRACKEN had visited the sub-fleet Officer's Cub in Hawaii before sailing and were particularly upset to hear talk of their "Top Secret Raid" being talked about openly as it was common knowledge Japanese spies were known to be on the islands. This appears to be a case of the enemy having too much knowledge in advance.

Special credit is due to the members of the Medical Corps, particularly to Lieutenants W.B. MacCRACKEN and STEPHEN L. STIGLER, (MC) USNR. On the night of the 17th Doctor STIGLER managed to get aboard the Argonaut, and he took charge of the wounded there. DR MacCRACKEN remained ashore until the final evacuation and then spent the next twenty-four hours operating. This operation justified in full the policy of assigning one medical officer to each Raider Co.

AUTHORS NOTE: The remaining part of the action report deals with comments and recommendations as to further combat operations.

Both Doctor's were rightly awarded Navy Cross Medals for their bravery and devotion to duty in this operation. It has never been explained however, why this is the only Raider assault in which NO Corpsman was awarded a medal.

JOHN M. HAINES, COMMANDER
U.S. NAVY TASK GROUP 7.15 ABOARD THE USS NAUTILUS THIS EXPEDITION, THE FIRST IN THE HISTORY OF THE NAVY AS FAR IS KNOWN, is considered to have successfully accomplished its mission. The measure of success is not as great as had been hoped for and The loss of men and equipment by our forces were greater than expected. Some of the reasons for this was the semi-alert state of the enemy, failure of ship to shore communications, change of landing plan because of debarking problems and difficulties encountered by the Raiders in clearing the reef upon landing.

It is most difficult to single out from such a group of officers and men where everyone from the unit commanders down to the newest mess cook or mess attendant gave of their utmost towards the success of the expedition. The group Commander submits for special consideration the performance of the LTCDR WM.H. BROCKMAN, CO, USS Nautilus, LTCDR J.H. PIERCE Captain, USS Argonaut, and LTCOL CARLSON, DR. W.B. MacCRACKEN and the five rescue boat volunteers of the Marine Raiders.

CAPTAIN MELVIN J. SPOTTS was a PLSGT of the 1st Platoon, A Company 2ND Marine Raider Bn during the Makin Island Battle 17 Aug 1942. The company commander 1LT MERWYN C. PLUMLEY and the 1st Platoon Leader was 2LT WILBUR S. LeFRANCOIS. This account was written on Espiritu Santo in October 1942 barely two months after these events occurred and while still fresh in PLSGT SPOTT's memory. This account was written before other published versions could have colored his memory. Your EDITOR, is re-typing a long hand account from the original notebook and has added correct full names and. rank to those named and made only minor changes in sentence structure and spelling. This transcript is verbatim and reflects this battle without pulling any punches. EDITOR, LOWELL V. BULGER, 13 May 1980.

"On 8 August 1942, the 2nd Raiders went aboard the USS Argonaut (Submarine) for our first raid. A" Company on the USS Argonaut B Company on the USS Nautilus. Spent the day studying maps and aerial photos of the islands we are to raid. The men like the submarine much better than the APD Destroyer transports on which we had formerly done duty (APD'S USS LITTLE, GREGORY AND COLHOUN). Lack of fresh water for bathing and space seem to be the biggest disappointments to the men.

At 0330 on 17 August 1942, we left the USS Argonaut to make our first raid on the island of MAKIN in the Gilbert Island group. We rendezvoused around the USS Nautilus until 0430 trying to get organized into some kind, of formation (we never did). Finally the order came to head straight in toward the beach. The swells were very rough and no boats were in their right positions. In the twenty rubber boats of the two companies only two motors were running. Two out of the twenty is not a very good average. Everyone made noise and there was much confusion from the time we left the sub until the landing on the beach.

The beach we landed on at 0515 was excellent, and we immediately carried our boats the 20 feet or so up under the cover of the coconut trees. All boats landed in a two-hundred yard area of the beach except two. One B Company boat with LT

PEATROSS and the demolition men of his company landed about one mile to our left. The second boat was that of CORPORAL HARRIS J. JOHNSON (3rd Squad, 2nd Plt, A Co. CPL JOHNSON and his boat landed some 400 yards to our right.

LT PEATROSS B CO men helped a great deal more than can be imagined. They struck the enemy from the rear and drew machine gun fire and bombs from the Jap planes, which if dropped on our main force, would certainly have caused several casualties.

After securing our boats under some coconut trees, we assembled on the beach in the center of the landing area and went about getting organized. About this time, two shots were heard. The whole outfit took cover. We soon learned the shots were an accidental discharge by one of our own men. With our chance of surprise lost, our LT Le FRANCOIS got the order to move out. LT Le FRANCOIS gave me the order to bring up the rear and drop a man off every 50 yards, so that LTCOL EVANS F. CARLSON and the rest of the main body could follow.

About 200 yards inland, LT LB FRANCOIS, SGT NORMAN J. LENZ, and SGT CLYDE THOMASON went into a small house to investigate it and upon coming out, were mistaken for Japs by some of our men who opened fire on them. Lucky for them no one was hurt. The firing had awakened some natives who came running out of the grass houses and down the road toward the northeast end of the island. Several of these natives were stopped and questioned. They said the Japs numbered 150-200 and were southwest of us toward the central part of the island. (We had landed in the northeast part.)

Upon hearing these reports, LT LeFRANCOIS led us in the direction of the Japs some 500 yards when he met the Japs. I was lying near the 2nd. Platoon Radioman when LT Le FRANCOIS reported that heavy fighting had begun. I couldn't see a thing that was going on so GYSGT ELLSBURY B. ELLIOTT, myself and a few others tried to move up and close some of the gap that was on our exposed left flank. The fighting had become more or less of a free for all. Every man was trying to move up to the front to get his score of Japs before they ran out, which they did before the two day battle was over.

I stayed on the left flank for two hours getting in a shot every now and then. I only got one shot at a visible target the rest of my firing was at things that could have been but probably weren't Japs. I can say here that the Japanese were near perfect at concealment and camouflage. I advanced about 20 feet and came up behind some bushes that screened my view ahead. I had to go 75-80 feet to the right. I ran into PLSGT VICTOR "TRANSPORT'" MAGHAKIAN who had been wounded in the arm and was on his way back to get medical aid. He told me that snipers were raising hell with our troops and that they needed all the help they could get. I advanced another 50 yards and found things in bad shape.

I found the A Company C.P. (Command Post) and 1LT PLUMLEY. He asked me a few questions and then ordered me to move up to the front line, some 20-40 yards ahead of the C. P. The distance depended on the holes, stumps and low places that our men had found for concealment. I made the section assigned to me in about two bounds. The first bound I stopped behind a coconut tree that became the target of a Jap machine gun. I moved, from that place in a hurry. On my next move forward I passed SGT CLYDE THOMASON, who unknown to me was already dead. I stopped just to the right of CPL HOWARD A. YOUNG. This was on the right flank but to the left of the road. I got my bearings and noticed there were six men to my left front about 10 feet ahead and spread over a ten-yard radius. They were doing a very good job of holding this sector. PFC JOHN A. BEVON was one of these six men He had been shot in the ass but wouldn't leave to go back for first aid.

I held this position for about an hour and a half when I crawled back to the C.P. On arriving there someone reported hearing planes and two Jap pontoon sea planes came in very low. These planes flew back and forth for 20 minutes and finally dropped their bombs on the Jap territory ahead. These bombs looked small but when they went off they made one helluva noise and shook the whole island. It was about 1400 when we got the order to fall back about 100 yards and form a new firing line. We made this move without a single casualty, but when we reached this position we got our first real scare. Planes came over in large numbers. I counted six seaplanes, five zero fighters, three or four dive bombers, two dual engine bombers and one large four motored flying boat. This big flying boat cruised, around for 15 minutes, and then landed in the lagoon along with one of the sea planes. The 4 motored plane tied up at ON CHONG'S Pier in Jap territory. The rest of the planes cruised back and forth over the front lines and then began to drop their bombs and strafe their own troops. It was an answer to our prayers. The Jap pilots had been misled as to the position of our front lines.

In this attack, the enemy planes came over so low, that you could plainly see the features of the pilots and their gunners. Before starting their strafing runs, they would clear their guns with short bursts in the distance. As these planes came in I could see they had dark gray tails and motor cowlings with a lighter gray color on the fuselage and Wings. The red ball of the Rising Sun stood out and was very bright in color. This was about three feet in front of the tail. If we had only had a 20mm anti-aircraft gun with us!

Another order came at 1430 to move back another 100 yards and form a new front line. Again the move was speedily accomplished without a single casualty. We dug in and waited. MAJOR JAMES ROOSEVELT gave me the order to have our 55 Cal anti tank gun crew (SGT HOWARD E. STIDHAM and CPL ROBERT E. POARCHE) fire on the big sea plane in the lagoon if they could reach it but to use their ammunition sparingly. TRANSFORT MAGHAKIAN ordered the 30 Cal machine guns to open fire also. Both of these planes started to take off but our fire knocked both of them out of commission.

CPL ALVIN J. WEIMER and myself took up a position behind a tree so as to compare notes. Up until now, I didn't know what to make of the fight, so I thought it wise to destroy the maps I had on me (so they wouldn't fall into enemy hands if the battle had been lost). I did this by shoving them down into a taro patch. I had brought a small camera and ten rolls of film with me but up until now I had been unable to take any pictures. I decided that now was the time. I shot a few at the house, shacks, trees, the front lines, wounded men and Jap planes. I had some good ones of the Jap planes but all were lost in the surf when leaving the island.

The natives had gotten quite used to the firing and came forward to help as much as possible. They seemed very eager to help. SGT HENRY A. HERERO had them climbing trees getting coconuts for us. CPL WEMER and I were thirsty so I got two coconuts for us. The milk in them was delicious but the meat wasn't quite ripe enough. The natives that I ran across could speak a little English; words like candy, gum, cigarettes, etc. they could say with ease. I gave my last two cigarettes for the two coconuts they gave me. GYSGT LAWRENCE A. LANG of B Company gave one native two dollars and he completely covered our rubber boats with frond and leaves. At 1730 (5:30 pm) I located, the Battalion CP and finally found our A Company C.P. LT PLUMLEY told me we were going to leave the island at 1915 provided it was dark enough and until then we would hold our front. We would then draw back slowly into a large semi-circle around our boats on the beach. Each rubber boat was to carry 14 men with the sick and wounded being distributed among the boats equally.

The evacuation began on schedule as soon and darkness fell and resulted in almost complete failure. The surf which was very good, for the landing was hell to get through. The huge waves broke about 100 yards from the beach and kept coming in rapidly with a very short interval between them. We would paddle until we struck the point where the surf broke and from there it was just a matter of time before we ended up back on the beach again. In my boat, we tried to get off for about five hours. We paddled steadily and were getting nowhere staying about 50 yards from the beach all the time. Finally around midnight we gave up and decided to wait until morning when the tide changed. Our boat and one other landed back on the beach together and we immediately took cover in a clump of bushes. This cover was a life saver for us, as a Jap patrol started firing their bolt action rifles at the noise we were making. This time we were in the cover and the advantage was on our side.

We opened fire with our automatic weapons and sprayed the area they were in. We must have scored several hits for they squealed like stuck hogs and didn't bother us in this position again. At about 0300 we moved about 500 yards up the beach to a new defensive position. I dug a small trench in the sand and covered myself up with flat rocks. The air was cool and my only clothing was a pair of very wet trousers. The rocks served two purposes they kept me warm and kept some of the water off me when it was raining. There was some talk of surrender as most of our weapons had been lost in our attempts to get off the island.

At about 0530 some natives reported that the remaining Japs numbered no more than 10 or 15. This greatly surprised us for we thought they numbered at least 50 fully armed men. Our automatic weapon fire must have done a much better job than we thought. The grazing fire before we attempted to leave must have caught the Japs in an open position. Yet I do recall that the barrage we laid down with our machine guns and BAR' was terrific but I never thought we could possibly have done so much damage. Our men were overjoyed and some said we can lick that many with rocks.

At 0600, Tuesday morning, 18 August a group of us decided to try again to get through the surf. MAJOR JAMES ROOSEVELT decided he would go with us. We began our battle with the surf and after about 2 1/2 hours of paddling we finally got through beyond the breakers. Our worries were not over because we were now in the open sea and any minute we expected Jap planes to appear and blast us right out of the water. No planes appeared then. We picked up a lone, swimmer about 100 yards from the submarine and we in turn, were taken aboard."

2ND RAIDERS KILLED IN ACTION ON MAKIN ISLAND

CASTLE,VERNON	EARLES, I.B.
GALLAGHER,WM.	GASTON, DANIEL
HICKS, ASHLEY	HOLTOM,GERALD
JOHNSON, HARRIS	KUNKLE, KENNETH
MACIEJEWSKI,ED D	MAULDING,ROBERT
MONTGOMERY,KEN	MORTENSON,NORMAN
NODLAND, FRANK	PIERSON, ROBERT
SELBY, CHARLES	THOMASON,CLYDE
VANDENBERG,JOHN	YARBBROUGH,MASON

TWELVE 2ND BN MARINE RAIDERS WERE MISSING IN ACTION ON MAKIN. IT WAS DISCOVERED THAT NINE WERE LATER BEHEADED ON KWAJALIEN ISLAND.

THE REMAINING THREE ARE NOW CLASSIFIED AS KIA.

ALLARD,ROBERT	BEECHER, JAMES
COOK, DALLAS	DAVIS, RICHARD
GIFFORD, JOSEPH	KERNS, JOHN I.
LARSON, CARLYLE*	MATTISON, ALDEN*
OLBERT,RICHARD	PALLESEN,W.*
ROBERTON,DON	SMITH, CLETUS

*CLASSIFIED AS KILLED IN ACTION

2ND RAIDERS AWARDED MEDALS ON MAKIN ISLAND

NAVY CROSS

CARLSON, EVANS	COYTE, RALPH H.
CRAVEN,HOWARD	ELLIOTT,ELLSBURY
FAULKNER, JAMES	LAMB, CHARLES T.
LANG, LAWRENCE A.	LE FRANCOIS,WILFRED
MAGHAKIAN, VICTOR	PEATROSS, OSCAR
PLUMLEY,MERWYN	ROOSEVELT,JAMES
SEBOCK, JOSEPH	WYGAL, EDWARD

TWO SECOND BN RAIDER DOCTOR HEROES
AWARDED THE NAVY CROSS MEDAL ON MAKIN ISLAND

Their citations read in part:

"For extraordinary heroism Doctor William B. MacCracken, Lt (MC) and Dr. Stephen L. Stigler Lt(MC) accompanying the Marine Raider Expedition agains Japanese held Makin Island braved intense enemy fire to help evacuate the helpless and injured on the front lines and to help evacuate them to their sumbarines. Upon returning to their ships both Doctors performed several major operations over a long number of hours that resulted in saving the lives of many of their Raider shipmates."

2AD LTCOL HOWARD E. STIDHAM, El Cajon, CA commented on two Makin Island Raider buddies. "I remember, vividly, both SGT NORMAN LENZ and P.G. LOCKE as well our newly located B Co Corpsman, JAMES M. CASEY. I'm happy that we have at last located these three Makin Raiders. I recall talking to badly wounded SGT LENZ (Paralyzed since 17 Aug 1942), on the submarine coming back from Makin. He related how he tried to tell his rescuers not to put him back into that rubber boat after his third dunking in that raging 18 foot high surf but he just couldn't talk."

LOWELL BULGER,PATCH EDITOR: "It took nearly 24 extra hours after the main battle to safely evacuate all the known wounded and survivors that were under repeated enemy air attack from nearby enemy air bases at Wotje, Jaliut and Mille, in the Marshall Islands. A very hazardous 24 hours for some 80 Carlson Raiders, who were unable to breach the surf with their wounded during the scheduled six-hour departure period of l800-2400 on the 17th of August."

2B3L BRIAN QUIRK remembers, " it was cold and rainy off Butaritari and rougher than we anticipated, and loading the 21 rubber boats was a pretty dicey operation. I was carrying about 160 pounds with all the demolition gear I had, and I knew if I slid off the slippery side of that sub and missed the boat it would take me straight to the bottom. The Raiders found the current far stronger than they anticipated and the outboard motors on the rubber boats wouldn't start. "So once they were loaded it was impossible for the rubber boats to keep stationary near the subs while the others loaded up. The result was that even with everybody paddling like hell the boats got out of place and landed in the wrong sequence on the beach, out of sight of the landmarks that were supposed to guide us to our objectives." "We started about 0630 and the battle was over by 0830," Quirk remembers.

The garrison on the island was supposed to consist of 45, but the Raiders counted 90 dead Japanese after the battle.18 Raiders were killed and several wounded. Carlson was certain more of the enemy were hidden somewhere else on the island. In addition, the Japanese soon landed two large flying boats in the lagoon. The Raiders managed to sink both with heavy weapons fire, but remained uncertain whether any of the reinforcements aboard had reached shore. Enemy planes bombed and strafed the island intermittently during the day, but Quirk, dug in beside the wooden stakes of a native pigpen, noticed that the pilots steadily overshot their targets and did little damage.

Around 1700 Carlson decided to withdraw the Raiders as planned, protected by a covering force of 20, but the effort soon proved disastrous. The surf had mounted ominously, the rubber boats rolled over repeatedly in the surf and the Raiders lost most of their weapons and supplies. "We must have overturned eight or 10 times before my boat got through the surf," Quirk says. Once through they finally got the motor started and made it to one of the submarines, which had stayed submerged most of the day. Other boats made it back finally in the darkness to one sub or the other, "but few of us made it to the right sub, we were all soaked, chilled and exhausted". 120 men, Carlson among them remained stranded on shore, unable to make it through the surf. Only the covering force and a handful of others still had weapons. "Other boatloads had made it out through the surf to the subs during the night, however, and with dawn Carlson and his troops on shore realized no organized enemy force remained. Dodging occasional air attacks during the day as they destroyed Japanese supplies and installations, they contacted the submarines, arranging a night rendezvous at the mouth of the lagoon where there was no surf to contend with. They dragged four rubber boats across to the lagoon, and with the help of a native outrigger got the remainder of the force back to the submarines.

However, during the transfer, five Raiders who had volunteered to return from one sub to the island to help the others through the surf were lost. While they were paddling in, Japanese fighters attacked, forcing the submarine to submerge. "When we came back up there was no trace of their boat," Quirk remembers. "We had to assume they'd been strafed or drowned."

2B3 KENNETH J. SEATON wrote, "My association with the Raiders is probably, the only bit of immortality that I will ever share and that is soon to be lost in a page of history. Most young adults where I work never heard of Guadalcanal, Iwo Jima, Makin Island and lesser actions important only to us. Some even inquire if you fought in World War ONE or TWO. I keep a Raider coffee mug in the lunch room and that occasionally sparks an inquiry and some conversation.

Here is my personal account I recall of Makin Island. I had been spilled out of a rubber boat twice in that nasty surf trying to get off the island and back aboard the submarine. I was swimming towards shore, nearly to the point of exhaustion when someone pulled me into another boat that was still afloat. I no longer remember who the Raiders were, but even without a paddle, we somehow managed to get back to shore where we clustered on the beach. I had only a knife and one hand grenade left. Someone else had a rifle and another a Tommy Gun but most were cold, wet, exhausted and without weapons.

We were miserable and scared. There were no personal heroics, just an effort to hang on until the next day. We wondered if we would be captured or killed by the expected Jap reinforcements. I found my old buddy JESS HAWKINS, 2B, who had a nasty gunshot wound clear across his chest. I helped make him a bit more comfortable and found some coconut milk for him to drink. We had lost our canteens in the heavy surf. I don't know how he survived but he was totally tough.

During the second day, there were a couple of air attacks but no more enemy landing attempts. We carried the wounded and the four sound rubber boats across the narrow neck of the island to the lagoon side. We lashed them to a native outrigger and waited for darkness so we could make it out to the submarines that waited near the calm lagoon to pick us up. There is no way to describe how it felt to be back aboard that submarine!"

After a short rest, Doctor MacCRACKEN set up his operating room on the officer's mess table and went to work caring for those Raiders in the most serious condition. As always, following a battle, there was no rest for the Doctos and Corpsmen. Pharmacist Mates Sparkman and Casey took care of the less serious, while Doctor MacCracken performed surgery for almost 20 hours straight.

BEN CARSON 2BC wrote, "On Makin I was a member of the beach perimeter as the Raiders were attempting to shoot the surf with the wounded. It was really dark but the phosphoresence of the churning surf still permitted some background for the events that unfolded there that night. The rubber boats would have one wounded who could sit up and another wounded draped over the center of the inflated seats. As the boats approached the curl in the biggest surf the boat would be swept up and completely turn over dumping the wounded and the rest of the crew into that churning surf. As the Raiders were swept back to shore each wounded had at least one and most often two people guiding that wounded person back to the beach. There the wounded would be carried to the tree line to await another try at the surf. The doctors were still on the beach to check for shock and bleeding as each patient returned to the beach. This attempt to shoot the surf continued until near daylight and the wounded were as eager to try again as were the boat crews. While keeping watch for any Japs that might decide to attack the beach scene I heard something stirring among the darkened coconut grove. All of a sudden there was a burst of fire from Jessie Hawkins and return fire from the Jap recon party. Jessie was hit pretty badly in the chest and as I crawled over to him I could hear his chest making a sucking sound as he tried to breathe. Directly Dr. MacCracken crawled over to Jessie and checked him over. I offered to help carry Jessie to the beach but was told to stay in position since there were now only 7 of us left to man the whole beach defense. Some of the Raiders who were resting on the beach from their surf penetration duties came and lugged Jessie to the beach where Dr. MacCracken bandaged him up and prepared him for the trip to the subs. When the initial attempt to shoot the surf took place, each of the severely wounded headed back to the subs had a Corpsman or Doctor in the rubber boat with them. As the boats upset and the wounded were dumped in the surf much of the medical supplies and related necessities went overboard and was lost.

2K Makin Raider, E. PHILIP DE LUCA, asked the Patch, "How come you haven't mentioned the "Seven Magnificent Raiders at Makin" led by SGT HAROLD O. "STUBBY" KLEIN CPL JOSEPH W. COTTEN and five other Raiders including my self. We volunteered to take a rubber boat back to the beach and try to rescue the 60 odd Raiders and wounded who couldn't get through the high surf. I was one of those 'Never Volunteer Dummies' who volunteered to leave the safety of the submarine and make the rescue attempt. We left the safety of the sub and took the rubber boat into the beach. SGT NORMAN J. LENZ had been shot and was later operated on the sub by DR WILLIAM MacCRACKEN. We spent the second day 18 Aug 42 on MAKIN and went out after dark on the lagoon side of the island. Our outboard motor ran like a clock and only stopped when we ran out of gas. One of the B Company boat's motors kept heating up and stopping. There were only 3 usable rubber boats and one native outrigger lashed together and loaded with wounded...The outrigger was loaded with new JAP RIFLES, still in cosmoline and we had to bail like hell to keep from foundering. When we reach the submarine USS NAUTILUS, the task force commander, CDR JOHN HAINES, confiscated the NEW JAP RIFLES. In retrospect and being prejudiced, I always thought that we should have received some recognition in our record books. Once we were safe aboard the sub USS ARGONAUT, it was a touch decision to volunteer to return to that island in a "Long Odds" rescue attempt. None of us received even a mention. AUTHOR: I agree with Phil about this."

Post war information revealed that nine Raiders were inadvertently left behind and captured by the Japanese reinforcements when they landed on Makin. These nine Raiders were taken to Kwajalein Island on 2 September and beheaded in an Execution Ceremony on 16 Oct 1942.

Vice Admiral Koso Abe, LtCdr Hisakichi Naiki and Captain Kosio Obara were arrested in Japan and transported to the Island of Guam to be tried by a U.S. Military Tribunal on May 15, 1946. A native, Lejena Lokot, a worker in the Japanese officer's kitchen witnessed the atrocity and after the war testified at the WAR CRIMES trial of the Japanese Officers who were responsible.

Captain Hiyoshi testified that nine American Marine prisoners were brought to Kwajalein in early September 1942, and he witnessed their execution.

LtCdr Hisakichi Naiki testified that when Admiral Abe was unable to obtain any volunteers from his troops to act as executioners, he was told by Captain Kosio Obara that he would probably be the executioneer, which he refused to do. He said that when he arrived at the execution site the execution had already taken place and the bodies were already in a common grave.

Captain Obara said he had objected strongly to the orders to have the prisoners killed, but had to obey in order to save his career. Several others testified that he was opposed to the executions.

Admiral Abe testified that his superiors had ordered him to execute the prisoners, but he was unable to name the person or persons who gave him the order. He further agreed that he had ordered Obara to carry out the executions even though Obara had objected.

Vice Admiral Koso Abe, Captain Yoshio Obara and Lieutenant Commander Hisakichi Naiki, all of the Imperial Japanese Navy were found guilty and punished. Vice Admiral Abe was hanged on 19 June 1947. Captain Obara was sentenced to 10 years imprisonment and LCdr Naiki was given a 5 year prison sentence. Naiki was paroled in 1950 and Obara in 1951.

The 2nd Battalion Makin Island Raiders rejoined the rest of their 2nd Battalion Midway Island Raiders in Hawaii to train for the battles to come in the Pacific.

NAVY TRANSPORT SUBMARINES
USS ARGONAUT AND USS NAUTILUS

Surviving Raiders know all too well what heroes the crew members of Nautilus and Argonaut were. Many Makin Raiders and the submarine crews became close friends. Friendships that transcended petty inter-service rivalries and even outlived the war itself for some.

For some, their submarine voyage was a one-way trip. For others, a bad roll of the dice would come on another Pacific shore or ocean depth on a later date. But for the survivors there will always be a special reverence for those gallant officers and men of the Submarine Service.

During both Nautilus' and Argonaut's return to Pearl Harbor after the Makin Raid, the officers and men of both subs did all possible to make the Raiders as comfortable as possible. They let us use their bunks, gave us their choice chow, you name it! All surviving Raiders were put up for a week of Rest and Recreation at the magnificent Royal Hawaiian Hotel (previously used exclusively by submarine crews). Raiders who were part of the Makin adventure were made honorary submariners. Many still wear the coveted sub-marine service pin presented to them by the sub crews.

The final bonding between these two widely different sets of warriors, Raiders and Submariners, came less than a year after the Makin Raid. Word reached Raiders on Guadalcanal that the USS Argonaut (SS-166) had been lost at sea with all hands. It was devastating news. Argonaut had departed Pearl Harbor on 15 December 1942 on her third war patrol. She was off New Britain when she sighted a convoy of five Jap ships escorted by three destroyers on 10 January 1943. The sub's skipper, Lt. Cdr. John 'Happy Jack" Pierce, bored into an attack and hit a destroyer head on.

The two other destroyers, Maikaze and Isokazc turned

immediately and attacked Argonaut with savage depth charging Argonaut's bow broke the surface and was heavily shelled by the Jap destroyers until she disappeared beneath the waves. The crew of a U. S. Army bomber, returning from a mission with empty bomb racks, watched in horror as that valiant mem-ber of America's Silent Service" sank with all hands lost.

Flushing the Officer's head on the Nautilus normally required nineteen separate steps done in exactly the same sequence. The Bougainville Nuns rescued by the Nautilus never mastered the art, just as the 2nd Raiders before them experienced some embarrassing moments while on board!

The Nuns and other refugees wrote the following letter prior to leaving the Submarine on 3 January 1942.

To: Captain Brockman and the Officers and Crew of the USS Nautilus.

"The evacuees from Bougainville desire to express to you all and to your Government our sincere gratitude and appreciation of your prompt and efficient response to our appeal for help and for the wonderful hospitality and friendship extended to us by all on board.

We shall never forget our unique experiences and the very happy association with you all. We thank you most sincerely and can only wish you Good Hunting and that we may be able to meet you again some day. 'Apres le Guerre'.

Again our most sincere thanks for all that you have done for us."

Coastwatcher Clemens & Natives

Guadalcanal Cemetary

6

Guadalcanal
Col. Merritt "Red Mike" Edson, USMC, Medal of Honor

Col. Merritt A. Edson, USMC, MOH

OFFICIAL MEDAL OF HONOR CITATION

Col. Merritt Austin Edson, 1HQ. Born 25 April 1897, Rutland, Vt.

"For extraordinary heroism and conspicuous intrepidity above and beyond the call of duty as Commanding Officer of the First Marine Raider Battalion, with Parachute Battalion attached, during action against enemy Japanese forces in the Solomon Islands on the night of 13-14 September 1942. After the airfield on Guadalcanal had been seized from the enemy on 8 August, Colonel Edson, with a force of 800 men, was assigned to the occupation and defense of a ridge dominating the jungle on either side of the airport. Facing a formidable Japanese attack which, augmented by infiltration, had crashed through our front lines, he, by skillful handling of this troops, successfully withdrew his forward units to a reserve line with minimum casualties. When the enemy, in a subsequent series of violent assaults, engaged our force in desperate hand-to-hand combat with bayonets, rifles, pistols, grenades and knives, Colonel Edson, although continuously exposed to hostile fire throughout the night, personally directed defense of the reserve position against a fanatical foe of greatly superior numbers. By his astute leadership and gallant devotion to duty, he enabled his men, despite severe losses, to cling tenaciously to their position on the vital ridge, thereby retaining command not only of the Guadalcanal airfield, but also of the FIRST Divisions entire offensive installations in the surrounding area."

Guadalcanal

Maj. Kenneth D. Bailey, USMC, Medal of Honor

Maj. Kenneth D. Bailey, USMC, MOH

OFFICIAL MEDAL OF HONOR CITATION

Maj. Kenneth D. Bailey (1HQC) was born 21 October 1910 in Pawnee, Oklahoma. *Official Citation:* "For extraordinary courage and heroic conduct above and beyond the call of duty as Commanding Officer of Company C, First Marine Raider Battalion, during the enemy Japanese attack on Henderson Field, Guadalcanal, Solomon Islands, on 12-13 September 1942. Completely reorganized following the severe engagement of the night before, Maj. Bailey's company, within an hour after taking its assigned position as reserve battalion between the main line and the coveted airport, was threatened on the right flank by the penetration of the enemy into a gap in the main line. In addition to repulsing this threat, while steadily improving his own desperately held position, he used every weapon at his command to cover the forced withdrawal of the main line before a hammering assault by superior enemy forces. After rendering invaluable service to the battalion commander in stemming the retreat, reorganizing the troops and extending the reverse position to the left, Maj. Bailey, despite a severe head wound, repeatedly led his troops in fierce hand-to-hand combat for a period of ten hours. His great personal valor while exposed to constant and merciless enemy fire, and his indomitable fighting spirit inspired his troops to heights of heroic endeavor which enabled them to repulse the enemy and hold Henderson Field. He gallantly gave his life in the service of his country."

INVASION OF GUADALCANAL
BRITISH SOLOMON ISLANDS
7 AUGUST 1942

The assault force organized for the capture of Guadalcanal was the First Marine Division reinforced by the Second Marine Regiment, the First Marine Raider Battalion, and the Third Marine Defense Battalion, under the command of Marine MAJGEN ALEXANDER VANDEGRIFT.

The 1st Marine Division captured the airfield on D-Day, 7 Aug 42, against minimal opposition. MAJ GEN A.A. VANDEGRIFT set up a beach defense along the shore with the eastern flank anchored along the muddy stream Alligator Creek mistakenly called the Tenaru River on the primitive sketches called "Maps" of the area.

To the west towards the Matanikau river the front extended some 5 miles to a point about 2000 yards beyond Kukum where the flanks were refused and anchored inland about 1000 yards. Inland, beyond the coconut grove the jungle's impenetrable growth permitted only spot defenses and a few high hills offering a limited field of defense or observation. Edsons Ridge was such a spot about one mile directly south of Henderson Field. It jutted out of the lush jungle, offering a dominant view of Airfield's defenses.

In the battle of Savo Island on the night of 8 Aug 1942, Japanese Naval forces inflicted a serious defeat to Task Force 61, and Admiral Fletcher withdrew his supporting Carriers PRIOR to the attack. He feared an aerial attack by the Japanese and used as a further reason, a supposed shortage of fuel. Historians have taken a dim view of his reasoning over the intervening years.

Fletcher's decision in effect abandoned the Marines on Guadalcanal with less than half of their heavy weapons and equipment, ammunition, aviation fuel, food and supplies. Much to their dismay, Gen Vandergrift and his Marines helplessly watched their supply transport ships sail away with half of their cargoes still onboard. This required they go on reduced rations right from the beginning.

When the Raiders arrived on Guadalcanal, General Vandergrift immediately put them to work. On 2 Sep 42, USS LITTLE and USS GREGORY ferried 2 Companies of the 1st Raiders to Savo Island to investigate rumors of a Japanese presence on the Island.

CAPT JOHN ANTONELLI led A Company down the Eastern Shore while LTCOL SAM GRIFFITH led Company B down the Western Shore, circled the island, found no Japs, re-embarked on the LITTLE and GREGORY and arrived at Guadalcanal after dark. They started to debark, when word came from LTCOL MERRITT EDSON to remain aboard as the Tasimboko raid was scheduled for the next morning. Since the unloading had already commenced, it was decided to complete it and all Raiders went ashore.

At 0130 3 Sep, three Japanese Destroyers entered the channel to shell Henderson Field. A PBY dropped 5 flares to illuminate, and the out gunned LITTLE (Division CDR HADLEY), and Skipper (LCDR LOFBERG) opened fire with one one 4" gun and some 20 mm guns. One enemy shot penetrated the steering engine room, one entered the after fuel tanks and another put the gun 4" out of action. Fuel oil burst into brilliant flames and GREGORY now drew the attention of accurate enemy 5" salvos which shredded her bridge, knocked down the after stack, pried open the galley deckhouse, burst a boiler, and killed seamen with jagged hunks of metal. Before Abandon Ship could be carried out both Skipper LOFBERG and DIV CDR HADLEY were killed on the bridge and the USS GREGORY was abandoned.

On the Gregory, the crew-members helped their badly wounded Skipper, LCDR HARRY F. BAUER over the side. He ordered them to go the aid of a drowning sailor and he was never seen again. With both ships burning and helpless the Japanese steamed between them at high speed firing shells which killed floating survivors. USS LITTLE lost 22 killed and 44 wounded. USS GREGORY lost 11 killed, 26 wounded. Survivors spent a miserable, night in overturned life rafts and shattered life jackets until rescued.

The Raiders were saddened by this turn of events as all four of the Raider Battalions had at one time or another served aboard these gallant old ladies of the sea and knew many of the crew members who perished. These sailors were the unsung heroes of the Guadalcanal campaign.

During the first week in Sep 42, the Japanese successfully landed sizeable forces by destroyers at night, both east and west of the Marine perimeter around the newly captured airfield, that was renamed Henderson Field by the Marines. To the west beyond the Matanikau River, Jap Col Oka assembled a force of some 2,000 men and prepared to launch a coordinated attack with a larger force of some 4,000 Japanese who were landed near the Village of Tasimboko. These enemy troops were enveloped and totally destroyed by the 1st Marines on 20 August 1942.

TASIMBOKO RAID
1ST MARINE RAIDER BN
8 Sept 1942

Native scouts reported the landings of thousands of Japanese near Tasimboko, but Intelligence discounted their ability to count and estimated the force to be in the hundreds.

The newly landed troops were under the command of MajGen Kyuotoke Kawaguchi and known as the Kawaguchi Brigade, which was to be soundly defeated by the 1st Raider Battalion and the 1st Parachute Battalion at Edsons Ridge on 12-13 September 1942.

Edsons Raiders newly arrived from Tulagi were given the task of making an amphibious landing to the east of Tasimboko and destroying this force. The 1st Parachute Bn was held in reserve to be moved into combat in a second landing.

On 7 September Companies A, B, and C, 1st Raider Battalion, embarked in the USS McKEAN, USS MANLEY and two YP (Yippie) boats. These last were converted tuna fishing boats from California. One of them, commanded by Portuguese Captain Joaquin S. Theodore loaded his small craft with Raiders, including LTCOL SAMUEL B. GRIFFITH II and delivered them to Tasimboko for the pre-dawn landing. He then retired to the harbor at Tulagi. That night 8 August, enemy destroyers shelled the harbor and set his tiny Yippie boat afire. Though suffering a chest wound, Captain Theodore beached his craft and kept it from sinking. Two Raiders and 27 Japanese were killed in this engagement.

RAIDERS KILLED IN ACTION
DURING THE TASIMBOKO RAID

CARNEY, WILLIAM D. CPL   SMITH, SERAPHINE B. PVT

The Raiders had a surprise waiting for them when they landed, for there were hundreds of Japanese soldiers packs lined up in neat rows just as they were abandoned when the soldiers vanished into the jungle. In an effort to find those troops A and B companies headed into the interior.

Meanwhile, the USS McKEAN and USS MANLEY made the second landing with Raider Co C and the 1st Parachute BN, who followed A and B Company into the jungle. As the Cactus Air Force bombed and strafed the area, a 77mm gun was captured by CAPT JOHN SWEENEY'S platoon. A second 77mm gun began firing directly at their Raider attackers until silenced by the accurate fire of PVT ANDREW J. KLEJNOT, but unfortunately not before 2 Raiders were seriously injured. CORPORAL CARNEY was killed by the gunfire and the arm of Raider MAURICE PION was almost completely severed. PION'S life was saved when two corpsmen, ALFRED W. CLEVELAND AND KARL B. COLEMAN amputated the jagged stump at the shoulder using only a penknife. Both Corpsmen then attended to the serious injuries suffered by PFC KENNETH BRUBAKER.

Everything in the supply dump was destroyed, except the food and medical supplies that were badly needed by the Marines, who were already on reduced food rations. The destruction of the supply base meant the Japanese were now dependent on the supplies remaining on their backs and condemned them to almost certain starvation.

KARL COLEMAN, PHM 1C BECAME THE FIRST RAIDER COMBAT CORPSMAN TO BE THE RECIPIENT OF THE NAVY CROSS, THE NATION'S SECOND HIGHEST AWARD FOR HEROISM, IN THE BATTLE OF TASIMBOKO.

His citation read in part:
"For exceptional heroism and devotion to duty in action against the enemy. During the attack on Tasimboko, Guadalcanal on 8 September 1952 Pharmacist Mate Third Class Coleman moved forward under hostile artillery, machine gun and sniper fire in order to render emergency aid to a wounded Marine whose artery had been completely severed by shrapnel, thereby saving the life of his comrade. During the hostile attack on the airport at Guadalcanal, British Solomon Islands, on the night of l3-l4 September l942. Pharmacist Mate Third Class Coleman, attached to a front line company as company Corpsman, constantly exposed himself to enemy fire to care for and the wounded to the rear, although at times his company was almost completely surrounded by the enemy and under fire in all directions. As a result of his devotion to duty and courageous action, the lives of many of the wounded were undoubtedly saved who otherwise might have perished."

BATTLE OF EDSONS RIDGE
1ST MARINE RAIDER BATTALION
12-14 Sep 1942

By the time the jubilant Raiders returned to the Marine perimeter after their successful mission GEN VANDEGRIFT was aware that the 3,000 man Kawaguchi Brigade would have to strike almost at once before their supplies ran out. He also knew that his Marines would be unable to sustain an attack for a very long period.

The Marine lines were subjected to daily air attacks and surface shelling as the enemy prepared to attack. MAJGEN VANDEGRIFT ordered EDSON and his gallant band of Raiders, together with a few of the decimated ranks of the Paramarines, to defend a prominent grassy ridge that emerged from the lush, green jungle about 1700 yards south of the airfield. EDSON believed that area would be the focus of enemy attacks. The Raiders moved into these positions after 3 days rest, on 12 Sep 42 and dug in.

MAJGEN A. A. VANDEGRIFT moved his Command Post into the jungle between the ridge and the airfield. COL EDSON placed the Paramarines on the left spur of the ridge facing south. On the right spur off the crest of the ridge he positioned his Raiders. First B Co, and to their right C Co, extended to the banks of the Lunga River. C Co was split up because of an impassable swamp. Co A was in reserve. D Co had nearly ceased to exist as its personnel were used to shore up gaping holes in the other companies. E Company's Machine Guns (the Weapons Co) were parceled out to the rifle companies.

At 2100 an enemy plane dropped a flare over the airfield and an intense, 20 minute shelling by four Japanese ships, opened the attack. At 2120 a flare arose out of the jungle in front of B Co. Preceeded by wild yells the Kawaguchi Brigade hurled their attack at the juncture of B Co and C Co. One platoon of C Co was cut off from its parent Company and forced back along the lagoon, while Co B's right flank was curled back. Another strong enemy attack down the LUNGA RIVER isolated the extreme right flank platoon of Co. C. At midnight another shelling from enemy Naval guns occurred. Small parties of the foe spent the rest of the night trying to envelope the dismembered C Co, but ignored B Co's exposed flank.

On 13 Sep 42. At daybreak, COL EDSON committed Co A and part of Co D in an attempt to restore his lines, but the Japanese had dug in and were strongly entrenched in the jungle flats. In the afternoon, EDSON withdrew the Raiders and Para-marines back along the ridge about 300 yards, and consolidated his defense line for the night onslaught. The Japanese throughout the war preferred to launch their attacks at night and consolidate any gains during daylight hours.

B Co (CAPT JOHN B. SWEENEY), was disposed across the grassy ridge and down the spur to the right and SWEENEY was given B Co 1st Engineers as reinforcements.

On SWEENEY's right flank, A Co, (CAPT JOHN B. ANTONELLI) was moved into position echeloned to the Lunga River. C Co had managed to cut its way back from its exposed position of the previous night and was now placed in reserve. D Co had ceased to exist.

As soon as darkness fell black as ink, the enemy launched their first attack and succeeded in driving a two-hundred yard wedge between B Co and A Co. As flares were dropped they launched attack after attack, 12 in all, mostly at B Co.

At 2100 the Japanese float plane, 'Washing Machine Charlie', dropped a flare over the airfield and enemy surface ships began shelling the Marine lines. To help stop the enemy attacks COL EDSON called in artillery fire from the 5th Bn, 11th Marines, 105mm guns. He directed the fire closer and closer until the shells were falling on Jap concentrations, within 200 yards of Co B. The Raiders line held as they slaughtered the enemy who came charging down the ridge and up its slopes. Everything that could fire was brought to bear against the two battalions of oncoming enemy.

At 2230, the foe laid down a heavy mortar barrage. Then yelling in English 'GAS ATTACK! GAS ATTACK!', they stormed the left flank Paramarine positions, who gave way to EDSON'S left rear, where the 2nd BN, 5th Marines were then thrown into the line to hold the last high position on the Ridge. A Co Raiders then fought there way back to where C Co was emplaced around the knoll that was EDSON'S Command Post.

E Co. Raiders were reduced to 60 men and ordered to withdraw to the knoll since both its flanks were exposed to the enemy. CAPT SWEENEY accomplished this difficult maneuver (for which he was awarded the Navy Cross), under heavy fire in the pitch black of the night. COL EDSON told JOHN SWEENEY, "this is it, we are the only ones between the Japs and the airfield, you must hold!" For the rest of the night of 14 Sep 42 the Raiders, with mortar, machine gun, grenades, small arms, even knives and bare hands withstood every enemy attack until daylight when the badly shattered remnants of the Kawaguchi Brigade broke off the attack and fled. The 11th Marines artillery fire increased all night long while the Japanese attempted to advance. In all, during the night they fired 1,992 rounds, some at ranges of only 1,600 yards. The 1st Marine Div. history says that, "The Battle of Edsons Ridge was the most critical and desperate battle of the entire Guadalcanal campaign!"

All during these furious enemy attacks the Raider Corpsmen were rushing to care for the wounded or to evacuate them as best they could, sometimes behind the lines, sometimes on the line and sometimes in front of the lines. Many Raider's foxhole buddies took care of their wounds, while others ignored theirs or had to wait for daylight to be treated.

At dawn Squad leader JOE SWEEDA was hit with mortar fragments but managed to fall in a foxhole where SGT TONY MASSAR managed to bandage his wounds. SWEEDA then crawled slowly and painfully toward a truck when he saw MAJ ROBERT BROWN headed the same way holding a bleeding hand that had one finger dangling. They and several other wounded were placed in the truck bed. When the truck moved out the Japs ambushed it and MAJ BROWN and two others were killed.

PVT EDWARD SHEPARD, while protecting a trail was wounded in the arm, shoulder and chest by the approaching Japs when the grenade he threw was a dud. PVT FRANK WHITTELESEY and others dragged him to safety in the jungle. WHITTELESY was killed when the position was overrun and was buried where he fell.

AUTHOR: His remains were not to be discovered until 1989, when a farmer digging a hole unearthed his dog tag and a few remains.

After crawling to safety through C Co's protective wire, SHEPERD was treated by Corpsman Karl Coleman. He was eventually transferred to a hospital in the United States. After recuperating he shipped out with the 1st Marine Division in time for landings at Cape Gloucester, Peleliu and Okinawa.

AUTHOR: Because of the small size of the Marine Corps, men who would never have been sent back into combat in an Army unit, were routinely sent back overseas as replacements to new Marine Divisions desperate for battle savvy infantrymen. It has been said, "Marines are either fighting, or they are on their way to fight!"

The Raiders withstood the main attempt to retake Henderson Field and the Army P40's (Aircobras) bombed and strafed the fleeing enemy troops as stragglers were hunted and killed. Enemy sources reveal that the Japanese suffered over 1500 casualties in the attack at Edson's Ridge. Over 600 dead Japs were counted in the immediate area of Edsons Ridge and several hundred more were later found on back trails, leading over Mt Austen to the Kokumbona area. The Kawaguchi Brigade had been badly defeated!

PATCH EDITOR BULGER'S NOTE: On TULAGI, 7- 8 August 1942, MAJOR KENNETH D. BAILEY while aggressively leading his Company C on the right flank of the action was WIA and subsequently evacuated to New Caledonia. While still recovering from his wounds on 12 Sep 42, he went AWOL from the hospital, rounded up the Raider mailbags and hitched a plane ride back to Guadalcanal. He arrived just in time to resume command of Company C and skillfully directed his men in what is now called the battle that saved Guadalcanal. The 1st Raider BN suffered 37 killed and 103 wounded in the battle of Bloody Ridge. There were many heroes in addition to COL MERRITT A. EDSON and MAJOR KENNETH D. BAILEY. 24 Navy Crosses were later awarded Edsons Raiders for this action, nearly half of which were posthumous.

RAIDERS KILLED IN ACTION AT EDSON'S RIDGE

ARNOLD, HERMAN	BENISH, JAMES A.
BERGSTRAND,WALY	BOONE, FRANK C.
BROWN, ROBERT S.	BUGALA, ANTON A.
COFFEY, DONALD J.	CHAMPOUX, NEIL G.
CORZINE, JIMMY W.	CRACCO,SALVATOR
DANOWSKI,MARTIN	DEES, HOWELL C.
FLOETER, HAROLD	FRINK, LESLIE V.
HOGAN,MALCOM	HUDSPETH, DAN
KEBLISH, WM.	KOPS, STANLEY
KAMINOWSKI, J.J	LANGDON, JOHN
MATTHEWS, WM	MAYNARD, L. A.
METRAS,ALBERT	POTTER,FRANCIS
QUIGLEY, JOHN	RATCLIFFE,PAUL
RILEY, JOSEPH	RITTER, K.E.
ROBERTS, CHAS	ROBERTS.FRANK
ROCK, JOHN C.	ROLLAG, AUSTIN
SMITH,ROBERT *	STACKPOLE,G.B.
STARK, JEROME	TARGOSZ, J. JR
WHITTELSEY,F.R.	

* Hospital Corpsman.

DR EDWARD P. McLARNEY, DR ROBERT W. SKINNER AND 8 FIRST RAIDER CORPSMEN RECEIVED THE NAVY CROSS FOR ATTENDING TO OVER 200 CASUALTIES AT EDSON'S RIDGE

DOCTOR McLARNEYS citation read in part:
"When his aid station became untenable because of enemy attacks he directed its displacement to the rear. Before this could be completed many severely wounded men began to arrive at the original station. With only a few Corpsmen to assist him and continually exposed to hostile rifle fire from the front and flank, he worked cooly and skillfully from midnight to morning, rendering first aid to approximately 200 Marine casualties."

DOCTOR SKINNERS CITATION FOR BRAVERY IN THE SIEZURE OF TULAGI, THE BATTLE OF EDSONS RIDGE, AND THE 1st AND 2nd BATTLE OF THE MATANIKAU read in part:
"During these battles DR SKINNER time after time exposed himself to enemy fire in rendering aid and supervising evacuation to his battalion. During the battle of EDSON'S RIDGE he made at least three trips from the forward to the rear dressing station."

RAIDER CORPSMEN AWARDED THE NAVY CROSS IN THE BATTLE OF EDSON'S RIDGE

Their citations read in part:
"The President of the United States takes great pleasure in presenting the NAVY CROSS, TO DELBERT D. EILERS PhM3, WILLIAM BRUCE KINCANNON PhM3, WILBUR L. MARSH PhM1, LOYD T. MATHIS PhM2c, THADDEUS PARKER HA1, GERALD E. ROEBUCK, PhM3 AND ALBERN M. POTTER PhM3, "For exceptional heroism and devotion to duty in action against the enemy on GUADALCANAL, SOLOMON ISLANDS. During the hostile attack on the airport on the night of 13-14 September 1942; these Pharmacist Mates attached to a front line company as company Corpsmen and constantly exposed themselves to enemy fire to care for and evacuate the wounded to the rear, although at times their company was almost completely surrounded by the enemy and under fire from all directions. As a result of their devotion to duty and courageous action, the lives of many of the wounded were undoubtedly saved."

RAIDER CORPSMEN AWARDED THE SILVER STAR AT EDSONS RIDGE

Their citations read in part:

"The President of the United States takes great pleasure in presenting the SILVER STAR TO:

JAY A. BROWN PhM2, ALFRED W. CLEVELAND PhM2, ROBERT W. CLUBB PhM2, KARL B. COLEMAN PhM2, JOHN W. FECHTER CPhM, GRIFFIN H. KERPER PhM3 AND ROBERT L. SMITH, PhM3, (KIA).

For service as set forth in the following CITATION:

"For exceptional heroism and devotion to duty in action against the enemy on Guadalcanal, Solomon Islands. During the hostile attack on the airport; on the night of 13-14 September 1942, these Pharmacist Mates stationed at the battalion aid station constantly exposed themselves to hostile machine gun, rifle and grenade fire, while caring for the wounded at the aid station and evacuating the wounded to the rear, well knowing that the road which they must traverse was under fire from groups of the enemy who had infiltrated around the flank although and rear of our position. As a result of their devotion to duty and courageous action, the lives of many of the wounded were undoubtedly saved."

Raider Hero Combat Corpsman DELBERT EILERS, PhM2 received the Silver Star Medal to go with the second highest award, the Navy Cross he had also been awarded,

The President of the United States takes great pleasure in presenting the
SILVER STAR TO
DELBERT D. EILERS PHARMACIST MATE SECOND CLASS, USN

For service as set forth in the following CITATION:

"During the First Marine Raider Battalion's operations against the enemy on 7-9 October 1942 at the mouth of the Matanikau River, Guadalcanal, B.S.I., PhM2c Eilers worked his way forward of the front lines to bring back and care for wounded personnel in his company, although in doing so, he was completely exposed to heavy hostile machine gun fire. As a result of his devotion to duty and courageous action, the lives of many of the wounded were undoubtedly saved."

IE KYLE Z. CASSIDY writes, "'About your brief on the Edsons Ridge Battle, SMITH, ROBERT L., was my Platoon

Corpsman and an outstanding one at that. The morning he was KIA, I told him, 'SMITH ', sit down and take a break, you have been removing wounded and giving first aid all night. We lit a cigarette as it was getting daylight. He looked up the crest and noticed a Raider down. He said, 'I'll go get him out and I said,' No, let the other Corpsmen go', but he was gone by then. I watched as he reached the wounded Raider and began giving first aid.

I looked away for a moment and then back to see if he was coming in, but he was lying prostrate over the wounded man. I sent someone to check but when we got them back. SMITH was dead. Later that day, I told both DR McLARNEY and DR SKINNER of SMITH's outstanding work and his courage, but they too had a long hard night. I hope they don't forget him. From the foregoing, you might think that I was a Corpsman but I am not. I just wanted to tell it like it was, so that all the great Raider Doctors & Corpsmen who served with us will know that we say. 'THANK YOU'!

1HQ JAMES "HORSECOLLAR" SMITH wrote from the American Embassy, "I can't tell you how much pleasure it was to read of old friends and see pictures of them. The article on MEDAL OF HONOR recipient Raider MAJOR KENNETH D. BAILEY brought back memories. He led a few charges on the night of The Ridge and was always in the van. THOMAS H. DRISCOLL and I carried him out in a poncho the day he caught it at the Matanikau river."

AUTHOR: JIM SMITH was awarded the Silver Star Medal for his heroics on both Tulagi and Guadalcanal. He remains as one of our many great Raider heroes.)

Some of the outstanding acts of courage were:

PLSGT STANLEY D. KOPS, 1C, led a platoon of his company which was hard hit in the center of the RIDGE. He held the position against great odds and when ordered to fall back he hurriedly organized another platoon of men separated from their parent companies in the chaos, then led this impromptu command in a successful charge with hand to-hand fighting to carry the enemy positions. He was KIA 14 Sep 42 and posthumously awarded the Navy Cross

CPL WALTER J. BURAK, (KIA 08 Oct 42) was LTCOL EDSON'S runner, and, constantly under fire, traversed the whole length of the Ridge twice. The first trip he strung a telephone line from the forward lines to the CP to restore severed communications. The second trip, he carried a case of hand grenades to the forward positions when they were most urgently needed. Awarded the Navy Cross, he was KIA three weeks later.

CAPTAIN HOUSTON STIFF, toting a half case of grenades, bolted down the slope of the Ridge and completely through the forward lines before realizing it, in the complete darkness, as Raider lines were stretched dangerously thin.

PFC WILLIAM BARNES, 1E gunner in a mortar section, kept up steady fire until his shells were exhausted, evacuated wounded from the front lines, and returned with more ammo to the extreme forward positions. He then joined in the close quarters fighting as a rifleman. Awarded the Navy Cross, he was KIA on 23 Feb 1945 at Iwo Jima.

SGT DANIEL W. HUDSPETH. 1C, repeatedly led attacks against the enemy infiltrations and inspired his men with his daring until he was finally killed. He was posthumously awarded the NAVY CROSS for his courage in action that night.

During the heaviest Japanese attacks on Edson's Ridge, one squad was reduced to four men, 3 unwounded and PFC RAMON HERNDON, who was badly wounded in the stomach. RAY asked for a 45 automatic and said, "You guys better move back as ordered, I'm done for anyhow, but I can take three or four of the bastards with me before I kick off. He was KIA 13 Sep 42.

1E FRANK W. (HASHMARK) GILBERT wrote, "I was under SGT FRANK O. "BOOZER" BOONE (KIA 15 Sep 42). May he rest in peace. The last time I saw him he was hit and went down.

1C ROGER A. SRAMKOSKI wrote, "I especially liked the account in the Nov 77 Patch of the Edson's Ridge battle on Guadalcanal. I was in the 3rd Platoon, C Company. On the first night we were on a knoll overlooking the Lunga River, when we were cut off by the Jap attack, we made our way under the overhanging rain forest along the river bank. On the 2nd night, I was with MAJOR KENNETH D. BAILEY and a gent named GRAHAM. We went out to recapture a gun position on the top of knoll. Both GRAHAM and MAJOR BAILEY got hit but I was lucky and made it to the position. I was heaving grenades as fast as I could pull the pins when I got hit. Fortunately, about that time, others came to join us. It was quite a night."

1ST MATANIKAU RIVER BATTLE
1ST MARINE RAIDER BATTALION BRIEF
27 Sep 1942

LOWELL BULGER, Patch Editor: Following the defeat of the Kawaguchi Brigade at Edsons Ridge, 13-14 Sep 42, COL MERRITT A. EDSON turned over command of the 1st Raider Battalion to his Executive Officer, LTCOL SAMUEL B. GRIFFITH II, while he assumed command of the 5th Marine Regiment. EDSON took with him to the 5th Marines, CAPT LEWIS W. WALT, 1A, as Operations Officer, and CAPT HENRY J. ADAMS, 1Hq, as his Intelligence Officer.

On 26 Sep 42, the 1st Raider Battalion was to move to Kumkumbona to establish a permanent base for patrol action. It became necessary to change their plans however when the 1st Bn 7th Marines under LTCOL CHESTY PULLER ordered to scout the Mt. Austen area discovered there were 2000 fresh Japanese troops in addition to those known to be there. GENERAL VANDEGRIFT sent COL "RED MIKE" EDSON to take command of the entire attack force and Puller became EDSON's Executive Officer.

The 1st Raider Battalion moved inland along the east bank of the Matanikau, and ran into a strong enemy force that had crossed to the east bank during the night and established a strong defensive position that controlled the Raiders' approach on three sides. The first blanket of heavy enemy mortar and machine gun fire wounded LTCOL SAMUEL B. GRIFFITH, II, in the shoulder and not far away killed the Executive Officer, MAJOR KENNETH D. BAILEY, who had won the Medal of Honor, at Edsons Ridge barely two weeks previously.

RAIDERS KILLED IN ACTION
AT 1ST MATANIKAU RIVER BATTLE
BAILEY, KENNETH D.   DOBSON, JULIAN K.

The details, surrounding MAJ BAILEY'S death have remained a mystery in all the published histories of the Guadalcanal CAMPAIGN until recently.

1CA LTCOL RICHARD E. SULLIVAN provided, us this first hand story, "I was a Buck SGT with C Company, on inception of the 1st Raider BN and my Company Commander was CAPT KEN BAILEY. He was my idol.

On the events leading to his death, that day 27 Sep 42. We left the perimeter and started up to the Matanikau River. I was a Lieutenant and had the 3rd Platoon of C Company. We had the point for the battalion and made first contact with the enemy when we reached what I would have to call a small creek. We were fired on by a sniper, deployed and moved up on the creek. Orders came to hold up there. Across the creek was a more or less open field with a ridge just beyond and angling towards the river. I searched the field and ridge with my glasses as did my men but we could see nothing.

The Company Commander came up with his runner and radioman, and I went back to meet him with my runner. We were standing up talking things over when KEN (MAJOR BAILEY) came rolling up the trail with his runner and radioman. He took one look at us standing there in the open and shook his head as much as to say, 'What a bunch of dumb clucks standing there in the open.' About that time orders came to move out, sniper or no. KEN BAILEY joined us as I moved back to my platoon and gave the orders to my squad leaders.

We were standing in a little circle, facing the creek, KEN was in the back of the circle. As I walked up beside him, I looked across at the ridge and saw some men in what looked like Marine helmets running along the ridge. I thought, 'Maybe this is a Marine flanking maneuver from the main body'.

I voiced this question to KEN and as he opened his mouth to answer me an enemy machine gun opened up. We all hit the deck. KEN went down in front of me his head was in his hands and he was propped up on his right knee. The machine gun was going like mad. I hollered for him to get down. He didn't move. I reached out grabbed his ankle and pulled it from under him. He was hit right between the eyes, dead-he never knew what hit him and no one else in that circle was touched.

Needless, to say, It was a great shock and loss to me as of course it was to all of us. MAJOR KENNETH D. BAILEY was truly a great officer and gentleman. The finest that I ever knew. Having witnessed his greatness in action so many times, it doubly hurt to see him go out with his hands in his pockets, so to speak. But GOD in his wisdom didn't give us time to brood over great losses in those days!" 1979 PATCH.

When LTCOL GRIFFITH was finally evacuated, he turned over command of the battalion to MAJOR IRA J. IRWIN. The piece meal attack of all Marine units bogged down and by nightfall they were ordered to withdraw to the perimeter. The failure of the Marine attack in all areas was accountable to "faulty intelligence" said LTCOL GRIFFITH. "It can be said that we had most faulty intelligence of Japanese strength and dispositions. No orders would ever have been given for the Raiders to go up to Kokumbona and patrol from there, had there been any realization that there were several thousand Japanese between the Matanikau and Kokumbona. Faulty intelligence was the cause of the whole breakdown at that time." All Marine units, grouped together, suffered 60 KIA and 100 WIA while enemy casualties are unknown.

2ND BATTLE OF THE MATANIKAU RIVER
1ST MARINE RAIDER BATTALION
7- 9 OCT 1942

GUADALCANAL BRIEF: Lowell V. Bulger, US Marine Raider Assn.

In late September, the Japanese landed and emplaced at least four big 150mm howitzers in the vicinity of Kokumbona, about five miles west of Point Cruz well out of reach of the 11th Marines' 105's counter-fire. These guns fired singularly and, at first, were thought to be a single gun called 'Pistol Pete.'pushed back beyond Kokumbona where their artillery could not reach the airfield.

EDSON then requested his former 1st Raider Battalion and GEN VANDEGRIFT ordered them forward by companies at 1530. In the two months of fighting at Tulagi and Guadalcanal, the casualties and malaria had reduced the Raiders total strength to about 200 men.

Company A, under 1LT ROBERT P. NEUFFER was quickly organized with a machine gun and mortar section of Company E attached advanced up the shore road and reported to EDSON, about 100 in all. Their bivouac that night near EDSON's CP was uneventful but full of misery from the rain, mosquitoes, over head artillery and mortar fire.

At 0500, 8 Oct 42, A Co 1st Raiders was ordered up into the line to relieve Co I, 5th Marines. Raider Company C (about 100 men) was ordered forward at this time and by early afternoon the balance of the weakened Raider Battalion had reported to former Raider, MAJOR LEWIS W. WALT of the 5th. The torrential rains continued and delayed the Marine attack. The muddy jungle trails were impossible and all supporting Marine aircraft were grounded.

The combined attack across the Matanikau was postponed until the next day, 09 October. In late afternoon LT NEUFFER's Co A was ordered to advance to the mouth of the river while the 2nd Platoon (LT RICHARD E SULLIVAN) dug in immediately behind the barbed wire. To SULLIVAN's right extending down the beach, was the 1st Platoon (2 LT CLIFFORD H. McGLOCKLIN) and tied in to McGLOCKIN's right, on down the beach was the 3rd Platoon (PLSGT JOSEPH M. BUNTIN).

LT SULLIVAN, was spotted placing a few Raiders from the mortar and headquarters section to his left rear flank just at dusk (1830), a horde of Japanese from the half-moon pocket broke out of the jungle in a banzai attack towards the sand spit at the mouth of the Matanikau river. With smoke grenades, automatic Nambu's and grenades the enemy charged at the Raiders rear positions. Fierce hand-to-hand fighting took place as the enemy charged through the Raider mortar men and on through the 2nd Platoon. When their charge reached the barbed wire they became confused and were cut to pieces by Raider fire. A few escaped across the river's mouth but 59 enemy dead were counted on the wire and among the Raider foxholes in the morning.

In the darkness, Raiders and Japs found themselves together in the same foxholes or in adjoining foxholes, fighting continued throughout the night. At first light, the last Japanese in the area were destroyed. The Raiders had suffered the full impact of Japanese Col. Nakaguma's force, east of the Matanikau and had successfully liquidated it at a cost of 12 Raiders killed and 22 wounded.

RAIDERS KILLED IN THE 8-9 OCT 42
2ND BATTLE OF THE MATANIKAU

BOWMAN, WARREN	CONNOLLY, JOSEPH
FRENCH, NELDON	HANNA, WILLIAM
HEYLIGER,GEORGE	POPE, BILL N.
SMITH, EDWARD	STEINAKER,DONALD
THOMAS, DENNIS	THOMPSON,W .R.
WOLF, DONALD D.	ZOPHY, JAMES A.

Later that morning, GENERAL A. A. VANDEGRIFT and COLONEL MERRITT A. EDSON walked over the area slowly viewing the night battle results. When they came to the area where many dead Japs and a few Raiders were concentrated, RED MIKE'S eyes clouded. GENERAL VANDEGRIFT asked "Who did this job?" Sadly, but proudly, RED MIKE clipped "My RAIDERS!" The General replied "They're MY RAIDERS now!"

2nd MATANIKAU BATTLE: By LTCOL RICHARD E. SULLIVAN, First account written 30 Nov 1956. "Late in the afternoon of 8 October 1942, we received barbed wire and hastily constructed a double apron barricade in front of my 2nd Platoon, A Co., 1st Raider BN. It was pretty close to dark when this was completed.

As I crawled towards the Co C.P. I was hit by mortar shell fragment. My PltSgt was wounded quite severely in the leg and was evacuated. NEUFFER ordered me to the rear also, but I refused to leave, as my wound was not really severe.

I returned to the 2nd Platoon positions along the Matanikau just before dark. I was worried about my open left flank so I again went to the C.P. where LT NEUFFER gave me CPL JOE CONNOLLY and 3 or 4 mortar and headquarters personnel to place in position on my angling flank as listening posts. On the way back to put these men in position I was slightly wounded again from another grenade fragment.

While busily engaged with JOE CONNOLLY, I heard a noise in the jungle. Thinking it might be some Marines, I challenged, and all hell broke loose. The Japs broke out of the jungle almost on top of us charging in solid waves. I screamed the alarm as I began firing my Reising gun. CPL JOE CONNOLLY was cut down right by my side by a Jap with a sword or bush knife before he even had a chance to get his pistol out of his holster. The rest of the mortar men were falling, as I emptied 2 magazines I reached for a third magazine while backing up to get in my foxhole. I was shot through the left shoulder with a Jap .25 caliber bullet.

As I reached my foxhole, I found another Raider in my hole with 2 Japs standing over him with swords and they were cutting him to pieces. SGT DONALD W. WOLF, 1D, had a foxhole right next to mine so I turned and dived in on top of him. He and a nearby CPL killed 3 pursuing Japs who were almost on top of me.

Now it was pitch black and the Japs had completely overran our lines. As they reached the barbed wire, they were surprised and my men were able to account for quite a few while tangled in the barbed wire, mostly by bayonets and rifle fire. I had my Reising gun in my left hand and had dropped it when I was shot. I gave SGT WOLF my ammunition and lay there with my knife, half in and on top of him in his foxhole.

The Nips launched a charge against a .30 caliber water cooled machine gun which had been set up in back of our right flank positions covering the sand spit. However the gun was disabled and the crew withdrawn towards the C.P. Half the Japs started to cross the river when someone came out of the jungle screaming and ordered them all back.

SGT WOLF and the corporal were almost out of ammunition so I ordered them to break from the river line and try to sneak away. This was the first and only time that a couple of Marine Raiders almost disobeyed my order. They knew I was hurt and refused to leave me! I finally convinced them that there was nothing wrong with my legs and that we should all break and run. I had lost my knife and could not find it in the dark.

The corporal bolted off down the river towards the beach, but I knew the platoon on the beach had pulled back and the area was full of Japs. The corporal never made it. SGT WOLF and myself ran towards the jungle but almost as soon as we left the foxhole, WOLF ran into a group of Nips. I could hear him cursing and scuffling with them.

At the same time, I ran into a Jap Officer. I caught a glimpse of his sword against the sky and kicked him as hard as I could. He fell back screaming and I turned and hit the jungle. I hit some vines, bounced back, and then crawled up under them as far as I could and lay quiet. The Japs probed in the vines over my head with bayonets and finally eased off searching elsewhere.

I slowly crawled away headed into the jungle then eased out until I could see the light from the sea and crawled on to the rear, keeping my direction in this manner. My left arm, of course, was useless and it began to hurt. It took me the rest of the night to crawl back to the 5th Marine's lines. My biggest worry was the fact that I was losing so much blood, I was afraid I would pass out and the Japs would finish me off in the morning and just about daylight I crawled over next to the road.

Not knowing the password when I came to the road, I jumped up and ran towards the Marine lines hollering that I was coming in. The Marines stood with their rifles at the ready but they didn't fire. Inside the lines, I was taken to RED MIKE EDSON and gave him as much of the story of the river as I knew it." The men moved out and trekked toward the Matanikau. As the Raiders left the shore road they passed through the forward units of the 5th Marines. The immediate objective was to eliminate a small pocket of Japanese resistance and then the wavering flank was to be extended to the Matanikau and anchored.

CPL FRANK J. GUIDONE, 1BDA, led his squad slowly through the jungle. GUIDONE'S squad was on the extreme left of 2LT CLIFFORD McGLOCKLIN's 1st Platoon and was tied in with the 3rd Bn 5th Marines.

His scouts were PETE G. SPARACINO, and ROBERT S. HUNT. A sudden burst of a Jap machine gun and the Raiders hit the deck. GUIDONE and his Assistant Squad Leader, WILLIAM O. GRIFFITH, Scranton PA, surveyed the situation.

About 20 yards ahead, GUIDONE saw something move

behind the root of a giant banyan tree. He sent his BAR man SYLVESTER L. NIEDBALSKI, to his right flank and when in position, the riflemen peppered the enemy position around the Nambu machine gun that was almost obscured by the jungle and the rain. NIEDBALSKI opened up with this BAR on full automatic and debris danced as the bullets sprayed the area. The jungle came alive with enemy small arms fire. The slightest RAIDER movement attracted even heavier Japanese counter fire.

GUIDONE ordered GRIFFITH and his squad to hold and began to crawl back to report to LT McGLOCKLIN. On the way he ran into COLONEL "RED MIKE" EDSON and MAJOR LEWIS W. WALT, both former Raiders, now of the 5th Marines. GUIDONE reported on the enemy small arms fire. RED MIKE warned that the fire would get heavier as the Japs were compressed in a pocket. GUIDONE continued and found LT McGLOCKLIN. He reported that his squad had knocked out a Jap machine gun but was now facing an impenetrable wall of enemy fire. McGLOCKLIN ordered him to advance if he could but to hold his position if advance proved impossible. FRANK returned to his squad in time to join BOB HUNT in cutting down a Jap who exposed himself about 25 yards ahead.

In support of the Raider's push, SGT ANTHONY MASSAR 1E & 4BO and a few of his mortar men were setting up their 60mm mortars. RED MIKE EDSON was standing nearby. Like the Officers, TONY MASSAR was carrying field glasses and was not armed with a rifle. Jap snipers were clipping twigs very close, to MASSAR and one of his mortar men warned. "I think they are shooting at you TONY." MASSAR replied, "You're crazy. Why would those Nips shoot at me when there is a BIRD COLONEL standing nearby." A few more enemy slugs convinced him and he took cover."

Later in the afternoon the Raiders reached the mouth of the Matanikau River and 1LT ROBERT P. NEUFFER, "A" Company CO issued his orders to extend the Raider Company line inland up the river bank from the mouth and along the beach of Lunga Channel. McGLOCKLIN's 1st Platoon was ordered to break contact with the 3rd Bn 5th Marines and report to NEUFFER at the mouth of the Matanikau. The platoon was extended from the sand spit along the Lunga Channel and tied in with the 3rd Platoon (PLT SGT JOSEPH S. BUNTIN, 1A4AN near two 37mm Anti Tank guns and the Company C.P. The Raider's 2nd Platoon, 2LT RICHARD E. SULLIVAN, 1CA tied in with McGLOCKLIN's at the river mouth and extended along the banks of the MATANIKAU some 200 yards inland.

MAJOR LEW WALT visited the Raider positions. He ordered FRANK GUIDONE and WARREN G. BEAVERS, to collect as many grenades as they could carry and creep up towards the Jap's jungle position and heave the grenades. When they heard Jap voices, the unloaded all of their grenades as fast as they could pull the pins and throw. High shrieks of pain told the tow Raiders that they aim had been good. They slowly crawled back to their own lines.

LT SULLIVAN became worried about this open left flank and was spot placing some mortar men when he heard a noise in the jungle and challenged. A holocaust of Jap fire shattered the jungle evening stillness and a solid wave of screaming Japs broke out of the jungle (Editor: Author PETE PETTUS here uses the direct account written by LT SULLIVAN.)

From his foxhole, WILLIAM L. DODAMEAD saw a light flash on the broad blade of a Jap officer's sword coming down as the Jap leaped into his foxhole. DODAMEAD slowed the stroke with his arm before the blade cut into his back. Although disarmed, DODAMEAD tore the windpipe from the Jap Officer's throat with his bare hands, while blood poured from his own wounds. DODAMEAD left the dead Jap and crawled away. He survived the attack. Most of the Japs headed for the sand spit but some veered off towards the Raiders beach positions. THOMAS ANDERSCAVAGE saw three Japs charging towards him. Andy pulled the trigger of his BAR and heard the click of a misfire. He raised his BAR and hurled it broadside into the face of the onrushing Japs. Two of them went down but the third rushed in, bayonet at the ready. ANDY sidestepped the Nip's thrust and wrenched the rifle from his enemy's hands and bayoneted the Jap. Now armed with the Japanese Arasaka .25 rifle and bayonet he jumped out of his foxhole and bayoneted the other two Japs.

McGLOCKLIN on the beach realized he had to risk hitting the mortar men to open fire on the charging Japs. MAC shouted, "Mortar men stay in your holes! We are going to open fire." When the 1st Platoon opened fire, the Jap attack changed direction towards the sandbar at the mouth of the Matanikau.

LT SULLIVAN'S 2nd PLATOON positions along the river worked frantically to reverse their machine gun positions towards the Jap charge out of the swamp to their rear. MIKE P. FEDORAK, was ready when the first Japs came into view. He squeezed off steady bursts of fire and fifteen Japs fell before his gun. When his gun jammed, he made it useless and changed his position.

CLIFFORD C. "RED" HILLS picked up a heavy machine gun and holding the barrel across the crook of his left arm sprayed a full blast of free fire into the charging enemy. As wounded and withdrawing Raiders arrived at the C.P., NEUFFER led them to new positions and set up a new line of defense. When NEUFFER finally reached Regimental HQ by field telephone. RED MIKE EDSON ordered, "NEUFFER, you will hold your position."

EDSON ordered MAJOR LEW WALT now in command of the 3rd Bn 5th Marines to move forward and take charge of the Raiders. MAJOR WALT and his runner slipped by undetected and reached NEUFFER's CP. McGLOCKLIN gave LEW WALT a picture of the situation and was ordered to withdraw to make room for half-tracs that were moving up to help repel the still expected tank attack across the sand spit.

A platoon of "C" Company under LT Robert P. NEUFFER moved into the half-moon Japanese defensive position from which the attack was launched. Battalion Intelligence Section was called to search the area and Raiders PETE PETTUS, TOM DRISCOLL and AL HAAS opened packs for maps diaries and orders. JOSEPH L. MURPHY, BOB LAVERTY and JOSEPH P. CUETARA examined the underground enemy defense system. C.P. and underground tunnels leading outward as radial spokes to stand-up machine gun positions - 12 in all. The enemy position had successfully held the 5th Marines at bay, even with half tracs firing at point blank range.

On 13 October the battered remnants of the 1st Raider Bn boarded the USS Zeilen and sailed for New Caledonia. They had battled heroically in five major battles in their 67 days on Tulagi and Guadalcanal. The battalion, initially about 800 strong had destroyed over 1136 enemy (counted) and wounded hundreds more who later died. 94 Edson Raider's were KIA and 200 WIA. They forever earned the love, honor and respect of America, the Marine Corps, and fighting men the world over.

SGT MAJ JOHN H. CARSON said, "Once on a forced march in Quantico, VA, LTCOL RED MIKE EDSON came along and asked, 'How's it going JOE?' CONNOLLOY replied with venom, 'That Ethiopian son-of-a-bitch that thought up this hike should be strung up by the balls.' It was LTCOL EDSON who thought it up, so he just laughed and moved on. Just before the Second Matanikau battle, JOE CONNOLLY was not feeling well when we left the Marine perimeter and moved out to support the 5th Marines at the Matanikau river, but he wouldn't turn himself in to sick bay. When we got into position along the Matanikau, JOE kept saying he heard the Japs in the jungle along the mortar front but I cannot remember hearing anything. I do remember walking towards the shoreline and asking, 'Where the hell is the 3rd Platoon?'

At that moment all hell broke loose behind me and I jumped behind a pile of empty boxes with my drawn pistol but I couldn't see anything to shoot at. It was dark by this time and when the initial firing died down, I made my way to the beach talking out loud all the way, like SAMMIE MITCHELL, so our own men would know who it was. I think SAMMIE made it before I did.

After I got through the wire and onto the beach the 37mm's and machine guns opened up. I had, unknowingly, come out in front of them but I wasn't hit. PFC JAMES A ZOPHY (KIA 9 OCT 42) and I shared a shelter-half together back in the coconut grove. During the battle he came running out with his poncho on but he was cut down. I saw PFC DENNIS F. THOMAS after he was killed that night. Another Raider in the Mortar Section was GEORGE A. SIMMONS, IE. He was wounded in the battle but I never saw him again. Needless to say, that was some night! It was bad but could have been worse.

On 17 October, the 1st Raider Battalion, battered and suffering from numerous tropical maladies returned to Camp St. Louis in Noumea, New Caledonia to recuperate and train for the battles that were to come all too soon.

1ST RAIDERS AWARDED MEDALS ON GUADALCANAL

NAVY CROSS

ARNOLD, HERMAN	BARNES, WILLIAM
BROWN, ROBERT	BURAK, WALTER
CONNOLLY, JOE	CORZINE, JIMMIE
FEDORAK,MICHAEL	FRENCH, NELSON
GAY, ROY M.	GRIFFITH,SAMUEL
HANNA, WILLIAM T.	HARRISON,LAWRENCE
HEYLIGER, GEORGE	HOLDREN, LAWRENCE
HUDSPETH, DANIEL	KOPS, STANLEY D.
MIELKE, JOHN W.	PETTUS, FRANCIS C.
SCHNEIDER, ROBERT	SMITH, EDWARD L.
STEINAKER, DON	STEVENSON,WM.
SULLIVAN, R.E.	SWEENEY, JOHN
THOMAS, D.F.	THOMPSON, W.R.
WILLOX,NICHOLAS	WOLF, DONALD

```
                     SILVER STAR
DE BOER,HENRY           FLYNN, LAWRENCE
GARRETT, NOLEN          JOHNSON, LEWIS
MADDOX, BRICE           MAITLAND, THOMAS
MAGHAHAKIAN, VICTOR     MAROTTA, ALEXANDER
MCAVOY, GEORGE          McCAFFERY,JOSEPH
MILANOWSKI,H.D          MURPHY, JOHN J.
NEUFFER, ROBERT         OSWALD, KENNETH
POLLARD, P.D.           REILLY, JOSEPH
SMITH, JAMES            SNYDER, MORRIS
STARK, JEROME           TABER, DAVID P.
THOMAS, R. H.
```

NAVY CORPSMEN AND DOCTORS

Prior to their departure from New Zealand and the invasion, any Marines physically unfit for any reason were left behind. All hands were inoculated for smallpox, yellow fever and typhoid fever plus tetanus toxoid.

During the battle for the control of the island while front line Corpsmen fought alongside the assault troops, Headquarter Doctors and Corpsmen faced new problems every day. Sickness and disease ravaged the troops to a much greater degree than had been anticipated, often exceeding the casualty rate of combat troops wounded or killed in action.

As field hospitals early in the Guadalcanal campaign were targets for almost daily aerial bombing and/or artillery fire it became necessary to evacuate patients a distance of some hundreds of miles before operations and other definitive measures could be carried out. Although some casualties were flown out in combat aircraft, regular air transports weren't available until almost a month following the initial landing and casualties were evacuated aboard APD's.

The food supply gradually improved and enemy supplies captured by the 1st Raiders added significantly to the limited stores. If Marine ingenuity had been unable to make use of captured enemy weapons and food, the success of the operation would have been in doubt. The 1st Raider Battalion on Guadalcanal reinforced the 1st Marine Division and played an important role in obtaining more food and supplies for the troops by capturing them before the Japs could destroy them. The Japanese Commanders were surprised by the attacks and were forced to leave behind a great deal of equipment in addition to food and supplies.

Because of the delay in the construction of proper sanitary facilities, and the time consuming, refuse clean up during the first few weeks, epidemic gastroenteritis often occurred. Later, catarrhal (cat) fever, dengue, malaria and filariasis were the major medical problems. Fungus infection of the foot and groin became a serious problem later on. Malaria did not appear until about 2 weeks after the landing. Treatment with atabrine was begun on 10 September 1942.

Many of these illnesses plagued Marines in island campaigns throughout the Pacific. Combating malaria however, was the most successful effort of the war. Preventative measures and the use of atabrine helped Marines not already infected escape this dreaded malady almost entirely.

Corpsmen attached to each Marine Company usually gave first aid on the spot where the Marines were wounded in combat. The combat Corpsman when hearing the cry of "Corpsman, Corpsman, or Corpsman Up!" would run or crawl forward with his first aid kit to treat a wounded Marine often while both were still under fire from the enemy. It was not unusual to see a corpsman lying beside or crouched over a Marine to protect him while treating his wound, or holding a life giving blood plasma bottle raised high in the air.

Tourniquets were used to stop the flow of blood, sulfanilimide powder placed in the wound, large compress's put in place and morphine administered. Often a splint had to be applied for broken bones and on rare occasions it was necessary to perform an amputation in the field with a Raider Knife without the benefit of anesthesia.

After receiving first aid the wounded they were placed on make shift stretchers taken to a first-aid station behind the front lines by the Corpsman or the stretcher-bearers. Once there they were given further treatment. If called; for surgical operations were performed by doctors and corpsmen, often while bullets were flying in all directions.

Suffocating heat, rain and deadly insects made the Solomon Islands one of the most unhealthy areas in the world. In a very short period of time malaria, dengue fever, tropical ulcers, ringworm, heat exhaustion, sunburn, diarrhea, dysentery, and insect bites began to exceed the casualties of battle. Post war records indicate 9 out of 10 of the men admitted to a hospital were suffering from a disease or illness rather than of wounds inflicted in battle.

Malaria with an incubation period of 5-9 days appeared

a couple of weeks after the landing. In mid September there were 48 cases in the hospital, where hundreds would soon join them. Military planners failed to realize at first that, a man infected with malaria was a casualty as surely as though he had been wounded by enemy action.

In the first few weeks catarrhal fever, dengue fever, and malaria were the main medical problems while sunburn, heat exhaustion, gastro-enteritis and fungus infection of the feet were secondary problems. Salt tablets were issued on a regular basis due to the excessive body perspiration resulting from performing the most simple of tasks.

Even though the Japanese continued to send in thousands of reinforcements, these illnesses and infections continued to cause more casualties that the Jap bullets.

Drinking water had to be treated chemically, heads (toilets) built and insect control programs established. Personal sanitation, very bad at it's best, was a terrible problem throughout the war. It was almost impossible for a Marine in the filth of battle to be able to keep either himself or his clothes clean. Until relieved and returned to a non-combat area it was very rare to be able to shave, bathe or have dry socks or a clean uniform to wear. Wearing wet socks often resulted in an infection that produced ulcers on their feet, which was usually referred to as " jungle rot or immersion foot."

COASTWATCHERS

Many Marines, including Raiders owe their lives to the advance information supplied by heroic Coastwatchers and their native scouts.

The Coastwatchers were first organized in 1919 to protect the shores of Australia. With the government increasingly concerned of Japanese activities in the Southwest Pacific it was decided in 1939 to extend the service to the islands stretching from New Guinea to the Solomons. The man entrusted to form the organization wasCommander Eric Feldt, Royal Australian Navy (RAN).

By 1942 when the Japanese juggernaut came rolling through the islands like an out of control hurricane Feldt had contacted every owner of a teleradio in the islands and trained them on setting up secret sites and how to avoid being captured by the Japanese. Although there were only 14 radios behind enemy lines the help of missionaries, locals and natives played a prominent part in saving Guadalcanal from the Japanese.

Their job was to transmit information about Japanese bases, enemy troupe activity, ship and aircraft locations and movements. With war, came survivors from ships sunk, and airplane pilots all hoping to escape and live to fight again. Submarines, PT Boats and PBY seaplanes were all used to evacuate these men as well as to supply the Coastwatcher stations. Nuns, missionaries and some Chinese were also rescued in this manner in order to escape Japanese atrocities. Over 100 airmen were rescued in the Solomons. Coast Watcher Reg Evans on Kolombangara Island rescued John F. Kennedy, after PT 109 was sunk in the Kula Gulf. Air-drops were also utilized to provide food, equipment and supplies when needed.

One amusing tale came to light, when three flyers were rescued from Mono Island by Coastwatchers Forbes Robertson and Frank Nash, the only American Coast Watcher. It seemed the 3 Americans had narrowly escaped the Japanese held island of Sterling and encountered Japanese troops before moving to Mono Island where they found villagers that spoke English. The leader led them to a cave, gave them Japanese soap and a razor and asked them if they would like "mates." When they looked funny he explained would you like "mates" for sleeping." They remembered all those indoctrination lectures about getting mixed up with native girls and virtuously declined. It was only after a restless night sleeping on the stone floor of the cave that they realized the natives English was limited. He meant "mats," not "mates!"

Radio operators used code to transmit military matters and ship movements. It was necessary however to use an open mike to give the number of planes and the direction they were headed so that possible targets would have time to prepare for an attack.

Native scouts and carriers were needed to protect Coastwatcher sites and on a short notice had to be able to carry the heavy radios, components, their fuel and batteries, food and supplies with their Japanese pursuers close behind.

It wasn't until after the first Coastwatchers were captured and executed by the Japanese as spies that, they were inducted as part of the Australian military.

Coastwatchers had knowledge of local areas that included mountains, swamps, jungles, treacherous trails, rain forests, crocodile infested inlets, shark laden waters, roaring mountain streams, mud and rain, coconut plantations, open kunai grass plains, muggy heat and the highest incidence of malaria in the entire world. They were able to provide very helpful information to Allied troops about the terrain and the weather.

The Marines and Raiders welcomed receiving advance notice of air raids, the movement of Japanese ships and barges in surrounding waters and Native troops and guides accompanying reconnaissance patrol missions throughout the war.

When the Japanese seized Tulagi and Guadalcanal in May 1952, a young British Officer, Captain MARTIN J. CLEMENS was the sole British official on Guadalcanal and the nearby islands. Following the Battle of the Tenaru, Clemens asked for laborers. The natives were anxious to do their part in helping to remove the Japanese from their islands and volunteered to help unload the ships.

As a link in the Coastwatcher organization, along with Don MacFarland and Snowy Rhoades, Clemens moved his observation post to Aola Bay and later to the highlands of Guadalcanal following the Japanese occupation of Tulagi.

AUTHOR: "Our old friend Martin Clemens and Sister Mary Theresa, a nun who was on Guadalcanal for over 30 years, were two special guests at the Raider Reunion held in Las Vegas in 1994, along with General C.E. Mundy, Jr, Commandant of the Marine Corps. I was the Master of Ceremonies, and it was my pleasure to have as my guest Patsy Lee (Fasano). Patsy, an 8 year old girl, was bayoneted by the Japanese in 1942, and carried through Jap lines, where she was treated by Marine Corpsmen. She recovered and became the "little sweet heart" of the men on the island, until she had to be evacuated. She, Sister Mary, and Martin Clemens had a great reunion of their own that evening. Patsy's unbelievable tale appeared in a book written by a Fr Goehring, a Marine FMF Chaplain, on Guadalcanal. He later became her benefactor and arranged for her to come to the United States, where she received her high school education in Williamsburg, VA."

On 15 August 42, following the Marines occupation of Guadalcanal, Clemens and his native scouts marched down the beach into a 1st Marine Division outpost. This began the heartwarming relationship of Clemens and his loyal islanders with the 1st Division Marines, and in particular with the Raider Marines. They provided information about enemy strength and movements, tracked General Kawaguchi's force as it slashed its way through the jungle on the way to what was to become the defining battle on Guadalcanal, the attack on Red Mike's men on Edson's Ridge.

Later Clemens, and our Solomon Islands friend SgtMaj

Jacob Vouza and his Native Scouts, accompanied patrols with Carlsons Raiders on their 30 day patrol behind enemy lines in Nov and Dec of 42. No Guadalcanal native ever betrayed and American.

On 4 Dec, Clemens was awarded Great Britains Military Cross and promoted to Major. The United States awarded him the Legion of Merit, Legionnaire in Feb 44.

When Japan surrendered, Clemens was the first to be sent home to Britain on leave. He had the longest combat service of anyone serving in the South Pacific Command.

In a later letter to the Patch Clemens said, "after the Battle of the Tenaru when the natives saw we were in earnest about knocking the Japs in the head, they were all prepared to help. When GEN VANDEGRIFT and COL GERALD C. THOMAS, D-3, admitted that Marines could not unload cargo all day and fight all night. I said, 'I will try to get some native ship unloaders.'

The answer to my appeal by the local natives was fantastic, and I arranged a special section of the front with instructions for them to come through the Marine Lines. 273 came and they dug their own fox-holes that night and worked very hard for a month. When I asked them if they wanted pay they said, "NO, that is our war effort." 500 more came in October by which time I had telegraphed Sydney for help. 5 or 6 ex-planters were sent up and started a labour corps of 3 Battalions of about 800 Natives each, from Malaita and Guadalcanal. These were paid the basic soldiers rate of the Australian Army."

On Tulagi, the 1st Raiders had three Sub Lts attached to them for the fight, they were DICK HORTON, HENRY JOSSELYN, and NICK WADDELL.

On Guadalcanal, MARTIN CLEMENS, JOHN MATHER, JACOB VOUZA, DANIEL PULE. SILAS SITAI and hundreds more served with either the 1st or 2ND RAIDER BN.

At Viru Harbor, New Georgia, DONALD KENNEDY, BILL BENNETT & GORDON Mc MANN, among others, helped the 4th Raiders. At Vangunu, it was HARRY WICKAM who provided the native scouts. Again at Rice Anchorage, Coast watcher CORRIGAN with the 1st Raiders, led the way for the assault at Enogai Inlet and Bairoko Harbor. The natives, everywhere, were evacuating wounded and carrying gear.

Coastwatcher DICK C. HORTON, Sussex, England was one of many heroic British Naval Officers who remained in the Solomons during the Japanese occupation. He, NICK WADDELL and HENRY JOSSELYN accompanied the 1st Raider Battalion in the initial assault on Tulagi 7 August 1942. He writes, 29 May

1977. "It was good of you to write, I was particularly interested in the account of the Tasimboko Raid (March 77 RAIDER PATCH) because RED MIKE EDSON asked me to guide that one and I did so with some of my Guadalcanal police. I particularly well remember the incredible blast of the close range Japanese artillery and RED MIKE'S anger when the first Japanese seen were shot instead of being captured for interrogation. Also SAM GRIFFITH'S asking me to slow down a bit when we were circling around behind Tasimboko, preliminary to attacking it from the rear, ' the men carrying the heavy weapons were having a hard time keeping up because of the weight of the weapons.'

It was because of that raid that the Japanese panicked and bayonetted Fathers Duhamel and Enberink and some nuns. One nun got away and was helped and looked after by KEN HAY on Gold Ridge. That episode was the basis of the film, 'Heaven Knows Mr Allison'.

1st Marine Division, Medal of Honor recipient COLONEL MITCHELL PAGE received a letter from our old friend Guadalcanal Coastwatcher, MARTIN CLEMENS in Toorak, Australia . "Well do I remember after being up two whole nights in succession in the pouring rain waiting for the Aola Bay Reinforcements. When they came ashore one Raider said, 'what disease is that native suffering from?' Michael, my cook had earlier been buried alive by a Jap bomb at the D2 shelter near Henderson Field. He was lacerated all down one side, since then his black skin was healing up with pink spots and blotches, from head to foot. Bomb Disease", I said."

EDITOR LOWELL BULGER: This writer was aboard the APD USS McKEAN along with LTCOL EVANS F. CARLSON and Charley Co, 2nd Raider Battalion. The convoy of about 6 ships was scheduled to land at dawn on 2 Nov but was delayed 24 hours by a severe tropical typhoon which played havoc with the convoy and damaged two of the ships. The convoy withdrew out of enemy plane range, rode out the storm, and came in the early morning hours of the 3rd.

MAJOR JOHN MATHER was a planter who, having spent several years in the Solomons, was recruited for Marine Intelligence purposes. Mather and his natives accompanied Carlsons Raiders on their 30 days of guerrilla activity from Aola to the Lunga River, killing 400 - 800 estimated Japanese. He writes: "Please give all my HQ friends warm salutations from "Down-Under'. It reminds me of the time when I joined 1st Mar Div (D2) on Guadalcanal. I had difficulty with my slang and was sent over to the island of Malaita to find some 20 odd Japs. They sent me over in a plane and I had to let them know when I was ready to return. I finished my job and was most anxious to return but I didn't know the Code and didn't want the Japs to read my message, so I sent this, "have the straight dope and this is no scuttle-but, send plane immediately." The D2, Cal Edward J. Buckley was so pleased, he rushed around Headquarters yelling. 'JOHN'S learnt the language, JOHN'S learnt the language." He was so excited he forgot to send the plane, and I had to wait 2 days before he remembered it."

In Admiral Halsey's words, "the Coastwatchers saved Guadalcanal, and Guadalcanal saved the Pacific!"

GUADALCANAL CAMPAIGN
2ND MARINE RAIDER BATTALION
AOLA BAY- MOUNT AUSTEN PATROL
4 NOVEMBER - 4 DECEMBER 1942

By LOWELL V. BULGER, Patch Editor
AUTHOR: Lowell Bulger could easily be called Mr. Raider or the founding father of the Marine Raider Association, as he worked tirelessly and served in every official capacity and as the voice of the Raiders, until his death from cancer, on 11 Sep 83.

The guerrilla campaign of Carlsons Raiders on Guadalcanal is usually simply called "30 Days behind Enemy Lines" or Carlsons Jungle Patrol." Suffice it to say that this Raider operation was unique because it was almost entirely conducted without back-up support from any other American unit. A small band of determined men waged a bitter, strenuous and debilitating war with the Japanese in a series of hit and run ambushes over a full month's continuous, tortuous, jungle campaign.

Over 400 enemy Japanese were destroyed with a minimum loss of Raider lives. Of far greater damage to the Raiders were the ravages of disease, hunger and the jungle itself. Malaria, Intestinal Parasites, Fungus, Jaundice, and Infections due to constant exposure along with totally inadequate food or nourishment to combat these insidious enemies wreaked havoc to our health. Seriously ill and delirious Raiders refused to give up. Brave men fought to carry their own part of the load, for just one more day until they were forced to turn in and be evacuated to the beach where Higgins boats picked them up and carried them to field hospitals inside the Marine perimeter.

Because the extended campaign was conducted over a long period and involved three Raider landings of different units, no factual accounts of the entire operation have appeared in print since these events, occurred nearly 40 years ago. Several of the principal Raider officers of this operation are alive at this writing and most of them have submitted their written accounts of their first hand recollections for inclusion in this chronological report. An unknown number of Japanese troops were still threatening a break through our lines that would threaten Henderson Field in the area that the 1st Raiders had recently fought.

Col Carlson's 2nd Raider Battalion, Companies C and E were embarked on the APD's USS McKEAN and USS Manley on 31 Oct 42 from Espiritu Santo for a landing at Aola Bay, Guadalcanal. Coast Watchers Martin Clemens, John Mather and their Native Scouts marked the landing area with bonfires on 4 Nov.

Enroute, very heavy seas and steering problems aboard one of the large trans-ports caused an hour delay in the scheduled landing. This writer was aboard the APD USS McKean with C Company, LTCOL EVANS F. CARLSON, CAPT JOHN APERGIS, 1A2DHQ, and a few other Headquarters Raiders.

When the storm hit on the second day at sea, those little TIN CANS were tossed about like corks. The bow plunged under 25 foot waves and doused the entire ship with sea water. These thin shelled, old World War I destroyers, shuddered, creaked and moaned as we zig-zagged around and about the slower bigger transports.

Nearly every Marine aboard suffered from seasickness. The jam-packed, holds were filled solid with deathly ill men who lay in their bunks and vomited in their helmets, gangways, decks, and the head were all slippery and wet with the puke of men who failed to make the toilets. The stench was almost overpowering and infected even the "old salts' of the ship's crew as well as the veteran Nicaragua and Guantanamo Bay veteran Raiders. 5 or 6 feet of water rushed over the gunwale and to port and then starboard as the little APD rolled in the heavy seas. The rain came down in torrents and it was very cold topside. To escape the sickness below, a few Raiders sought refuge topside.

With the anticipation of a short fast assault of 24 hours and orders to return aboard ship if no serious enemy opposition occurred, the Raiders took only the top half of their field pack. 3 cans of C-Rations, 1 pair of socks, 1 white T-shirt oil and cleaning gear, a poncho, shelter-half, 2 grenades and our weapon with one unit of fire (160 rounds) and our GUNG HO KNIFE. All else was left behind in our bunks aboard the APD. We piled over the side into the Higgins boats and stormed abreast into the landing beaches, open stretches of sand about 20 yards deep and easily marked between two burning pylon fires set by CLEMENS and his native scouts.

The remnants of two Japanese outposts were known to be in the area so Coast watcher MARTIN CLEMENS, JOHN MATHER and his natives were exposed in a dangerous poaition and vulnerable to enemy attack. We quickly spread out and. pushed inland, searching some empty native huts, and advanced about one mile inland to the banks of the muddy Kola river. These fire group outposts were about 100 yards apart and we were barely positioned when night fell and pitch black darkness descended. My fire group was sitting on a 20 foot wide knoll about 3 feet above the Aola river to our front and surrounded by swamp from 2 to 3 feet deep.

Raiders at Aola became quickly indoctrinated to the pattern of life familiar to the jungle. Daily drenching rains, eerie jungle noises, huge crawling land crabs, two-foot long tree lizards, crocodiles swimming in the hundreds of rivers, creeks and slews, millions of insects, voracious mosquito's the carriers of malaria, swarmed about our faces. When asleep in the mud and rain any exposed piece of skin area would be one huge mass of itching bites. If scratched they became open running sores which refused to heal in the jungle.

Many Raiders refused to take atabrine, the bitter medicine used to treat malaria, because of an unfounded rumor that it induced sterility and nearly all paid the price and fell ill with malaria in a very short time. We had been warned to drink only fresh rainwater, or boiled river water. When no fires could be kindled deep in enemy territory, river or stagnant pool water in each canteen was to receive two drops of IODINE to kill some the parasites. In spite of precautions taken two out of three became ill with some form of gastro-enteritis, diarrhoea, dysenterey and hook-worm.

No jungle hammocks or mosquito nets were available to us out in the bush and nobody escaped. Officers and men alike equally fell prey to these jungle hazards. Our only consolation was in knowing that the enemy was equally falling prey to insects, parasites, infections and disease and they had far less medical supplies from what we saw of the condition of some of the enemy we encountered at every battle site. When daylight arrived along the Aola river we all breathed a sigh of relief but it was 1300 before we were relieved by army troops.

During the morning a big crocodile approached in the river and appeared to be coming to our little island for a meal and to sun bathe; both RED MELAND and BUCK LOVELAND hurled a grenade that exploded under water. We saw no more of that crocodile.

When we were relieved we returned to the landing beach area. COL CARLSON called us all together and told us ' the change of plans. The rest of the Battalion arrived soon and instead of returning aboard the APD's we were to launch an inland guerrilla patrol to ascertain the extent of enemy troops in the area. The patrol would last 2 or 3 days and we would come out of jungle at Taivu Pt about 15 miles west of Aola. We did not have time to retrieve the balance of our gear left aboard ship. The APD's had immediately weighed anchor to return to Santos for another load of Raiders. ADMIRAL TURNER had relinquished control of the 2nd Raider Battalion to MAJGEN VANDEGRIFT's Henderson Field command. VANDEGRIFT ordered COL CARLSON to begin the patrol at dawn 6 Nov 1942.

On or about 7 Oct 1942 a seven man scouting patrol of 1st Raiders under PLSGT FRANCIS C. PETTUS; provided enough necessary intelligence concerning two enemy outposts, for GEN VANDEGRIFT to send Co A, B, & C of the 1st Raider Battalion, to cross Sealark Channel and eliminate these outposts.

LTCOL Robert E. Hill and his 1st Bn, 2nd Marines, landed at Koilotumaria, killed one JAP officer then attacked Gurabusa and killed another 30 Japanese. The balance of these two enemy outposts were scattered inland in small groups. One casualty was Lt Ishimoto who had lived and worked on Tulagi prior to the war while gathering data for the Japanese Naval Intelligence. It was the hated Ishimoto who directed the torture of SGTMAJ VOUZA on 19-20 Aug.

It was also Ishimoto who led a Japanese patrol into the Marist Mission at Ruavatau on 1 Sep 42 and for a week tortured two priests, and three nuns. Sister Edmee was rescued and hidden by loyal natives but Ishimoto directed the execution of Father Henry Oude-Engerink of France, Father Arthur C. Duhamel, Sisters Mary Odilia and Mary Sylvia of France. Ishimoto was killed on 10 October 42 by the COL HILL force!

The 2nd Raiders drew 6 cans of C-ration (Beans-Biscuit—Hash) and two D-ration bars (Vitamin enriched chocolate bars) from the US Army and begin the inland patrol 6 Nov 42 at dawn. 1st and 2nd Squads of 2nd Plt (LT LAMB) alternated every four hours on "the point". One native scout, familiar with the trails, travelled with the Point Squad. Each swamp, river, creek slowed the Raider's single file advance. Point, could easily outdistance the main body and regularly had to slow up and wait for the main body to cross. a swamp on a slippery-log bridge.

The Raiders were strung out for a mile at 3 paces apart. At each river or creek a 4 or 5 foot river bank became a slippery-as-ice slide after 20 or 30 men had scaled it in their dripping wet boots and the steady falling rain. At every trail branch our native scout would investigate several yards each way before directing which route to take. These little used overgrown trails had to be steadily cleared with our Gung Ho knives. One deadly little liana vine, full of thousands of fish-hook barbs lined every trail and constantly hung across the narrow openings of the trail. Visibility was limited to a few feet. A Raider who slipped into one of those fish hook vines, simply could not move and it would require several minutes to free himself and continue. Those vines would rip and tear your face or hands or arms right through your dungarees. The lacerations would quickly fester and become a running sore that remained during our entire stay on Guadalcanal.

We passed two isolated camps, merely a couple of grass shacks. One of them was still occupied by a native and his wife. She was one of the very few native women we saw on our 150 mile jungle hike. The Japs had raided native villages and molested women and young boys. They commandeered the native pigs and chickens, stripped his gardens of melons, yams, corn and food stores. The Nips would chop down a pau-pau (Papaya) tree to obtain ripe fruit. The natives deserted nearly all of their coastal villages and gardens, often moving inland many miles up into the mountains.

Four of SGTMAJ JACOB VOUZA's youngest children died of disease and malnutrition during that first year of Japanese occupation. Only his wife and two oldest daughters (10 and 9) survived. The natives hated the Japanese and were 100% loyal to their British Government and the American Marines. Any stray Jap was killed, but downed American pilots and sea-battle survivors were rescued and hidden until they could be returned to the Marine perimeter safely. We travelled barely 5 miles during our first day in the bush. No fires, smoking-lamp was out, we fell exhausted asleep in the rain. One man of three awake at all times.

Coastwatchers W.F. Martin Clemens, Toorak, Australia, Maj John Mather and SgtMaj Jacob Vouza and his Native Scouts led the Raiders on a 150 mile jaunt over mountains and through dense jungle for the next 30 out of 45 days. I am proud to say we dearly loved Vouza and all of his brave men The patrol began on 6 Nov 1942 with Companies C and E plus a few HQ CO personnel. The problems in jungle missions moving 300 or more men over unknown and unused trails developed early and the unit covered barely 5 miles during the first day of the debilitating campaign.

At dawn 7 Nov 1942 LTCOL CARLSON informed the two Raider companies that the units progress was too slow. He chose the 2nd Platoon of C Company (2LT CHARLEY LAMB) to become an advance patrol without waiting for the main body which slowed at every obstacle. A C ration breakfast bolted in haste, and the LAMB platoon trotted out in single file, 3 paces apart. Two native scouts who knew the trails and the terrain accompanied the point squad.

COL CARLSON chose to accompany this advance platoon together with his runner-bodyguard CPL ADRIAN E. SCHOFIELD with a total of 37 men. By traveling light and fast we covered several miles through dense, almost impenetrable rain forest. We investigated every side trail for a distance of 200 yards and found no enemy sign. We crossed and re-crossed the Bokokimbo River arid the unoccupied village of Gegende and finally reached the Village of Reko where our first action occurred.

It was here at Reko where we found much evidence of recent enemy presence. We, in the point squad, hurriedly searched each grass hut and one large communal-type grass meeting hall. A strange stillness of an ominous and eerie nature raised the hairs on the back of my neck. Even the macaws and myna birds were strangely silent as we conducted the search. The Japanese had shredded English bibles arid bibles printed in the Solomon Island dialect and scattered the pages throughout the huts. I saved some pages along with fragments of rosary beads and a letter written in pencil by a Pelisse from another mission. Empty Japanese field ration boxes and cigarette packages indicated that the enemy was well supplied and equipped. We estimated the force to be of a 20 man patrol size from footprints and various signs.

It was high noon, and the heat and humidity was accentuated by our own sweat and adrenalin. CARLSON posted sentries, and decided to wait for the main body to catch up to us. We bathed and washed our sweaty clothes as best we could. We estimated our position at about two hours ahead of the main body but in reality we were more like 4 hours out in front.

Always hungry and searching for food, the reader will

note in every account, a constant, impelling, ever-present urgency with the search for food. CARLSON believed his Raider's should be able to live off the land and we were about to prove it. One of our natives disappeared in the jungle and. reappeared carrying a huge bundle of ngali nuts with a meat not unlike avocado, oily, soft and nourishing.

As we waited, about 1100, suddenly the quiet was punctured by a single rifle shot which echoed and re-echoed down the river valley. The strange sound was obviously not American and sounded to be about 200 or 300 yards away across the river and along the trail ahead. We, now on the alert, moved out on the double. We advanced about 200 yards on our side of the river to a point where the trail crossed. The river crossing was neck deep and each man lifted his pack and weapon above his head as he bolted into the river to cross and get on with the war. However when the lead starts to fly, every Marine is faced with the decision to go forward into the fray or take cover.

A flurry of rifle shots rang out when I was nearly to the middle of the river with pack and. weapon overhead and more or less totally vulnerable to a sniper's fire. I forged ahead with the water feeling like pushing against a brick wall against my chest until I reached the opposite shore of the river. We immediately charged off in hot pursuit of the enemy patrol. Our point, moving at a dog-trot had entered a small glade and ran into 10 or 12 Japanese who were gathered around a wild pig and busy skinning the dead animal. After a brief encounter our lead native scout, PIU was wounded in the arm. The Raider's heavy automatic fire rapidly scattered the enemy in the bush in all directions. The surprise over, the Raiders hotly pursued the remnants of the enemy force. Two dying Japs were quickly isolated and blood stained leaves some 200 yards up the trail indicated that others had been wounded.

A humorous incident! WARREN G. ALGER, a BAR man, dove for cover with the first blast of rifle fire...He dove into a heavy cluster of vines which turned out to be the fish hook liana vine. He stopped like a man trying to slide on barbed wire and remained suspended about 3 or feet above ground in a most precarious position if grenades started to go off. After being trapped a full ten minutes and cussing for help, we cut him free amidst our laughter at his plight.

Much needed rations were delivered by the Tetere patrol and dispensed per fire groups so men could do their own cooking. 1 sock full of rice, 1 pound of bacon, 1 sock of tea, A few raisins and some sugar was to last three men for 14 days and could easily have been wolfed down in one day's sitting. From this point on food in any form became the number one obsession and constant topic of conversation. As hunger pains gnawed cases of thievery occurred and COL CARLSON warned... "If any Raider is caught stealing food from another Raider, I hereby authorize you to shoot him dead. Or if you can't shoot a buddy, bring him to me and I'll shoot him!"

On 11 Nov, patrols were launched by C, D, E and F Companies, after learning that enemy reinforcements had landed in the Metapona area, with C Co going toward Asamana. Captain Washburn's D Co engaged two Jap Companies in the Metapona area and 1Lt Cleland Early's 2nd Platoon lost three men.

RAIDERS KILLED IN ACTION AT METAPONA

ANDERSON, LORENZO   AUMAN , JOSEPH M.
MILLER, JERRALD B.

The morning of 11 Nov 42, E company, was ordered to move from Binu to try and locate any more enemy along the Metapona River. The camp at Binu was located in a large grove of trees and our E Company route was across a large open field covered with kunai grass. It was the consensus between WASHBURN, EARLY and BURNETTE that the best alternative was to cross the Metapona and move towards the battle because we believed we might get behind the enemy.

A machine gun section of the light MG's under SGT NATHAN LIPSCOMB was deployed in an area the Japanese were attempting Japanese were wading across the river in various stages of undress, with clothing and weapons held high. Other enemy were assembling and resting in a clearing directly to the front and to the right of our position. The Japs were not aware of our presence, so we were in a good position to ambush them. The platoon was placed in an L shaped defensive position anchored by two machine guns on the river bank overlooking the river crossing and protecting the right flank from the rear.

SGT LIPSCOMB got our machine gun in operation and commenced firing on the Nips in the river. Members of the left front squad also took the enemy under fire. The Japanese reacted at once and our entire platoon was raked with small arms fire. BOB BURNETTE observed a Jap with a nambu move into position at the base of a huge banyan tree. BURNETTE was stationed in a native hut and just as he pointed out the enemy position the nambu opened up just missing us both by inches. I placed my Platoon Sergeant ALBERT O. KAMINSKI in charge of the right side of the line and formed an attack group of SGT NATHAN LIPSCOMB, PFC WILBUR N. WHITAKER, a BAR man, PVT CARL L. CANTRELL, and PVT EDWARD GREJCZIK, a rifle man to destroy the machine gun nest. We attacked by placing a high volume of fire from our MG on the left and the BAR on the right.

This was one hell of a skirmish as each time we killed one Jap, another took his place on the Nambu. I was informed that PFC'S JERROLD MILLER AND LORENZO D. ANDERSON had been hit. Corpsman PHM1 WESTLEY PROCTOR came forward. We moved forward and found the Raiders. Both had been shot in the head. MILLER was still alive but ANDERSON had been hit between the eyes and was dead. MILLER died soon afterward. We moved forward to take out the nambu machine gun nest. Several bodies were around the gun and a Sgt was holding the gun. I turned him over and narrowly escaped death when a grenade he was holding went "puff "and was activated. I was hit in the left hand with shrapnel.

COL CLELAND EARLY continues, "As we pulled out of Asamana the last thing I remember was an increase in mortar fire and the movement of Japs towards us. I did not look back. Our only hope was that we could get back to Binu before dark and that we would not be fired on by either the enemy or our own troops. I do not remember much of what happened when we returned to Binu as we were told to rest and make ready to return to Asamana the next day.

On the 12th we moved back to the same positions of the day before. The Japs had cleared the battlefield and there was little evidence of the battle from the day before. The bodies of ANDERSON, AUBAN and MILLER were undisturbed. We buried them in graves in the open field where they fell."

Meanwhile C Co ran into 700 Japs of the 228th Infantry, troops that had escaped the 7th Marine's trap the night before and Carlson ordered B Co to go forward to Asamana, followed by E Co.

PETE ARIAS states, "I was in JOHN D. BENNETT'S squad. We entered that open field of kunai grass with some misgivings and just as we finished, crossing the open mile field, we approached more heavy jungle. We could hear the enemy clanking on something and jabbering. J.D. ordered us into a scrimmage line and then all hell broke loose, he was killed when machine gun fire raked his chest and LARRY SPILLAN and JOE

HARRISON were killed. Man I never heard so goddamn much firing. I couldn't get close enough to the ground. One machine gun didn't sound too damned friendly directly in front of me. LT MAITLAND ordered "Okay men let's get up and charge them!" SGT "BULL DOG" EVANS said, "Okay, Lieutenant, you get up first and we will follow you, " but that ended any foolish charge talk. I was one of those who didn't get the word when everyone withdrew. HAPPY SANCHEZ and everybody thought I was killed but HAPPY kept saying, "Nobody can kill that goddamn Mexican!"

On Guadalcanal on the way to Asamana the 228th Infantry enemy force was hit for the third time by a Raider unit within a two-hour period. The special platoon of D Company under CAPT CHARLES P. McAULIFFE led his D Co patrol across another open grassy field and ran head on into large units of the enemy well hidden in heavy jungle.

The Raiders found themselves caught in the open field with the enemy well concealed in the jungle to their front and both right and left flanks. Two lead men in the point were immediately killed and a third wounded. The slain Raiders, were PFC LEROY I. FANSLOW, and a big Indian BAR man named PFC FRANK S. MERCADO. It was a perilous position for this small Raider patrol.

A first hand account of those moments comes from LTCOL HUBERT D. FALTYN 2DG who writes "I was a squad leader of one of the Mortar Squads am CPL CHARLEY VAN HOOSE, 2DG, had one of the (MG) Machine Gun squads. The kunai grass in that open field was 4 or 5 feet tall and we were following a 2 foot wide trail when our point reached the jungle and the firing started. We were strung out in single file and only about one third of our patrol actually reached the jungle when all hell broke loose. They had machine guns, mortars, rifle grenades and small arms to our front and, on both sides of us, and knee mortars sighted down the trail when we were pinned down. If you moved a blade, of grass you drew enemy fire. The mortars hit right near us showering us with dirt but thank goodness the trail wasn't straight. We snaked through the grass and my belly never left the ground. Finally the word was passed to 'Get the hell out of here', and we did just that.

We moved, well out into the field and laid out about 20 white T-shirts in a large arrow. Within 10 minutes a flight of six S82EY and P-400 American planes arrived from Henderson Field and made several passes over the enemy positions, bombing and strafing and firing cannon into the enemy positions. A group of 3 or 4 Raiders, who had missed the main action approached me and asked me to lead them into the area where they might help recover more of our wounded. At this time, I surmised that the right flank woods would most likely conceal some wounded survivors. I led a 5 man group about 400 yards down the right side of that horseshoe shaped Sudan which will always be known as Bloody Plains to those who were there. CPL IRA D. MILLER (KIA Okinawa) led the group of would be rescuers and PVT BROOKS POWERS was also in the party.

When we failed to find any survivors, I was amazed as my whole 2nd Platoon was unaccounted for and I knew that both WARREN GLEN ALGER (KIA Iwo Jima) and VIRGIL S. LEEMAN had been hit by mortar fragments but should have been able to reach that right flank jungle. CPL RICHARD FYE appeared and stated there were many dead but no known Raiders still alive.

I returned to the Coconut Grove and learned that my 2nd Platoon had withdrawn almost intact on orders and had been assigned a defensive jungle position guarding the C. P. and Field Dressing Station in the Coconut Grove.

RAIDERS KILLED IN ACTION AT BLOODY PLAINS

BARBER,OWEN	BENNETT ,JOHN
CLUSKER,JAMES	FANSLOW, LEROY
HARRISON,JOSEPH	MERCADO, FRANK
MYERS, CHARLES M.	SPILLMAN,LAWRENCE

One C Co Raider, PVT JAMES P. CLUSKER JR. was so badly wounded he was unable to crawl away and remained within a few yards of the searching enemy Japs during the night. He over-heard the screams of PVT OWEN BARBER who was captured, castrated, tortured and finally killed by the enemy only a few yards from his hiding place. JIM CLUSKER was rescued the next morning. (The above account was related by Lowell Bulger, Patch Editor).

COL OSCAR PEATROSS, "Upon our capture of Asamana my Command Post was located in a thatched roof hut in the Village with a muddy floor. After two tense days and a sleepless night I returned and the sky opened up and heavy tropical rain began to fall. Too tired to dig a foxhole I lay down after eating a D bar and drinking some tea and immediately fell asleep. Our hut was fired upon and we rushed out without finding anyone, but decided I should dig a foxhole for my own safety. After excavating only eight or so inches of the muddy earth, my entrenching tool hit something firm but it wasn't a rock. I probed around in the clammy dirt with my fingers, only to my great revulsion realize my fingers were tracing the features of a human head, face, lips eyes, nose and eyes. The obstacle to my digging was with out a doubt, the body of a recently buried corpse of a Japanese soldier. I hastily scraped back the earth and moved over a couple of yards to dig into another, and then another and another. The floor of our hut was literally a Japanese cemetery.

On the 13 Nov, E Company returned to Asamana and, occupied it for several days. It was very eerie duty with Japanese being sighted daily on all sides of the Raiders positions. 1LT WILLIAM L. LANSFORD, 2E stated, "I was plenty scared until I looked, up and saw our CO, CAPT RICHARD T. WASHBURN, standing in an open glade, calmly shaving his face, while bullets were whistling around. Our leaders bravery was most reassuring to those of us who were nervous

Meanwhile back at base camp Binu, LTCOL EVANS F. CARLSON, received a native scouting report which is best related in a first hand account of PFC PAUL R. JOPLIN. On the morning of 11 Nov at Binu, COL CARLSON received word via a native scout that a small band of 15-20 Japs were holed up in a jungle hideaway about four miles away. CARLSON ordered CAPT WILLIAM E. SCHWERIN, 2F, to take a couple of squads of Raiders and eliminate the hidden Japanese. I was runner-radio man with CAPT 'WILD BILL SCHWERIN.' He carried a 12 gauge shotgun and two 45 Caliber pistols. I carried two 45 Cal pistols as spares and a walkie-talkie radio.

At about 1100 we left Binu and following our native scouts who were armed with captured Jap rifles, bayonets and their bush knives, we reached the enemy position by about 1400. We noted a single Jap sentry guarding the narrow mouth of a ravine between two steep jungle cove hills on either side. We lay still on our bellies. We watched and waited. Finally, after two or three hours the sentry was called in for chow and we made our move into the ravine. Wild Bill sent us into the ravine by three man fire-groups, and in short order we reached assault position undetected. The enemy soldiers were clustered around two camp fires busily eating their rice balls Their arms were leaning against trees and well out of easy reach. Wild Bill directed half of us to open fire on one group and the second half of us to fir on the other group of enemy. He had previously told us, "When you hear my shotgun. that's the signal to give 'em hell!"

The Japs were 75-80 feet away in an open glade so we split into two groups and crawled forward to close a bit more ground. Suddenly CAPT SCHWERIN opened with his shotgun and every Raider poured a clip of ammo into the exposed enemy M-1 rifles, BAR's and Thompson MG (Tommy Guns) made short work of the surprised Japs. The heavy firing lasted less than a minute. Our native scouts dropped their rifles and charged in swinging their bush knives to finish off any survivors. All the Japanese were killed and no Raiders or natives were even scratched. It was a perfect ambush!

We searched the bodies and gathered enemy maps and intelligence data. We gave native scouts the enemy weapons. Among the dead, we found one enemy officer', a sergeant and a corporal. The Japanese were bearded and somewhat ragged but appeared to be well fed and an organized patrol."

The Raiders had slept in their clothes and been soaked daily. Jungle rot and fungus, fevers, jaundice and dysentery ran rampant through our ranks and nearly every Raider suffered one or more malady. COL EVANS CARLSON was ordered to continue the guerrilla mission but he wanted only reasonably healthy, determined men to continue. Sick and. ailing men would only hamper the lives of healthy men and could only hamper the continued success of the mission. CARLSON ordered a medical inspection and a survey of all physically sick. Strong brave men wept when they were told they would be sent back to the beach and perimeter hospital. Those that refused to turn themselves in were turned in by their buddies if it was evident the man could not continue another extended period of patrolling and battle. Nearly one half of the original first men landed, were found unfit for further action. Rotting jungle sores covered their feet, legs and jocks. CARLS also permitted the survey of the gripers and. the faint hearted as he repeatedly stated, 'I would rather have ten stout hearted men who are ready and eager to fight than a hundred men who think only of saving their own lives.'

Daily patrols and minor actions continued for a week until the Raiders reach the Engineers Ferry that consisted of raft and a rope hawser across the Tenaru river. It was located about two miles outside the Marine Perimeter. This became our new base camp from which we daily patrolled from 2 Nov to 27 Nov. Only scattered messengers and stragglers were encountered, captured, interrogated, and dispatched. Food supply was critical during this whole period. Two wild native cows were butchered and fresh meat made us all violently ill with the runs. On every fourth day ice, bacon, and tea, were brought in to us by native bearers. They then evacuated our sick and stretcher cases. Once we received some canned New Zealand Corned Beef, the most highly desirable ration of all, which again made us all sick with intestinal cramps and diarrhea for almost 3 weeks.

On their patrols in the Mount Austen area of the Lunga Gorge and Tenaru River areas they discovered a 75 mm mountain gun known as Pistol Pete during the last days of November and the first days of December.

RAIDERS KILLED IN ACTION AT
MOUNT AUSTEN (MAMBULA)

FARRAR, RICHARD C.	HERMISTON, ALBERT
MATELSKI, CYRILL A.	MILLER, JACK
MITCHELL, GLENN	VAN BUREN,STUVEYSANT

LT MILLER and PVT VAN BUREN who were seriously wounded on 4 Dec, concerned both Doctors, ROBINSON and MacCRACKEN, while being carried on stretchers along the trail. They stopped the litter bearers to check on them and LT MILLER died shortly after. When COL CARLSON was notified, he came back from the front of the column with his bible and conducted a service and MILLER was buried on the North Slope of Mombula Mountain. Unfortunately, VAN BUREN would also to die that day.

During this time A, B and F Company's had come across many dead Japanese that were emaciated with their uniforms tattered. Even though they were all armed, none of them had a full clip of ammunition.

The Raiders hiked the last eight miles to their bivouac area where they were given a complete head to feet issue of clothing and shoes, followed by a bath, shave and a haircut. Playing cards and writing materials helped to bring about miracles in their appearance and morale in a very short time.

This was a classic example of a successful 150 mile Raider Operation in which 488 Japanese soldiers had been killed, and enemy weapons, ammunition, equipment and supplies for some 4000 Japanese troops were destroyed, that doomed their effort to sustain an attack to retake Henderson Field,

The issue of who would win the Battle of Guadalcanal was still in serious doubt in Oct, when only one bomber and ten fighter planes were flyable and they were unable to stop six transports from coming in. If reinforcements hadn't arrived we could have been forced from Guadalcanal, which would have opened the route to Australia for the Japanese.

Following the humiliating defeats inflicted upon them by the Raider 1st and 2nd Battalions, and other Marine and Army units, the Japanese forces were in total disarray on Guadalcanal. Jap Commanders still convinced of their invincibility led poorly planned banzai attacks which resulted in a shocking number of deaths and wounds to their fighting men. Following defeat after defeat their troops were struggling to escape by cutting their own trails through mountainous terrain, while poorly fed and suffering from untreated wounds and illnesses such as malaria and dysentery.

Recognizing their plight, Japanese planners arranged a rescue mission to evacuate over 12,000 men aboard speedy destroyers, in a nighttime maneuver, that was a complete success. The starving, wounded and sick troops unable to fight their way to the evacuation site however, were left to die in the unforgiving jungles of the island.

The remaining American troops on the island commanded by Army General Patch were caught completely by surprise at the escape of the doomed Jap troops. Many American lives were saved because of the reduced number of enemy troops, while mop up operations continued until the island was secure. They had fought several battles and killed over 500 Japanese while losing only 16 KIA themselves.

On the thirty-day guerrilla mission of LTCOL EVANS F. CARLSON'S Raiders on Guadalcanal during Nov 1942, over 200 loyal natives were recruited by Australian MAJ JOHN MATHER and SGTMAJ JACOB VOUZA to serve as scouts, bearers and fighters during the extended campaign. They foraged for food, built shelters, carried out our sick and wounded and brought us food, ammunition and medicines from the beach drops at Tasimboko. These brave natives served without pay, retaining the slain enemy weapons and bayonets to protect their women and villages. When Carlson's Raiders reached the relative safety of the Marine lines around Henderson Field. These natives served as Beach Gangs unloading much needed cargo. For this they were paid meagerly, a shilling and a twist of black tobacco per native per day.

MEDALS AWARDED 2ND RAIDERS ON GUADALCANAL

NAVY CROSS

AUMAN,JOSEPH	CARLSON,EVANS F.*
MILLER, JACK	SLUSSER,JOHN
YANCEY, JOHN	

* Silver Star awarded for the second time.

SILVER STAR

BURNETTE,R.W.	CAMPBELL,STUART
CARLSON, EVANS C.	CIANCI, JOSEPH J.
CRANDALL, B.W.	CROFT, ORIN
EARLY,CLELAND	GARY,ALBERT V.*
HUTTON, C.W.	JACOBSON, J. P.
LEARY, JOHN J.	MAGHAKIAN, V.
MAITLAND, T.F.	MONTE, ARTHUR
ROBINSON, J.N.	TASSONE, FRANK
VAUGHT, E.E.	WASHBURN,R.T.

2E JOHN A. SCHOCH, wrote, "When we were behind the Jap lines on Guadalcanal in November 1942, we spent one night in a deserted native village. When we lined up for head count in the morning we were given a G.I. chocolate bar, (D Ration) which was a real treat after 3 weeks of rice and tea. I don't think any of us were aware of the date (You lose track of time under extended battle conditions), until CAPT DICK WASHBURN said, enjoy your dinner, TODAY IS THANKSGIVING!

2FE ARTHUR DON GARDNER Twin Falls, ID sends us a clarification on our 2nd Raider Battalion on Guadalcanal story Nov 81 RAIDER PATCH.

"You give the impression that only A & B Companies took the East-West trail over Mount Austen where LT JACK MILLER and the others were killed and wounded.

CAPT WILLIAM SCHWERIN and I were also with them although we brought up the rear as reserve that afternoon and the next morning. When the dead were buried, FOX COMPANY took the point and we led the main body back to the Marine lines around Henderson Field. I was the first man in that procession when we entered the lines and some Army troops were standing guard. A soldier had just returned from chow and had a canteen full of scalding hot coffee. I hadn't had a drink of anything for more than 24 hours. I tipped up his offered canteen and drank about half before pausing. Our mouths and throats were calloused and immune from gulping down hot rice and tea for 30 days. When PVT GLEN "BLACKIE" MITCHELL was killed on the Upper Lunqa. (1 Dec 42) CPL JOHN YANCEY, PVT EDWARD E. VAUGHT and myself were about 20 feet away. We were the first at his side and he had a massive wound in his throat where the bullet had exited. YANCEY yelled, 'Corpsman-Corpsman' but BLACKIE was gone. I helped bury him. We made a cross covered with tin from a hardtack can to mark his grave."

Jungle Creeper Vines - Guadalcanal

USS Thaddeus Parker

APD Colhoun
Sunk just after Raiders Disembarked - 30 AUG 1942

Chow Down on Guadalcanal

Coastwatcher Seton

Native Payday - Guadalcanal

7

Assault on New Georgia

Raiders Disembarking from APD

Raiders disembark from APD transport by descending rope nets
to enter higgins boats for assault on New Georgia

NEW GEORGIA, BRITISH SOLOMON ISLANDS.
1ST MARINE RAIDER REGIMENT
1ST MARINE RAIDER BATTALION
4TH MARINE RAIDER BATTALION
7 Aug 42 - 8 Feb 43

Following the defeat of the Japanese at Guadalcanal, it was the turn of the 4th Marine Raider Battalion to follow the stirring example shown by the 1st and the 2nd Marine Raider Battalion's in their 1942 assaults against Japanese Forces in the Solomon Islands and on Makin Island (Butaratari).

The nearly completed airfield at Munda, and the start of construction on another airfield at Kolombangara in the New Georgia chain of islands, threatened the possibility of continued air attacks on Guadalcanal, so they became the next targets to be attacked.

New Georgia and it's Islands, only 180 miles from Guadalcanal, were protected by coral reefs with the only access being Viru Harbor, Bairoko Harbor, Rice Anchorage and Enogai Inlet, all sites of future Raider battles. The dense jungle and swamps of the islands made it difficult for even the natives to travel and they generally avoided the interior of the island. Viru Harbor, for instance, had an annual 200 inches of rainfall per year.

The Japanese were not to be the only enemy on New Georgia. The real enemy was the terrain itself. The never ending tropical heat, rain and smothering humidity quickly drained the strength from the proud Raiders, leaving them dripping with water, just like the trees and bushes.

Swamps concealed the twisted roots of trees and vines under the muck. Murky water that was hip to shoulder deep had to be slowly traversed in total darkness, by the slipping, falling and cursing Raiders. The halo of flies and other pests around each mans head during the day in the 10 to 12 feet guinea grass jungle, was replaced with swarms of angry mosquitoes covering every bit of exposed flesh at night. The in-penetrable tropical forest, with clusters of gigantic tree trunks rose straight up to a ceiling a hundred feet or more from the ground with little or no sunlight showing through. Pale orchids hanging from dripping tree trunks, presented a contrast to a forest seemingly full of clouds of flitting bats. Underfoot was a stewing, steaming mass of rotting vegetation, damp and musty from centuries of never drying rain. Huge white slugs could be seen crawling through the muck.

The islands were occupied by Japanese troops in Nov 1942. Japanese engineers immediately began construction of the airstrip and nearly succeeded in completing it in secrecy, by cleverly hiding view of the construction from the air, by cutting the tops of trees and stringing them on cables above the work on the runways. Only after receiving information from Australian Coast Watcher Donald Kennedy located on Segi plantation was the airfield identified.

Upon receiving this information from Kennedy, several recon missions were then scheduled for New Georgia. The first recon team visiting Kennedy's base to obtain intelligence information included Navy Lieutenant William Coultis who had been in the Solomons on a scientific expedition and knew the islands well. Raiders included 1st Battalon, CLAY A. BOYD, CHARLES E. JAMES, FRANK J. GUIDONE AND ROBERT C. LAVERTY. They were followed by the team of 2LT HAROLD SCHRIER, CPL JOLLY AND PFC SCHMID, who visited Vangunu and Wickham Island sites, while another team under the Command of LT COL MICHAEL S. CURRIN were also transported to New Georgia to lay the groundwork for the invasion.

The 4th Raider Bn was organized at Camp Pendleton, CA in October 1942. Marine Major James Roosevelt the son of the President of the United States was the Commanding Officer. Much to his chagrin however, Jimmy Roosevelt was not to see the culmination of his efforts to prepare the 4th Battalion for battle. Already suffering from poor vision, with part of his stomach removed, he had flat feet and was forced to wear tennis shoes most of the time. He became ill with malaria and was then evacuated back to the States on 28 Apr 1943, with his replacement being Marine LTCOL MICHAEL S. CURRIN.

Former Raider MAJGEN OSCAR PEATROSS, USMC said in his book "bless 'em all", "the 4th Eaider Battalion, under the Command of Major JAMES ROOSEVELT well may have been the best trained battalion in the Raiders and perhaps in the entire Marine Corps.

4th BN, O Co Hospital Corpsman 2, LYLE C. McDERMOTT Jr. has permitted your author to excerpt portions of his manuscript written about his service with the Marine Raiders. "The morale of the 4th Raiders was the highest I have ever seen in one group of men. As we embarked for New Georgia we were to carry our poncho's, 4 days K-rations, 79 rounds of ammunition, hand grenades, rifle, bayonet (Yes Corpsmen were armed), canteen, dungarees, shorts, and sox. Raiders have to travle light. We wore a camouflage jungle suit and special boots with rubber soles and canvas tops. We found out the boots weren't worth a damn.

Corpsmen also carried two Unit Three, medical kits. They hung on the side like a pack-saddle. I was issued a carbine rifle weighing 4 1/2 lbs. We clambered aboard our APD, a converted Fast Transport Destroyer. We left Guadalcanal about 1900 and arrived at Segi and arrived at Segi Point before dawn the next day. Coastwatcher Kennedy's natives guided us into the beach where O Company dug there foxholes in solid coral. At six inches deep they filled with water, but we slept in them anyway.

On 28 May 43, about 1900, we launched our rubber boats and left Segi Point for Viru Harbor. The night was the darkest I ever experienced. As we paddled the phosphorescence followed our path like a million stars in the Milky Way. We paddled for about five hours that night. COL CURRINS, MAJOR BATTERTON AND THOMAS were aboard a large Native War canoe.

We arrived at a village and searched for any place at all where we could sleep. Sgt ZWICK, the best Marine I ever knew, set his platoon in position. The men didn't argue with him but they may have sworn at him later. Half of the men were on watch at all times. I used my helmet as a pillow. We were up before dawn, cleaned our weapons and ate a breakfast unit of our K-rations.

Native guides led off in the morning followed by the 1st and 2nd and 3rd platoons, then Headquarters Company and P Company bringing up the rear. Within 100 yards we were in a swamp that was up to our knees and soon got up around our hips and butts. If we stepped on slippery roots we fell in the water. The brush was thick and the trees had twisted roots hidden below the muck. As usual the mosquitoes were terrible, and the flies were even worse, the biting, stinging kind, like horseflies.

We finally got out of the swamp in the afternoon and began following a path through tall grass. The line was moving slow, because the remaining men were still in the swamp. We had to hold up a little and messages were passed from man to man by mouth, as we always seemed to have problems with our radios. Special messages had to be carried by runners who were on the go, double time, almost always.

Our column was intact when we ran into an ambush that took us about three hours to eliminate. They hit P Company and killed 5 men while we killed eighteen of them. We continued, on over a mountain range and underneath towering trees so dense we never saw the sky. At the top of the range the trail led us into a valley that followed a river. The men had been drinking their chlorinated water and were now about out, so many were dipping their helmets in the stream and using it for a cup.

Another swamp loomed in our way through which we struggled late into the night. We fell exhausted on a hillside where we were able to sleep a little in spite of the pounding rain. Our march the next day was similar and P Company left us to go around the harbor to attack it from behind.

Following a Navy bombing run on Viru, we began our attack. Top Sgt PETE KOSOVICH, PlSgt ZWICK and Cpl THOMACK, were killed by a machine gun that was soon silenced. DUNHORN was hit in the shoulder and refused medical aid until the battle was finished. When I came upon a Raider machine gunner shot in the hand he also refused treatment. As soon as the battle was over he rushed up and demanded I treat him immediately, so he could get back to his gun before the battle could start again.

The battle for Viru Harbor lasted about 6 very tough hours. We lost many men killed in action and about the same number wounded. Early in the battle each side were shouting insults at the other. The Japanese soldiers spoke pretty good English. Corpsman STONEWALL SPARLIN was tops with me. Stoney was with the Headquarters Platoon at Viru and I had to marvel at his endurance. He could carry a heavy load and do many things to help the men that were wounded. As tired as he was, I watched him carry water up a slick hill to the patients being treated, late into the night. He did everything possible to make BUTLER a boy of 17 or 18, who was hit in both kidneys, comfortable. He made sure BUTLER had his Raider knife with him and that it was buried with him later when he died.

The fighting on my right flank became pretty hot and I climbed in a small hole for protection. In a few minutes, word was passed along the line that HAUSER was hit. I started out to find him, keeping very low to the ground. Once I asked a head sticking out of the ground where I was and JACK BRASWELL threatened to blow off part of my ass if I didn't get back behind the front line.

Time must have passed fast, but it seemed ages before I got near to where I could see HAUSER. He was riddled with machine gun bullets and was located about 75 yards in front of the lines. There were other men hit with the same machine gun including, OLSEN, CHILDRESS, DECKER, ANDERSON, SWEDE, BLOMBERG, and a couple of other Raiders.

I left my Unit Three with those guys; put a morphine syrette in my teeth and a few battle dressings in my dungaree jacket. When I reached Hauser all I had was the morphine syrette. I tried all the fancy holds we were taught in Hospital Corps School to get HAUSER turned on my back, but nothing seemed to work. I somehow managed to wrestle him behind a large log just before another full blast of the machine gun took the top off it. CALLAHAN was hit in his extremities after LT ANDERWALD sent him crawling to take out the Nip gun. He threw three grenades into the nest that didn't go off because of the mud. While he was cussing, I was able to see one of the snipers and killed him with my carbine. DON HARPER was also out looking for the machine gun, and my shots at the sniper gave him the location. He said 'Thanks, Doc', and hurled his demolition charge into the nest and destroyed it. CALAHAN rushed the other sniper and that ended the action on our flank."

AUTHOR: Both, Corpsmen McDERMOTT and SPARLIN, were Awarded Letters of Commendation for their bravery during this battle.

The 4th Raider Battalion's initiation into combat began with the occupation of Segi Point and continued with assaults on Viru Harbor, Vangunu and Bairoko Harbor, New Georgia, British Solomon Islands in 1943. Military historians in general usually describe the battle for New Georgia as one operation, and generally ignore the three separate objectives of the Raiders.

Because of the large number of Raiders suffering from malaria from their stay on Guadalcanal, even stricter orders were handed down in order help limit any new cases. Not only were Corpsmen responsible for tossing atabrine in a mans mouth while he was in the chow line, but an officer had to stand alongside, and observe that both the Corpsman hit his target and the Raider swallowed the atabrine. This was a bitter pill for the Raiders to take, but it proved very successful in helping to limit new cases of malaria.

The coral nature of the islands resulted in many instances of nasty coral cuts and abrasions that became easily infected. Swarming flies were a constant problem. They would quickly cover any food and often refused to move even when the food was swallowed. Many a Raider fought a silent and often fierce battle in his foxhole when the very large land crabs that were everywhere, dropped in on him in the dead of night.

Corpsmen and officers were issued medical kits, as was every 4th Marine. The value of doing this was proven early in battle. Battle casualties were taken by stretcher and on foot to be evacuated by LCT's, LST's and PBY's to Guadalcanal.

Malaria, acute infections, gastro-enteritis, jaundice, dysentery, diarrhea, tonsillitis, fungus infections, ring worm, and open sores, kept medical personnel busy long after the wounded received treatment.

War neuroses; was the most serious medical problem encountered on New Georgia.
Of the reported 2,500 cases, 1,950 occuurred in the 43rd Army Division, 200 in the 37th Division, and 200 in Navy and Marine units. The 43rd Division represented 40% of the attacking force, and contributed 80% of the total number of cases. Perhaps as many as 50% of these cases could have probably been classified as combat fatigue.

The first operation was the 4th Raider Battalion capture of Viru Harbor by O and P Company on 1 July 43, following their landing on 21 June at Segi Point. Then came the 30 June attack at Vangunu Island and Gavutu by N and Q Co of the 4th Battalion. The third operation was that of the 1st Raider Battalion and their assault at Enogai Inlet on 5 Jul 43. When their continued push to capture Bairoko Harbor bogged down, a decision was made to rush the battered 4th Raider Battalion back to New Georgia from Guadalcanal to reinforce them.

The lack of heavy weapons and the absence of artillery or aerial support doomed their effort to capture the heavily reinforced Bairoko garrison where the Raiders were outnumbered almost five to one. The heavy casualties during the earlier fighting on New Georgia left the 1st and 4th Raider Battalions with a combined strength of less than one Battalion for the assault on Bairoko.

Generally overlooked however, is the 4th Battalion had successfully completed both of their missions by capturing Vangunu Island and Viru Harbor before the initial 1st Raider Battalion landing on Rice Anchorage, New Georgia.

In the first phase of the New Georgia operation, the 4th Battalion O, P and HQ Company landed off the APD's USS Dent and Waters at Segi Point, New Georgia Island on 20 June 43. Army infantry and supporting troops arrived two days later to take over their positions.

The Raider's left Segi Pt on 27 June 43 using rubber boats for the eight mile night trip to Regi (the longest combat assault by rubber boat in WW II), that was completed the next day. With Native scouts as guides they then plunged into a three-day march, through nearly impassable swamp, while fighting off Japanese ambushes along the way. The Villages of Tombe and

Tetamara fell and Viru was seized on 1 July 43.

During this time N, Q and _ HQ Company, under the command of MAJ JAMES R. CLARK was assigned to support the Army's 103rd Infantry Regiment under the command of LTCOL Lester E. Brown in the capture of Wickham Anchorage, Vangunu Island. The Raider assault began on 30 June 43, as they disembarked from the APD's USS Schley and McKean.

The 43rd Army Division, along with the 24th Naval Construction Bn (SeaBee's) were to land 30 June 43 in the third phase of the operation at Rendova Island, aboard the APD's Schley, KILTY, CROSBY AND DD USS McCALLA. They were to be followed by the 5 July 43, 1st Raider Battalion assault on Rice Anchorage, New Georgia.

After the 4th Marine Raider Battalion made their initial landing at Segi Point, the Army 43rd Division came ashore to become the New Georgia Occupation Force. They were joined by the Army 37th Division and Medical elements of the Army 25th Division, plus the 17th Field Hospital which was to set up in mid July, after the Army XIV Corps assumed command of the Rendova Occupation Force.

Of great concern prior to the invasion was the health of the troops. On Guadalcanal during the first 6 months of 1943, malaria was still the major medical problem for the Marines, with over 65% being afflicted. Added to this was the need to control and treat other medical problems such as dengue fever, diarrhea, dysentery, fungus infections, ring worm, heat stroke, etc. Preventative measures taken, such as the carefully observed daily disbursement of Atabrine tablets aided in holding down the incidents of malaria.

Plans were made to handle the anticipated battle casualties so the problems of their immediate care until evacuation by sea or air could be arranged. Evacuating casualties over jungle trails was never easy and four to six men per litter were needed to carry the wounded with the litter bearers having to stop and rest every 300 to 500 yards.

Combat corpsmen carried unit 3 medical kits while each battalion member had a supply of atabrine, halazone, salt tablets, aspirin, band-aids, and a morphine syrette, all in a metal container.

VIRU HARBOR ASSAULT, NEW GEORGIA ISLAND
COMMANDING OFFICER COL MICHAEL S. CURRIN

"When we set out for Viru, a number of War Correspondents

wanted to accom-pany us but they decided, on just three. Clay Gowran (Chicago Tribune); Gordon Walker (Christian Science Monitor), and Walter Farr (London Daily Mail). Their stories were carried pretty much all over. After we captured Viru Harbor, I made all three Honorary Raiders.

It was a difficult operation, which was carried out by as fine a group of officers and men as I have ever served with. I would especially like to mention the Doctors and Corpsmen. There has always been a special relationship be-tween the Medical Corps (MC), the Hospital Corps (HC) and the Marines. They never let us down when help was needed on the battlefield or off."

When we returned to Guadalcanal after Viru, I remember when, Lieutenant General M.F. Harmon, Commanding General, Unites States Army Forces In South Pacific Area flew up to Guadalcanal from his headquarters in Noumea, New Caledonia. The Army 143rd Infantry Division under Major General John H. Hester was having great trouble in the approaches to Munda Airfield. General Harmon sent for me and we talked privately for about 45 minutes at the Headquarters of Rear Admiral Richmond Kelly Turner, Commander of the South Pacific Amphibious Forces. The gist of the conversation was that the General wanted to know why the 4th Raiders did so well in the difficult operations of Viru Harbor and Wickham Anchorage under the same conditions as the Army troops that were having so much trouble at Munda.

I told him that our officers and men were of high caliber, thoroughly trained and conditioned. And that we were MARINES. General Harmon was a very nice man and he thanked me for having my frank discussion with him."

AUTHOR: General Hester was later relieved of his command by the Army.

One of the more serious Army concerns was combat fatigue, exhaustion related problems, and temporary mental disturbances. It was reported to be the most serious medical problem in the New Georgia campaign. Approximately 2,500 Army troops were admitted with this diagnosis. This alone accounted for more men than the combined 1st and 4th Marine Raider Battalions combat force on the island!

Twenty-one Raiders were awarded the Army Distinguished Service Cross, second only to the Medal of Honor, for their bravery on New Georgia. Those medals were more than the Army awarded to all Marine units combined during the rest of the war!

At Segi Plantation in early 1943, New Zealand. Coastwatcher, DONALD KENNEDY trained a small band of loyal natives to harass the enemy troops in defense of the Japanese airfield at Munda Point, New Georgia. Segi is located about 70 miles east of Munda Airstrip and is about midway between two enemy bases at Viru Harbor and Wickham Anchorage.

These natives were called the Solomon Island Defense Force. They ambushed enemy patrols, raided their camps and, interrupted the barge traffic between bases. They armed and, equipped themselves with captured enemy rifles, bayonets and helmets. They were a constant thorn in the side of General Sasaki, the enemy commander at Munda, so he took steps to eliminate KENNEDY'S Segi base by sending Major Hara and the 1st Bn, 229th Infantry Regiment to reinforce Lt Takagi and his 225 man command at Viru.

Admiral Turner had originally intended to launch the New Georgia landings on 30 June l943 at both Rendova and Segi where the Seabees were to prepare a fighter strip to support the attack on Munda. At KENNEDY'S urging Turner ordered the Segi landing and envelopment to begin on 20 June to deny this base to the Japanese while it was still in allied hands.

At Guadalcanal, LTCOL MICHAEL S. CURRIN, HQ Company, Company O, (1LT RAYMOND L. LUCKEL) and Company P, (CAPT ANTHONY WALKER) of the 4th Marine Raider BN were hastily loaded aboard the APD'S, USS Dent and USS Waters. They rushed up "the slot' to land at Segi on 21 Jun l943 landing at 0550.

The next day at 745, Two Army companies of the 103 Infantry Regiment and a survey party landed to replace the Raiders at the Segi base, while the Raiders moved out to attacked Viru Harbor. Immediate construction of a fighter strip at Segi was begun and completed by 11 July.

The Raiders set up a perimeter defense around Segi and undertook vigorous patrol action in preparation for the Viru Harbor attack that was scheduled for capture by 30 June. Although Viru lay only 11 miles to the west of Segi the overland jungle route would require the Raiders to cover many times this distance in heavy jungle and waist deep mangrove swamps.

AUTHOR: This article written by War Correspondent Clay Gowran, describing in detail, the 4th Raider Battalion attack on Viru Harbor allows readers the opportunity of seeing this battle through the eyes of an on the spot War Correspondent. It is a story written by a brave UNARMED correspondent in a battle, where even Corpsmen removed our Red Cross armbands and carried a weapon, as they had become targets for the Japanese troops while treating their wounded comrades when they were hit by enemy gunfire.

As published in three installments, November 7,14, 21, 1943 in the Chicago Tribune. The late Clay Gowran of the Chicago Tribune accompanied this tough, gallant band of 4th Marine Raiders assigned to capture the important Japanese base at Viru Harbor. Their objective did not bulk large on any map. Indeed, it is only a tiny cove fringed by high coral cliffs on which stand bomb torn trees and a few tumble-down thatched huts. But on that day, 1 July 1943, it loomed strategically important.

WE STORM VIRU, By Clay Gowran

"An official communique told the story in 57 words: "UNITED STATES MARINE RAIDERS yesterday captured the important Japanese base at Viru Harbor on the mainland of New Georgia, 30 miles east of Munda Point air field, after severe fighting. Viru Harbor was attacked from the rear by the RAIDERS who emerged from the jungle after a grueling four day march to strike the defending Japanese garrison.' It is an epic of the impossible, a chronicle to be repeated wherever brave men gather or patriots speak of the days of war." The first rays of the tropical sun were just touching the blue waters of Florida Island's Halava Bay as the ponderous Catalina flying boat gathered speed, kissed the sea for the last time, and was airborne. Above droned 10 Corsairs and 8 Aircobras, the fighter escort that would screen the big boat on her 140 mile flight thru the Japanese held central Solomons to Segi Plantation, on the south-eastern tip of New Georgia. It was 27 June 1943, three days before America's offensive operation (Codename: TOENAILS) in the Central Solomons was to begin. At dawn on 30 June, United States forces would strike simultaneously at Rendova Island, at Wickham Anchorage on Vangunu Island and at Viru Harbor.

The stage was set and I was on my way to join a unit of the 4th Marine Raiders made up of Headquarters Company, O Company commanded by 1LT RAYMOND L. LUCKELL and P Company commanded by CAPT ANTHONY WALKER and the overall command under LTCOL MICHAEL S. CURRIN).

The Raiders were concealed at Segi, awaiting D-day. They had been landed there in the dead of night from fast destroyers several days before, to be ready just in case the Japs got any notions about Segi Plantation (Headquarters of Coastwatcher, Donald Kennedy, District Officer for the Western Solomons) where our forces planned to build an air strip.

If nothing developed at Segi, they would push off thru the jungles and smash at Viru Harbor, 20 air miles west up the coast. Viru was defended by hand picked Japanese Imperial marines, so it was fitting that the Raiders were given the task of capturing the harbor.

With me in the plane were two members of the SEGI unit, carrying confid-ential dispatches to their commanding officer from the General Staff directing the New Georgia show. They were 1LT MALCOLM N. MC CARTHY, 4CP, of San Francisco, a small, wiry young Irishman, and MARINE GUNNER JAMES J. GARRISON, 4 BO of San Diego, who had spent 13 of his 30 years in the Corps, and looked the part. He was tough, how tough I did not realize, until later.

They spent the time drinking coffee from the plane's thermos jugs, and polishing and cleaning the short .30 caliber carbines with which the Raider officers had been armed. Over the roar of the motors they talked about what was coming. GARRISON had heard lead fly in Nicaragua and Cuba, but it would be McCARTHY's first experience. "These Japs may be good, but we'll give 'em a few pointers in the finer art of real toughness yelled GARRISON, You know, the old RAIDER heave-ho. Wait until you see the gift's BATTERTON's boys are fixing up for them."

BATTERTON, it turned out, was the 25 year old Operations Officer of the unit MAJ ROY J. BATTERTON JR. of Lexington, KY. He had spent 18 months with the British Commandos, taking a post-graduate course in organized murder, with emphasis on the use of demolitions. He was typical of the youthful, deadly efficient type of officer who commands these special units. Youth and guts, those are the attributes the Marine Corps wants in its men with rank on their shoulders.-

Slipping out between Guadalcanal's Cape Esperance and the jutting volcanic cone of Savo Island, the PBY Catalina flattened out 30 feet above the water and poured on the coal. Down there, with the waves almost kissing her duraluminum belly was her safest bet against any wandering Japanese Zeros which might be interested.

Above the F4U Corsairs and P400 Aircobras wove intricate designs in the morning sky as they flew a crisscross patrol to protect the flying boat. In three groups the army Aircobras roamed 3,000 feet above us. (This unloved version of the P38 manufactured for export to the British was equipped with the British high-pressure oxygen system for which no equipment was available in the South Pacific). Six thousand feet over them, wings glinting silver in the strengthening sunlight, the high altitude, faster Corsair's banked and turned in the precision pattern of the screen.

Big and clumsy, like a crazy streetcar with wings, the Catalina hedge hopped the Pacific toward her goal. Wings almost touching the waves in her turns, she tore thru the tiny islands, of the Russells group, mounted like lovely green emeralds in settings of white coral reefs and blue water, soon the densely wooded slopes of Gatukai Island, southeastern most of the New Georgia group, rose from the sea dead ahead.

The fighters tightened in around us, and our gunners swung open the blister hatches and fired test bursts from their weapons. This was enemy air, the young, sandy haired Navy pilot held the Catalina's ugly blunt nose on Gatukai until the island was only a few miles away, then banked to the west. We tore past the enemy base at Wickham Anchorage, rounded the south flank of Vangunu, and raced into the islet strewn waters of the Heda bar, and further away loomed the tip of Tetiparo which lies adjacent to Rendova. The waves, thundered, into white foam on the reefs of Fury shoal. Ninety minutes out of Halava, the Catalina roared low over the treetops of a coconut Plantation on a tiny arm of land extending into the sea, banked steeply in a 180 degree turn, and cut her engines for the landing at SEGI. Above the Fighter planes moved away so they would not call attention to us.

Young Marine Raiders in camouflaged, jungle dungarees paddled out to us in rubber landing boats shaped like elongated doughnuts. Within a few minutes, we were standing by the copra sheds of Segi Plantation, waiting for the boats bringing our duffel. When they came we climbed the coral path leading to the plantation house, set on the crest of a hill overlooking the bay.

Segi had been a rich plantation before the Nips came to the Solomons. Its master's house was large and well built, but Jap patrols had carried of every scrap of furniture and even parts of the building itself.

Under the coconut trees that bordered the long path leading to the house lay the Raiders. They looked like boys at a summer camp rather than members of one of the toughest combat units in the Pacific. Many were not more than 18 to 19 Years old. Some played mumblety-peg with the deadly stilettos which all carried. Some Raiders sprawled asleep on ponchos. Others' cleaned rifles, read dog-eared magazines, or just sat and talked about the coming mission. There was no tense-ness, no foreboding about what lay ahead.

On the porch of the abandoned house, sprawled in a deck chair made from saplings and a canvas shelter half, I found LCOL MICHAEL S. CURRIN, 32 years old of San Diego. 'MICKEY' CURRIN the cigar smoking, mustache-twitching Irishman who had risen from private to his present rank in 15 years with the Marines was to lead us against the Japs at VIRU.

This short heavy set man was right out of Devil Dog history. He had seen service over half the world, and he had a personal and bitter grudge against the Japs. In 1940, when he was touring the interior of Japan on his own, they had arrested him and held him for 24 hours in a cold, miserable cell as a suspected spy. Their later apologies were profuse, of course, but it still rankled. In a sweat-stained undershirt and jungle pants, with his feet comfortably bare, CURRIN sat there reading dispatches, giving orders, checking on food supplies, and ammunition, attending to the tedious bookkeeping of war. All the while twisting his tiny, tired looking mustache. That mustache must have aided his thinking', like chewing a pencil or scratching your head. So many times in the days of battle and toil that followed, I watched him meet difficult, dangerous situations in the same manner.

An officer would bring in bad news. MICKEY CURRIN would stand there in the drizzling jungle rain, worrying the small mustache for a moment, staring at nothing. Then in a few clipped words he would give his decision. It was the right one. Perhaps those fat black cigars helped too. They would have knocked down an ordinary man.

Around CURRIN that morning, his officers sprawled on the floor or sat on empty ammunition boxes. BATTERTON was there, deceptively young and mild, looking like a boy dressed up for war. Suave, handsome CAPT FOSTER C. LA HUE, 25, of Corydon IN, the Rudolf Valentino of the force. 1LT DE VILLO BROWN, a shy young man from Hollywood, CA who wasn't at all shy two days later when his platoon deliberately rushed a Japanese ambush to wipe out a heavy machine gun nest. Big, bluff CAPT ANTHONY WALKER, 24, of Washington DC who looked like a punch drunk heavyweight and later fought like a madman. 1LT RAYMOND L. LUCKEL, 35, of Richmond CA, whose platoon on the point of our attack bore the brunt of the fighting at Viru Harbor.

One of the two U.S. Navy surgeons accompanying the

Raiders was RAY L. NOURIE of Kankakee, IL, a young man not long out of medical school. I watched him at work later in a jungle hut, ministering to wounded men as coolly and efficiently as tho in an office on Michigan Avenue. (Dr Nourie remained a Fleet Marine Force doctor throughout WW II, and the Korean War, were he was killed in action in January 1950.)

Present also, was FATHER PAUL J. REDMOND of New Haven, CT. and San Francisco, formerly of the Holy Name Society, and the brother of the noted golfer. He was 42 years old, twice the age of most of the Raiders. The grueling forced marches that lay ahead were to be harder on him than on any of the rest of us. But, like the real Irish padre that he was, he kept on. And when he was needed he was there, soiled and unshaven, but with strong, vibrant words and tender hands to make the last moments easier for a man dying in the mire of a jungle trail.

Then there was 1LT CYRIL M. ANDREWS of Los Angeles, who by all the rules should not have been there at all. Branded physically unfit when he tried to enter the Army because he was almost blind without his glasses. He had been commissioned by some shrewd Marine recruiting officer because of the 14 years he had spent in Japan, and the thorough knowledge he had gained of the Japs' queer singsong speech and their picture writing. With his spectacles, alternately soaked from the rain or fogged by jungle steam, he stumbled to Viru with us, falling over logs the rest of us could see, crashing his lean bruised body against coral outcroppings he could not discern thru his thick befogged lenses. If he ever lost those glasses he might have ended up marching with the Japs.

These, men and officers, were the Marine Raiders who would carry the war to the Japanese at Viru Harbor. America breeds good fighting men, but man for man the Raiders are her best. They should be, because each man and officer is handpicked, selected from the cream of the regular Marine units, and then given a five months course adroitly designed to break him down. If he breaks, he goes back to his old unit; if he carries through, he is a Raider.

During those months of training the Raiders who were ALL VOLUNTEERS, learned many things. He learned to master every type of weapon with deadly accuracy. He learned to stoke his body enormously when there is food, and to make it carry him on without food for days when there is none. He learned to cripple and kill silently with knife, noose, or his bare hands if need be. He learned to march mile after mile, hour after hour with a heavy load on his back until his body and brain are aflame with pain and ex-haustion. He learned to march on and on until the pain and exhaustion die and he is a human machine, dead on its feet, but still moving forward. These are the skills the Raiders took to Viru.

All that day of 27 June we rested there at the house, talking and sleeping. Poking amid the rubbish of the deserted rooms, I found a 15 year old London almanac and a moldering copy of J.B. Priestley's 'Angel Street'. The rats and insects were literary minded, Priestley's novel scarcely had a page left intact. Late that afternoon we ate our last hot meal, sauerkraut, sausage, asparagus, and coffee prepared in a field kitchen hidden in the grove. We sat on the ground bal-ancing mess kits on our knees, and as we ate COLONEL CURRIN explained, what lay ahead. "We shove off at dusk tonight," he said, "In native canoes and rubber boats we'll travel to the village of Regi eight miles further up Panga Bay. It will be the longest trip ever made with so many rubber boats, but we will get there along about midnight.

Tomorrow we push into the jungle. All reports are that the trails are good, with no swamps and few rivers to ford. We've been told we may meet two or three man Jap patrols; between here and Viru, but they can't bother us much. We are due to attack Viru Harbor at 0630 on 30 June. There is one main objective we must knock out a three inch gun the Japanese have spotted to defend the harbor entrance. When that gun is destroyed and only then, ships will be able to reach us with supplies, and relief troops. But remember this: 'We can expect no help, at all until we get thru the Jungle and get that gun. We've got to clean out Viru ourselves. '

I've wondered since if COLONEL CURRIN has ever met those staff officers who gave him the reports of the trails with no swamps and few rivers to ford, and of those "two or three man Jap patrols" we might meet. I would like to be at such a meeting. Those trails simply disappeared in the jungle, time and again. We mucked thru mangrove swamps up to our hips, thick black foul mud woven thru with treacherous roots. More than one river was chin deep. The two or three man Jap patrols invariably brought along 20 or 30 of their brothers, with machine guns. The native scouts who had been assigned to guide us to Viru finally admitted one day deep in the jungle, they had never been there before either!

We left at 1800. With MAJOR BATTERTON, I rode in one 40 foot, high-powered Native canoe with 16 fuzzy haired, ebony paddlers. COLONEL CURRIN and FATHER REDMOND were in the other. Behind the canoes came the scores of rubber boats, clumsy affairs hard to propel, and always ready to upset if a man drove his paddle too vigorously.

It was a weird, ghostly trip on a moon less tropical night. Like black shadows amid deeper shadow, the convoy slipped, silently thru the many islets of Panga bay over glass still water. BATTERTON and I conversed in whispers. The only sound was the occasional cry of a sea bird alarmed by our passage. Except for one scare the 8 mile trip was uneventful. It came at about 2300. All the little boats were lying still in the bay half a mile from Regi, waiting for word from the scouts who had gone ahead to make certain no Japanese were in the village. A half moon now gleamed down upon us thru a thin layer of clouds. The channel and the surrounding islands lay exposed under its sickly bluish light.

I noticed a long, narrow island a few hundred yards away, which I had not seen before. Suddenly that island changed shape and became a destroyer cutting through the seas with white water peeling from her prow. I could make out her rakish superstructure, her five inch gun batteries, her twin funnels. Alarmed, I grabbed BATTERTON, he, too, was excited until he had made a careful study thru his binoculars. Imagination had aided tricky shadows in transforming the island into a Jap warship. When we realized this, superstructure and guns changed back to coconut trees and underbrush.

From midnight until dawn we slept on the earthen floors, of the native huts of Regi. Because Japanese patrols might be about, we could use no light, smoke no cigarettes. It was cold and clammy, and no man had more than a poncho. Six inch land crabs that seemed to have a strange affinity for the human body added to our discomfort.

At dawn on 28 June began the march, which was to become nightmarish and an ordeal for us all. That day we hiked not quite six miles over those 'good trails.' It took us 11 hours, and every foot was a struggle. As we hiked out of Regi, gnawing on the chocolate ration bars that were breakfast, we plunged into a mangrove swamp. It was two miles wide. LT ANDREWS was ahead of me in the column. We were not more than 200 yards into the swamp when his nearsighted eyes missed a protruding root, which tumbled him onto his face in the foul black mud. Without complaint he picked himself up, wiped off as much of the goo as he could, and plunged on. He was going to show the Army come what may that they made a mis-take when they turned down ANDREWS.

The struggling, sweating column of men almost a mile

long wound thru the jungle like a tremendous snake. There was no talking, no sound but the suck of our boots in the mud. When a man hit a soft spot and sunk to his hips, the next man in the line seized him and dragged him out without a word. Three hours later we struck our first Japs. It was during a 10 minute rest break. I was in the center of the column with COL CURRIN and MAJOR BATTERTON when suddenly from somewhere behind us on the trail, there was a rifle shot then another, followed by the staccato chatter of a machine gun.

CURRIN seized his carbine and was off to have a look. Before he had been gone 10 minutes the shooting stopped. Unconcernedly, BATTERTON gave the order to move out knowing CURRIN would catch up later. At 1130 while the Major and I were sitting in the mud under a tree, nibbling on ration cheese and hard biscuits, and washing them down with muddy water taken from a jungle stream, CURRIN came in. Just as the rest break started, a native runner had come in to CAPTAIN WALKER and reported that a 20 man Japanese patrol was moving up the trail behind the column.

WALKER tried to lay an ambush for them, but his riflemen still were preparing it when the first Jap rounded a bend in the trail. "WALKER said it was funny," CURRIN related, "The Nip apparently thought we were miles ahead. He suddenly popped around that bend, and there were three Marines standing in the trail. The Jap stared at them and, they stared at him. Our boys stopped staring first. Before the Nip could raise his rifle he was full of lead. Three others ran up to see what was, going on and got it the same way. The rest hit the bush."

But it was not all such good news. Five Raiders on a scouting mission down a side trail had been cut off by the patrol and were missing. "Don't worry about them" said CURRIN, they're good boys. You'll see, they'll turn up, probably back at SEGI." 'He was right, SGT JOHN F. SUDRO and his men joined the rear echelon force at SEGI 48 hours later. Smart, the SGT had kept his men away from the trails where the Japanese waited, and traveled straight thru the jungle to the plantation.

By this time my attention was directed else-where as I had been sitting on the home grounds of a colony of tiny red ants of the Solomons, which have a bite like the puncture of a red hot needle. I had a worrisome half-hour. CURRIN planned to depend entirely on the native guides, but several times that first day they fell to quarreling among themselves about the route, and once we had to backtrack when one of them picked the wrong trail. CURRIN kept checking the route with map and compass. At 1700, with night settling over the jungle, we reached the Mohi River, a sullen, silent stream wending its way thru a gash in the solid walls of the jungle. Night comes early in the bush, where even the days are shrouded in a green half-light.

After the machine guns were emplaced on a tight defensive line around the bivouac area, some of us slogged down to the river to fill our canteens and try to wash some of the mud off our hands and faces. By the time we got back the rain, which had heckled us off and on all day, began to rain in earnest. Miserably we crouched under our ponchos, eating scraps of cheese and a peculiarly unappetizing pork paste.

FATHER REDMOND saved me that night when a vicious chill, hangover from an old bout with malaria, shook me and set my teeth to chattering. Sidling up, inconspicuously the tired Irish Priest slipped me a tiny 2 ounce bottle of medicinal brandy. "Drink this, it'll warm you a bit," he whispered, don't tell the other boys. There's only a little of it with us and they might get peeved at the old PADRE if they thought I was playing favorites, bless their hard young hearts. As we sat together amid the interlacing roots of a giant native mahogany tree I sipped the brandy and FATHER REDMOND talked. Like any Irishman, he loved to tell stories. He described his work back in the United States, talked about his brother's prowess with a golf club, talked about anything and everything, there under that tree in the cold, driving rain. I asked him how he happened to join the Raiders.

"Well. I've always liked a good fight and good fighters, he said after a moment, and my lads here are the best fighters in the world. They're so young and full of life and crazy that they need and older fellow like me around. You know, sort of a godfather on a mass basis." A few minutes later we wrapped our-selves in our wet ponchos and half lay, half sat amid the roots. FATHER REDMOND's brandy enabled me to sleep a few hours despite the rain that poured down upon us all night long.

Late in the black jungle night we heard the muffled roar of machine guns far away. Next day native scouts reported that a strong Japanese patrol, angry with the natives of REGI for assisting us, had machine gunned the helpless unarmed village. Before dawn 29 June 43 we were up and breakfasting. Two square inches of chocolate and more muddy water. This was destined to be a tough day. We would spend the 12 hours from dawn to dusk struggling thru 7 miles of swamp to the village of Libo, at the headwaters of the Choi river. And, we would have our first real battle with the Japs the main preliminary before the big bout at Viru.

139

It happened like this, COLONEL CURRIN decided LT DE VILLO BROWN, Hollywood CA with his platoon should scout another trail leading to the CHOI River. They left us shortly before noon. A few minutes later, sporadic firing began in the jungle somewhere off to our left. This was heavier stuff than yesterday machine guns, grenades, the duller explosions, of demolition bombs. Calling a walky talky operator CURRIN tried to make radio contact with BROWN. But the dense blanket of the jungle effectively prevented communication. The firing increased in volume. Whatever it was, it was a good battle. The CURRIN mustache suffered.

I was lying on the ground near two young Raiders, PFC DONALD J. BALFOUR, 22, Hq Co, Chevalis, WA, and Battalion Runner, WILLARD R. GOODSQN, 20, Monroe, MI. Hiding our nervousness, we talked while the guns roared louder and louder." Golly this is the kind, of an adventure you'll be telling our kids about or the next 25 years," said BALOUR: "Yeah. if you live to have any," was young GOODSON'S pessimistic reply. BALFOUR stopped grinning and sat there, looking off into the jungle. Two hours later BROWN'S runner brought in a report.

The platoon had moved up the side trail only 200 yards when Jap machine gunners opened fire on them from a ridge above, the trail. "We went right up that ridge into the muzzle of that damned gun," the runner told CURRIN. "There wasn't any withdrawal or second charge, or anything like that. Five of the boys died going up but another STEVE M. KLOS kept right on going. You should have seen that guy sir. A bullet tore into his left leg and smacked him down so hard it sprained his right ankle, but he kept on going on his hands and knees. He had one or those homemade bombs in each fist and a lighted cigarette in his mouth. 'When he got within throwing distance he lit the fuses and heaved them. That settled the hash of those gunners. With only sniper fire to heckle us we went on up and over. There were 15 Jap bodies lying around the gun, sprawled out just the way the bomb had tossed them. We found the packs of about 35 others a abandoned further back along the trail. Those bombs sure do a job sir."

I saw one of them later, deadly handmade affairs that are the Raiders' pride and joy. MAJOR ROY J. BATTERTON JR, (Berryville, VA) taught them how to make them. This one was four packages of TNT bound together, with a half-inch fuse attached. Around the bundle, about half the size of a man's head, a 6 foot length of tire chain had been wrapped. The concussion alone would kill a man at 15 feet.

4TH BATTALION RAIDERS KILLED IN ACTION
AT CHOI RIVER

GILBERT,ORRA   JOHNSON, MARTY
ROSSITER,GEORGE   TOWER, EVERETTE
WARREN, RASE

The story of STEVE M. KLOS is an epic in itself. That Jap .25 caliber bullet smashed his leg and the fall had hurt his right ankle badly. He knew no Raiders could be spared to carry him and that to be left behind with that Jap patrol on the loose meant to die. So, with a native boy to help him, he decided to walk it. We could not even wait for him. It would have endangered the whole force as well as the objective, everyone had been so forewarned, so he carried on as best he could. That night he staggered into camp four hours after we had arrived. Those miles had been grim torture for him, but he arrived cheerful and uncomplaining. The next day, with his left leg swollen to twice its normal size and the color of a skinned haunch of beef, he hiked seven miles; and the next, six miles more. He was with the column when we hit Viru.

By mid afternoon, as the long line of tired men alternately crawled up and tobogganed down the greasy ridges, leading to the Choi River, CURRIN knew he could never reach our objective at the appointed hour, even if we kept on all night. You could not march men 24 hours thru that kind of jungle, then throw them forward into battle. Food and ammunition were looming problems too. We had left Segi with three days jungle rations a piece, which might make one halfway decent meal if eaten all at the same time. But most of us had shared with the natives, thinking we would be in Viru 30 June. I had only one 6 by 3 inch chocolate bar and eight moldy biscuits left. And a stick of gum which I later lost. The others were in about the same boat.

We had started with one unit of fire for the machine guns, all that could be carried on the backs of men in such a march. The two unexpected, encounters with the Japs had eaten into this reserve, which was to have been saved for the actual attack on Viru. That day of 29 June we forded 14 jungle streams, four of them sizable rivers. Three were up to our shoulders and one, the last, was almost over our heads. Those river crossings would have sent any Hollywood movie director with an instinct for realism into ecstasies. Approaching a river, the long winding column of men halted momentarily on the brink, then slid, forward into the water like a serpent. Always the banks were 10 or 15 feet above the stream. There was only one way to get down, sit on the bank and give yourself a shove and toboggan down the slope over rocks, roots, and occasionally a startled land crab, until you landed with a splash waist-deep in the water. LT CYRIL M. ANDREWS, by now beaten to a pulp, suffered another of his incredible mishaps at the last stream. Spectacles befogged as usual, he was unable to see the lip of a high bank and walked right off it. His long, lean body somersaulted in midair before he hit on his face in three feet of water and mud. Grimly he righted himself, recovered his rifle that had landed near by, and splashed on across the stream. He still was going to show that damn Army, by God.

Despite the repeated torture of plunging into the icy stream, to emerge wet and dripping on the other side, the fordings had their comic touches. At the deepest river a little mite of a Marine weighed down with a .30 caliber machine gun, for some reason it's always the smallest men who get the heaviest loads, waded out and simplv disappeared beneath the surface. Behind in the column was a mountain of a Second Lieutenant. The big fellow stretched a long powerful arm down into the water and brought up the little man sputtering and gasping, but still clinging for dear life to his gun. By the scruff of the neck and the seat of the pants the Lieutenant quickly marched the little gunner to shallower water. With no further trouble from the Japs, we made camp that night in the abandoned village of Libo, two ramshackle thatched huts and a vegetable garden gutted by the Japan-ese.

It was a bad night. We all had been soaked to the skin repeatedly that day, and after nightfall the jungle becomes piercingly chilly. I ate my biscuits, paper wrappings and all because the river fordings had melted them into an indistin-guishable lump. The chocolate bar I preserved for one big feast the next day and then it made me ill. I thought I was fortunate that night because I drew as a bed one of the low bamboo platforms on which the natives had slept. Carefully I gathered fern leaves, and spread them for a crude mattress, laying my wet poncho over them. Then I climbed in, and platform and all crashed to the floor. The rest of the night I spent among the broken slats and the harder rocks of the hut floor.

At dawn the next day, 30 June, CURRIN tried again to contact headquarters to tell them of our predicament, but still could not establish communication. While the rest of us sat around snatching a last few minutes of rest before the day's ordeal, COL CURRIN stood beside the hard working radio operator, alternately gnawing on a fuzzy bit of chocolate and worrying his mustache. By now, with three days' growth of heavy black beard around it, the mustache seemed almost nonexistent in the general foliage.

As the exhausted little groups of Raiders struggled to their feet, and filed slowly out of the tiny clearing, the rain that had dogged us since the start of the mission began again. It added to the misery of the march, to the days without hot food or drink, to the mosquitoes that torment-ed us at night. We did not know it when we started, it was a good thing, but this was to be our worst day. Before it ended it would bring sheer physical tort-ure to us that would make the actual battle of Viru Harbor, fought the next day an anticlimax.

The nightmare of that 30 June was not Jap devised. It was the racking struggle of overtired muscles and empty bellies against the inanimate viciousness of the jungle itself. Against the snake-like roots which reached out to trip us. Against the damnable mud which sucked us down. Against the million and one vines and creepers which clawed at a man and threw him off balance. That day I heard men curse the jungle; curse it in hoarse hysterical whispers in a way they had never cursed the enemy. As we tired it seemed to gain strength in its silent war against us. The smallest vine was enough to throw a man onto his face in the mud if it caught his foot. The tentacles took vicious pleasure in sweeping our helmets from our heads, or snagging rifle barrels from our shoulders. It seems like a little thing probably, to people back home. But too much of it could drive an exhausted, starving man mad.

CURRIN must have hiked three times as far as the rest of us that day. Back and forth from the head of the column to the rear guard, he struggled stopping to talk to a 19 year old boy laboring under a load of machine gun ammunition. Giving a bit of his own slim supply of chocolate to a lad that had lost his crossing a river the previous day. He knew this was the psychological crisis, for his men if the jungle whipped us now, fresh Japanese troops would have only a cleaning up job to do later. He knew something else too. The Raiders had become a misplaced cog in the smoothly synchronized machinery of the New Georgia battle plan. That plan directed that we attack Viru Harbor shortly after dawn 30 June. Zero hour had come and gone, and we still were miles from the harbor. Our radios had failed; we already had expended much of the ammunition earmarked for Viru; our food was almost gone. Headquarters could have no way of knowing what had happened to us, for all that the commanding officers there knew, we might have been wiped out by the Japs. We were on our own.

CURRIN made up his mind to do the only thing possible, drive forward to Viru. That 30 June we started hiking at 0600 with only two rest periods, 20 minutes at noon and another 20 minutes at 1800. We kept on until 2200. In those 16 hours of brutally hard going, we managed to travel only seven miles. Shortly before noon I found myself hiking behind CURRIN. I told him we were all wondering why we had not met any more Japs. "We're on a different trail," he said, "The Japs probably don't know about this one. You see I began yesterday to have suspicions about the ability of these natives, so this morning I rounded them up and put it to 'em point blank, 'How many of you actually have been over these trails? Not your grandfathers or your sister's husband, but how many of you men yourselves?' And do you know, they finally admitted that not one of them had made this trip," the COLONEL went on. "So I began picking the route myself, selecting paths by compass. Hope it works." We all did!

During the noon break I remembered I had a clean pair of socks in my pocket and removed my shoes for the first time since leaving Segi After almost three days of hard going and constant soaking my feet looked as tho they had been thru a grinder. The old socks were wet with blood and stuck to great broken blisters when I tried to pull them off. I wrapped my feet in pieces of my undershirt, pulled the clean and also wet socks over them, and replaced the shoes. I never dared take them off again until after Viru. While I was thus engaged a Marine Officer came up, sat down beside me, and started to talk. I couldn't remember having seen him before and asked him his name. Hurt, he told me he was MALCOLM MC CARTHY. But he was a different, ages older MCCARTHY than the clean young Lieutenant from San Francisco who had ridden to SEGI with me so many long days - or was it years ago? This man's face was streaked with dried mud and stubbled with a dirty black beard. His mouth hung open as if he were too tired to close it; his cheeks were drawn hollows; his eyes were staring and bloodshot. I suddenly realized that I undoubtedly looked the same to him. After the Battle of Viru, I found a Japanese mirror and took a look. Frightful!

CAPT FOSTER C. LA HUE came up and dropped to the ground beside us. In his hands he had several small oval metal discs. "They're the dog tags of the five men killed yesterday." he

144

explained soberly, "We couldn't bring the bodies with us so we hid them in the jungle. Later we'll send men back to bury them." A few minutes afterward LA HUE and I wandered up to where MAJOR BATTERTON sprawled against a tree. He had his wallet out and was staring at a picture that he showed to us. It was the photograph of a lovely girl in a light summer frock, sitting on a smooth lawn of green grass. She looked so sweet and immaculate that it was hard to believe, here in the filth of the jungle, that there could be another world with people like her. It was very far away and unreal. BATTERTON, in his dirty, wet jungle suit, didn't say anything. He just held that picture in his mud caked hands and stared at it. "I know how you feel ROY," LA HUE said, "Here's a picture of the girl I married 18 months ago, 18 months ago today, by God, and it seems centuries since I've seen her.

I sat there in the mire and thought about my own wife and baby daughter. I had not seen them for nine months and it had been more than a month since a letter had found its way up to me. They seemed like people in a dream. Reality was the dripping, brown-green jungle with its mud, it's tangled vegetation, its lizards, crabs, and insects. I felt as though I had lived for years in the deep black slime of the mangrove swamps, and the bush trails. Trails, which led a long column of desperately tired, desperately hungry men on and on to nowhere. About noon our force split for the first time, COL CURRIN sent CAPT TONY WALKER, and 60 men off on a side trail leading almost straight south. WALKER'S unit would strike the small Japanese force encamped at TOMBE, on the eastern Cliff of Viru Harbor while we engaged the main body at Tetemara on the western aide. CURRIN wanted to make sure no Japs escaped to pester us with sniping after VIRU had been secured.

Big TONY WALKER even said good by like a prize fighter. Nervously rubbing his feet in the mud as tho he were standing in a resin box, he stood before CURRIN getting final orders. Then he saluted the Colonel, winked at BATTERTON, poked the no longer suave LA HUE in the ribs and was gone. We could hear his men moving out along the side trail, the rhythmic suck of their feet in the mud punctuating the stillness. Then that, too, was gone.

All afternoon we moved forward along the trail CURRIN had found. Luck had been with him; it held almost a true compass course in the right direction. By now we were almost due north of Viru Harbor and moving on it from the rear. The blackness of the jungle night was descending upon us when our mile long column broke out of the bush onto the banks. of the MangoRriver, far back in the New Georgia hinterland. The next few hours were to be worse than a nightmare.

Across the river deep and foul, stretched a barrier that seemed insur-mountable in the gathering darkness. Another mangrove swamp. Interlacing snakelike roots by the million's, lay upon its surface, Under the roots were apparently bottom-less depths of oily black mud. CURRIN viewed, the river and swamp with utter disgust. "We have three miles to go to reach a high ridge on which I had planned to bivouac, he muttered, "That damned swamp is at least two miles wide, and night will be on us before we can even get the men across the river. If we get into that swamp in the blackness, God knows how we'll be able to maintain contact with each other. The men are too tired to hold on to each other's packs while they're stumbling and falling in the muck of the swamp. And they'll surer than hell get lost if they don't." We stood there and watched the night come down. It looked as tho we never would be able to reach Viru the next day. Then age-old native lore came to our aid.

Our chief native scout, a wiry, middle aged, black bush man who had come from his inland village to lead us in our attack on the harbor, jabbered excitedly to CURRIN in pidgin English and pointed across the river. CURRIN, who could not understand pidgin, looked, blank. The native jabbered some more and pointed again. Then we saw it. The blackness of the night was complete, by now. Across the stream the swamp lay a dark ebony mass. But at the spot to which the bushman pointed, strange, wavering lights glowed in the darkness. Their pale fluorescence was unholy there in the jungle night. Those strange glowing's were to save us. The native scouts plunged into the river, forded it, and disappeared into the swamp. At CURRIN'S orders we followed, up to our necks in the stinking, slow-moving water, several times going under completely when we hit potholes, ammunition and weapons we carried on our heads.

As the first unit reached the opposite bank the native scouts emerged from the swamp. They staggered under great armfuls of "LIGHT". Their loads were fragments torn from rotting tree stumps that apparently had become soaked with phosphorus from decaying jungle vegetation. The loads glowed green in the blackness. As the tired men staggered past the scouts handed to each a chunk of the rotting, luminous wood.

In single file the Raiders moved off, each man following the glow of the fragment held by the man before him. It was like a weirdly regimented column of giant fireflies, moving into the swamp, moving pathetically slow, stumbling and falling in the mud, but moving. With night contact assured by the glowing wood, we fought our way thru. It took us three hours to cross those two miles of swamp, and when we reached the other side we were more dead than alive.

But it was not over yet. Before us, as we emerged from the slime and filth of the swamp, lay a mile of dense jungle that we had to traverse to reach the ridge. Somehow, afterward no one remembered just how, we struggled thru. The last 200 yards were almost vertical, and the muddy trail was as slick and greasy as a toboggan slide. Crawling on hands and knees, the shivering, feverish Raiders fought with screaming muscles and pain racked bones to reach the ridge. It was like a scene from Dante's "Inferno." Time after time half a dozen men would get within a few yards of the crest. Then, unable to see in the blackness, the leading man would hit a slick spot and tumble the whole lot to the bottom of the ridge. Sliding men smashed against machine guns, rocks and trees, and other men. Finally we crawled over the crest onto the flat top of the ridge and fell exhausted into the mud. No one tried to eat. No one had any water left in his canteen. We flopped in the goo and slept like dead men. Tomorrow we were to attack. "Christ, those Jap bastards are going to pay for this," groaned the Marine lying beside me. "They're going to pay, and plenty, for every foot of that son of a bitching mud, I'm going to drive my bayonet right thru the guts of the first bastard I see. They're going to pay and pay and." I looked over at him. He was asleep, his dirty blond head pressed flat against the stock of a Garand rifle.

On 1 July 1943 at dawn we moved out. The worst of the trek was behind us. Swiftly the column completed the encirclement of Viru and by 0900 was driving straight toward the Japs from the west. There was a change in the men this day. As they hiked they checked the action of their Garands and submachine guns. Cartridge bandolier slung far back over their shoulders during the last few days, were shifted forward to fighting position. Exhausted, sick, and hungry tho they might be, the Raiders quickened their step along the narrow trail. The staring deadness disappeared from their faces. They were men who, in hours or minutes would face the test for which they had been conditioned during long grueling months of training.

Shortly after 0900, we were not more than two miles from Viru at the time, we heard the tremendous explosions of heavy bombs somewhere ahead and the whining roar of diving planes. CURRIN stopped the column and went forward to talk to MAJ ROY J. BATTERTON JR. and I went with him. BATTERTON was the expedition's demolition expert. "What do you think that is, ROY"? CURRIN asked, "There was no dive bombing called for in our plans. Hell, this gets more confused every minute." It might be Jap planes attacking WALKER, if the Nips at VIRU learned his position BATTERTON replied. "But there; is no way of telling for sure out here." "Damnit whatever it is, we've got a job to do so let's go do it," grunted CURRN. We'll die of old age if we don't knock off that harbor soon."

We moved on, and within 20 minutes the last bomb had fallen and the planes had left. Then, so far away that it sounded like the crackling of branches, we heard a machine gun begin the battle of Viru Harbor, WALKER'S men had struck. By the grace of God the dive bombers had been ours, (Six SBD Douglas Dive Bomber, from VMSB-132 and VB-1l3) were sent out by worried commanders on the slim hope of helping us if we were facing an enemy too strong for our small Raider band. WALKER reached the fringe of the tiny clearing on the east side of the harbor at almost the exact minute the first plane peeled off from its lazy circle and dropped, like a diving hawk for the center of Viru Village. On its tail came another and another, diving at intervals of only a few seconds. Giant geysers of earth and rock streamed skyward from the big bombs. The Japs on the east bank were too busy getting themselves underground to become aware of WALKER'S men.

When the bombing ended the Nips climbed from their holes, only a few yards in front of his machine guns. Those were the last foxholes they ever left. Those planes helped us on the west side as well. When the heavy bombs tore into the village, the Japs there deserted the bivouac area and poured back into the jungle to the west towards us. Apparently they stayed there, expecting another air attack, for we met them in the jungle half an hour later, instead of in their prepared defensive positions.

The rain had begun again, a steady cold downpour. At a half run we moved up the trail, dense jungle on both sides of us, no signs of life. Then, from somewhere ahead of the point of the column, came the crack of a rifle. The light and vicious 'spang' of a Jap 25! Two men in the point were hit immediately but long months of training saved the rest. Without thinking they fanned off into the thick underbrush. The attack began. Nip machine guns, heavies this time, commanded the trail approaches. Sniper's 50 feet up in the trees protected the gun emplacements. They were our greatest danger, those snipers, because their range of fire from those high positions enabled them to snipe at men far back in the main body of the column. Their bullets whined around us, chipping bits off the trees, making funny little plopping sounds in the mud of the trail.

That 4 hour battle lives in my mind as a series of kaleidoscopic flashes. I have no continuous over all picture. Things happened too fast. At the beginning I was about 50 yards behind the point. The advance had stopped, and we were lying in the ooze at the roots of jungle trees, pressed flat on our faces. I saw CURRIN go by on a dead run. Peeping out, I saw him charge 50 yards up the trail, then make a running dive behind a fallen tree where LT RAY LUCKEL, in command of the point awaited orders.

Beside me was young WILLARD R. GOODSON, the runner. He nudged me as CURRIN rushed by. 'Now, watch what happens, he said. The old, man will have us on our way in no time. We might as well take it easy while we can. Got a match?" I handed him a match box and watched him as he rolled over onto his back, lit a cigarette, and lay smoking peacefully. Within a few minutes the RAIDERS spread over a 200-yard front and began the envelopment of the first machine gun nest. Soon they were only a few yards away from the gun muzzles, flattened on the ground behind stumps and fallen trees, waiting for the final push.

SGT LOREN W. SCHOFIELD, 22, Omaha, Nebraska got tired of waiting, of listening to the chatter of the Nip guns, of hearing their bullets whining over him. When the firing ceased for a moment, while the nips changed belts, SCHOFIELD jumped forward with his BAR (Browning Automatic Rifle), hoping to wipe out the nest before it got him. He told me about it 20 minutes later as a Corpsman taped his chest. "I'd no sooner gotten to my feet and begun to move when something hit me in the chest and slammed me flat on my back. Jeez it was like a punch from Joe Louis. I felt no damn pain and couldn't figure what the hell had happened. When my head cleared I ducked behind, a stump, then looked down at my chest. Cripes, do you know what it was? I had a grenade in the left breast pocket of my dungarees, and a bullet had smashed right into it. The force of impact knocked me right on my rear, but the grenade was all right but chipped a little and, the firing handle twisted. The Nips were still firing, so I took the grenade, moved up a few yards and let em have it. There were four gunners there and it got em all. And all I got out of it was a couple of broken ribs.'

By now the Raiders were performing like a Knute Rockne backfield. LT LUCKEL'S men moved forward until a machine,

149

gun opened on them. Then they flatten-ed out, and with their own rifles and machine guns settled down to keep the Japs occupied. While they held the attention of the enemy gunners, four or five Raiders from the demolition unit, the homemade bomb boys slipped around on each side. Closing, by sound, they hurled their TNT concoctions into the enemy emplacement. Then everyone set out to look for a new gun position.

All of the Raiders were tough, but these men of the demolition squads had an extra special brand of toughness. Lying there in the mud, I watched them moving up in the driving rain. They crawled on their hands and knees. In each dirty face was stuck a lighted cigarette, part of their combat equipment. Every man had a demolition bomb in each hand and across each chest was strapped a canvas, bag filled with additional charges. If a bullet had hit one of those sacks, there wouldn't have been even a dog tag left. When a man got within throwing distance of an enemy emplacement, he touched the half-inch fuse of a bomb to the cigarette and threw the charge like a gigantic firecracker.

Later I discovered that two men of the demolition unit underwent what was probably the most peculiar experience of the entire battle, they were PRIVATES DONZEL HARKER, 18, of Morgantown, W.VA. and. WILLIAM A. CHANCE, 23, Boone, KY. HARKER and CHANCE were ordered forward about an hour after the fight started to knock out a pillbox well concealed in the jungle about a hundred yards to the left of the trail. Alone they crawled toward it. The Japs must have been been at lunch or something, because the two Raiders crawled right past it without seeing it or drawing fire and kept on going.

We crawled on and on until all the shooting was behind us, "HARKER told me. It didn't seem right but what the hell. Then, by golly, we came out in a little clearing, and on the other side was a big emplacement facing the sea. Inside was that damned 3 inch gun, guarding the harbor entrance, which the old man told us about." The two Raiders had moved past our own front lines thru the Jap front, thru the enemy rear positions, and down to where the heavy gun was emplaced. By that time my knees were doing a rumba," HARKER continued. "We decided to get the hell out of there and right now. Turning around we crawled back, and after 20 minutes managed to get back inside our own lines without getting shot. Oh yeah on the way back we bagged a sniper.' He was perched in a tree with his back to us, and he never knew what hit him. He came down like a shot gunned duck."

Slowly we moved forward. The advance was sporadic.

Sometimes we lay along the trail for 30 minutes at a time; then the order would be whispered back down the line. "MOVING UP, LET'S GO, MOP UP." We were fighting an unseen enemy. We never saw a Jap, but their bullets, whined and echoed over our heads. I always had imagined the roar of the guns never ceased once a battle had started. But it was not like that at all. Thus for Viru, one of the most vicious in the New Georgia campaign, it really was a series of little battles lasting from a minute to 15 at the most, with long periods of silence between. A machine gun would open fire somewhere ahead, and we would hug the ground. Other weapons would take it up, and the jungle would resound with their chattering roar. The sharper crack of rifles and pop of grenades, then the heavier, duller wumph-wumph of demolition bombs would punctuate the racket. For minutes all hell would break loose over and around us.

Then, so suddenly you could not believe it, the guns would stop and the jungle would be still again. Not a sound, but the dripping of the rain. Not a movement to be seen anywhere just the silence of death.

It was during one of these periods when both sides were awaiting a move that GOODSON showed what a good little man he was. He had left me shortly before to take a message to CURRIN, somewhere ahead. During the lull he decided to beat his way back. I heard someone coming and raised my head to look. GOODSON, carrying his rifle in his right hand, was moving as fast as he could while bent over. Suddenly a Jap rifle cracked somewhere to his right I saw the bullet bite a hole in the mud at his feet, then another struck a tree beside him. The Michigan boy slid to a halt, swinging his, rifle up as he stopped. Still crouching, he fired twice from the hip. Then he ducked behind a tree. I was sure he had missed. I couldn't see anything in the direction he had sent his bullets. I waited too. In a minute there was a slight rustle from one of the trees on the right of the trail, another rustle. Then a heavy object toppled like a stone from the crotch 60 feet up. It was the Jap sniper. "I always wanted to get me one of those bastards, and I sure nailed, him, right through the head," GOODSON whispered as he flopped beside me, "how about a cigarette? I'm out."

In the next rush forward, I lost contact with the man ahead of me in the column. I was going at a run, slipping and sliding in the mud, when I tore around a bend in the trail and, ran into my first Jap. With a yelp I jumped off the trail and behind a tree. I had seen a big, powerful yellow man clad in a brown-green uniform, crouched beside the trail, a rifle in his hands and his eyes staring straight into mine. For a minute or so I lay there, wishing somebody with a rifle would come, cursing the regulation which insists that correspondents go unarmed.

Then I realized nothing had happened, although this Nip had had time to shoot ten people. Cautiously, I sneaked around the tree until I could see ahead with one eye. He was still there, still crouching, still staring at me. Then I saw it for the first time a little round hole centered almost directly between the eyes. Further up the trail I passed several little groups of five, to ten Japs, huddled around, their guns where grenades and demolition bombs had caught them. But none was so startling as that first one, crouching there in the mud and looking at me with still unglazed eyes.

Despite the grimness and death that enveloped us, even those four hours of bitter, vicious fighting had their moments of comedy. Comedy dabbed with blood to be sure, but still comedy. PFC JAMES CALLAHAN, became involved with a Jap heavy machine gun. Vainly he dived, from one fallen tree to another, trying to get away from its fire, but the bullets continued, to chip bark around him and throw dirt and. rock into his face. He dived for another fallen tree, but unfortunately this one was not quite thick enough to shield all of the rather obese CALLAHAN body. Hugging the ground behind the tree, his head, trunk, and legs were safe; the Jap bullet creased him across the only portion of his anatomy he had forgotten. He didn't sit down for a week afterwards, and that's one war wound he'll never show his friends.

Then there was CPL FLORIAN J. BARTOSCZEICZ, Handling a light machine gun, he hammered away for five minutes at a concealed Jap machine gun, all to no avail. Suddenly the Jap opened up on him. One bullet creased him across the shoulder. BARTOSZEWICZ angered by the wound was about to begin firing again when a second bullet hit his other shoulder. That second wound apparently aroused the fighting blood of generations of BARTOSZEWICZ'S. Roaring curses, he seized his machine gun and ran forward, lugging tripod and all, firing as he ran. With his left hand burning to a crisp on the hot barrel, he cleaned out that nest.

Three hours after the battle started, we were within a few hundred yards of Tetemara village. I was behind a mahogany tree, awaiting the order to move up again and, hoping that a sniper working nearby would not see me. Beside me, his face covered with a poncho, lay a young Raider dying from a bullet wound thru his head. He had been hit under this same tree a few minutes earlier. Some one hurled himself down almost on top of me. Rolling over, I saw it was FATHER PAUL J. REDMOND of San Francisco and New Haven, CT the Chaplain. Motioning me out of the way, he crawled in beside the dying Raider. With his body pressed down into the mud, he fished a stole from his uniform pocket, hauled it up around his neck, and began his last rites of the Catholic Church. Coolly and peacefully, there amid the machine gun and sniper fire and the mud and smell of the jungle, came the sonorous Latin words of the extreme unction: "PER ISTAM SANCTAM UNCTIONEM INDITOGEAT TIBI DOMINUS QUIDQUID DELEQUISTI." While he was intoning the soft rolling words of the death chant the rattle of the guns died, away and jungle became still, Some where a small tropical bird gave a frightened cry. The silence was a blanket.

Then, 75 yards ahead there was a muffled howling, beginning on the margin of sound and growing louder and louder. It had a queer, subhuman quality the mouthing's of mad things preparing for slaughter. It was the Japanese working themselves into a fanatical frenzy for a final desperate attempt to stop the Raiders. For three minutes they howled and shrieked and, all the while the guns were still. Then, at the climax they charged. The staccato chatter of one of our guns began, then another, and another, and another, swelling into a clamoring rush of sound as the Marines smashed lead into the onrushing Japanese. For 30 seconds the guns roared unceasingly; then the firing stopped. The howling began again but this time it was different. It was the screams and, groans of men mortally torn and ripped by the Raider guns. In those 30 seconds the backbone of Japanese resistance was broken.

The next hour was a mopping up operation, cleaning Japs out of coral caves; finding and killing isolated snipers, now and then flushing a lone, frightened rifleman from his jungle hiding place. Half a dozen or so Japanese chose to plunge to their death from the one hundred-fifty foot cliffs of the harbor rather than face the Raider's guns and bombs. That was all right with the Marines, it saved ammunition. When the last Jap had been killed we turned our attention to their bivouac area. It was smashed and gutted from the morning bombing. There were craters 140 feet across and 25 feet deep. But we did find what we were looking for, food and water. Sitting there on the earthen floors of the little thatched huts, we gulped down Japanese tinned salmon and clear cold water. I know this sounds coarse and brutal, crouching there and stuffing ourselves with captured food while our enemies lay dead around us. But it did not hurt them any and we had been without real food for four days.

That night we brought in our dead from the mud and slime of the trail. There on that high bluff overlooking the little harbor the Marine Raiders who died in the final attack on VIRU were laid in shallow graves, in the tiny clearing amid the coconut palms. It was a fitting resting place for Marines, who since the founding of their Corps have given their lives in the lonely, forgotten places of the world. COLONEL CURRIN, MAJOR BATTERTON, and the rest of us stood there in the growing darkness of that forsaken little spot as the thin, worn bodies of our friends were wrapped in ponchos and lowered into graves. FATHER REDMOND was dirty, needed a shave, and his eyes were red and tired as he stood there in the coming night, reading the burial service by flashlight. But his words were strong, and they transformed the little clearing into a special kind of church as he spoke to them:

" I AM THE RESURRECTION AND THE LIFE; HE WHO BELIEVETH IN ME, ALTHOUGH HE BE DEAD, SHALL LIVE; AND EVERY ONE WHO LIVETH AND BELIEVETH IN ME SHALL NOT DIE FOREVER. "You men who have given your lives here in the jungles of Viru were of all races and religions. But you were comrades in life, and here in this spot you shall remain comrades. May you rest in peace; you have served your country well. God Bless You!

Rifles which a few hours earlier had dealt death to the Japanese roared over the graves of the dead. The United States Marines once again had the situation well in hand.

4TH RAIDERS KILLED IN ACTION AT VIRU HARBOR

BUCKLEY,THOMAS	CHATFIELD.JOHN
HILL, JOHN W.	HOUSER,ELWOD
KOSOVICH,PETER	THOMACK,WALTER
THORNSBERRY,SAM	SNYDER, EUGENE
ZWICK, FRED I.	

The Viru Harbor Raid had cost the Raiders a total of 14 killed (all were O Co) and 16 wounded. Counted enemy dead were 83, with 166 enemy survivors, 100 of whom were wounded, arrived overland at Munda on 18 July and were totally destroyed in the final defense of Munda Airfield.

Chaplain PAUL REDMOND received his first Medal for his heroics on New Georgia.

The citation read in part:

By direction of the President a LEGION OF MERIT is awarded by the Commanding

General, United States Army Forces in the South Pacific Area to:

LIEUTENANT PAUL J. REDMOND. (ChC) UNITED STATES NAVAL RESERVE

"For exceptionally meritorious conduct in the performance of outstanding services while serving with the FOURTH MARINE RAIDER BATTALION 1st MARINE RAIDER REGIMENT on NEW GEORGIA Solomon Islands, on 1 and 20 July 1943 during the heavy fighting against enemy Japanese forces at both Viru Harbor and Bairoko Harbor, he repeatedly ignored intense machine gun, rifle and mortar fire so that he might comfort the wounded and administer last rites to the dying in the front lines. When the fighting had subsided, he helped. in the hazardous work of recovering the dead and preparing a proper place for their burial. Throughout both actions, CHAPLAIN REDMOND'S calm demeanor and his willingness to proceed to any point, however dangerous where his presence was needed were a constant inspiration to the men."

By Command of Lieutenant General Harmon /s/ A.J. Barnett Brigadier General,GSC, Chief of Staff

---

RAIDER CORPSMEN AWARDED THE ARMY SILVER STAR AT VIRU HARBOR AND VANGUNU

EDWARD M. ELLINGTON JR.   LEONARD J. PELTON

Corpsman WILLIAM G. LACY, Dresden, OH talked with PhM1c JERRY SITTON, 4HQ and sent Jerry's story. "I was on the spot when PLSGT FRED ZWICK, 4BO was killed 1 July l943 at Viru Harbor. He didn't have to be that far up in front but he was a very courageous leader. As I went back for more first aid gear FATHER REDMOND, came flying through with white scapular straight out in the air to administer EXTREME UNCTION. ZWICK had a hand-knitted brown sweater rolled on top of his pack and I covered his face with it. Passing Raiders uttered violent curses and vows of vengeance. I was also the last man aboard that PBY full of wounded at Enogai Inlet that was shot down 21 July 1943. "

4CP FRANCIS A. HEPBURN, San Diego, CA wrote two

most interesting accounts to your PATCH EDITOR "I remember those war years. NEIL STILES 4CP was a squad sergeant in the first platoon when we landed at Segi, New Georgia on 20 June l943 to make that sneak attack on the Japs at Viru Harbor. That four day trek in the swamps and jungle was a nightmare. We were so hungry when we captured the Jap facility at Viru we ate canned sea weed. PVT GEORGE A. ROSSITER 4CP was the first man killed at the Choi River on 29 Jun 43 and STEVE KLOS. 4CP was wounded in the right knee. When KLOS hobbled in late that night I offered him my foxhole and the corpsman dressed his wound. FATHER REDMOND noticed me standing in the rain with no poncho and he called for me to get in his shelter that he shared with 3 other men. It was a thatched native structure with a wood floor and I lay down beside FATHER REDMOND and I suddenly felt a great sensation of security and ease with the world. I slept well that night!"

AUTHOR. Another FR Redmond tale. One of the major problems in jungle warfare is keeping mud, water and sand from clogging up your weapon. At Viru Harbor, Father Redmond said, "I solved the problem by giving each Raider a condom to stretch over the end of his rifle barrel. He laughingly adds, another visiting Chaplain on New Georia, threatened to have me excommunicated for advocating the use of contraceptives.

4 BO SYLVESTER J. NELSON writes "I joined the Raiders in Sep 42. CAPT R.L. LUCKEL was my C.O. and GUNNER JAMES J. GARRISON was Platoon Leader in the Machine gun Platoon. I remember Chaplain FATHER PAUL REDMOND very well and I was his protection under an old bamboo shack at Viru Harbor, when an Army Colonel stormed in and bellowed. 'We have THIEVES on this island! We came ashore with 150 cases of Jungle Rations and in one half hour they are all gone'. COLONEL M. S. CURRIN and FATHER REDMOND were each sitting on one of the missing cases at the time and COL CURRIN replied, "We will have to look into this reported thievery!" 77 Patch

4 HQ Corpsman HAROLD C. FERRIN, "I participated at Viru Harbor and Bairoko Harbor battles. I was WIA at Bairoko on 20 July 43 and evacuated to the states. When recovered, I went on to 1st Bn 26th Marines, 5th Marine Division. I noted BILL MOUSER'S comments in the PATCH story about the strafing and evacuation of the PBY's at ENOGAI. I too was one of the wounded on that plane that was hit and shot down."

FERRIN also wrote, "This Coastwatcher Kennedy Scout named PETER PAN had traveled extensively throughout the world as a steward on the merchant ships. He had a tremendous vocabulary with a very British accent. His command of the language generally put us all to shame. When the firing started at Viru Harbor, the unarmed scouts started back down the trail to the rear. I was moving up the trail as they were coming back. When one of those "All Hell is Breaking Loose' situations started, I made a dive for cover at the side of the trail. PETER PAN zeroed in on the same piece of real estate and dove in on top of me. After untangling, both of us bellied up to mother earth as close as possible. This fellow PETER PAN in a calm voice very matter-of-factly said, 'My, but there does seem to be a great deal of promiscuous firing up ahead.' Home to PETER PAN was in one of the islands somewhere up north. When the Japs invaded his island, he hid his wife and children inland in the isolated mountains and made his way down through the island until he met up with Coastwatcher DONALD KENNEDY. There he volunteered his services as a scout and part of the Solomon Island Defense Force that KENNEDY was training at Segi. I learned his background from conversations with him at Segi and on the trail to Viru

VAN GUNU-WICKHAM ANCHORAGE BATTLE
4TH MARINE RAIDER BATTALION
30 Jun 1943

While Companies P, O and Hq Co under LTCOL MICHAELS. CURRIN, were attacking Viru Harbor, the balance of the 4th Raider Battalion, loaded aboard the APD's, USS SCHLEY and USS McKEAN and left Gualcanal under command of MAJOR JAMES CLARK.

The force consisted of Co N under CAPT EARLE O. SNELL Jr., Co Q under CAPT WILLIAM FLAKE; the Demolition Plt under 2LT ROBERT P. SMITH; Hq Co: 20th NOB (Seabees), and the re-enforced 2nd Bn 103rd Infantry. Overall command was given to USA LtCol Lester E. Brown.

On 30 June at 0335 the force arrived off Oloana Bay, Vangunu which was the landing beach selected by a pre-invasion scouting party under 2LT HAROLD SCHRIER, 2DG. Heavy seas and pitch-black darkness caused great difficulty in maintaining contact. Some landing craft's coxswains headed in the wrong direction and landed far away from SCHRIER and the assigned beaches. Two boats grounded on a reef seven miles east of Oloana. 1Plt Q Co boat ,(2LT ERIC S. HOLMGRAIN) grounded, broached and was abandoned.

The Raiders had to wade and swim 2 miles in to shore. 2Plt. Q Co, boat (2LT JAMES BROWN) lost its rudder on the reef but remained afloat as the Raiders steered their boat with buckets trailed on lines, At dawn BROWN'S boat was sighted by the USS McKEAN and a replacement boat was provided. Six other boats were lost in the landing.

The enemy force, the Kure 6 SNLF (Special Naval Landing Force, commonly called Japanese Marines) were entrenched at Kaeruka, Wickham Anchorage, overland some 10 miles from Oloana. LtCol Brown, 2 Army companies and the Raiders began the overland jungle approach at 0715. Crossing the Vura River and the Kaeruka River by rope lines in chest deep water they reached the line of departure by 1320. Amazingly all the missing Raiders heavily laden with arms and ammunition; having covered great distances from their landing beaches, caught up with the main body and rejoined their parent companies.

The sudden attack launched at 1105 was a complete surprise to the enemy as SNELL, on the east bank of the Kaeruka River and FLAKE on the west succeeded in completing the envelop-ment. By 1730, FLAKE forces raced through the enemy camp at Kaeruka to the sea, killing 120 Japanese. It was here that LT FLAKE was seriously wounded and evacuated from the beach the following morning. The Raiders lost 12 Killed, and 21 Wounded. The Army lost 10 Killed and 22 Wounded. A hasty beach defense was set up as darkness fell.

At 0200 that night (1 Jul), 3 barges loaded with food, supplies and 120 Jap troops tried to land in the Raider Demolition Platoon positions on the beach. The Raiders hail of fire killed the barge coxswains. As the barges drifted helplessly, Grenades, Rifle Grenades and Raider Machine Gunners had a field day, killing all but six of the enemy that escaped by swimming. Over a month later, on 2 August at Rice Anchorage, New Georgia (Over 80 miles away) these last six Japanese in a native canoe tried to land against the same 4th Raider Demolition platoon. Five were killed and 1 Captured. One of war's crazy coincidences!

4TH RAIDERS KILLED IN ACTION AT WICKHAM ANCHORAGE, VANGUNU

BURKHOLDER, M.M.	COSTELLO, RAY F.
COURTWAY,A. JR	FENTON, ROBERT

HAGGERTY, WM	HOLFORD, RAY C.
HUFF, ROBERT J.	JURGENS,FRED
KELLEY, FRANKLIN	LALLY, WILLIAM C.
MEYER,THEODORE	SCHOEPPEL, FRED

On 9 July O and P Co's of the 4th Raider Battalion, left Viru Harbor aboard LCI 23 and LCI 331 and returned toTetere Point, Guadalcanal the following day. N and Q Co's left Vangunu Island, aboard LST 331 and LST 332 on 13 July to return to Guadalcanal.

The attempt to rescue Coastwatcher Kennedy and keep his operation active, as well as securing Segi Point as the location for an airstrip was a complete success. The two battles resulted in more than 100 Raider casualties while over 150 men were felled by malaria seriously weakening their combat readiness.

4E ARTHUR T. KOLOINI JR. told how popular he was with MAJ CLARK. It seems KOLOINI always carried toilet paper with him no matter where he was. On Vangunu in the thick of battle, MAJ CLARK'S call rang out loud and clear-"KOILINI, KOILINI", front and center."

4DQ JAMES R. HEARN, in a letter to JAMES STRAWBRIDGE, Pensacola Fla. wrote, "After 30 years almost to the day I found out where you were. I have been trying to find you to thank you for helping to save my life on Vangunu Island, New Georgia, 30 June 1943. I received a letter from the Raider Association telling of ROBERT THORNTON'S letter, your inquiry and concern about my wounds. I had my right shoulder blown off, hit in the back and left leg. I spent a total of 3 years in the hospital and am disabled 90%, but still have some use of my right arm, I had to learned to be left handed and boy was that a job! My left leg is partly stiff with a steel plate in it. I remember after I was wounded that some Army boys were carrying me out and you told them if they bumped me into a tree you would kill them. Also on the way out, FATHER REDMOND thought I had died and was giving me the last rights, and when I opened my eyes and he almost fainted. I was wounded the same day as 1SGT LOWELL A. "PAPPY" JOHNSON, also spent time in the hospital with DON MAJERUS and a SGT MOUSER, I want to thank you again and was so happy to find out that you made it OK! (Patch 1973)

4DQ JAMES R. HEARN, wrote, " About your brief of the VANGUNU battle. One of the dead was a boy named BOOTH. He was shot the first night and I was with him when he died. I was a PLSGT under 2LT JAMES BROWN, 1DQ, (Mustang). After CAPT WILLIAM FLAKE was wounded he became C.O. and I took over the 1st Platoon. LT ERIC HOLMGRAIN had the 4th Platoon. I was talking to WM. L.M. "RED" TOWNSEND, of the Weapons. Platoon when I was hit in the right shoulder and back with two 37 mm anti tank shells. The first did not go off but the second exploded and I was badly hit.

On the way out I was being carried along with LOWELL "PAPPY" JOHNSON (1SGT who received the Army DSC), when WIA while breaking up a Jap Ambush). PADRE REDMOND is the best as far as I'm concerned. Glad to see JOHN ALLEN COOPER is on the Raider ROSTER. He and JIM STRAWBRIDGE got me out when I was hit.

4 BO ALBERT H. DOSCHER JR wrote, "Your Viru Harbor brief in the July 77 PATCH was very interesting. A complete story would be something to have. Of those listed as KIA at Tetamara, it was right on. All were from the 1st Squad, 1st Platoon except KOSOVICH, THOMACK and THORNSBERRY. This was the point when we moved out that morning. PLTSGT ZWICK was in the lead and the first man KIA. THORNSBERBY was a communicator attached to the 1st Platoon. We came on the Japs very suddenly and they were waiting for us. The fire-fight was hot and heavy for awhile. I'm surprised that we didn't lose more men than we did.

Those days in the approach through the swamp after we landed at Regi in rubber boats, will never be forgotten. Our food D Ration Chocolate Bars, all went moldy and we were on short rations from the start. The GUNG HO rule was 'share whatever you had with your buddy.' After the battle at Viru we were all part of that burial detail for the KIA's. It was no picnic digging those graves. We all had jungle rot from immersion of our feet and we were hobbling around with two pair of woolen socks because we couldn't get our shoes on. The burial site was on the crest of a ridge overlooking the harbor. The incident about the Army Colonel missing his jungle rations brought many a laugh. The best was when COL CURRIN offered the Army Colonel a few of his own ARMY RATION PEANUTS."

RICE ANCHORAGE, ENOGAI INLET
1ST MARINE RAIDER BATTALION
5 July 1943

The 1st Raider Battalion landed at Rice Anchorage, New Georgia on 5 July 1943 and began a tortuous four day jungle approach towards the Japanese sea coast artillery base at Enogai Inlet. After 4 days of preliminary battles at Triri and the jungle approaches leading to the enemy strong-hold, there were 18 KIA and 28 WIA Raiders by nightfall of 9 July.

1ST RAIDERS KILLED IN ACTION AT TRIRI

ABBOTT, LLOYD	CORBETT,JAMES *
CROSLAND,MAUREL	FLAUM, MARTIN
FLYNN, L. H.	HARPER,JAMES JR
HODGES,BURRELL	INGLEBURGER,T.O
KINGSBURY, JOHN	LE BLEU, ELMO
OLDHAM, PHILIPP	PATRICK, ERSEL
PELKEY,WILLIAM	RETZCH,NORMAN
ROOSEVELT,J. H.	SZAKOVICS,JOE
WILLIAMS,PAUL	ZINCKEVICH,BARNEY
* CORPSMAN	

At 0630 LTCOL S.B. GRIFFITH ordered the main attack on 10 July to begin with Co A, under CAPT THOMAS F. MULLAHEY on the left; Co C, under CAPT JOHN SALMON in the center; and Co B, under CAPT EDWIN B. WHEELER on the right. Co D under CAPT CLAY A. BOYD was in reserve. Co B advanced rapidly and within two hours had captured the village of Baekineru, killed 12 Japanese and captured 1 heavy and 5 light machine guns. LT BOB KENNEDY'S 1st Platoon on the point, crossed two small streams and reached a point overlooking the enemy campsite, where they were pinned down by heavy enemy machine gun fire.

On the left and center MULLAHEY and SALMON reached high ground some 600 yards from the point. GRIFFITH ordered the Demolitions Platoon under WO ANGUS R. GOSS to assist Co B, and one platoon of Co D under 1LT THOMAS D. POLLARD to pass through Co C and attack towards KENNEDY'S forward position.

Following a heavy mortar barrage, POLLARD'S men charged down the slopes, over running a key Japanese machine gun that was bothering KENNEDY and continuing on through the enemy coral camp street. The unwounded enemy raced to the Inlet and attempted to swim to an adjoining island as RAIDER machine guns slaughtered them. POLLARDS bold assault had broken the back of the enemy resistance as it divided the enemy into two surrounded pockets. As KENNEDY saw POLLARDS charge approach. He stood up in the open to stop POLLARD'S fire from falling on his own men. KENNEDY says with a laugh, "the bravest thing I did during the whole war was to step out in front of that mad charging POLLARD." At 1600 a carrying party of REGT HQ and some Army arrived with some food air -dropped at Triri and the hungry Raiders wolfed down their first food in over 30 hours.

The Raiders had captured: four 140-mm Naval Coastal guns; 3 Anti-aircraft guns, four heavy and 14 light machine guns, 2 tractors, a searchlight, small arms ammunition, food and supplies. They killed 350 Japanese.

1ST RAIDERS KILLED IN ACTION AT ENOGAI POINT

ANDERSON, SAMUEL	ANDRZEJEWSKI,L. S.
ASHDOWN,GERALD	BOOTH, ALFRED J.
BUNN, BENNIE M.	CAIN, WILLIAM F.
COMBS, JOHN G. A.	DANIELS, CHARLES
ERICKSON, HARRY	FLYNN, LAWRENCE
JOHNSON, JAMES	JORDAN, JAY
KAUFMAN,ROBERT	KENNEDY,JAMES
LEWIS,KENNETH	MAKIN, GEORGE
MCSWEENEY,HUGH	MEDICIS, HARVEY
MULFORD,ROBERT	OLLER, GEORGE
PELKEY, WILLIAM	PYNE, HAROLD
SCOTT,WALTER	SEATON, HARLEY
SMITH, HAROLD.	SZAKOVICS,JOE
VISCO,JERRY W.	WABSCHALL, DAN
WAHLERS, FLOYD	

ENOGAI INLET BATTLE AFTERMATH
Raider Patch, Bulger.

The 1st Raider Regiment, under COL HARRY B. "THE HORSE" LIVERSEDGE was composed of Regimental H&S and the 1st Raider Battalion, under the command of LTCOL SAMUEL B. GRIFFITH II, when they assaulted enemy Japanese bases at Rice Anchorage Maranusa I, Triri and Enogai Inlet. (The 4th Raider Battalion under the command of LTCOL MICHAEL S. CURRIN was busy elsewhere destroying enemy bases at Viru Harbor, New Georgia and Wickham Anchorage, Vangunu, and did not reinforce the 1st Raider Battalion on Enogai, until 18 July 43 for the assault on Bairoko Harbor.)

When the initial assault was launched 5 July 43, COL LIVERSEDGE had two US Army Battalions under his command at Rice Anchorage, and for all subsequent battles on New Georgia. The Army units involved were, 3rd Bn 145th Infantry under command of LtCol G. G. Freer and 3rd Bn 148th Infantry under command of LtCol D. E. Schultz; both Army 43rd Division units.

The Raider and Army troops clambered down the sides of the APD's into Higgins boats for the trip ashore in driving rain, where they were to be met by Capt CLAY BOYD'S recon patrol that included Flight Lt J.A. Corrigan, RAAF and his native guides. The landing took longer than usual because the Higgins boats kept getting hung up on the sandbars. Unable to get close to shore the Raiders plunged from their boats into water, waist and sometimes shoulder deep, pelted with a driving rain in pitch black darkness.

After the destroyer Strong was sunk by a Jap torpedo while standing by, the remaining ships waited anxiously for the troops to get ashore, so they could clear the island. Not wanting to expose the ships to Japanese fire any longer, COL LIVERSEDGE released them after 90% of the supplies were ashore. To his chagrin, he later found out that a high powered TCS radio allocated only for this assault had been left aboard ship. This was to cost the troops dearly later on.

By nightfall, Raider Co D under the command of Capt BOYD, had established a bridgehead on the opposite side of the Giza Giza River. The next day, new trails had to be cut through the heavy underbrush, slowing progress considerably.

When the Raiders, and 2 companies of the 145th Infantry moving through swamps, reached the Tamakau River, they found it to be swollen and 9 feet deep from the incessant rains. Fortunately they found a tree that had fallen to the other side and managed to cross the river safely, one man at a time however they were forced to remain in the damp swamp for the rest of the night.

One company of the 148th Infantry was directed to establish a roadblock at the Munda-Bairoko Trail. Army COL Schultz reported he was in position late that evening.

On 7 Jul, the target date for the attack on Enogai, BOYDS men came upon the worst terrain they had encountered in the campaign that delayed the attack for one day. While still in the swamp, they heard sounds of the air attack laid on to help soften up the Japs before the Raider assault. After finally breaking out of the swamp, there was only a narrow trail at the base of a high coral ridge to use in their approach. Maranusa I was occupied by D Co before noon and Triri later in the day.

COL GRIFFITH set up an ambush that broke up an attack by a company of Japs that fled down the trail toward Bairoko.

On 8 Jul, after repulsing a Jap counter attack on Triri, GRIFFITH'S Raiders moved forward toward Enogai, where they launched an attack that split the Jap defenders, allowing them to completely surround both groups and captured their objective.

When the Raiders received an air-drop of food on Jul 9th, COL LIVERSEDGE attempted to reach Army General Hester to tell him of the fall of Enogai, and to request planes be sent to evacuate the wounded. The NET control station stubbornly refused his message and requested he end radio traffic until the following morning. LIVERSEDGE ignored this order and continued to send messages until they reached the right persons.

The following day after a Jap strafing and bombing attack on Enogai, 3 Dumbo Flying Boats landed to evacuate the wounded, who were taken out to the planes in rubber boats. Although attacked by 2 Japanese planes, the PBY's were able to take off with over 100 wounded and ill men.

With the fall of Enogai Inlet, an estimated 350 Japanese had been killed at a cost to the Raider Regiment of 50 killed, 91 wounded, and four missing in action that were later declared dead

1C Doctor BYRON ELLER (former Corpsman) wrote, " I was assigned to 1st BN C Co 3rd Platoon. During the battle for Enogai Inlet 9 and 10 Jul 43, the first man hit was, CRAIG, followed by PATRICK, BOOTH, BUBELNICK and FLYNN. LT OLDHAM AND ALFRED J. BOOTH were dead on the field. SGT LAWRENCE H. FLYNN and CPL ERSEL T. PATRICK passed away in the aid station. It is of interest to note that WALTER B. SCOTT was KIA 10 Jul 43, because on 8 Jul, he sprained his ankle very badly and was able to walk only with great difficulty. After taping it as best I could, I sent him to the rear but later in the day I found him again with his squad barely able to keep up, he was determined to stay in there! That's what the Raiders were like, a magnificent bunch of men. I was proud to be with them! The Raiders accepted their Corpsmen wholeheartedly and saw to it we were well taken care of."

AUTHOR: Pharmacist Mate 2c BYRON ELLER was awarded the Army Silver Star Medal for his bravery at Enogai, New Georgia Island on 9 Jul 43.

4CP HAROLD C. "HAL" FERRIN, Denver, CO, sends us a partial clipping from a Saturday Evening Post article (Date and Author unknown). That describes the above incident and other heroic missions of the PBY's called Dumbos, on their many close support missions of supply and rescue of the Marine Raiders.

"Dumbo fliers still talk with amused awe about the taxi hop and grocery run combined which Lt. J.E. White flew to Coastwatcher Donald Kennedy. He took off from Florida Island with his regular crew of nine, a ton of supplies and two passengers. His mission being to deliver the passengers and supplies to Marine Raiders on New Georgia. He was then to return to Guadalcanal with four American fliers, survivors of downed planes that had been rescued by loyal natives and had managed to reach Donald Kennedy and the Marine Raiders at Segi. It was a routine mission but when Lt. White landed at Guadalcanal, his plane's cramped and gear-encumbered interior disgorged four fliers, two Jap prisoners and twenty-two Chinamen, a whole colony of them, with all their worldly goods. (EDITOR: IN 1974 there were over 800 Chinese residents and merchants in Honiara's China Town).

Of Dumbo's other duties, none was so important and none certainly so in keeping with their growing traditions as the evacuation of the wounded. In the early days of the war in the Solomons, calls would come frequently, urgent calls, asking Dumbo to fly the severely wounded directly from the beachheads to the base hospitals, where their lives might be saved as they could not be in the field. More often, Dumbo was called upon to fly to secret rendezvous in bays or inlets of Jap held islands to carry out wounded or sick Raiders who, if they had not been evacuated, would have seriously hampered the swift movements essential to all the Marine Raider operations."

AUTHOR: 4 CP HAROLD FERRIN, Pharmacist Mate 2c, was awarded the Army Silver Star Medal for bravery at Bairoko New Georgia Island on 20 Jul 43, and later served on Iwo Jima.

Unknown contributor- "Can you Raiders who crossed the river near Enogai ever forget how approximately 600 men crossed the Tamakau River over one lone log within six and one-half hours? Of course when many fell in, toggle ropes were linked together and stretched across the river, and while the line generally expedited the crossing it was responsible for several immersions, when it suddenly snapped during this crossing. LIEUTENANT FRANK KEMP, SERGEANT SIMONICH, and SERGEANT WALSH distinguished themselves by pulling out of the water eleven men who had slipped from the log and who would have inevitably drowned had it not been for their quick action.

It rained and rained and rained all that night in all forms, and on into the next day where the trail they followed was a coral ridge for approximately a mile, that was tortuous. The footing was slippery and dangerous, and many men tripped over roots and fell heavily, cutting their hands, knees, and other parts of their bodies on the razor sharp coral.

After what seemed an endless trail, we marched into a swamp about six hundred feet wide. This finally led to the ridge that lay just south of the Enogai Inlet. Several bombs landed in the swamp shattering huge banyan trees and injuring several Marines as we moved forward the battle. We met strong enemy patrols, but by evening Triri was occupied and organized for defense. Our Corpsmen and Doctors cared for the wounded that were sheltered from the rain in a large grass shack.

FATHER MURPHY conducted a digni-fied service for our dead, after which they were buried beneath a large banyan tree. Mission accomplished, with a part of the enemy "back door" effectively closed.

The Raiders and the Army troops were withdrawn, and the area was turned over to an Army defense battalion for operation and maintenance."

4 CP MILTON GRIGGERS, "When we were set up on the line at Viru Harbor, HUFFSTUTTER and CARMODYS fox hole was just up the slope from TOBY'S and mine. We had a good foxhole. It was deep and covered with bamboo and silk parachute cloth from when they dropped 'K' rations for us. One night when 'piss call Charlie' was circling overhead, CARMODY got the dysentery urge, and as you know when you bend over the rest is automatic. CARMODY had to bend over of course getting out of his hole and his aim was right down on our silk cover. We slept fitfully that night, but a rain the next day cleaned things up. LT POPELKA detailed TOBY and me to be responsible for some surplus food, raisins, nuts, dry fruit and such and we were getting along pretty good until one morning the Lt accused us of tapping the goodies we were guarding. So we were soon out of the supply business, but never did figure out how they counted peanuts and raisins.

BAIROKO HARBOR, NEW GEORGIA, B.S.I.
1ST MARINE RAIDER BATTALION
4TH MARINE RAIDER BATTALION

The under manned 1st Raiders organized 2 full strength companies and a Demolition Platoon of WO ANGUS R. GOSS, Co B, CAPT EDWIN B. WHEELER and Co D, 1LT FRANK A.

KEMP in preparation fir the attack on Bairoko. To reinforce them, the banged up 4th Raider Battalion was recalled from Guadalcanal where they had returned after capturing Viru Harbor and Vangunu. The 4th arrived at Enogai on 18 Jul, aboard the APD's Kilty, McKean, Ward and Waters and quickly unloaded their supplies.

The Raiders attack was to be supported by air attacks from Navy planes with the two Army Battalions attacking from the south. Neither materialized, as Col Schultz advised COL GRIFFITH he was held up by four machine gun emplacements, and could not advance.

AUTHOR: LTCOL McCAFFREY led a recon unit of highly trained Marine Intelligence scouts and Natives to the roadblock. Here they determined it was actually 2 rather than 4 machine guns that kept Army Col Schultz from arriving to help in the Raider attack, even though his unit had experienced very few casualties.

The battle began at 1000 on 20 Jul, and continued all day. With nothing but guts, and small infantry weapons about 800 Raidersattacked the enemy force, who were well emplaced in a series of four parallel ridges with interlocking bunkers and cleverly concealed cross fire machine gun fire lanes. The Raiders drove the enemy back into a pocket some 300 by 600 yards, but at a very heavy cost in casualties. It was here on New Georgia, the Navajo Code Talkers were first used and they were active throughout the battle, but were hampered by broken wires all day long.

At 1730 with darkness coming on, the Raiders upon the orders of COL GRIFFITH broke off the attack with the harbor only 300 yards away, and ordered a withdrawal. The Raiders suffered over 30% casualties. More than 250 men were killed or wounded, with half of the remaining men needed to care for the many casualties.

Following a fairly quiet night except for the work of the Corpsmen, Doctors and Chaplains struggling to save the wounded, and a small Japanese probe killing one Raider and wounding nine, the withdrawal began at daylight. Eighty walking wounded Raiders set out for Enogai, mostly providing their own security along the trail. The walking wounded helped by their buddies, were followed by the stretcher cases carried by Marines or the Natives.

The next morning, 1LT GEORGE LEPPIG led the 80 walking wounded back in to the base at Enogai. Seventy natives brought up water and supplies and carried out the litter cases. They made two trips and saved many lives with their continuing aid.

"At 1500 on 21 July 43 three PBY's landed to evacuate the wounded. When the first of these planes departed it had on board LTCOL SAMUEL B. GRIFFITH, bound to Koli Point, Guadalcanal to make a personal report to Rear Admiral Theodore S. Wilkinson. The second plane left without incident at 1600, but 30 minutes later, but just as the last PBY was preparing to take off, a radio report was received of 25 enemy planes heading for Enogai Inlet, the Raiders base of operations. No sooner had the PBY become air-borne than it was attacked by two Zero's and received many hits which damaged its port oil line and wounded two crewmen and one Raider, who was himself previously wounded. The plane was forced to return and spend 3 nights at Enogai Inlet. (This is our first story of some of the brave USN pilots who flew these Angel of Mercy, mission's that saved many Marine Raider lives.

1ST MARINE RAIDERS KILLED IN ACTION AT BAIROKO HARBOR

ARMSTRONG, ORVAL	BALDIGA, WALTER
CARPENTER RALPH	DODSON, VIRGIL R.
GOSS, ANGUS R.	HOLLADAY, JOHN B.
HUNTER, JOHN W.	LOSHEK, JAMES R.
MACLEAN, JOHN	STATES, GEORGE
MOCK, GEORGE F.	NEILL, WILLIAM K.
PARKER,THADDEUS*	SELFRIDGE, CALVIN
SIM, ALEC M.	WALSH, JAMES F.
WINN, AUDREY G.	WHEELER,EUGENE
WHITNEY,THOMAS	WOOD, GEORGE
*CORPSMAN	

4TH MARINE RAIDERS KILLED IN ACTION AT BAIROKO HARBOR

ALLEN, CARROLL	AYERS, GERALD
BARNES, DONALD	BRUCK, EDWARD
BRYANT,EVERETT	CASH, ROBERT D.
CORBET, JOHN R.	EASTON,CHARLES
FIZUR, FRANK J.	GIBBONS, WALTER
GOJMERAC,NICHOLAS	GARDNER, JOHN
HANCOCK, ELZIE J.	HOGUE, FRED
JOHNSON, JAMES W.	LAROCHELLE,ROGER

LARSON, BERENT L	LEWIS, JOHN O.
MAASSEN, DALE G.	OLIVER, FLOYD A.
PHILLIPS, CARL	POWERS, WILLIAM
REGAN, WILLIAM	REYNOLDS,JAMES
SHUEMATE,JAMES	SIKKEN, JOHN L.
TATUM, CURTIS A.	THORNBURG,VIRGIL
TROHA, FRANK E.	WATSON,JEFFERSN

RAIDER CORPSMEN AND DOCTORS AWARDED SILVER STAR MEDALS AT BAIROKO HARBOR

BROWN,RICHARD	FERRIN, HAROLD
KNOX, STUART	MAYFIELD, JAMES
MILLER, HARRY A.	PARKER,THADDEUS
SITTON, LEWIS W.	THOMPSON,STANLEY
WOOD, SAMUEL D.	

1ST AND 4TH MARINE RAIDER BATTALION AND ARMY CASUALTIES AT BAIROKO

1ST RAIDER BN	17	KIA	29	WIA
4TH RAIDER BN	29	KIA	127	WIA
RAIDER TOTALS	47	KIA	198	WIA
ARMY	3	KIA	10	WIA

When the 1st Raider Regiment boarded APD's on 29 Aug 1943 to return to Guadalcanal there was plenty of space onboard the ships. Casualties and illness had reduced the 4th Raider Battalion to 150 men well enough to be considered capable of engaging in combat, and the 1st Raider Battalion to 250 men.

THE JOINT CHIEFS OF STAFF REPORT ON BAIROKO IN PART STATED, "THE MARINE RAIDERS ARE EQUIPPED FOR SURPRISE OPERATIONS. THEIR HEAVIEST WEAPON IS A 60MM MORTAR. SUCH LIGHTLY ARMED TROOPS CANNOT BE EXPECTED TO ATTACK FIXED POSITIONS DEFENDED BY HEAVY AUTOMATIC WEAPONS, MORTARS AND HEAVY ARTILLERY.

FAILURE TO RELIEVE THE MARINE RAIDERS BY REGULAR INFANTRY UNITS IS ON A PARALLEL WITH THE FAILURE TO RELIEVE THE FIRST MARINE DIVISION AT GUADALCANAL."

AUTHOR: At the ripe old age of 17, I had participated in the successful capture of Viru Harbor. Now at age 18, the order to withdraw when we were within 300 yards of victory at Bairoko was a bitter pill for everyone to swallow!

"We Raiders contend that we would have taken Bairoko Harbor had we received the air and naval support asked for. Even with the failure of COL SCHULTZ and the Army 3rd BN 148th Infantry, with their 81mm mortars, that allowed TWO MACHINE GUN NESTS STOP THEM FROM ARRIVING IN TIME TO SUPPORT OUR ATTACK!

Should readers believe we feel strongly about this, you're damned right we do! Many brave Raiders died needlessly in this attack because of a failure to give us the support we needed to capture Bairoko Harbor."

On 11 August, the 1st Raider Regiment doctors reported that of the 956 Marines on the rolls, only 436 of 2,000 were fit for duty. There was a high incidence of recurrent malaria, with a large number of cases of sheer, utter exhaustion complicating the problem.

The Corpsmen, Doctors and Dentists worked 24 hour days, drenched by rain, knee-deep in mud, with little shelter, yet losing only a handful of the wounded. Fortunately for Navy medical men, combat fatigue was almost unknown among the Marines.

On 20 September the 4th Raider Battalion left for Auckland, New Zealand for a month's rest and recreation. The 1st Raider Battalion followed 30 days later.

4 HQ FATHER PAUL J. REDMOND, Carmel, CA writes, "At Bairoko Harbor, COL HARRY LIVERSEDGE' was leading a small patrol around the Jap positions. On the way back, we heard a noise in the bush ahead. Someone challenged who is it? 'A voice answered, 'RITES', and our men immediately opened fire. It was a small enemy ambush. We found a DOG TAG on one of the dead enemy with the name of one of our RAIDERS PFC NORTON P. RETZCH, 1C MIA 9 Jul at Enogai Inlet. He had always insisted his name was pronounced 'REETZ', that is why we opened fire immediately after the enemy said, RITES'. We were about a dozen Marines including myself."

IRA GILLIAND, 1E, was one of the wounded Raiders being evacuated aboard a PBY from New Georgia, which was attacked and damaged by Japanese Zero's while in the air. Gilliand became one of the three newly wounded before being flown out the next day. The other 2 Raiders were WILLARD GOODSON, 4HQ, and ROBERT KENNEDY 1B. 76 Patch

Corpsman, JAMES E. BOREN 1B, Clifton, TX wrote, " I was assigned to the 1st Raider Battalion on New Caledonia in April 1943. I was delighted to see the name of LT ROBERT KENNEDY 1B, Reno NV in the March 82 RAIDER PATCH. I was in B Co 1st BN, and my Platoon Leader was LT BOB "PLOW-JOCKS" KENNEDY. It just has to be him. I haven' t seen or heard of him since that day on the Enogai-Bairoko trail on New Georgia. He got badly shot up in both elbows when we were ambushed. We got him out on a PBY the next day and that's the last I heard of him. He was a fine and courageous Officer. Happy to know he is still around.

AUTHOR: Corpsman James Boren was an accomplished western artist who became very successful following the war.

4HQ WILLARD R. GOODSON writes, " Sorry to hear about the trouble FATHER REDMOND was having. I was with him and the rest of the gang on the Segi Point to Viru Harbor stroll...We had a very enjoyable time. I received a fractured skull at Bairoko Harbor. I was on that PBY that started to fly us wounded out and was shot down at 300 feet. We stayed in two Higgins boats at Enogai Inlet for a couple of days before we made a go for it. (Patch 1974)

4HQ THOMAS J. LANNEN WROTE," I was saddened to hear of the death of Dr. JESSIE LOCKHART 4HQ. I got to know him well as he nursed me through a few malarial attacks. I can still see him at Bairoko Harbor desperately trying to save the life of 2LT CURTIS A. TATUM, KIA 20 Jul 43. Bullets were coming from everywhere, sniper and machine gun, but he never wavered nor hardly hunched over as he worked furiously to save his comrade."

1ST AND 4TH MARINE RAIDERS
AWARDED MEDALS ON NEW GEORGIA

LTCOL HARRY LIVERSEDGE, COMMANDING
OFFICER OF THE 1ST RAIDER REGIMENT
RECEIVED THE NAVY CROSS

ARMY DISTINGUISHED SERVICE CROSS	
AYERS,GERALD L.	BUNN, BENNIE M.
CAIN, WILLIAM JR.	CORBETT, JOHN R.
COSTELLO, RAY F.	EASTON, CHARLES
GILBERT,ORRA E.	GRAY, OLIN M.
GRIFFITH,SAMUEL	HASH, CHESTER

HOLMGRAIN,ERIC
MAASSEN, DALE G.
PHILLIPS,CARL
POLLARD,THOMAS
SIM, ALEC M.
TOWER,EVERETTE

JOHNSON,LOWELL
NOVINA, JOHN
PHILLIPS,WESLIE
REGAN,WILLIAM
TEAGUE, WAUSS

ARMY SILVER STAR

ABBOTT, LLOYD B.
ANDERWALD,FRANK
BARNES,CHARLES
BELLMAN,MERRIL
BROWN, DEVILLE
BUNTIN, JOSEPH
CALLAHAN, JAMES
CARSON, JOHN H.
CONNOR,THOMAS
DESFORGES,ROBERT
DOW, ROBERT E.
ERGUSON,PHILLIP
FLEMING, PATRICK
FORCINIO, HARRY
GRIER, ROY M.
HANCOCK, ELZIE
HUNT, WILFRED A.
KEES, ELZY JR.
KENDALL, JOHN
LARSON, BERENT
LINTON, FRED C.
McCARTHY,MALCOM
McSWEENE,HUGHIE
MITCHIE, CHARLES
MUNDELL, SAMUEL
OAKES, JOHN J.
OLDHAM, PHILLIP A.
PINCKNEY, JAY J
SARTAIN, MELVIN
SMITH, HAROLD
STONAKER, JAMES
TATUM, CURTIS
VAHEY, WILLIAM E.
WALKER, ANTHONY

ALFORD,LEONARD
BANKS, CHARLES
BARNES, DONALD
BRASSWELL, JACK
BRYANT, EVERETT
CALKINS, HARRY
CARROLL, DANIEL
COMBS, JOHN G.
CURRIN,MICHAEL S
DION, HUBERT E.
ERICKSON,HARRY
FLAKE, WILLIAM L.
FLYNN, LAWRENCE
GLEASON, WM.
HALL, KENNETH C.
HONOHAN, WM.J.
JOLLY, WILLIAM T.
KEMP, FRANK A.
LAMBUTH,WARREN
LENZI, JOSEPH
LUCKEL,RAYMOND
McGOVERN, JACK
MITCHELL,GEORGE
MULFORD,ROBERT
NEILL, WILLIAM K.
OGRODNIK,STANLEY
PALONIS,ANTHONY
ROBERT,MILTON
SCAVERA, JAMES
SMITH, THOMAS W.
SZEWCZAK, HENRY
TINKER, BUD
VANNATER, LLOYD
WALKER, JAMES O.

WALTRIP, WILLIAM	WEAVER, ROBERT
WHEELER, EDWIN	WINN, AUDREY G.

MARINE AND NAVY CHAPLAINS

When President Franklin D. Roosevelt declared a national emergency in 1939 the United States was totally unprepared for war. With only 150,000 men in the Navy and 25,000 in the Marines, Roosevelt authorized an increase in all services.

The Chaplain Corps as directed in 1939, began preparing for the need of more volunteers but was overwhelmed following the Japanese attack on Pearl Harbor on 7 December 1941. During that catastrophe the Navy District Chaplain in Hawaii was given the responsibility of burying over 2100 Navy and Marine officers and enlisted personnel who were killed. Over 960 were also missing and presumed dead.

There were few caskets available, and the existing Nuuanu Cemetery could accomodate only 300 gravesites for burial. Thus the bodies were placed in cold storage while pine boxes were being built and additional plots were made available for burial services.

The Navy owned a parcel of land called Halawa, which was then immediately prepared as a cemetery. Every day at 1500, 3 Chaplains...Protestant, Catholic and Jewish stood together and buried the dead. It is little known that burial services continued on a daily basis there for a period of 3 months.

Back home in February 1942,the Navy established Chaplain Training School's at the Naval Operating Base in Norfolk, VA and Fort Schuyler, Bronx, N.Y. Future Raider Chaplains McGowan and Redmond attended the first Chaplains School in Norfolk.

With the continuing demand for more and more Chaplains, the Navy authorized moving the Chaplains School to the campus of the College of William and Mary, in Williamsburg, VA. in early 1943. AUTHOR- I was to teach at the college many years later.

In order to inject some reality in the course sometimes brought this typical remark from an instructor: "The last Sunday you preached from your pulpit a nice old lady came up to you and said, 'that was a nice message preacher.' The first sermon you preach after you leave this school, a Marine may come up to you and say "Damn good sermon Padre." You must realize there is as much sincerity in one as in the other."

In 1939, there were 94 Navy Chaplains in the Navy, only 4 of whom were attached to the Marine Corps. Before the end of the war 2,934 Chaplain had served in the Corps. Of those volunteers over 200 were attached to the Marine Corps.

MARINE RAIDER CHAPLAINS

Nine Silver Stars were awarded Chaplains for heroism in combat during World War II. Four of these men were attached to the Fleet Marine Force and two, Chaplain William M. McCorkle and William M. McCorkle served with the Marine Raiders.

Eleven Legion of Merit Medals were awarded to Chaplains for heroic service in WWII. Six of whom were attached to the Fleet Marine Force. Marine Raider Chaplain Paul J. Redmond was awarded this medal for his bravery and devotion to duty.

Of the forty-six Navy Chaplains who received the Purple Heart during World War II, sixteen were attached to the Fleet Marine Force. Marine Raider Chaplain William M. McCorkle was wounded on Bougainville and Chaplain Robert J. Cronin was wounded on Guam.

Fr Redmond was first awarded the Army Legion of Merit for bravery on New Georgia in July 1943, and later received the Bronze Star Medal on Guam in July 1944, followed by the second Bronze Star awarded on Okinawa in 1945.

Although Chaplain's, Hospital Corpsmen, Doctors and Nurses were all classified as non-combatants. Each learned early in combat that Japanese troops would not honor the Geneva Convention and would try to wound or kill them when they came to the aid of a wounded Marine. They chose to ignore that danger and distinguished themselves throughout the War with their selfless devotion to duty and in particular, while serving with the Fleet Marine Force, their bravery under fire.

Navy Chaplains were detached to the Marine Corps, just as Navy Corpsmen, Doctors and Dentists. Though held in high regard aboard ships afloat they were revered even more for their contributions while attached to the Fleet Marine Force (FMF) in the field.

The goal of the Raiders was to provide fast, hard-hitting assault units that could land from submarines, destroyers, air transport, or regular Navy transports. The men all volunteers, in preparing for these hit and run raids underwent four months of rigorous, specialized training in blistering heat and torrential rain.

They marched day after day and after a 30-mile hike they were expected to be battle ready. They swam streams and stormed beaches. They played "games" like diving over double-apron barbed-wire fences. Their rigorous training prepared them for hand-to-hand combat with the Japanese.

Chaplains with the Raiders trained and became part of the front line troops, suffered the same deprivations in battle, and agonized over every casualty, just as Corpsmen did. Our Chaplains received medals for bravery while with the Raiders and continued to add to their laurels when the Raiders became a part of the 4th Marine Regiment

Regardless of respective faiths they conducted religious services, gave last rites to mortally wounded Marines, provided for rest and recreation, called on the sick, gave moral support and guidance to the troops plus a myriad of other unspecified duties. Some of the activities they helped arrange were movies, shows, boxing matches and baseball, basketball and football games.

Without a doubt, in the eyes of the Raiders, Chaplains ranked right up with our Commanding Officers. To observe their utter lack of fear while giving last rites to the seriously wounded on the battlefield was an inspiration to all of us. We honored, respected and loved them.

WARRIOR PRIEST

One Priest however, became the most beloved of all the Raider Chaplains. He was FATHER PAUL J. REDMOND, a 4th Marine Raider Battalion officer, who was actually old enough to have been a real father of most of the young Marines in the Raiders. Why, the top brass must have wondered, would a 42-year-old Catholic priest request duty with this outfit?

When Father Redmond entered the Navy as a Chaplain in 1942, he requested duty with the Marines. His first assignment was the Marine base at Quantico, Va., where he served as Post Chaplain from April to September 1942. He then became the Corps Chaplain of the Amphibious Corps, Pacific Fleet.

"I was a staff chaplain at Camp Elliott, CA and had no congregation," Father Redmond recalled from his home in Carmel, Calif. "I'd go to Camp Pendleton where the Raiders were training. They had no Chaplain because they were too mobile and couldn't have a chaplain. I got interested in what they were going to do." He asked to be assigned to the Raiders.

"I was MAJGEN. HOLLAND SMITH'S Chaplain at the

time, and he would release anyone for a promotion, but he never liked anyone to go backward," he said, referring to the fact that he would have to be demoted from Corps Chaplain to battalion chaplain to serve the Raiders. "Between Holland Smith and LTCOL JIMMY ROOSEVELT, they let me go." Recalling an old friend, Father Redmond added, "Jimmy Roosevelt was a very brave man. He always led the point. I told him that the men were worrying about him, and he said, 'You pray for me and I'll be all right.'

Having gotten his wish, Fr Redmond began the training required of all the Raiders. Tall, robust, and athletic, he appeared as one of his Marine comrades, except that his hair was thinner. A story about Father Redmond written during the war reported that before he became conditioned to the Raider's pace, he said he traveled on will power alone. "I soon found the only way to keep up with them was to relax completely. When we stopped for a short rest I would topple over backwards and lie there until the order was given to march on." On marches, he kept up the men's spirits with witty comments and stories.

FATHER REDMOND was always solicitous of "his" Marines. When JIMMY ROOSEVELT ordered them to work seven days a week, Father Redmond scheduled church services for Wednesday. It is rumored that when questioned about countermanding Roosevelt's orders, FATHER REDMOND replied, "If a Marine Colonel can make Sunday a work day, I guess God can make Wednesday a Sunday!"

Father was known as a most charitable man of the cloth unless something threatened his boys, as he called them. It was then that he became a veritable tiger, a true WARRIOR PRIEST. Absolutely fearless, he was constantly on the front lines giving last rites to the men where they had been shot with no thought whatsoever about his own safety. When fired upon by enemy troops there would be no hesitation in using his sidearm, a .45 cal revolver, to protect his own life or that of a comrade.

The 4th Raider Battalion was rushed back from Guadalcanal to Rice Landing, New Georgia on 18 July 1943 to reinforce the 1st Marine Raider Battalion who were reduced to less than 300 effective fighting men in their battle for Enogai. The 4th Battalion had less than 7 days rest on the Canal following their battles at Vangunu Island and Viru Harbor. They were to join the Bairoko Harbor attack the next day in which 156 officers and men became casualties.

Father Paul J. Redmond Raider Chaplain later conducted the 4th Raider Memorial Service in a Coconut Grove, at Enogai

Inlet, New Georgia Island 19 July 1943. He had landed on 18 July from the APD1 USS Ward, along with COL MICHAEL S. CURRIN, 35 Officers and 666 enlisted personnel.

A picture of these services in the Coconut Grove made some sort of history of a sort when published. The only one Fr. Redmond could identify was COLONEL CURRIN, but one of the boys kneeling with his back to the camera was identified by at least 30 Mothers as their son that was lost in action. They recognized him from the back of his head. Father always felt badly that he could not confirm their beliefs.

Fr Redmond went on to conduct burial services for over 3,000 Marines during World War II. This represented 8% of the total number of burials conducted by the entire Navy Chaplains Corps, both ashore and afloat during the war years from 1941 to 1946.

About two weeks after the battle at Viru Harbor, FATHER REDMOND and a force of Raiders led by LTCOL MICHAEL CURRIN joined other Marines at Enogai. Here the priest was assigned a runner, a husky, tobacco chewing Texan, Oail "Bum" Phillips. Armed with a carbine, Phillips protected himself and the chaplain. Bum Phillips, who later became football coach of the San Diego Chargers, the Houston Oilers, and the New Orleans Saints, recalled his special assignment. "I thought it was a real honor to work with him," Phillips said from his home in Sugarland, Texas. When he first saw Father Redmond, he remembers thinking, "Boy, this fellow's going to have a hard time, but he didn't. He could pretty well do what everyone else could do. He had more strength inside."

One incident that both Father Redmond and Phillips recall took place after an attack on Bairoko. "One of the things that stuck out in my mind is when we made a push on New Georgia. Phillips said. "We lost a lot of boys with a couple hundred wounded. We pulled back. Next day, he came and got me and said, 'We're going to get the dog tags from those boys.' AUTHOR: Unless dog tags are removed from a Marine to prove his death, or he or his body is recovered and identified, he is carried on Marine muster rolls as Missing in Action, "Phillips said that they almost went into the middle of the Japanese camp and it took quite a while to do. We looked all the way until dark, until we couldn't see anything at all." What if Bum Phillips hadn't been there to protect the priest? "He would've gone anyway. He had no regard for his own life. His regard was for the kids." He was one of the real heroes during the war," emphasized Phillips. He had courage. He wasn't afraid to meet his maker. He simply wasn't afraid of anything."

One of the most enduring and humorous tales of World War II, involving FR REDMOND was the story of the MISSING PIANO!

4HQ FATHER PAUL J. REDMOND, sends us THE 'GOSPEL ACCORDING TO PAUL'.

"The MISSING PIANO will follow us forever. It started with the fact that we had this entertainer (Jimmy Joyce)who later became famous in Hollywood as a song writer. WE NEEDED A PIANO and like Mt Everest, it was there. Plans were made, but I was only an innocent bystander.

For off "transport", I happened to know a Navy Coxswain who had been a Marine at Mare Island or Quantico. My part in the actual removal was unusual. All I had to do was tell COLONEL ROOSEVELT that the Captain wanted to talk to him or vice versa, I forget which. The timing was important to keep them both off deck. 2E happened to be on deck when a large object came topside and was placed in the Coxswain's boat all by hand. I told the robbers not to tell me where they had placed it ashore so that I could truthfully tell the COLONEL or the Ship's Captain that I didn't know where it was. Several days later COLONEL ROOSEVELT asked me to return the MISSING PIANO. I truthfully told him I did not know where it was. Meanwhile, before the men and their cargo went ashore, I had been saying Mass for the natives in a Native Church. The altar was very convenient in size and height, covered, with a tarp which should have made me suspicious, but didn't. The Captain threatened to contact Washington if THE PIANO was not returned, so it was on a direct order from COLONEL ROOSEVELT that I made inquiries and much to my surprise, I had been saying Holy Mass on stolen property. It was returned with great regret To me a Marine is never guilty, he is either innocent or ignorant. In this case believe me, I was an innocent marine."

THE MYSTERY OF THE MISSING SHIP'S PIANO
By LOWELL V. BULGER Patch Editor

Espiritu Santo, New Hebrides, 28 February 1943. Following the arrival of the USS PRESIDENT POLK (AP 103) and the subsequent debarkation of LTCOL JAMES ROOSEVELT and his 4th Marine Raider Battalion, a violently angry, sputtering, ship's Captain, hit the battalion headquarters ashore and demanded the return of ONE (1) only, MISSING SHIPS PIANO. COL ROOSEVELT repeatedly denied that so large an article could have found Its way into Raider gear, but all logic failed to placate the irate Skipper who threatened dire repercussions. An exten-sive search was launched and the missing heavily wrapped article was found in of all places, The Raider's Chapel, it was being used as an altar by the unknowing Raider Padre FATHER PAUL J. REDMOND.

The unwitting Raider stevedores had reportedly mistaken the piano for the Chaplain's Altar. It was returned to the ship along with the BLESSING OF THE LORD."

EDITOR: In an effort to shed some light on this 34 year old mystery we requested information from the troops and the following first hand accounts reveal:

4DQ JAMES GLEASON, PhM2. "JIMMY JOYCE, a young 4th Raider from Ohio, was the cause of the glint in FATHER REDMOND'S eye when he looked with envious eyes upon the piano aboard the USS Polk. Jimmy had entertained aboard ship, primarily with the harmonica, on the trip across the Pacific. Father Redmond knew he also played piano and had an excellent voice, so he had grand plans for using Jim's talent.

After the war ended, Jimmy went back to California to seek his fame and fortune as an entertainer, and became very successful. He and his lovely wife Betty toured with Alvino Rey's Orchestra and later appeared with the Kings Family and dubbed in their voices for various movie stars who were not accomplished singers. Jimmy was choral director for the Smothers Brothers Show, Hollywood Palace and many movies." Their young sons later became the voices in the original sountrack for the musical "Sound of Music"

4AN WESTON A. HARTMAN writes, "Regarding the lost or MISSING PIANO. On our last night aboard the USS POLK, 2LT THOMAS S. CONNOR, approached several of us in his company and said he needed some volunteers to help out our Chaplain FATHER PAUL REDMOND on a little detail. Myself, SGT STANLEY KONDRACKI, 4 AN, SGT GEORGE J. HUDOCK, 4AN, GUNNIE LOUIS L. BARNHART, HQ, and two or three others reported to an office on the Main Deck. TOMMY CONNOR showed us a rather large item, that was covered with shelter halves and ponchos. He said he would like it taken ashore. The PLAN was for LT CONNOR to get the ship's deck officer (O.D.) to go forward with him to check on an unloading problem in the forward hatch. When the coast was clear we rolled the PIANO across the main deck to the port gangway. We had some juggling to do in order to get it on the gangway and finally had to turn it up side down to slide it down. THE PIANO played an unwritten symphony all the way down.

A lighter, LCVP, was circling off the port side and as soon as the PIANO reached the bottom of the gangway it was loaded for the beach. Ashore a RAIDER RECON truck was waiting, where with the PIANO safely aboard, it was whisked away to a Native Church where the Padre had conducted Mass. The PIANO was secreted under the Altar Cloth that hid it very well. The only thing the Padre had said was. "It would be nice to have a PIANO for Mass AND IT WAS DONE."

4DQ HAROLD P. HART, writes "Re the Allegedly Stolen PIANO. THE PIANO was filched sure nuff. I had a 32 man Guard Mount on the beach supposedly to guard all that rubble we had to 'Off Load' to get at our own gear, which was, of course, on the bottom of the heap. A couple of RAIDERS hopped off a cargo barge and confronted me with a request to leave a spot open right on the beach for a 'SPECIAL OFF LOAD', Can do! Precisely on the hour, here comes an unloading barge from the President Polk with one huge object well covered and escorted by several RAIDERS. As she beached a RECON truck backed up to the barge and the mysterious object was loaded. The operation was short and sweet. No need for me to ask questions as the operation looked 'Neat to me'. I did not know what it was but if it came off the Polk, I was all for it. They had treated us like dogs' aboard when we left the ship, "We lifted everything that was loose and if it wasn't loose, we LOOSED it!"

4DQ CAPT DONALD S. FLOYD wrote, "I was in ship's Sick Bay with an ear infection when the USS POLK was off loaded at Espiritu Santo. Before they would let me leave the ship THEY SHOOK ME DOWN. When I asked the reason for this unwarranted action, they wouldn't tell me but I remember somebody saying. "ROOSEVELT and his THOUSAND THIEVES!"

AUTHOR: The term "Father Redmond and his Thousand Thieves was also used frequently."

4DQ CHARLES L. KILGORE, Carmel, IN says, " FATHER PAUL REDMOND is certainly a legend. I once picked up a hitchhiker, who had recently moved from California. I told him about being in San Francisco at the RAIDER REUNION. He said, 'Since you're a Raider, you probably know FATHER REDMOND. We were both in the 6th Marine Division on Okinawa. He asked if the PIANO STORY is true," I replied it certainly was."

Editor's Note: This article was picked up from a rare copy of "GISMO", a short-lived publication for servicemen in the Pacific Theater. The issue was Vol. 1, No. 1 — I have no idea if there were other issues.

THE GOOD PADRE AND HIS "BOYS"
Ralph Liberato, USMC

Many of you know the Story of the famous Father Duffy, the chaplain who served in World War I with the "Fighting 69th." He was always doing things for his men and keeping them happy. Well, so was the Padre in our outfit doing things for us. He was another Father Duffy, a true Raider. He is FATHER PAUL REDMOND, Lt. USMC.

The name of FATHER REDMOND is on the lips of every man in the Fourth Marine Raider Battalion. Every time someone mentioned the Padre's name to a Raider or anyone who knew him well, a twinkle would come into their eyes. Many stories can be told about the Padre, but only in words. You could never put just what you feel down on paper.

You could never forget the funny things the Father did. "Father Redmond and his Thousand Thieves" was the name given to the 4th Marine Raiders and their chaplain.

A corporal by the name of FRANK MORROW had an infection in the nail of his left thumb from boxing. This made things look bad for Frankie. It meant he wouldn't go on the raid with the battalion he had trained so hard with from the beginning. Corporal Morrow was broken hearted till the Padre had a talk with the Colonel, and fixed it up so Frankie could go on the raid by being his assistant. They were of different religions but they loved each other like father and son. I visited Father Redmond's tent often, to see my buddy Corporal Morrow, and find out how our Padre made out on his daylight raids.

You could always have a good time with the Father. He would have you laughing no matter how blue you were. You wouldn't need a morale officer if every outfit had a chaplain like Paul Redmond. Every outfit should have a chaplain like the Padre, but there is only one, and we have him.

When the boys were being evacuated from the front lines to the hospitals, the man they talked about most of the time was the Padre. A living hell was turned into a heaven when Father' Redmond was there. Many Marines who went up north without religion, came back with religion. Every time the Padre would see you, he'd ask if you had been to church. One day Father grabbed a certain corporal by the neck of his collar and led him

181

Raider Jimmy Joyce Playing Piano in New Zealand

to church. Whenever the name of FATHER REDMOND is spoken, it is with great respect. One of the many good things our Lord has given us, was Father Redmond, the kindest, and finest man to be found.

1C KENNETH FRIED, "During the invasion of Guam, Father Redmond was aboard our Landing Ship Tank, LST as we moved toward D-Day. On the morning we made the beach landing, FATHER REDMOND was holding services. SCHULTZ, LOFFEL and I were down below in our hammocks and LOFFEL said, "We've never been to a service." I said, "Okay, let's go. "Up the gangway and through the hatch we went. As we approached the services FATHER REDMOND stopped us and looked us right in the eyes and said, "AT THE LAST MOMENT OUT OF THE DARKNESS, THEY CAME TO BE SAVED" We were so embarrassed we turned around and returned right back down the hatch. Years later I met him at a reunion and brought that up. He said, "If I said that, it must have been the truth."

4D 1LT CHARLES L. KILGORE, Carmel, Ind., writes about FATHER REDMOND, "It was on the second day of the campaign and my outfit had turned left and attacked Orote Peninsula. About noon, or a little later, we were in a JAPANESE defensive area of fortified bunkers and houses just south of Orote. A Marine was hit by a sniper, and FATHER REDMOND pulled him to cover, on the safe side of a small house. In doing so, THE

GOOD PADRE attracted the fire of the sniper, but was not hit - too bad for the sniper. As soon as FATHER saw the wounded Raider was properly cared for, he crouched at the corner of the house and returned the enemy fire. This was the last time I saw FATHER REDMOND blazing away at an enemy. He was involved, he was always where the action was.

1D FRANK KEMP and later Company Commander of A Co. 2nd Bn, 4th Regiment tells these experiences with FR REDMOND: Before the invasion of Guam, we were on the LST convoys for fifty six days waiting to go in. FATHER REDMOND could have stayed on the Command ship along with General Shepherd and other staff but he preferred to be with us. It was on this trip that I got to know him.

Returning from a 30 day leave before we invaded Okinawa, I stopped at Honolulu waiting for transportation to Guadalcanal. While there I went to FMF Headquarters to see Fr. Redmond and he spent a lot of time showing me around. He took me to meet GEN. HOLLAND SMITH AND GENERAL MERRITT EDSON.

Fr. Redmond gave me a pair of silver bars that were given to him by 'Howlin' Mad that General Smith wore in the first World war. We went to the Schofield barracks and later had lunch with Jimmy Roosevelt.

I received a shrapnel wound on Okinawa in May and by August was in the Mare Island Hospital. FATHER REDMOND came to the Hospital and visited with all the 6th MarDiv patients as well as others. At horse racing time he came with two cars and took us to Bay Meadows to watch the races. I visited he and his wonderful sister Marion at Carmel where he showed me the garden that he planted and cared for himself.

FATHER REDMOND was a very intelligent man, had a genuine interest in the Marine enlisted men and was often there before any one when they were wounded. He took great pride in serving with the Marines and only lived to serve his God and others. We were all privileged to have known him. "

4HQ CHARLES H. SMITH wrote to FR REDMOND, "There is something I should have done a long time ago and that is to thank you for what you did for me on Guam. The morning we landed we moved up the beach. It was eerie. Every inch of ground was pulverized and cratered. Old coconut trees were shredded stumps. We encountered Japs at the first rise of hills. We threw grenades at each other. I don't know how it happened but I saw four Jap grenades come over the hill and bounce along the hard ground right toward me. I only had time to flatten to the ground and hold my arm against my heart to protect it. When the grenades went off they shredded all my clothes along the right side and blood spurted from my head. A buddy put a bandage on the head wound.

I was able to slide down the hill and stagger to the aid station on the beach. When I got there they told me to lie down and I saw you there. I remember a flurry of bullets came over and I began to gasp. You saw me FR, and called for a Corpsman to come give me blood. If it hadn't been for you I wouldn't have lasted very long. The aid station was so busy no one would have noticed me. I owe my life to you FATHER REDMOND. You watched over all of us like that. I want you to know that we are thankful you were our Chaplain."

This is the letter FATHER REDMOND wrote in reply on Feb. 21, 1990:Thank you for your letter. It made me feel years younger. At 91 my eyesight is not so good. As I was twice the age of all the men in our outfit, excepting a few officers, I felt like a father as well as a priest.

When I was young I thought if I ever had sons, I would want them to be brilliant and successful. When I was with the Raiders I wanted sons that would be good, courageous and compassionate. Some Raiders later became successful and well to do, but all my sons in the Raiders were compassionate and courageous. Your goodness is my reward in life. I send a prayer for your happiness and health. God Bless. Paul

1AB MELVIN HECKT writes The second day on Okinawa, April 2, 1945 while the 1st platoon, Baker Company, 1st Bn 4th Marines was fighting on Okinawa, I heard but could not see a Marine calling for help. ED DUNHAM, ED COPELAND, CHET COOPER, JOHN ACUNA, PALMER CANFIELD and I started down a tree and brush infested hill to rescue this Marine who was way out in front of our lines. He became impatient and requested that we hurry up. His request was peppered with profanity that would make even an old salt blush

I swore back at the Marine and told him we were coming as fast as we could. We finally fought through the brush and found him lying in a shallow ditch, pinned down by Japanese machine gun fire. We threw grenades and a satchel charge in a nearby cave and the machine gun stopped shooting. Who was this very profane Marine? He was none other than our most beloved Father Paul J. Redmond. My face is red to this day for having sworn at the most beloved man in the Corps.

I had the privilege of attending FATHER REDMOND'S 91st birthday party. He was sitting in a wheel chair as I approached him. I said, "Father Redmond, my name is MEL HECKT. I promise not to swear at you tonight, if you will promise not to swear at me." He smiled - he agreed - he remembered.

4OP JAKE MOODY says "While I was overseas, I saw Father Redmond around camp but had little contact with him. My real association with him began during my stay at Mare Island Hospital after I was wounded. In September 1945, I was in my bunk reading, when I looked up and saw a beautifully dressed lady, wearing diamonds and furs, accompanied by a Marine Officer. When they stopped to chat with one of the patients, I thought I recognized FR REDMOND so I got in my wheelchair and went over to them. And so began our association which lasted for more than a year.

Father had something going for us every weekend. Two or three times a month we spent the weekend at a large estate in Redwood City owned by Mr. & Mrs. Jenanyan. There were usually ten or twelve of us patients from the hospital who went. There were also girls from the area and ladies who would help serve us home cooked meals and booze, and we played games and swam. Best of all it was great just to be out of the hospital for awhile.

Thanksgiving Day, FATHER REDMOND took three of us to Los Angeles where we stayed at the Wilshire Hotel. (He had borrowed someone's 3-bedroom suite.) He got us tickets for everything going on in San Francisco; Stage shows, football games, meals at the best restaurants. We saw Pajama Game and Voice of the Turtle. The cast of Voice of the Turtle came out to meet us instead of us going backstage. He had also arranged at a very fine restaurant for us to go there anytime and eat and just sign the tab.

We were introduced to Admirals, Medal of Honor winners, movie stars and radio personalities. Even though we were held back by our disabilities he pushed us forward and gave us a great feeling of worth.

After a year at the hospital, as we were discharged Fr. Redmond arranged for our transportation home. This allowed us the money we got for transportation as money in pocket. I could go on and on, but the best thing he gave us was pride in being a Marine." (Jake was a 60-mm mortar crewman, wounded on Okinawa and lost a leg. Ed)

(Excerpt from The Chicago Daily Tribune 1/26/61, by CLAY GOWRAN)

A SAINTLY MAN

"Tonight an airplane from California will land at O'Hare field with a white haired man who is "saintly" in his own unusual way.

His name is Father Paul Redmond, and he is a Catholic priest who in 1943 helped steal a piano, and in 1960 landed behind penitentiary walls. It's all right, though he was a chaplain with the tough Marine Raiders when he took part in the piano-napping, and last year it was as a Chaplain that he went to the state prison at Soledad, Cal.

He's coming here for the 1961 installation of Officers of the United States Marine Raiders Association Saturday night in the Hotel Sherman.

Now about that piano. The Padre and the 4th raiders were sitting in the mud in the New Hebrides slands in the early summer of1943, waiting to go in as spearheads on the invasion of New Georgia in the central Solomons. You should have seen their camp. Nothing to do. Redmond discovered the Raiders had several good piano players, while a Navy transport out in the harbor had a good piano but no pianists. So, on a nice dark night, Redmond went out to the ship and somehow kept its officers and men entertained, he is a good story teller, while some of his Raiders crept aboard, manhandled the piano into a landing boat, and lugged it ashore.

"I told then to hide it where I wouldn't know where it was," said the priest. "Where do you think they put it under the altar in my makeshift chapel."

Like all Chaplains, he had to console guys who received "Dear John" letters from the girls back borne. One Raider Redmond will never forget. "This boy had real trouble," the Padre recalls. "He had received 'Dear John's' from three different girls at about the same time. Each told him she was breaking 'their engagement.' The boy told me, 'You just can't trust women, Padre.'"

Here's one that is unfunny. In 1945, upon returning from Okinawa, Padre Redmond said he had helped bury some 3,000 Marines. Their average age was 19 years, he said.

Chaplain REDMOND was very discreet. He didn't prowl through the tent area on Sunday mornings before Mass to roust out the Catholics for worship. However, after Mass at a more decent hour, he would occasionally on a Sunday, go up and down the rows of tents with a baseball bat thumping the tent poles and ropes, calling out for the Protestants to get up and go to church. Many did.

He knew the procedure for last rites in the Catholic, Protestant and Jewish manner and probably other religions as well. When the dead Marine's faith was unknown, because of missing dog tags, he would recite all three and it has been said that if a dead Marine was so young as to show no sign of whiskers on the face, Fr. Redmond softly wept during the rite.

2E FRANK CANNISTRACI has this to say, "I feel privileged and honored to pay homage to a great man, a legend within our Corps history and our Raider history. Many words of upon praise have been bestowed upon him, enough to fill many books. His name and words have been featured in newsletters of the Sixth Marine Division Association, the U.S. Marine Raider Association, The Marine Corps Gazette, The Marine Corps League Magazine the Leatherneck Magazine and news media publications across the country.

He was one of us, an enlisted man before he became a priest. He was 42 years old when the Raiders were formed, an age far beyond that allowed for combat duty, especially in Raider units, but he prevailed on COL JAMES ROOSEVELT to allow him to accompany the Raiders wherever they went. He took a demotion from the rank of Corps Chaplain to sail overseas with the Raiders."

Recollections of Joy and Sadness

At the Marine Raider reunion in Omaha, Father Paul Redmond described his role as Raider Chaplain as "not conventional." Judging by the priest's stories of that period, shepherding the Raider flock was more akin to riding herd over a group of run-away steers. Given a warm greeting by the Raiders, Father Redmond told of his World War II experiences "a time of joy and sadness both, they joy and sadness and friend-ship that were all exaggerated."

He had amusing stories to share with his audience. He remembered that the Raiders had a genius for "appropriating" alcohol. Navy medical lockers were often the targets of thirsty Raiders."

AUTHOR: Our name for "appropriating", was "liberating" and it applied mostly to food, weapon's, ammunition and clothing.

The Marine Corps always seemed to be last in the food and supply chain while the Army and Navy owned the mother lode of the items we desperately needed so their inventory became fair game.

Merchant Marine ships crews often treated Raiders and other Marine troops as second class citizens throughout the war in the Pacific. They were heartily disliked by all Raiders so it became a game to "liberate" anything that wasn't bolted down, and some times things that were bolted down! ROBERT A. BUERLEIN, President, American Historical Foundation a co-author along with COL MARTIN J. SEXTON and RUDY ROSENQUIST of "OUR KIND OF WAR", the definitive history of the U.S. Marine Raiders.

AUTHOR: Bob Buerlein was instrumental in establishing the Marine Raider Museum located in Richmond, VA.

This beautiful Eulogy for our Dead Raiders was given by Father Redmond in 1974.

"The bodies of MARINE RAIDERS who gave their lives for their country are scattered over land and sea in known and unknown graves. Please GOD, send your HOLY ANGELS to guard their honored remains...By a single... act of ultimate CHARITY they gained citizenship in YOUR KINGDOM... a realm for brave and selfless men...They have left a history of unselfish SERVICE to their COUNTRY. They were youthful men, but no man is TOO YOUNG to die to protect the things that make life worth living...Life, Liberty and the Pursuit of Happiness for all our citizens... Some men live to an old age without ever giving SERVICE or CHARITY to any man or country... These youths in a brief lifetime earned the gratitude of all our countrymen and the right to a dwelling place with YOU.

For those who have died after their re-turn to home and loved ones...LET The Wings of YOUR ANGELS be above them...around them...so that they may be lifted up into the MORNING SUN to join their brothers... already with you...Make a humble prayer of our proud boast in our Marine Hymn...that these men and women stand guard with YOUR ANGELS in the Streets of Heaven...Brave men die once...Grant to all Marines a brave death and an HONORED MEMORY...We ask this with humility...LORD GOD of the BRAVE and UNSELFISH who serve you and their beloved country in the UNITED STATES MARINE CORPS.

Final TAPS was sounded by a Military Bugler, with RAIDER RUSS CALVO, lst & 3rd Bn playing TAPS ECHO...One half mile, away on the span of the GOLDEN GATE BRIDGE, the Raider wreathes were hurled from the huge span into the swift, outgoing tide. Joe Rosenthal who took the historic picture of the Marine Flag Raising on Iwo Jima in 1945 was present and snapped many pictures.

ANOTHER UNFORGETABLE FR PAUL REDMOND EULOGY

Delivered at Golden Gate National Cemetery Sunday 20 July 1980.

"How can we come together for so many years to remember a past that was so cold with hunger and thirst. Bloody and muddy with toil and danger a past that we now wish to protect our children and women folk from ever experiencing. It is because, in that past we found our Camelot, that Camelot was not a magnificent castle with shining streets of gold and. silver. What we remember is a past when we were stripped of all pretenses, all the silly glitter of a plastic world, `all the comforts of a shabby world. A time when no emotion, no bodily function, no weakness, was a secret from those about us. We were stripped of all the veils that conceal what we really are. We saw each other as God sees us. And what we saw we liked, we LOVED another human being stripped of all protection, with nothing to give each other but our lives.

In song and poetry we see our Country as a heroic figure in flowing robes, a shining light. But the reality was a dirty young man with tired eyes, muddy and bloody, ready to throw himself on a live grenade to save his fellow Marine. The sadness of war to me was one Father's Day on Okinawa when GENERAL FENTON knelt by the body of his dead son praying. With no regret for a wayward son, but with a Father's sadness and pride in a son in whose short life has spanned all that was worth while.

I am not brave or more unselfish than any man, but every night I prayed God would take me and spare some boy to live a long and useful life.

Today it is the fashion for some youths to sneer and snigger at patriotism, service and discipline, but those despised virtues, were commonplace among us then. We and our departed brothers formed a thin red line that finally became a wall covered with the banners of victory.

4HQ FATHER PAUL J. REDMOND, Writes from London. "A friend took me on this trip, Copenhagen, Berlin, London and Dublin. Have been all over England the last two weeks, in spite of the rain and the cold. Friends here remember London in 1917-18, when I was a radio operator on the old USS WYOMING. Was in the Battle of Zeebrugen on the USS TEXAS and was in London when they bombed it from Zeppelins." 75 Patch

Several Raiders were certainly influenced by the example set by our Raider Chaplains. They too became men of the cloth later in life as Priests, missionaries and ministers. The REVEREND SHIRL BUTLER our present Raider Chaplain served in combat with the 4th Raider Battalion and 4th Marine Regiment on New Georgia, Guam and Okinawa.

NAVAJO CODE TALKERS

Navajo code talkers took part in many of the assaults the U.S. Marines conducted in the Pacific from 1942 to 1945 at New Georgia, Tarawa, Peleliu, Iwo Jima, and Okinawa. They served in all six Marine divisions, Marine Raider battalions and Marine parachute units, transmitting messages by telephone and radio in their native language, a code that the Japanese never broke.

The idea to use Navajo, for secure communications came from Philip Johnston, the son of a missionary to the Navajos and one of the few non-Navajos who spoke their language fluently. Johnston, reared on the Navajo reservation, was a World War I veteran who knew of the military's search for a code that would withstand all attempts to decipher it. He also knew that Native American languages--notably Choctaw--had been used in World War I to encode messages.

Johnston believed Navajo answered the military requirement for an un-decipherable code because Navajo is an unwritten language of extreme complexity. Its syntax and tonal qualities, not to mention dialects, make it unintelligible to anyone without extensive exposure and training. It has no alphabet or symbols, and is spoken only on the Navajo lands of the American Southwest. One estimate indicates that less than 30 non-Navajos, none of them Japanese, could understand the language at the outbreak of World War II.

Early in 1942, Johnston met with Major General Clayton B. Vogel, the commanding general of Amphibious Corps, Pacific Fleet, and his staff to convince them of the Navajo language's value as code. Johnston staged tests under simulated combat conditions, demonstrating that Navajos could encode, transmit, and decode a three-line English message in 20 seconds. Machines of the time required 30 minutes to perform the same job. Convinced, Vogel recommended to the Commandant of the Marine Corps that the Marines recruit 200 Navajos.

In May 1942, 29 Navajo recruits first attended boot camp. Then, at Camp Pendleton, Oceanside, California, this first group created the Navajo code. They developed a dictionary and numerous words for military terms. The dictionary and all code words had to be memorized during training. Once a Navajo code talker completed his training, he was sent to a Marine unit deployed in the Pacific Theater. The code talkers' primary job was to talk, transmitting information on tactics and troop movements, orders and other vital battlefield communications over telephones and radios. They also acted as messengers, and performed general Marine duties. Praise for their skill, speed and accuracy accrued throughout the war. At Iwo Jima, Major Howard Connor, 5th Marine Division signal officer, declared, "Were it not for the Navajos, the Marines would never have taken Iwo Jima." Connor had six Navajo code talkers working around the clock during the first two days of the battle. Those six sent and received over 800 messages, all without error. The Japanese, who were skilled code breakers, remained baffled by the Navajo language. The Japanese chief of intelligence, Lieutenant General Seizo Arisue, said that while they were able to decipher the codes used by the U.S. Army and Army Air Corps, they never cracked the code used by the Marines.

Raider Navajo "Code Talkers " host, CECIL E. McCLELLAND, 1E writes, "The first reunion of Marine Corps Code Talkers took place in July 1971 in Window Rock, AZ. Those attending were: JOHN BENALLY, SIDNEY BENONI, WILFRED BILLIE, PAUL BLATCHFORD, CARL GORMAN, JIMMIE KING SR., ALEX WILLIAMS SR., JUDGE W. DEAN WILSON (YAZZIE)

1E CECIL MC CLELLAND, Farmington, NM writes, "I was invited to attend the first Marine Birthday party, 11 Nov 78 at the Red Rock, NM Convention Center, near Gallup. One of he Navajo Code Talkers was EUGENE ROANHORSE CRAWFORD, of Hawaiian Village. Ga1lup, NM . In the Nov 78 RAIDER PATCH, HARRY L. FORBES, 1C HQ asked about Navajo Code Talkers. They are alive and well. This party was the best I have ever attended. We had CODE TALKER speeches, banquet, cake cermony and dance, a Navajo Drill Team and a Navajo Color Guard. The Navajo's have a very fine ROTC program for Marines at Kienta, AZ. It makes big tears come into your eyes when you see these fine young Marines. I travel all over the UTE, NAVAJO and ZUNY Reservations and am aquainted with many Indian Marines. My friends just couldn't believe we still had the 03 SPRINGFIELD rifles, in 1942 on Guadalcanal. They should have tried the chow. Patch 79

1 H&S EUGENE ROANHORSE CRAWFORD, " I joined, the 1st Raiders in time for New Georgia, and was at Rice Anchorage, Enogai Inlet, Bairoko Harbor, Auckland, NZ. Stand by for Iwo Jima and then into Okinawa." EDITOR: The FIRST use of Navajo Language CODE TALKERS in the Pacific occurred on New Georgia, although Code Talkers were with the 2nd Raiders on Guadalcanal, but not used in that capacity.

Paul J. Redmond, Legion of Merit, Bronze Star.

Robert J. Cronin, Silver Star, Purple Heart.

USS Little - WWI 4 Stack Destroyer Before Being Converted to APD High Speed Destroyer Transport

Water, Water Everywhere on Bougainville

Walking Wounded Going to Aid Station

War Dog Patrol

Navajo Code Talkers

8

Russell Islands

Assault on Pavuvu

Finally, a break! Marines landing on Pavuvu were unopposed.

OCCUPATION OF PAVUVU, RUSSELL ISLANDS
3RD MARINE RAIDER BATTALION
21 FEBRUARY 1943

As part of a defensive effort to keep the Russell Islands from being used as an airfield from which to attack Guadalcanal only 50 miles away, Admiral Halsey ordered they be seized.

The Army 43rd Infantry Division, 3rd Marine Raider Battalion, 11th Marine Defense Bn and one half 35th Naval Construction Bn were chosen for the task. The Raiders were to seize Pavuvu while the Army was to land on Banika. As no Japanese Naval or Air Force appeared to protect the islands it was anticipated the landings would be unopposed.

The Raiders went ashore in their rubber boats before dawn on 21 February 1943 without a shot being fired. Several worn trails suggested heavy Japanese activity on the island, but no Japanese were to be found on the island in the 30 days the Raiders remained there.

The native islanders told the Raiders that the Japanese had left the island a few weeks before their landing. As on most of the islands occupied by the Japanese the islanders told of being mistreated, with their crops destroyed and their pigs killed. They were close to starvation when the Raiders arrived and began to share their food with them. Later on both survived on Japanese rations found on the island.

As on most of the Pacific Islands, medical problems surfaced in a short period of time. Sickbay visits for treatment of malaria, jaundice, acute infections, gastro-enteritis, pharyngitis, fungus infection, and infected body ulcers, kept the Corpsmen and Doctors busy.

A Navy torpedo base was established on the island, with the Raiders providing security and labor parties, before they were withdrawn on 21 March and returned to their base on Espiritu Santo for further training prior to their assault on Bougainville.

New Georgia
Captured Emaciated Japanese Prisoner of War

9

Bougainville

Pfc Henry Gurke, 3DM, Medal of Honor

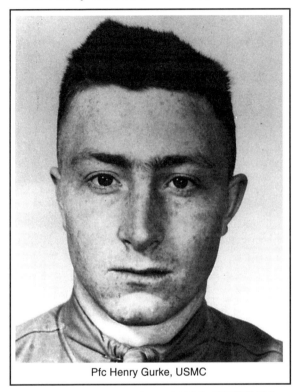

Pfc Henry Gurke, USMC

OFFICIAL MEDAL OF HONOR CITATION

"For extraordinary heroism and courage above and beyond the call of duty while attached to the Third Marine Raider Battalion during action against enemy Japanese forces in the Solomon Islands area on 9 November 1943. While his platoon was engaged in the defense of a vital road block near Empress Augusta Bay on Bougainville Island, Private First Class Gurke, in company with another Marine, was delivering a fierce stream of fire against the main vanguard of the Japanese. Concluding from the increasing ferocity of grenade barrages that the enemy was determined to annihilate their small, two-man foxhole, he resorted to a bold and desperate measure for holding out despite the torrential hail of shells. When a Japanese grenade dropped squarely into the foxhole, Private Gurke, mindful that his companion manned an automatic weapon of superior fire power and therefore could provide more effective resistance, thrust him roughly aside and flung his own body over the missile to smother the explosion. With unswerving devotion to duty and superb valor, Private Gurke sacrificed himself in order that his comrade might live to carry on the fight. He gallantly gave his life in the service of his country."

BOUGAINVILLE, EMPRESS AUGUSTA BAY
CAPE TOROKINA, PURUATA ISLAND, KOIARA
RAID AND THE BATTLES OF PIVA FORKS,
COCONUT GROVE AND NUMA NUMA TRAIL

1ST MARINE RAIDER REGIMENT
2ND MARINE RAIDER BATTALION
3RD MARINE RAIDER BATTALION
1 NOVEMBER 1943-12 JANUARY 1944

Bougainville was the largest of the Solomon Islands but not a British run island. The natives there would prove to be no friends of the Americans as were the other Solomon Islanders. It had to be in back of the minds of the planners that unlike the natives of Malaita it was unknown if they had ceased being fierce head hunters.

The low swampy, timbered coast had limited protection from onshore winds and was very poor for digging in. There were meager, muddy foot trails not conducive for vehicular traffic.

Three medical companies landed on D-Day and were able to set up each field hospital by 13 Nov. There was a low incidence of malaria however, Marines that had been in Samoa, had a high incidence of filariasis. Combat fatigue and war neurosis caused a larger number of casualties on Bougainville than any other disease. These cases outnumbered malaria 3 to 1.The main cause was determined to be lack of confidence in leaders, lack of training and physical exhaustion. Although there is no breakdown available, the incidence among Raiders was almost non-existent.

The wounded were again mostly evacuated; 1,190 by LST's, 309 DD's,313 APD's, 99 AP's and 236 APA's. PBY's played a minor roll and for the first time DC transport planes were used in larger numbers to determine their usefulness. The Marine Corps surgeon cast doubt on their use for evacuating the seriously wounded. The DC's proved very effective later in the war in the southwest pacific island hopping campaigns.

Japanese forces occupied the Island in 1941 and set up defensive perimeters far superior to anything the Raiders had yet faced. Bougainville had six heavily defended airfields all within easy reach of Truk considered to be the strongest of all the Japanese held Islands.

Rear Admiral Theodore Wilkinson of the South Pacific Command was responsible for the planning of the operation, with Marine LtGen Vandergrift, in charge of the Third Amphibious

Force. The 3rd Marine Division, including Seabee and Pioneer units, was reinforced by the Second Marine Raider Regiment 2nd Marine Raider Bn, and 3rd Marine Raider Bn, 1st Marine Parachute Regiment, with the 37th Army Infantry Division in reserve. There were three Medical Companies prepared to set up field hospitals. The 8th New Zealand Brigade Reinforced was assigned the task of attacking the Treasury Islands.

THE PURUATA CAMPAIGN

Puruata was just offshore from the beaches of Bougainville Island, about 300 by 500 yards in size. On 1 Nov l943 at Empress Augusta Bay the 3rd Raider Battalion (Less M Co), under LTCOL J. FRED BEANS landed on Puruata Island, some 800 yards from the main Japanese defenses at Buretoni Mission. And on Cape Torokina fought in the battles of Piva Forks, Coconut Grove and Numa Numa Trail. On 22-23 Nov 43. K Co conducted a reconnaissance mission in the vicinity of Reini-Tehessi River areas East of Cape Torokina.

They landed at Green Beach 1 and by 1800 on 2 November had destroyed the defending enemy troops including a few who tried to swim to a small neighboring island called Torokina some 400 yards off Cape Torokina and the mainland.

The island was fiercely defended by about 100 well dug in enemy units. Heavy anti-boat gunfire from Puruata played havoc with the landing craft as they passed the island. There was light firing until about 200 yards inland where they met heavy resistance from over 25 bunkers that had survived the Naval bombardment, and suffered their first casualties. PVT OSBORN CAMMACK, though wounded, destroyed a machine gun nest and was able to wipe out the position.

I Co surged forward through enemy opposition to secure the Village, but discovered GYSGT LEYDEN was missing. It was here Corpsman MARVIN SOMMERS PHM3 volunteered to go back and find him. SOMMERS found him critically wounded and while dressing his wounds was himself hit by sniper fire. When nothing was heard from the Corpsman back in the village, FATHER CRONIN and Pvt RED HOWARD volunteered to go back and look for them. After finding them they had to fight their way back to the village while carrying the two wounded men. GySgt LEYDEN died with Corpsman SOMMERS desperately clinging to life until his death on 28 Mar 44. On the night of 2 Nov PhM3 JOHN G. HOWARD was killed when a Jap bomber made a near direct hit on a nearby anti aircraft gun.

Nine Raider's were KIA on D-Day and eight others were killed D-Day +1 and D-Day +2, with 22 wounded. Corpsmen MANGRUM and SOMMERS were killed. Corpsman MANUEL MAYA, was wounded while treating a wounded Raider but refused to be evacuated. Raider, PVT ALFRED TSOSIE, was the first Navajo Code Talker to lose his life. Most of the wounded were evacuated to the USS Fuller before night fell.

The 3rd Raiders were then returned to Bougainville where they moved to a position in the center of the island and started to secure that area.

RAIDERS KILLED IN ACTION AT PURUATA
1 NOV- 3 NOV

BREWER, BOBBY	HEFNER,ROBERT
HOWARD, JOHN	HUDSON,GEORGE
KAFUT, WALTER	LEYDEN, JOHN
MANGUM, CECIL*	McCAFFERY,JOSEPH
MCCOMBE, WILLIAM	RUSSELL,CARLETON
SCANLON,RAYMOND	SCIANICALAPORE, S.
SOMMERS,MELVIN*	STUDER,JOHN
TSOSIE, ALFRED	WISEMAN, EMMETT
WHEELER, JAMES	
*CORPSMEN	

RAIDER CHAPLAIN ROBERT J. CRONIN
The President of the United States takes pleasure in presenting the SILVER STAR TO ROBERT J. CRONIN
LIEUTENANT LTJG, CHC, USNR
For service in the following CITATION:
For conspicuous gallantry and intrepidity in action against the enemy while serving with the Third Marine Raider Bn., during a landing on Puruata Island, British Solomon Islands on 1 November 1943. After a landing had been effected, Chaplain Cronin was informed that a Marine was dying of wounds received in the interior of an enemy infested area. Although not required by duty to do so, he organized a stretcher party and without regard for his personal safety proceeded to the side of the wounded man. He administered the Last Sacraments and remained with him until he died. His conduct and personal courage were in keeping with the highest traditions of the United States Naval Service.
For the President, /s/ W.F. HALSEY, Admiral, USN

SILVER STAR MEDAL AWARDED TO
CORPSMAN HERO ON PURUATA ISLAND

The President of the United States takes pleasure in presenting the SILVER STAR TO MANUEL M. MAYA PHARMACIST MATE THIRD CLASS, USN

For service in the following CITATION:

"For extraordinary heroism in connection with military operations against the Japanese forces, while attached to the 3rd Marine Raider Battalion during the landing attack of the 3rd Marine Division, reinforced, at Puruata Island, British Solomon Islands, on 1 November 1943. Pharmacist Mate Maya accompanied a platoon engaged in and assault on the Japanese position consisting of 3 pill boxes, strongly organized for defense and protected by snipers armed with light machine guns and grenades, in trees and on the ground. Having been wounded himself during the fire fight while assisting the Marine wounded, he gave himself cursory first aid and continued to treat the other wounded under fire until he believed the fighting had ceased, whereupon he arranged for his own evacuation. Before this could be accomplished the fire-fight was resumed with the full intensity with every weapon the enemy could bring to bear. Maya thereupon refused to be evacuated, and with complete disregard for his own safety, moved among the assault troops as they fell wounded, rendering first aid under a constant hail of enemy fire. The high order of courage he displayed and his prompt assistance of those wounded, materially contributed to the morale of the troops and aided in reducing the enemy position. His gallant conduct was in keeping with the highest traditions of the U.S. Naval Service.

3I PFC M. W. "DUTCH" DOORNBOS, "A BAR man in the 1st Squad, 1st Platoon, "I" Company, under MARINE GUNNER YELANICH, New York, NY, tells it like it was, D-Day on Puruata Island, Bougainville. "GYSGT JOHN R. LEYDEN, (KIA 01 Nov 1943) was a real Marine. He got it on Puruata, a little island that lies just across the channel from Bougainville. The 3rd Raiders "I" and K" Co's assaulted Puruata on the channel side. We advanced 200 yards in skirmish formation against light opposition until "K" Co. on our right ran into heavy machine guns and several light Nambu's. We continued to advance across the native village compound while the Japs laid, down a knee mortar barrage. We had a lot of casualties but charged on through to the beach. The enemy had disappeared into the dense jungle. It wasn't until we'd moved back to the village that we learned

GUNNY LEYDEN had been hit. One of the "K" Co Corpsmen, MELVIN SOMMERS (KIA 1 Nov 1943) went out in the brush and found him. AUTHOR - as is often noted by Marine Officers, "many men who performed courageous acts never received a medal." This is certainly the case of Corpsman MELVIN SOMMERS, who was killed when treating Leyden's wounds, but received no recognition, while Chaplin Cronin and MAYA were both awarded the Silver Star for their rescue attempt.

My buddy, PFC O.L. "RED" HOWARD and our Chaplain, FATHER ROBERT J. CRONIN went after the wounded men. LEYDEN was dying but he kept training his field glasses around trying to locate the sniper. A couple of minutes later they hit the deck as about a dozen Japs passed by. As soon as they had passed HOWARD heaved every grenade he had. And charged firing his M-1. LEYDEN lived long enough to see the JAPS get theirs, although RED was wounded in the hand. About that time a Jap Banzai charge on our positions in the village ended with their total destruction. We mowed them down like falling dominoes. After that only a few snipers were left. FATHER CRONIN and RED HOWARD came in carrying the wounded Corpsman and told us about LEYDEN. None of us will ever forget him he was so cool and fearless. A few days later at the Piva Trail Roadblock I was wounded in the elbow and leg. RED HOWARD'S hand had became infected and both of us were evacuated back to Guadalcanal."

3L&4 Hq Daniel Scheer was a Sgt Radioman in the 3rd Raiders. He wrote, "I had two Navaho Code Talkers attached to my radio team on Bougainville. 3Hq – Alfred Tsosie was KIA on Puruata 01 Nov 43 and one of the Yazzie's. (Editor: Dan Yazzie and Joe S. Yazzie were both Code Talkers with the 3rd Raiders on Bougainville). We had 13 Code Talkers attached to the Raider Regiment at that time."

BOUGAINVILLE, BRITISH SOLOMON ISLANDS
2ND MARINE RAIDER REGIMENT
2ND MARINE RAIDER BATTALION
1 NOV 1943

The 2nd Marine Raider Battalion reinforced with Co M, 3rd Marine Raider Battalion went aboard the USS George Clymer (APA-27) at Guadalcanal on 30 Oct 43. They participated in the assault landing at Cape Torokina, Empress Augusta Bay, Bougainville, BSI on 1 Nov 43 that was spearheaded by Co M, 3rd Raiders. The Bay that was located some distance from the heavily defended airfields at either end of the island, had what appeared to be the most suitable beaches for a landing. The plan was to establish a beachhead, then bring in supplies and equipment to build a landing strip for fighters. Invasion forces consisted of 14,321 troops included the 1st Marine Dog Platoon with their 24 Dobermans and German shepherds.

The landing met with several obstacles. The Japanese defense of the beaches was stronger than anticipated. The 40,000 troops on the island had been reported stationed mainly around the airfields, and aerial reconnaissance photos did not reveal the extensive system of bunkers in the jungles above the beaches.

The Marines who landed west of the mouth of the Koromokina River encountered steep slopes and shoals on which more than 80 of their amphibious craft foundered. Those landing east of the Koromokina were caught in crossfire from machine guns on the offshore islet of Puruata and on Cape Torokina east of the beach. A small contingent of Marines knocked out the gun emplacement on the Cape after it had destroyed or damaged 14 landing craft; the 3rd Raiders captured Puruata.

It was here that a Japanese bullet struck the helmet of CHAPLAIN McCORKLE, gone through the helmet, and ricocheted around in it and exited out the rear while leaving just a scratch on his ear. McCorkle was awarded the Silver Star for his heroism on Cape Torokina.

Washburn was ordered to move the battalion inland and M Co, 3rd BN were to set up a road block further up the trail to stop any enemy approach. The 2nd BN would soon find out the value of the 1st War Dog Platoon with Clyde Henderson in charge. The first night ashore the men were able to get a good nights sleep as the dogs would warn them of any enemy attempts to infiltrate their lines.

Two Raiders were KIA on patrol but more lives were saved when Otto a Doberman scout dog alerted the men to a hidden machine gun position. Caesar a messenger dog twice alerted his handlers of Jap infiltrator's before being wounded as the Japs shot him twice and he was evacuated on a stretcher to the aid station. Prior to that Caesar had delivered 9 messages safely. Jack, a Belgian Shepherd even though wounded carried an urgent message requesting reinforcements. Rex a Doberman Scout dog alerted the Raiders of infiltrator's several times before his handler William N. Hendrickson was KIA, becoming the first War Dog Platoon fatality.

3RD RAIDERS KILLED ON CAPE TOROKINA AND THE BEACH ON D - DAY

KAFUT, WALTER   SILER, JOSEPH B.
WHEELER, JAMES

Captain Joe Griffiths G Co went on a patrol to protect an engineer party on the west bank of the Piva River that resulted in the death of 2 Raiders and 3 wounded.

RAIDERS KILLED ON SURVEY PARTY PATROL

HATT, WALTER D.   MORRELL, WILLIAM R.

2ND RAIDERS KILLED IN ACTION

BEHNISCH, LESTER   HATT, WALTER D.
HENDRICKSON,WM.   HOWARD, JOHN*
MCCAFFREY,JOSEPH   MORRELL, WILLIAM
RIEGEL, JAMES   ROGERS, WILLIAM
STUDER, JOHN   WISEMAN,E.P,
*CORPSMAN

JACK, a messenger dog, and his handler were wounded but still managed to carry a message requesting reinforcements needed at the roadblock. The Japanese continued to attack the roadblock and attacked with infiltration groups supported by 90mm mortars. REX a scout dog detected the Japanese approach and alerted the Raiders before the attack. His handler was killed and Rex suffered a loss of hearing.

2ND RAIDERS KILLED IN ACTION AT THE ROAD BLOCK

ANKELE, ROBERT   CAMPBELL,STUART
DARNELL, JAMES   FORD, RICHARD
GORACK, IGNATIUS   HAJIC, ROBERT E
HENDERSON,WM.*   WALKER, FRANK
WARD, JAMES J.   WATSON, FRANK
* War Dog Handler

Doctor Stigler was then the only original Regimental Raider doctor left. He, Corpsmen Olsen, Cantral, Casey,

Favinger, Hart, Hogan, Proctor and Reite were left with 2nd
Raider doctor's Knox and Ware to treat the wounded and face
the island's myriad of diseases such as malaria, polio, dengue
fever, hookworm and yaws. Purple feet, armpits and crotches
were everywhere after being treated with gentian violet. Few
had any premonition of the 2nd and 3rd Bn Corpsmen who would
be killed during this operation.

When there was a lull in the battle the Corpsmen and
Doctors had more work to do than ever as men who had ignored
problems during battle would line up to have their jungle rot and
immersion feet treated. Doctor McGowen, the BN dentist always
had a long line waiting for his expertise.

It had rained constantly for 7 days adding greatly to the
discomfort of the men as it was most difficult to find a place to
dig a foxhole. Most nights they spent the night sitting in water.

The most difficult job was in evacuating the wounded.
Walking wounded could often evacuate them selves. It took 4
men to handle a stretcher even if the man was small, through
several hundred yards of mud holes 4 - 5 feet deep in some
places. Cooks and bakers and band members were most often
used as stretcher bearers.

If tanks were available it was a godsend as it took 2 extra
men for security or relief to make their way stumbling over hidden
roots through pouring rain, falling in the mud and dropping the
stretcher. Even aboard the tanks the ride was extremely rough
and it often took several hours to reach the field hospital. Enemy
infiltrators managed to get through to the field hospital and bullets
poured through the tents as Doctors and Corpsmen performed
surgery and attended the wounded.

PIVA AND NUMA NUMA TRAIL BATTLE

Both Raider Battalions now battled to reach the junction
of the Piva and Numa Numa trails losing 14 men and their first
War Dog in the process. Attacks were slow to develop as the
men had to cut their way though vegetation mixed with many
thorny vines. One razor type vine called the "wait a bit", could
bring an attack to a standstill as the men figured a way to escape
it. Aid stations were stuck any place a clearing and somewhat
dry ground could be found, It was here that Pfc HENRY GURKE
earned the Medal of Honor when he threw himself on a grenade
to protect his foxhole buddy during an attack.

2ND AND 3RD MARINE RAIDERS KILLED IN ACTION AT THE PIVA TRAIL AND NUMA NUMA JUNCTION

BIBAEFF, WILLIE	COUPE,JAMES
DIERKER,STANLEY	GOEHRI, HOMER
GURKE, HENRY	GURNEY, DONALD
KELLERMAN,HUGH	KUNG WAR DOG
LARSON, JOHN M.	MARKO, ROBERT
MATTHEWS,THOMAS	PACE, EUGENE W.
REYNOLDS,HAROLD	RICE , WILLIAM M.
SWANK, FOREST R.	

On 10 Nov after warding off attacks on the division flank, the 2nd Raider Regiment moved into bivouac. This didn't mean any rest for Corpsmen, Doctors or Dentists, On the contrary, sick calls were always larger after a battle. Raiders ignored their minor ills while in combat. They lined up for any number of problems when they came off the line.

While patrolling in the vicinity of the Piva River M Co 3rd Raiders lost 4 KIA and 2 WIA.

3RD MARINE RAIDERS KILLED IN ACTION AT COCONUT GROVE 13-14 NOV 1943

DENNIS, LEONARD	KOWALSKI, ARTHUR
PAINTER,THOMAS	WOOD, ALLEN

L Co of the 3rd RAIDERS reinforced Cibik's Ridge when the Japanese launched an attack supported by 90 mm mortars and artillery just before dawn. 3 men were killed and several wounded.

RAIDERS KILLED IN ACTION AT CIBICK'S RIDGE

GIBSON, WALTER	HUGHES,RICHARD
MOSEBRUCKER, J.*	
*CORPSMAN	

Japanese artillery wounded 2 and killed 2 Raiders during the battle of the Piva Forks

---

RAIDERS KILLED IN ACTION AT THE BATTLE OF PIVA FORKS 19-20 NOV AND 21-25 NOV 1943

BARRITT, EARL E.   MEISTER, ARMIN
TULLOS, C.B.

On 21 December the 2nd Raider Battalion relieved the 3rd Marines. They also assumed control of an outpost manned by the Army Co B 145th Infantry. On 22 Dec the Army sent, a platoon size patrol that included ROLO, one of the best scout dogs and his 2 handlers. ROLO made an excellent alert the patrol leader did not believe, and he ordered his men on. The patrol was hit by an ambush a few yards further and in the fire fight ROLLO was killed and his 2 handlers were hit with one later dying of his wounds.

Following the end of fighting on the island, Col Shapley stated, "the War Dog Platoon has proven itself to be an unqualified success!"

WAR DOG AND HANDLER KILLED IN ACTION

FRIEDRICH, RUSSELL T.   ROLLO

During the period 26-30 Nov, 4 Raiders were killed by enemy mortar fire.

RAIDERS KILLED BY MORTAR FIRE IN DEC 1943

CAIN, CHARLES   MADSEN,CLAIRE
NELSON,CARMEN   KELSO, JAMES

**KOIARI RAID
M CO 3RD MARINE RAIDER BATTALION
1ST MARINE PARACHUTE BATTALION
29 NOV 1943**

(EDITOR: 76 PATCH) "The Koiari Raid was an operation similar to the Tasimboko Raid on Guadalcanal on 8 Sep 1942. For Koiari, M Company 3rd Raiders accompanied the 1st Parachute Battalion and landed in a Japanese supply dump, only this time the Marines were pinned down on three sides by heavy machine gun and mortar fire. The fierce battle raged for several hours, the Marines fighting with their backs to the ocean. Finally 3 Destroyers arrived and opened direct fire on the enemy at the flanks of the Marine perimeter while 155mm guns at Cape Torokina fired parallel to the shore. As darkness approached the Marines were able to safely evacuate the tenuous position. The landing force that had numbered 24 Officers and 505 enlisted, suffered total casualties of 22 KIA and 99 WIA.

3RD RAIDERS KILLED IN ACTION AT KOIARI

DAVIS, TED A. WILLIAMS, HERBERT
WOODALL, DONALD

MEDALS AWARDED 2ND & 3RD RAIDERS ON PURUATA, BOUGAINVILLE AND KOIARI

NAVY CROSS

BEANS, FRED BRODERICK,JOHN
CAMMACK,OSBORN DIERKER,STANLEY
McCAFFERY,J.P MENTCH, C. E.
QUIRK, BRYAN RIEGEL,JAMES
SABINI, JOHN WARNER,GORDON
WHERRY, JOHN

SILVER STAR

BAKER, WILLIAM BANGSER,LAWRENCE
BRACKETT,LANSFORD GORACK,IGNATIUS
HENDERSON,ROGER STEWART, S.G.
STUDER, JOHN WASHBURN,R.T
WILLARD,R.G. YOUNT, WM.

MEDALS AWARDED TO CORPSMEN HEROES ON BOUGAINVILLE

The President of the United States takes pleasure in presenting the SILVER STAR TO GERALD W. WARD, PHARMACIST MATE SECOND CLASS, USNR, JOSEPH R. WOOLDRIDGE PHARMACIST MATE THIRD CLASS USNR AND DANIEL WEBSTER, PHARMACIST MATE 2C, USNR
For service in the following CITATION:
"For conspicuous gallantry and intrepidity while serving with the 3rd Marine Raider Battalion during action against enemy Japanese forces in the Solomon Islands Area on 09 November 1943. While the platoon to which WARD, WOOLDRIDGE, and

WEBSTER were attached was engaged in the defense of a vital roadblock, the enemy, fanatically intent upon annihilating the Marine unit, kept up a merciless barrage from machine guns and mortar grenades. As wounded men began to fall under the torrential hail of Japanese shells, these men, throughout the duration of the action, made their way from one to the other across the exposed battle area, cheerfully rendering first aid under a deadly curtain of hostile fire. Their courageous devotion to duty, maintained with utter disregard for their personal safety, undoubtedly saved the lives of many of his comrades who other wise might have perished."

The Army Americal and 37th Infantry Divisions took over as the occupying forces with the withdrawal of the 3rd Marine Division and the 2nd, and 3rd Raider Battalions.

The 3rd Raider Bn was withdrawn from the combat zone on 12 Jan 44 and embarked aboard the SS President Adams, APA 19 for Tassafaronga, Guadalcanal, while the Second Raider Bn returned to Tassafaronga, Guadalcanal, BSI on 14 Jan 44 aboard the USS President Hayes (APA-21).

The Bougainville campaign remains one of the most resounding successes of the war in the Pacific in terms of the smooth coordination between the Navy and Marine Corps.

3K COL MARTIN J. "STORMY" SEXTON WROTE, " Jim, I had the privilege of observing Corpsmen in three wars and they were always there when needed. On Bougainville when I was hit at about 2330 I called out for our platoon Corpsman. He answered in the pitch black night, 'I'll see you in the morning.' I spent the time until daylight rationalizing whether I should be mad or reasonable. In the morning I was carried to the beach evacuation station and thanked the Corpsman with sincerity and appreciation." AUTHOR: Knowing that COL SEXTON didn't carry the nickname 'Stormy', without reason; I'm not sure I would have been more willing to face the Japs than incur his anger.

Stormy had a soft side though when it came to his Raider Marines.

At Bougainville, on 1 Nov 43, 1&3 BN RAIDER PFC FRANKLIN FITZ and EDWARD J. SITTING were isolated by enemy troops. FITZ killed 3 of the enemy and dragged the seriously wounded SITTING to a less exposed position. SITTING suffered additional critical wounds as FITZ attempted to treat his wounds while fighting off another attack. FITZ, unhesitatingly crossed fields of enemy fire several times, despite wounds he received in defending PVT SILLING, in order to find someone to help him get SILLING to a safe area and medical aid. Another

Raider was found and the 2 Marines removed SILLING from the area of hostile fire. FRANK FITZ was recommended for the Navy Cross, for this action, only to never hear anything about it again.

It wasn't until he mentioned the oversight to RAIDER COL MARTIN SEXTON IN 1995, the lost recommendation was resubmitted. Unfortunately the review board reduced his Medal from the Navy Cross to the Bronze Star on 28 April 1998. FITZ was once again a victim of sloppy paperwork. He later discovered a typo in his application left out the fact he was wounded while protecting SILLING. Had that statement been included, it would have made a profound effect on the decision by the Review Board, and FITZ would probably have been awarded the Navy Cross!

AUTHOR: It has been an honor for me to know STORMY SEXTON and FRANK FITZ. They each typify the best of the Marine Corps, both on and off the field of battle!

2FHQ Former Corpsman, DR ROBERT B. KRAUSE (MD) wrote, " I joined the 2nd Raider Battalion in March 1943 on New Caledonia and served through Bougainville, Emirau, Guam & Okinawa, campaigns. I see DR DRUE WARE regularly at our annual State Medical Meeting, but I will never forget how he looked on 3 Nov 43 on Bougainville when our Jeep driver, TONY RELJA was killed by an artillery shell which landed on his head. We were in an L-shaped foxhole. DR WARE was in the other half of the foxhole and was uninjured. There are no atheists in foxholes. I recognized 2 fellow corpsmen on the Raider Roster Rolls, JOHN W. FASANA AND BERT FARBER. FARBER certainly did a fine job with G Company PIVA TRAIL on 8-9 Nov 43. My first casualty was, JOHN W. "BILL" STUDER 2F, Baker, OR who was mangled in both legs and scrotum from a Jap grenade that he saw the Jap throw. He rolled right over on top of it. When I reached him he was chewing his sulfa tablets and he asked, 'Doc, will I be able to have kids?' I made a stretcher with two small tree trunks and a Jap blanket from a nearby hut and sent him back to the beach. He died aboard ship that night 1 Nov 43. ROBERT ANKELE 2CF, was captured on 8 Nov and found two days later with a stake driven through his mouth. On New Caledonia, BOB ANKELE swiped my beer ration one night and got drunk. Later he apologized and explained that he knew his luck had run out and that he wouldn't make it through Bougainville."

3K COLONEL ARCHIE B. RACKERBY wrote, "I owe my life to WM. M. JANSSEN our K Co Corpsman. When I took a large chunk of anti-personnel rifle grenade in the neck during a training accident on Guadalcanal in 1944 my jugular vein was severed and the vocal cords paralyzed. As I was bleeding like a stuck pig, JANSSEN was beside me in seconds, quickly stopping the blood flow with several compresses from my kit and his medical bag. He administered two syrettes of morphine which stabilized me until GySgt ELDON MANEY AND Raiders from my platoon carried me through the jungle on a makeshift stretcher back to the battalion aid station where LT ROBERT PAINTER immediately sent me to MOB #8 hospital for surgery. Corpsmen MAYA AND WARD, were awarded the Silver Star on Bougainville. JIM CONNOLLY, Chestnut Hill, MA, was as night blind as anyone I have known, but he had the most amazing daytime distance visions! He spotted incoming flights of Jap aircraft long before anyone else could see them, or warning sirens were sounded. PHILIP ANDERSON, received and sent more mail than an entire squad. What great friends he had. JIM THOMAS, our supply sergeant, without whom we would have starved, under extremely adverse conditions got our "C" & "K" rations to us our ammo and even an occasional pair of socks."

3M DANIEL WEBSTER wrote, "I was a PHM2 in the initial landing on Bougainville, 1 Nov 43. Got the Silver Star for the Battle of Piva Trail, 9 Nov 43. SGT MIKE STRANK, Iwo Jima Flag Raiser, KIA Iwo Jima was my Platoon SGT and PFC HENRY GURKE was a Medal of Honor recipient in the same action." He adds, "As I look back at those days, I realize what a privilege and honor it was to be attached to the BEST USMC outfit EVER!" Patch 78

2HQ Dentist MARVIN C. McGOWEN wrote of his experiences with the Raiders in February 1990. "About an hour after I landed on Bougainville I received a Marine patient who had been in the forward group when his higgins boat beached. He was knocked down in the rush to get ashore and he fell on the metal ramp and broke off a tooth at the gum line. I proceeded to deaden his mouth and extract the root. When CHARLES LAMB received a promotion that required a medical exam, part of which was to read an eye chart, he said ' I can do that standing on my head', and he did just that! On one of our transports that had a dentist, we agreed to use one dental chair for the Marines and the other for the ships crew. When he started to complain about his duty aboard ship, I mentioned I could get him a transfer to the Marines and he quickly replied, 'Oh No, not that!' On Guam, another dentist and I, Harper Jung, were the only ones left to receive the casualties as they came in as the doctors and corpsmen were busy in surgery. Harper came over to me and asked, 'will you see if you can get this plasma needle in, I can't'. I tried and tried to penetrate that Marines skin but I couldn't either. THAT WAS ONE TOUGH MARINE, A REAL LEATHERNECK!"

AUTHOR: The rosters in this book do not differentiate between doctors and dentists because of space restrictions. Dentists provided an unheralded service to all Raider and Marine units. They were always there to give quick relief to their patients before, during and after every battle, and deserve more recognition than they ever received.

3M PHILIP O. IRVINE wrote, "How many N Co RAIDERS are around who remember the Koiari Raid on Bougainville. We went by sea about 10 miles down the coast from Cape Torokina in landing craft and landed right in the middle of a Japanese supply dump. Not likely to forget that little jaunt! I was on that last boat leaving the beach."

3HQ CHESTER MALINOWSKI in a 1990 letter said, " I never thought I would be talking about something that happened 47 years ago. We landed on Bougainville in time to be caught by the earthquake. I jumped out of my foxhole and reached back in it in the morning to look for my shoes. They weren't there, but buried and I found them. Glad that wasn't me! I found that being assigned to a heavy weapons platoon meant they had another body to load with ammunition. I believe the over-the-head carrier was meant for 4 shells, they gave me 6."

2E & 3L CAPT THOMAS P. DALY, "I joined the 2nd Raiders as Platoon Leader, 1st Platoon, E Co 2d Raiders on New Caledonia before the Bougainville operation. My Platoon was supposed to be the right flank of the assault wave at Empress Augusta Bay, but the Wave Commander, I think, lost his nerve and we landed about 1,000 yards up the beach. This left the second wave with the Battalion Commander LTCOL JOSEPH P. McCAFFERY and his staff to land where all the shooting was. COL McCAFFERY was killed; Chaplain WM H. McCORKLE, 2Hq, was wounded in the head, and Corpsman PHM3 JOHN G. HOWARD was killed. The assault companies marched down the beach, hit the mission defenses from the side and reduced the enemy forces with minimal casualties, in a very short time. Inland, my platoon was the first contact with the enemy in the Battle of Piva Trail. I was completely too close to an enemy mortar shell when it landed, about six yards away, knocking out one of my front teeth and rupturing my ear drum. The same mortar shell killed one of my squad leaders with a piece of shrapnel that hit him in the neck.

After Bougainville, I was transferred to 3rd Battalion, 4th

Marines, serving as Mortar Platoon Leader of L Co then Exec and Company Commander of I Co 3rd Bn, 4th Marines. I had a lucky wound on Guam from a knee mortar that landed between me and another fellow who was lying on the ground while I was kneeling talking on a field telephone. I had only a shallow wound in my leg but he died in the hospital from a multitude of shrapnel wounds. I got hit again on Okinawa on Sugar Loaf Ridge from a machine gun burst, the bullet hitting about an inch to the left of my spine and coming out underneath my armpit, but I was back to duty in 3 weeks. I was the first officer hit in my company, and when I got back, there was only one officer left who had been there 3 weeks before. "

3L HARRIS F. WALLACE, JR., PFC wrote, "I will always remember my first Christmas on Bougainvile. I was a late arrival and was assigned to group with LARRY SELIG and BILL REYNOLDS. I was promptly assigned to mess duty at the L Co. mess hall. The snipers were around and everyone had to carry his weapon. I was scrubbing out a big pot with sand and a sniper shot my pot! One of our guys got him immediately. My ears rang for hours. I know he could have hit me instead but he must have been a joker. Also remember the Christmas tree decorated by the cook tent guys and was decorated with shiny, curly strips from "C" rations and playing cards were also hung on the tree. The tree was a big leaf jungle tree like a magnolia."

3K GEORGE MacRAE, Virginia Beach, VA has permitted your author to use portions of his autobiography describing the Bougainville campaign and how he volunteered for the Raiders while in a replacement battalion in Noumea. "A Marine in jungle dress camouflage walked up to the evening chow line and announced they needed some replacements for the Raider Battalions. You had to be unmarried and no higher in rank than private to be accepted. When he added that their camp was having steak for dinner, I was third in line at the designated coconut tree to sign up for the Raiders.

One thing I shall always remember during field training were the giant spiders and the tough webs across the trails that could bring you to an abrupt halt. Often the spiders sitting in the middle of these large webs were of a size where the span of their legs would have covered a large dinner plate. The body could be as large as your fist and often marines shot them with rifles. Native fishermen rolled the web between their palms and used this for making nets and lines.

In early November we boarded a ship, the Bloemfontain, and sailed north. The ship stopped at Espiritu Santo for a few hours and than on to the island of Guadalcanal where we landed at Lunga Beach and went south by trucks to a camp along the coast. This was the "rear echelon" since the rest of the battalion had already gone north for the landing on Bougainville at Empress Augusta Bay on 1 November.

During our wait to go to Bougainville there was training in the form of conditioning hikes and firing on the rifle range. After the days work we would go to the river to swim or wash clothes. Before we arrived, the river was closed for a while when patrols found Japanese bodies in the upper part of the river. This was a risk in any river on any island during the war, you never knew what was upstream. It often paid to send a patrol to check out the territory even on a "secured" island.

We again boarded a Navy transport ship APA 19, the President Adams, I think, for Bougainville in early December and upon arrival at Empress Augusta Bay, where we were put on the front line of the perimeter along the Torokina River. Our company commander was Mike Nolan, a big man who was once a sparring partner for Lou Nova the boxer. Mike carried a BAR with such ease as if it were a child's BB gun. Normally whenever I saw him, he had a single barreled shotgun. I was first assigned to the Second Raiders headquarters company but a day later was transferred the first platoon of K Company, Third Raider Battalion, Second Raider Regiment. Our foxholes were under the jungle cover of ninety foot tall trees. We were assigned in fire teams of three men each. My two team members were Andy Mante from Brooklyn and "Muzzy" Marcellino from the Bronx. All I heard day after day was arguments about baseball until I finally banned it as a topic of conversation in our foxhole.

Our position was to cover a wide jungle trail leading to the river. This was almost a road and appeared to have been made earlier by an amtrak. With some effort we constructed a "block house" sort of defense by making our foxhole six feet square and about four feet deep and surrounded by tree trunks with gun ports. Mildew from the dampness got on all equipment especially leather items. The mildew would form overnight on your boots. Cleaning your weapon was a daily ritual. The odor of the jungle still can be remembered today.

We were allowed to go back to a rear area with a cook tent for a hot Christmas dinner. I ran across Corpsman Manuel Maya who had been awarded the Silver Star on Puruata. He stayed in the service and went to Korea and was at the Chosin Reservoir taking care of the Marines. He was discharged and returned to Avalon but when the Viet Nam thing happened,

Manuel wrote to the President when the Navy would not let him back in the service. He finally got in and went to Viet Nam for two tours. When I returned found Manuel working as a gardener at the country club. Most of the people at Avalon never knew of his part in those three wars.

Later when we returned to Guadalcanal I hung my 45 on the center tent post. One day when there was a surprise "shakedown" to locate any "liberated" paratrooper weapons, a Marine lieutenant eagerly grabbed it from its holster and upon checking the serial number asked who owned it. When I admitted to it being mine, he asked where I got it. I said it was my father's from World War One. He knew from the serial number being C-12063 that it was not a current war weapon and placed it back in it's holster.

The "old timers" told us about an event in the same chow line where we had our holiday dinner. It seems some of the Japanese, due to hunger, would dress in dungarees taken from dead marines and get in the chow line with the rest of the company. This one day a cooks helper, who kept a carbine on the serving table, suddenly grabbed his weapon and fired at one of the people in the chow line. All the rest of the men scattered thinking he had flipped his lid. When someone turned the body over, it turned out to be a Japanese who could have passed for a Mexican. They constantly tried to infiltrate our lines at night looking for food. The "word" was passed that if you fired your weapon at night you had better have a body handy at daybreak or else you automatically got thirty days "mess duty". I would have rather used a knife if necessary rather than risk getting put on mess duty.

There were patrols sent out across the river to probe for Japanese to see if they were building up for a major attack. I volunteered for these because I felt I needed the practice, as I had not gone through the regular stateside Raider training. The Japanese had a gun on rails in a tunnel dug in the side of a mountain. Each evening they would run the gun out and fire four or five rounds inside our perimeter. Navy dive bombers could not get them so some island natives went out one night with a patrol of Marines from K company. The patrol waited in Japanese territory while the natives went on in the darkness, found the gun, killed the guards and took the breech block from the gun. No more sporadic fire from that area and those inside the perimeter could go about their work.

At night I would lie half awake and listen to the deep sound of artillery back near the beach. First would be the muffled boom and then you would hear the swoosh of the projectile as it passed overhead and landed somewhere deep in the jungle across the river from our position. The explosion's were also muffled by the dense jungle but you hoped they were on target. As a line company, we never learned what was going on or the results of such activity. Our war was only fifty yards wide in front of us --- although we also looked to the rear.

We made a long foray across the river one day, to bury a Navy flier who had crashed in the wide valley while strafing the enemy. All the plane's instruments and weapons were smashed to keep them from the Japanese. On the way back to our lines we were alerted by our Doberman dogs and tumbled into a gully just in time to avoid being strafed --- by our own planes. Arriving at our lines after dark, the patrol had a few anxious moments since the pass word had been changed. But after some questions about who played for what baseball team, the line troops were convinced the incoming men were truly Raiders.

On 6 Dec 1943 there was a violent earthquake. The eighty foot tall trees in the jungle around us swayed back and forth. The two Marines from New York jumped out of our hole and grabbed nearby trees to keep their feet and yelling at me "What's happening, Mac?" I almost thought that I could see the floor of our bunker roll and pitch. Being from California and having experienced such tremors, I had an answer for them and kidded them about their concern. In other parts of our perimeter, several men were injured by falling trees. All our telephone lines, strung on trees, were knocked out.

There was an order calling for 100 percent alert on New Years Eve as the Japanese were expected to attack our perimeter by floating down the river on logs and trying to infiltrate our lines at night while the Americans were all supposedly celebrating and drunk. Almost everyone was awake that night but nothing happened.

When I was not "on watch", I slept with my 45 automatic under my left armpit. The exit to a small trench was on my left. I told Andy Mante, who was on watch, to wake me if he ever left the foxhole. This night I woke to see a figure stooped over to come in the entrance and had cocked my 45 ready to fire when I recognized the outline and ears of Andy Mante. He really got chewed out by me as I could have killed him. I told him I would not have minded killing him but I was afraid what would happen to me if I could not convince my superiors that he had left the hole without waking me. He never left again without making sure I was awake

The night noises in the jungle will long be remembered. It was difficult to tell the difference between a bird that made a sound like two hard sticks being knocked together and which was also a trick of the Japanese when probing our lines at night. Then there were other birds that had a raucous cry or screech. Then there were the rustlings and small noises of unknown animals such as the "banana bears" a sort of possum or rat like animal. All this kept you alert on your "watch" and I was too keyed up to ever think of nodding off. Moonlight nights were the worst as the moving of the trees in the wind created all sorts of shadows in motion and your imagination could discern all shapes of Japanese crawling through the undergrowth. The discipline in regard to firing at night was amazing. Most men preferred to rely on their combat knives rather than fire their weapon at night and risk 30 days mess duty at the galley behind the lines if no Japanese body was found by daylight.

On the 12 January 1944, we turned our positions over to the Army. I can still remember our lieutenant telling an Army captain that we had three riflemen in this pillbox but that they would probably want to put an anti-tank gun to cover the road! The final straw was that the army would not take our positions until we had strung a double apron of barbed wire in front of our lines with fire blackened tin cans holding pebbles attached. Also we had to "tidy up" the area before the Army would come in to take over! Someone in the cleanup detail threw a belt of ammo in a fire and we all hit the deck until the whirr of exploding ammo subsided.

The Army rode from the landing beach to the front lines in trucks but the trucks were sent back empty and we marched the three miles to the beach to show the army that we were still in good shape. All I had was my rifle, a bandoleer of ammo and a tooth brush and the clothes I was wearing. Everything else had rotted away from the humidity and mildew. As we passed a Seabee camp the cooks helpers brought us scrambled egg sandwiches on white bread -- it sure tasted great after all the C rations we had eaten on the line. They also offered clean socks and shirts to those who needed them, that's the reason Marines and Seabees are so close. Sort of a mutual admiration society.

We left from the beach aboard landing craft and boarded Navy transports off the bay for the trip back to Guadalcanal. Our APA 19, was the President Adams one of the Unholy Four, the others being the President Hayes (APA 20) and APA 18, the President Jackson. The fourth was APA 21 the Crescent City. From the beach to the transports our route was off the end of a fighter strip and we all ducked as Marine F4U's roared a few feet above us in taking off on a mission. On the way south to our new camp at Guadalcanal we heard on the ships loud speaker system that the Japanese had made an all out attack on the Army at the perimeter around Empress August Bay after the Marines left. Scuttlebutt had it that we were going to have to turn around and go back which fortunately did not happen as the Army held their ground.

Arriving at the 'Canal on 14 Jan, we were put ashore well north of all the other military camps and told to build our own camp. For some reason the Raiders were always isolated from the other Marine Units. Several of us were put on a work detail to take some supplies such as galley stoves and various boxes and crates ashore. A large tank landing craft came alongside and we unloaded gear from the cargo net lowered to the boat from our ship. At the beach we unloaded the many crates and boxes above the water line. After three trips to the ship the work detail was secured and we were told we could sleep ashore. All we had were ponchos in which to roll up in and we were all so tired we slept on the ground under the coconuts trees lining he beach. The man next to me said, "Mac, something is crawling on my poncho". I lit my Ronson lighter and in the faint glow we say this huge coconut crab on his chest. Needless to say he jumped up and fell over several other men and got roundly cussed for waking them. I threw the crab toward the water and pulled my poncho tightly around my neck to avoid any more of these ugly things and drifted off to sleep.

It was during this time that I had my first toothache and went across the road to the battalion dentist who was, of course, an officer. When you sat in the dental chair you also had to supply the foot power to pedal a bicycle contraption which powered the dental drill. You were told that, no matter what happened, you were not to stop peddling. That was an order given by the dentist. This type of Marine powered dental chair was similar to the unit described by 4 DQ PAT ALMOND, originally set up by Raider Dentist Tessman, Navy Dental Corps, on Espiritu Santo in 1943.

It was during January and February that the training continued for whatever the next assignment would be. One day in late January all Third battalion troops were assembled in the movie area -- coconut logs for seats -- and we were told the Raiders were to be disbanded effective on 1 February. We were stunned at the news but knew that some of the higher ups in the Corps did not agree with the Raider type organization. We were told that the four Raider Battalions were to be formed into the old Fourth Marine Regiment. This was the old China regiment. Some of their men had been captured on Corregidor and Bataan while some others were taken prisoner at Tiensen and Tsingtao, China before the Japanese invaded the Philippines.

3L Corpsman, PHM1C JOHN J. SMITH, JR., "I started with the 3rd Raiders on Samoa and went through Bougainville. I didn't do anything outstanding except use up a lot of Band-Aids and Aspirin. I was recalled to active duty for Korea and sure enough back to the Marines, but that is another story! I was sure sorry to read of the death of Medal of Honor Raider, GYSGT WILLIAM G "RED" WALSH, 3L, (KIA 27 Feb 45 Iwo Jima). He and I dug in together a lot of nights on Bougainville. I still have a Catholic medal he gave me which was sent to him by his brother, a Catholic priest."

1ST MARINE WAR DOG PLATOON

A War Dog Training Center was set up at Camp Knox, Camp Lejeune, NC in January 1943 and the first dog sworn and signed into the Marine Corps was a Boxer named Fritz who was joined by 14 Doberman Pinschers that were donated by Baltimore, MD and Canton, OH Pinscher Club of America members.

The Marine Corps was the only service to have a service record book for their dogs. Their service number was tatooed inside their right ear and entered in their service record along with date of birth, date of enlistment, call name, breed and dates and type of training received. Following physicals they went through a six week obedience training course.

Dogs enlisted as Privates just like Marines and were promoted on the basis of their length of service. After three months the Dogs became a Private First Class, one year a Corporal, two years a Sergeant, three years a Platoon Sergeant, four years a Gunny Sergeant, and after five years a Master Gunny Sergeant. The Dogs could eventually outrank their handlers. Marine Devil Dogs lived a military life in the Corps. Roll call and inspection was a daily routine, except in combat. One dog, 4th Marines WWII Mascot Soochow, was a Jap POW for 3 Years!

The dog handlers were just out of boot camp or transfers from other outfits. Prior handling of dogs was not a requirement. The dogs were taught to heel, down, crawl, come, or stay on both voice commands and arm and hand signals. During this early training, no Marine was allowed to molest or play with another Marine's dog.

Messenger dogs had two handlers and were taught to carry messages, ammunition or special medical supplies from one handler to the other handler, avoiding all other men. They were subjected to overhead rifle and machine gun fire and explosions of heavy charges of dynamite and TNT to simulate nearly as possible actual battlefield conditions.

The scout dogs had only one handler and were trained to alert the troops of the enemy, but not to bark and tell the enemy where the troops were. The detection of the enemy was signaled by the dogs, not by barking, but in different ways.The dogs were trained not to attack as this part of the dog's job was so important that the Marines did not want to risk them by getting them involved in an attack. The Marines stated that they had enough weapons to attack the Japanese with, they did not need dogs to do that.

Upon their arrival overseas the 1st War Dog Platoon commander, Lt. Henderson said, 'We felt lost when we came out here, everyone looked on us as a curiosity and wondered what we were supposed to do. We weren't too sure ourselves." Lucky for the First Platoon, Colonel Shapley and his 1st Marine Raider Regiment was billeted near where the dog platoon setup camp. One day, the Colonel saw an exhibition of how the dogs delivered messages and immediately asked that the dogs be attached to his Raiders. Eager for a "sponsor" and knowing the Raiders reputation, Lt. Henderson quickly agreed. Neither outfit ever regretted the move. The two groups trained together at the advance base, which was the jumping off spot for Bougainville, the dogs and their handlers learning the ways of the Raiders and the Raiders learning how to work with the dog teams.

The 1st War Dog Platoon served with the 2nd Raider Battalion on Bougainville. It was here the 1st Marine Dog Platoon proved it's worth to the Corps in combat . The Marines landed on Bougainville, the largest island in the Solomons, on November 1, 1943. The 24 canine members of the 1st Marine Dog Platoon was sent ashore under heavy mortar and rifle fire just one hour after the first Marines hit the beach, and were dispatched to various companies according to prearranged plans. The 1st Marine Dog Platoon consisted of 48 enlisted men working in pairs as handlers for the 21 Dobermans and three Shepherds, plus six enlisted instructors and headquarters personnel.

The First War Dog Platoon saw action on Bougainville, Guam, and Okinawa. The 2nd War Dog Plt and 3rd War Dog Platoons, commanded by 1 st Lt. William W. Putney, saw action on Guam (Lt. Putney was also the vet for both the 2nd and 3rd platoon), Morotai, Guadalcanal, Aitape, Kwajalein, and Eniwetok.

There was one thing that quickly changed the Marines' view of the dogs to a very positive one. In landing and fighting on islands quite often the Marines were stopped for a time on the beaches. It was a common tactic for the Japanese to infiltrate the beach positions at night and attempt to kill the Marines. The dogs were called in. It was a quiet night and the Marines got some sleep.

The Dobermans keen sense of smell and hearing could detect the presence of men several hundred yards away. In one instance, the dogs detected the presence of troops one half mile away. Their handlers always had help digging their foxholes, the other Marines always wanted the handler and their dogs nearby. No unit protected by one of the dogs was ever ambushed by the Japanese or was there ever a case of Japanese infiltration.

During the battles, the dogs led infantry points on advances, explored caves, pill boxes, dugouts, and scouted fortified positions. They did sentry duty with military police at crossroads day and night. They occupied foxholes in forward outposts at night. They were officially credited with leading three hundred and fifty patrols during the mop up phases of the battles. The handlers accounted for over three hundred enemy soldiers killed.

On Guam fourteen dogs were killed in action and ten more died from exhaustion, tropical maladies, heat stroke, accidents, and anemia from hookworm. All were buried there on Guam, at what was to become the first War Dog Memorial years later. The U.S. Marine Corps maintains a War Memorial on Guam, for those 24 War Dogs that served and died there during WW 11.

More than 1,000 dogs had trained as Marine War Dogs during World War II with 29 war dogs listed as killed in action.

Many Raiders owe their lives to the bravery of both the War Dogs and their handlers.

RAIDER PHOTOGRAPHERS

Prior to August 1942, the 1st and 2nd Raider Battalions were so secret that no photographers or cameras were allowed near a Marine Raider base, thus the sparsity of a picture record of COL EDSON, COL CARLSON, MAJ BAILEY and all the other heroes that were to make the name Raider famous. Many died without ever having a picture taken in Marine uniform.

221

In 1942, Marine General Robert Denig, the Public Relations Officer of the Corps, realized there was a need to get the story of the fighting Marines in front of the world. In all of General Douglas MacArthur's news releases from the Philippines, for instance, there was no mention of the 4th Marine Regiment's participation in the battles for Bataan or Corregidor.

The American people and the Allies had heard nothing but bad news for months. They were hungry for news of their boys overseas and everyone was hoping to hear of any good news at all.

Denig had the right idea at the right time, for very soon, in lightning like fashion, came the stories of the victory at Midway. Then the exploits of the previously hush, hush U.S. Marine Raiders with the first attack on Japanese held territory at Tulagi, the first ever submarine raid at Makin Island, and the Raider and Paratrooper battle at Edson's Ridge that saved Henderson Field on Guadalcanal.

None of this came easy for Denig's Marine Photographers and War Correspondents however. Most of his recruits had newspaper experience and were in there late 20's as compared to the average age of 19 in the Marine Corps. As with all Marines the correspondents had to successfully complete Marine boot camp and regardless of their specialty become a Marine infantryman.

Following graduation they faced problems reaching the Pacific War zones and when arriving, experienced the same uncertaincies as Navajo Code Talkers and the Marine War Dog Platoon, for the Marines didn't seem to know what to do with them. They were placed on office duties, watch duties and even acted as stevedores unloading ships until word from Washington straightened things out.

From that time on the Marine Correspondents and photographers were everywhere. They joined Raider and regular Marine units in battle on the islands and sent stories home about the wounded, submariners, tankers, artillerymen, airmen, sailors, seabees, ships, hospitals, doctors, corpsman, chaplains, nurses, cooks, Red Cross and any other story available.

And talk about the irony, both MacArthur, Eisenhower and later even President Truman all protested loudly about the Marine "propaganda "machine" that incidentally never numbered more than 23 photographers and fewer correspondents than MacArthur had in his Melbourne command center, let alone those in the field.

There were four Raider Regimental photographers at

Camp St Louis, New Caledonia in April 1943: J. D. WASDEN, 3RD BN. FRANK CANNISTRACI. 2ND BN, JACK LARTZ 1ST BN, WM. "HERB" BALL 3RD BN. SGT JOE WRIGHT, HANK GOOTEE and MILTON A. FORD 4TH BN.

Correspondent SAM STAVISKY of the Washington Post later became a 3rd Raider.

Nearly 99% of all Marine Raider photographs, both training and in combat, were taken by the above men. They seemed to be every where, seemingly oblivious to danger, trying not to miss putting any of the "real story" on film.

Thanks to those few correspondents and photographers, military historians have a mother lode of material with which to work.

Two Raider Photographers

Cape Torokina

Marine War Dogs Offoaded Ship to Higgins Boat

Marine War Dog and Handler

The Raiders were blessed with great leaders - military and spiritual. In this photo are two of the many wonderful chaplains. Left to right: Lieutenant Commander William McCorkle, 2nd Battalion; and Lieutenant Commander Robert J. Cronin, 3rd Battalion. Photo was taken on Bougainville in 1943.

Captain William H. McCorkle - Silver Star, Bronze Star, Purple Heart - examines his helmet, pierced by a machine gun bullet at Bougainville.

Cleaning Pots in Soupy Soup Kitchen

Raiders on Bougainville

10

Tarawa Beachhead

Marine's clinging to beach head on Tarawa

TARAWA ATOLL
20-23 N0VEMBER 1943

24 RAIDERS WERE KILLED IN ACTION ON TARAWA

BLANCHETTE,A.M	BURILL, RUSSELL
CAIN, THOMAS D.	CLARK, RICHARD
CLARK, WALLACE	COLEMAN, A.E.
CULP, WILLIAM C	HAYDEN,HAROLD
HEDGER, REUBEN	LAFRANCE, FRED
LEIDEL, HUGH P.	MILLER, CHARLES
MILLER, HARLEY	PALOPALI,ORLANDO
RICHTER, LEROY	ROBERTS, RAY C.
VEECK, WILLIAM	WALKER,CHARLES
WALLACE, FRED	WANER, ROBERT
WATSON, WILLIAM	WELLS, WINSTON
WILLIAMS,LEONARD	

11 Raiders remain missing in action on Tarawa

A United Nations mandate in 1920 following the end of World War I, directed that Japan was given possession of the Gilbert, Marshall, Mariana and Caroline Islands. The Japanese military immediately placed a cloak of secrecy around them. No foreign ships were allowed in port. Foreigners were not allowed to visit, even those arriving aboard Japanese ships. This enabled Japan to build ports and military facilities in complete secrecy.

Under these circumstances, with no knowledge of secret island fortifications, the Marines launched an amphibious landing 20 Nov 43, on Tarawa. It was the first landing in the Pacific; against an enemy so deeply entrenched in fortifications, that had been built during the previous 20 years

The Commanding Marine General H.M. SMITH, had recommended additional Navy bombardment of the island and was particularly fearful that his assault boats would be unable to clear the coral reefs at low tide.

While aboard their troop transports prior to the assault, the battle hardened non-commissioned officers found it hard to suppress their smiles. If Marines weren't bitching before a battle there was something wrong and they would be worried. And these leaders knew that no matter how many times the Navy would say they were going to shell an island into oblivion, it was their Marines who would have to lead the assault and root the enemy out of his fortifications with his rifle and his grenades. The Marines were bitching about everything under the sun! They complained about the crowded and sweaty holds below decks, the smells, the heat, and the poor food. They fought among themselves and with anyone else they could find. By the time their ships anchored offshore they couldn't wait to find some damn Japs to kill!

Leaving a ship wearing full combat gear and crawling down a rope ladder thrown over the side to get into your landing boat always results in injuries. With the waves often raising and lowering the boats from 5 to 10 feet or more it is hard to time your jump. This often results in someone getting a chipped tooth, a black eye or a swollen jaw from being hit by a rifle butt. When you do get aboard you are packed in like sardines and must stand for the entire trip into the beach, sometimes miles away.

After the boat is loaded the coxswain must then circle around sometimes for as long as 1, 2 or even 3 hours to join with his assault wave. Many of the Marines aboard become ill from the diesel fumes and others get sea sick, puking all over themselves and others. This, and the stinging salt water spray when they head in to the beach, just adds to the anger and everyone wants to get off this slippery, stinking boat as fast as they can.

As the boats headed in to Tarawa, the landing quickly became a nightmare, and General Smith's fears became a reality as 20 of the amphtracs in the first 3 waves were blasted out of the water by Japanese artillery. And almost all of the Higgins boats were unable to get over the coral reef. As the Marines tumbled out of their boats into chest deep water they held their weapons high above their heads to protect them from getting wet and started the agonizing duck walk to the beach 400-500 yards away. They had absolutely no cover and it soon became a nightmare much like a slow moving shooting gallery at a carnival. A scream could be heard and a head would disappear beneath the water, a Marine would step in hole and his heavy equipment would pull him under to drown, close by, an underwater explosion and two or three more men would go to their watery grave. There was no escape, just an agonizingly slow walk in the face of death. The few who did make it were exhausted by the time they reached the beach.

The amphtracs disgorged their men as rapidly as possible and headed back to the ships as fast as possible, but the coxswains were also suffering heavy casualties.

Marines were met at the shoreline with every weapon the enemy had in his arsenal. The beach was lined with small pillboxes and backed up with huge blockhouses. Each of these had to be reduced one by one. Many troops were pinned down and as the beach became more crowded, Corpsman and Doctors struggled to find any indentation or shell hole where they could treat the wounded. The noise became unbearable mixed with chattering machine guns, mortars, rifle fire, artillery, screams of the wounded and shouted orders and curses. Blue hazy smoke and acrid fumes burned the eyes and filled your lungs.

Tarawa was less than one square mile and 800-900 yards wide, only half the size of Central Park in New York City, yet this small island would take a terrible toll in Marines killed and wounded in action. There were Japs in front of and behind the men on the beach. It was impossible to escape the sweet smell of the nearly 1000 dead bodies at the waters edge and floating in the water. Fewer than 150 prisoners taken with no more than 20 being Jap troops and the rest Korean laborers.

27 Corpsmen and 2 Doctor's were among the 997 Marines killed, died of wounds or were missing and presumed dead on Tarawa. Over 2,000 casualties were treated on the island and evacuated to ships for further treatment.

8,643 Marines of the 2nd Marine Division had a history of malaria before sailing for Tarawa. Of an average 90 sick bay patients per day on Tarawa, 70 were malaria rated.

In an after action report, a Navy Commander Herring (obviously a desk warrior) pointed out once again, that Corpsmen must be better trained on how to handle themselves in battle with the FMF. Translated that meant...let the Marines bring their casualties to you", to which all FMF Corpsmen say Horse s--t! If the Commander had ever come out from behind his desk and was brave enough to visit the front lines it is doubtful he would say that to a Corpsman. If he did so, he may well have had a rifle barrel thrust under his chin and told to take his ideas and get the hell out of there while he was still alive. For it is only the Combat Marine, Corpsman, Doctor, and Chaplain who knows of the love and the willingness to die for each other that exists in the Fleet Marine Force!

The burial of the American and Japanese dead proceeded slowly. Corpses were putrefying on all sections of the island. The stench of the rotting and burned dead bodies inside the large block houses presented the largest problem. Identification of the Marines was difficult as bodies bloated rapidly in the warm climate and soon became unrecognizable. Many of the Marines, were able to be identified only the use of their dental records.

AUTHOR: I am indebted to PhM1 Stanley Bowen, 2nd Battalion, 8th Marines, 2nd Marine Division, for allowing me to excerpt portions of his book, "My War." It was written for his children and grandchildren so they would know of his experiences as an FMF Corpsman on Tarawa, Saipan and Tinian during WW II. Semper Fi Stan!

Bowens Story: "I drew the second wave. Johnny Snyder drew the second wave too (Johnny had the 1st platoon of "F" CO, I had the 2nd platoon.) Howard drew the first wave. Our wave was probably 20 to 30 yards behind the first wave, 2 to 3 minutes.

That afternoon Howard drew me aside and said, "Stan, I'm scared, I'm not going to make it, I know it." To which I said, "Bullshit, Howard, we're all gonna make it, I know it." He said, "I don't even have camouflage dungarees." So, I traded him, I gave him my camouflage dungarees and took his plain green ones, which seemed to settle him down. I don't know if Howard was psychic or not, but he didn't make it.

As we went in with our assigned wave, the operation or goal for the Marines was simple, get on shore, move forward, kill Japs and secure the island. For us Pharmacists Mates it wasn't so simple we didn't know what to expect. My Amtrac pulled up along side the ship, finally, I got in okay and the 12 to 15 of us headed out at daybreak for our position in the 2nd wave. We had Coast Guardsmen drive us in, a miserably dangerous job. Our Sergeant kept saying, "Stay down!" but no one did. It was a fantastic sight, the tree covered island ahead, hundreds of Amtracs, Hjggins boats, destroyers and cruisers all around. Overhead, as we got closer to shore, the planes started their bombing runs when the big guns from the battleship stopped. Noisy, very noisy, but really exciting, I couldn't wait to get ashore.

There was a real jolt when we hit the coral reef 500 yards from shore. There was an old sunken ship on the reef to our left, that we were getting fire from.

About half way to the reef I saw the amphtrac to our left literally blown out of the water, with body parts flying all over. Just before our amphtrac came to a stop I saw the first wave of amphtracs on the sand and I ducked down and jumped over the side when the Sergeant yelled, "Let's go!" I remember hoping I didn't sprain my ankle or break a leg in the jump. It was about five feet down, but seemed like 15. The first thing I saw was a great big Jap, I swear he was 6 foot or over, naked above the waist, swinging a long saber at Marines jumping over the side of the amphtracs. I know he cut one guy but someone shot him right away.

We had been told to move forward during our ship board briefings, so I did.   As it worked out that was lucky, because I ran right by those mounds in the sand that were the small pillboxes. I saw them and for a fleeting moment wondered, "Why were there piles of sand strung out down the beach?" These pillboxes, until they were discovered for what they were, caused hundreds of Marine deaths, for the Marines jumping out of Amphtracs and wading into shore from the edge of the reef were easy targets to the bastard Jap sharpshooters.

With incredulous luck, John and I spotted each other probably 25 yards or so moving forward. The noise was incredible, what with rifles firing and hand grenades going off. All of a sudden I spotted a guy from my platoon, Joe Varnado, laying face down, but his foot was turned upward instead of downward. Thinking he had a broken leg I yelled at John to, on the count of three, "turn his foot down while I hold his knee and lower leg steady." On the count of three I gently lifted where his knee should be and my hands came away with blood, tendons and bone splinters. His leg was completely blown off! I couldn't believe it. I looked at John and the look on his face was probably the same horror as on mine. What do we do now? I thought tourniquet" and grabbed his belt, strapped it around his upper leg and cinched it up as tight as I could. I recall, vividly, telling Joe his leg was broken.I just couldn't tell him the truth. I asked him if it hurt and he said, "No, it just feels numb." Johnny said we ought to give him a shot of morphine, so I grabbed a syrette out of my pack, pulled the cap off, stuck it in his leg, squeezed and gave him his shot. I told Joe to just lay there; some one would be by to get him back to the beach and to a hospital ship. Joe didn't make it.

Johnny and I quickly learned how to sprinkle sulfa powder, bandage and tape up guys. That's about all a frontline corpsman can do. Casualties were really heavy. It was noisy, it was hot, God it was hot! John and I took care of guys together for, I guess, an hour or so but then, because there were so many hurt guys we kind of split up.

The Japs were so well dug in on Red Beach Three (ours) and Red Beach Two and One that we had to pull back to the shore line, as did Red Beach Two and One. Movement against the Japs began from our right, way down at the end of Betio on Green Beach. From about noon, I guess, of the first day we, on Red Beach Three, "hugged" our shore line. The Japs had laid a two to three foot high, coconut sea wall to keep our tanks from getting on shore. This log wall was, as I recall, about 15 to 20 feet from the water at low tide. For the next two and a half days we were down behind the sea wall shooting and throwing hand grenades at the Japs behind the wall and they at us. Our grenades could be set for how many seconds you wanted before it exploded. We'd set them real short so none of ours came back at us.

At high tide we got wet and were still held down behind the wall. Thank God for that sea wall or there would have been hand to hand fighting and the advantage would have been theirs. All day long two of our destroyers steamed back and forth firing their guns, over our heads, at the Japs, while Navy fighter planes strafed them.

That afternoon a Marine shouted at me, "Doc, there's a guy out in that Amtrac thats hurt." Behind us, out about 25 to 30 yards or so was a "dead" amphtrac sitting in the water. I dropped all my gear, rifle, pack, rifle belt, grabbed my first aid pack and ran out to the amphtrac. As I got closer I saw little splashes of water near me, all of the sudden I realized those were shots being fired at me and I broke the world's record for the 25 yard water dash. Hiding behind the amphtrac were Marines, all hit, but not too bad. One said that a guy was in the amphtrac and hurt. I climbed up and there was, a guy I knew, a Corporal as I recall, who had stayed in the amphtrac when it got hit and continued to fire its 50 caliber machine gun at the Japs until he caught one right in the middle of his chest, he had a large hole right through him. There was nothing I could do for him but give him a shot of morphine and tell him to "hang on." He was dying and he knew it and so did I. He was calm and asked me to stay with him. I did for a few minutes but then told him to "hang-on," I had to get out of there as all hell was breaking loose. So he died by himself - as we all have to someday.

Back in the water I told two of the hurt Marines to "drop their gear, rifles and all, put their arm closest to me around my shoulder and get ready to run." At my shout of "now" we took off. One of them got hit on the way back to the beach. I dropped them off and headed back for the other two. This time there was more shooting and I recall that both of them got hit on our way back to the beach. Talk about God being on my side, I never got hurt on Tarawa. I had guys hit while I was patching them up. I had guys hit when I was helping them back to the aid station. I got sunburned real bad, got scratches on my hands, but never got hurt until we were in Hawaii about a month later I was "pooped," the guys on the beach all said, "Good job Doc, you're OK," and I forgot about it until later on. On the ship heading for Hawaii, after the battle, our Battalion Doctor came up to me and asked if it was true I'd run out to a disabled amphtrac and rescued some Marines. I replied "yes" thinking I was going to get "chewed out." I was stunned to hear him say, "I've heard the story from several Marines and I'm putting you in for a Silver Star", which I got. I also got spot promotion to Pharmacist Mate Third.

Later in the afternoon of the first day, still crouched down behind the sea wall throwing grenades, we began to wonder "what the night would bring?" We were to the extreme left of the operation, as I mentioned before. No "friendlies" on our left, my platoon was it. We couldn't more forward, no one had gotten to shore since the daybreak landing. The tide had washed in. (God what a horrible sight it was that morning all those waves of Marines flying to get to shore, wading, swimming, crawling and getting shot, mortared and killed. Thank the Lord I was in the 2nd wave and we got over the reef in our amphtrac and didn't have to come in on a Higgins boat.

We were getting low on ammunition and water. We decided if we got no reinforcements and ammo, we'd just charge in and hope for the best. We had no idea what was happening on the beaches to our right or what was going on with the rest of the battle. During this first day, and the second, the Navy fighter planes made strafing runs right over our heads, I mean right over our heads! I fired my carbine, threw hand grenades and patched guys up all day that first day. Our wounded lay in the sun behind the sea wall with the rest of us.

That night brought little fighting. We could hear the Japs moving around and once in a while we would get a grenade and then we'd respond. I guess the Japs didn't want night fighting anymore than we did.

When darkness fell we got the word to help carry our wounded down the beach to the pier, out to the end of it where they'd be picked up by the Navy and taken out to hospital ships. After dropping the wounded off at the end of the pier, we'd carry and ammunition back to our platoon. Thank God we had the cover of darkness to do this, as we were nearly out of both water and ammo.

That morning I ran down the beach to our Battalion Aid Station. It was a dangerous thing to do, but I was low on sulfa, tape, etc. Was I happy to see my buddies still alive!

Later that morning at the Aid Station, which was also pinned down behind the sea wall, I was sitting down having a canteen of coffee and talking to my buddy Ken Peebles, when all of the sudden he got a surprised look on his face and slumped over dead. He'd taken a sniper bullet right in the middle of the forehead. What a shame, Ken was a nice guy, quiet, not a rowdy like most of us. The bullet had to have gone right over my head into Ken (I was sitting with my back to the sea wall, Ken was facing it). I grabbed my carbine and thought I saw the SOB in a tree (one of the few still standing) and fired off three or four rounds. I yelled when I saw something drop, I think a rifle, he didn't drop though because they tie themselves to the tree.

The second day was a continuation of the first, noise, heat, shooting and planes strafing. Our outfit had no replacements but we "got the word" that "the battle was in doubt" and they were trying to land replacements (the 6th Marines) at the end of the island and that is what happened. The sweep began, as I recall, up the island from the right, toward us. The third day was a "zinger," because we finally moved up and over the sea wall

This third and final day was tough. I was tired, bone tired, and here we were moving up and guys were getting hit everywhere. John Snyder, my best buddy, got sprayed with shrapnel while working on a hurt Marine. I patched John up at the foot of the Jap Command Post, a huge concrete bunker with walls so thick not even the Navy shells penetrated it. Japs were everywhere; we shot them in their foxholes and pillboxes. It seemed like once the momentum started, nothing could stop us. We killed them all; we hated the bastards for what they had done to our buddies. They killed themselves too. Many of them committed hari-kari, which is suicide by putting the barrel of their rifle in their mouth and pulling the trigger with a toe.

And so, the battle came to a close. I recall the quiet all of a sudden. God, I was tired. I walked all around the island and really couldn't believe the destruction. Nothing was left, no trees, no buildings and, oh God, how the place smelled from dead Marines and Japs. A sweet sickly smell everywhere and the ugliness of death in that hot climate was very pronounced. Bodies bursting from their dungarees, none recognizable. I thought, "Thank God I don't have to strip these guys, find out who they are, bury them, etc."

That's when I thought about Howard and went to look for him when the island was secured, three days later, I asked a half dozen guys if they had seen Howard. Neither Johnny nor I had. I started a search for him that took an hour or so. I found him where he had landed, probably 15 feet from where he had jumped out of his amphtrac, face down, body horribly bloated, like all of the hundreds of dead Japs and Marines, unrecognizable, but it was Howard alright. He had been machine gunned as he ran forward. The Japs had little 2 and 3 man pillboxes, of metal, covered by sand, with a window just inches above ground level that they shot out of at the landing Marines.

And so it was over. My platoon, what was left of it, six guys out of forty-five that hit the beach only three days before! Six out of forty-five, not all killed, but still way too high a price to pay for that stinking little piece of sand.

The way Medals are awarded is strange, I saw guys do things that deserved Silver Stars, Navy Crosses and even the Medal of Honor, but received nothing. We had several guys who gave their lives for their buddies by throwing themselves on a hand grenade and getting blown up.

Scuttlebutt was that we were going home! But we landed in Hilo, Hawaii about midnight, trucked to our new home on the Parker Ranch. We were dropped off at two in the morning in the middle of a God damned desert (that we ended up walking every inch of). No one there, nothing! I remember being given a tooth brush, a tube of tooth paste and a blanket. There were no tents up, no camp, it was cold and we were dirty, tired and really mad that no one seemed to care. We later learned that the Army in Hilo had rejected our request for blankets, but it was approved by a General in Honolulu. We would have killed the Army C.O. if we could have gotten back to Hilo (65 miles). And so, we got to work and built our camp, soon to be known as Camp Tarawa." Stanley Bowen.

The initial landing 20 Nov 43, at Tarawa in the Gilbert Islands, was made on the north coast of Betio by the 2nd. Marine Division Reinforced. This was followed by the capture of Apamama Atoll on 26 Nov 43. Major General Julian C, Smith announced the capture of Tarawa on 27 Nov 1943. Many former Raiders fought here and died, as they did on all the islands invaded by the Marines in WW II.

Meanwhile, at home, Americans were appalled by the losses at Tarawa, flooding Admiral Nimitz's mail with angry letters. But Tarawa had taught the Navy and the Marines some vital lessons in amphibious warfare that in the near future would save thousands of lives. More Amphtracs were to be built with better armor, including side protection for Marines. Higgins boats were removed from landing operations. Landing craft were converted into supporting gunboats, able to come in close on the beach. Underwater demolition teams were organized to destroy natural and artificial obstacles before future atoll landings would take place.

The price for Betio had been very high, but within days, Betio was converted into a forward base for the assault on the Marshalls, with bomber and fighter sorties flying out within hours of the Marines victory. And within nine weeks of the battle, an invasion task force under Admiral Nimitz left Tarawa to take the Marshall Islands.

Meanwhile at BUTARITARI (MAKIN ISLAND), 6,500 U.S. ARMY TROOPS facing LESS THAN 300 JAP TROOPS AND 300 LABORERS were held up for 3 days before securing the Island. It took the 165th Army Regiment (Reinforced), approximately the same time it took for the Marines to take Tarawa, one of the most heavily fortified islands in the Pacific. Marines took Engebi, a much harder objective in 7 hours with the 22nd Marine Regiment.

On Tarawa, Marines faced pillboxes or blockhouses with concrete walls and roofs of palm tree trunks reinforced with several feet of coral, rock, and dirt piled on for protection from aerial attacks and shelling from Navy ships lying offshore. Almost all had to be destroyed with explosive charges and hand grenades in frontal attacks by Marines.

The Army also experienced problems with their dead. A Regimental Colonel and the bodies of other soldiers lay just 25 yards from a road that had heavy vehicle traffic from 1600 D-Day until 1100 D-Day Plus -1, before they were retrieved.

Serious Thinking Aboard Troop Ship

Chaplain Conducting Church Service on Battlefront

Stretcher Bearers Carrying Dead Marine From Tarawa Beach

Corpsman Administering Blood Plasma to Prevent Shock

11

Peleliu & Other Island Campaigns

Marines during battle for Peleliu

PELELIU AND OTHER PACIFIC ISLANDS

AUTHOR: Raiders and former Raiders fought in every major battle in the South Pacific Theater of War during World War II. Raider Historian Jerry Beau has researched Marine Corps Muster Rolls that show where former Raiders sacrificed their lives in combat on other islands and those who were awarded medals for their bravery. While these figures evolve from year to year, this represents the information currently available.

CAPE GLOUCESTER, NEW BRITAIN ISLAND
24 DEC 1943-1 MARCH 1944

RAIDERS KILLED IN ACTION ON NEW BRITAIN
FINLEY, GORDON A. *   HOLMES, JOSEPH P.
* Corpsman

RAIDERS AWARDED THE NAVY CROSS
FOR BRAVERY ON NEW BRITAIN
GORDON, FINLEY A.*   WALT, LOUIS W.
* Corpsman

Marine General Rupertus' 1st Marine Division Western and Eastern Assault Groups landed on Cape Gloucester with 24,000 Marines on 24 Dec 43 and secured the very narrow beachhead. The main objective was to seize the Capes airfields.

The Marines were surprised at the density of the swamp forest just behind the beach that provided perfect cover for the enemy. The roots of many trees left standing presented a natural hazard along with the hundreds of trees knocked down in the naval bombardment. They reached the end of one swamp only to face another one. As darkness fell and the veteran's tried to tie in their lines it seemed like Guadalcanal all over again.

Things went badly at first with both the C.O. and the X.O. of one company killed. However, first day casualties in the assault were light with 6 killed, 37 wounded and 124 missing. After receiving initial treatment, casualties were evacuated by APD's to LST's and later to the Base Hospital at Milne Bay.

That night, a violent storm that lasted 5 days, hit the beachhead area and wiped out all traces of landmarks forcing the men delivering ammunition to hold onto each others belts in order to find the command post. They arrived at 0805 and were immediately sent to plug the gap between the 2nd and 3rd Battalions. On 27-28 Dec the 1st Marines captured Hell's Point a stronghold defending the Cape Gloucester Airdrome.

On 29 Dec Airfields No's 1 and 2 were declared secure. Fighting continued until Army and Marine patrols from Arawe and Cape Gloucester met at Gilnit securing western New Britain on 31 December 1943. Marine units continued to engage the retreating Japanese troops until the area was cleared of Japs by the end of February. Raider LTCOL LEWIS W. WALT earned the Navy Cross for leading an attack on Aogiri Ridge one of the Japanese strongholds.

The 1st Marine Division lost 310 men killed and 1,083 wounded in action during the four month campaign on New Britain.

KWAJALEIN, NAMUR AND ROI ISLANDS
31 JANUARY 8 FEBRUARY 1944

MARINE RAIDER ARTHUR ERVIN WAS AWARDED
THE NAVY CROSS ON NAMUR ISLAND

The Japanese were building a bomber strip on Kwajalein, the world's largest Atoll made up of some 90 islands and the government center of the Marshall Islands. The capture of the Marshalls would bring the Allied Forces 700 miles closer to Japan.

On 31 Jan - 2 Feb 44 Kwajalein Island, Roi and Namur Islands and several smaller Islands of the Kwajalein Atoll, Marshall Islands, were attacked and occupied by the 4th Marine Division and the Army's 7th Division troops.

Japanese Forces, led by Admiral Koyabashi lost 7,300 men on Kwajalein and Roi Namur. Marine losses in the campaign were 190 killed and 737 wounded. Navy Underwater Demolition Teams were used here for the first time to swim in and check the beaches prior to the initial assault.

Several Marine platoons participated in assaults of three separate islands in one day. Navajo Code Talkers were among the troops, but little is known about their contribution as available historical material on these operations is very limited.

Amphtrack crews operated daily for 14 to 16 hours while continuously under fire during the assault period. Only a few of the LST's provided warm food, hot coffee and brandy to the men returning from the beaches. One LST Captain refused to give the Marines even one cup of coffee.

In general the Marines were in excellent health for these assaults although many men were lost prior to the invasion suffering from malaria and filariasis. In treating certain wounds it was necessary to remove some of the patients clothing resulting in some cases suffering from severe sunburn, which was aggravated by being completely soaked by salt water during operations. This resulted in many severe cases of skin irritation and eye conjunctivitis. One of the most painful causes of distress was lip sunburn that resulted in cracking, peeling and often ulceration. It was here that plasma was found to possess great and definite value in the treatment of cases of battle fatigue. More than 1,500 men were suffering from dysentery when they left the islands.

One Marine fell to the ground, hit by a Jap bullet, only to discover the bullet had entered his helmet just above the right ear and injured him just below his cheekbone. Bleeding badly, he sprinkled sulfa on his wound, bandaged his right eye and cheekbone and continued going forward. LT JACK POWERS attacked a pillbox single handed although severely wounded in the stomach, and dying in the effort. He was awarded the Medal Of Honor posthumously for his bravery and dedication to duty. Three other Marines received the Medal of Honor, two that threw their bodies on grenades, in order to save the lives of their comrades.

As soon as landings were affected, battalion aid stations were set up near the beaches, utilizing deep shell craters, pillboxes and dugouts. On Namur, casualties were heavy and Marine bands men were used as litter bearers. Casualties were first taken aboard their APA landing ships and then transferred to the hospital ship's USS Relief or USS Solace within 3 hours of being wounded.

ENIWETOK ATOLL, MARSHALL ISLANDS
ENGEBI AND PARRY ISLANDS
17 FEBRUARY - 2 MARCH 1944

The swift victory at Kwajalein allowed the planners to move forward the attack on Eniwetok Atoll to 17 Feb 44. Eniwetok had forty islands and a lagoon 17 x 20 miles long.

The Japanese had secretly brought in over 2,500 troops, so the plans were for the 22nd Marines to take care of Engebi, while the Army reinforced by one battalion of the 22nd Marines would assault Eniwetok and Parry Islands.

On the morning of the 18th the Marines seized Engebi by 1500. Most of the defenders fought from spider holes, but the Marines had figured a way to literally smoke them out. The spider holes were made up of oil drums set up underground and camouflaged so they could let Marines go past them and then they would pop up and shoot them in the back. Marines soon learned to toss in smoke grenades and as the smoke outlined the tunnels they would blow them up with demolition charges. The Marines lost 145 men while the Japs lost 1000 killed and 19 captured.

On 19 Feb, the 106th Infantry of the 27th Army Division and the 3rd Battalion 27th Marines went ashore and fought side by side. The island was secured the next day after a night of the Army firing at everything in sight as the Marines were dug in for the night. Fortunately only a few Marines were wounded by the Army troops.

After a three day bombardment, the 3 Battalions 22nd

Marines went ashore on Parry Island on 22 Feb. The battles were hard fought with machine guns, mortars, and hand to hand combat. Over a several week period the 22nd Marines killed over 25% of 13,000 troops in 29 landings. The rest of the enemy was left to starve.

RAIDERS AWARDED MEDALS ON ENIWETOK ATOLL

SILVER STAR

ENGEBI ISLAND	HOWARD,CHARLES
ENIWETOK ISLAND	SMITH,CHARLES
PARRY ISLAND	WIDDECKS, CHARLES F.

EMIRAU ISLAND ST. MATTHIAS GROUP
20 MARCH - 9 APRIL 1944

Emirau was an irregular shaped heavily wooded and hilly island 8 miles long considered to be lightly defended by the Japanese.

Plans for operations following Bougainville included General MacArthur's demand that Kavieng must be taken to neutralize Rabaul. Admiral Halsey proposed the seizure of an airfield sight on Emirau would neutralize both Rabaul and Kavieng and his proposal won over the Joint Chiefs of Staff. This avoided a blood bath and saved many Raider lives as the 4th Marines had been chosen to spearhead the attack on heavily defended Kavieng.

Instead of the 3rd Marine Division and the Army 40th Infantry Division destined for the attack on Kavieng, it was decided to use the newly formed 4th Marine Regiment's 1st and 2nd battalions made up mostly of Marine Raiders. They were reinforced by a pack howitzer battalion, engineer, tank, motor transport and medical companies and War Dog, ordinance and service and supply platoons.

Landing the 4th Marines quickly seized the island, but were to remain on the island for 20 more days. Raider SAMUEL C. LOWERY JR was killed when his demolition kit accidentally exploded.

PELELIU, PALAU ISLANDS
15 SEPTEMBER 1944

The 1st Marine Division, Reinforced by the Army 81st Division, landed on the White and Orange Beaches against heavy opposition. Where the 2nd BN 5th Marines reached the opposite shore cutting the island in half.

The 10,000 Japs on the Island withdrew to cleverly hidden caves and tunnels to repel the Marine attacks. Four of every ten Marines were killed or wounded. Many of the dead were so badly injured they could only be identified by fingerprints. The air was filled with the screams of the wounded should one corner of their stretcher would be lowered or dropped if one or more of the stretcher bearers tripped over a vine or tree limb and fell, while evacuating them to the rear for treatment.

In some of the most bitterly contested battles of World War II in the Pacific, Japanese casualties were 13,600 and 400 captured.

The Marine and Army casualty rate was the highest of any amphibious attack in American history at that time. The 1st Marine Division lost 6,256 men including 1,252 killed. The Army lost 1,393 casualties, with 208 killed.

The airfield was captured on 16 Sep by the 5th Marines, Hill 200 was seized by the 1st Marines on 17 Sep, and Hill 210 were gained on 18 Sep by the 1st and 7th Marines and Hill 205 was seized by the 1st Marines. On 19 Sep the elements of the 1st Marines gained Hill 100, and the 7th Marines gained the crest of Hill 260.

The 1st Marines, due to heavy casualties, were temporarily relieved of assault duty so they might recuperate, on 21 Sep.

Leading up to 25 Sep, several small islands off the coast of Peleliu were seized. On 26 Sep several elements of the 5th Marines secured Hills 2 and 80 and sealed off the North tip of the island.

The flag was raised at the 1st Marine Division command post on 27 Sep. As on all islands however, attacks continued until mop up was completed 25 Nov 44, although all Marine units departed by 30 Oct.

RAIDERS KILLED IN ACTION ON PELELIU

Fournier, Joseph A. L.   Nelson, William

RAIDERS AWARDED MEDALS ON PELELIU

NAVY CROSS

FOURNIER, JOSEPH A.   WALT, LEWIS W. *

* Second Navy Cross Award

SILVER STAR

ANDERSON, R. E. CAMPBELL,JAMES
CLARK,EDWARD HARRIS, RICHARD
JOHNSON,R.W. KELLY, THOMAS J.
NELSON, WILLIAM STACEY, R. H.*
* Second Silver Star Award

RAIDERS KILLED IN ACTION - ISLAND AND DATE UNKNOWN - MOST LIKELY GUAM OR OKINAWA

BARRY, JOHN BUGG, JOHN A.
GREEN, WAYNE HARTMAN, JOHN
LECLAIR, HERBERT MORRIS, MILTON S.
PETERS, ROBERT PETERSON,ROBERT
PIPER, NATE A. SULLIVAN, JOHN
YOUNG, DONALD

MAY THEY REST IN PEACE. NEVER FORGOTTEN
BY THEIR RAIDER COMRADES!

Invasion Beach - Tarawa

Foxhole Buddies - Both Wounded

Bunks Aboard Troop Transport Ship

12

Saipan & Tinian

Immediate transfusion of blood plasma by Corpsmen often meant the difference between life and death for wounded Marines

SAIPAN
MARSHALL ISLANDS
15 June - 9 July, 1944

RAIDERS KILLED IN ACTION ON SAIPAN

BROWN, KENNETH	BYRNES, JOSEPH
DOUGAN,DESMAND	DUNN, JAMES B.
ERVIN, ARTHUR B.	HART, JAMES E.
LASSITER,EMORY	MARSHALL,WALT
McARDLE, JAMES	McPHERSON,C.R.
MITCHELL, R. R.	NIX, JOHN D.
REED, ZENO O.	SHEETS, JACK
SINCLAIR, ALVIN	SWEET, C. N.

3 Raiders remain missing in action on Saipan

2HQ,RAIDER LEA BELL was blinded during a Japanese Banzai attack at Saipan on 7 Jul 44.

RAIDER PVT ROBERT J. JAMISON WAS
AWARDED THE NAVY CROSS ON SAIPAN

RAIDERS AWARDED THE SILVER STAR
FOR HEROISM ON SAIPAN

ARTZ, KENNETH E.	BARRON, STANLEY
BROWN, JOSEPH B.	EDSON,MERRITT A.
FLYNN, JOHN J.	NABER, BAILEY C.
SABO, ALEX	STIFF, HOUSTON

THE MARIANAS offensive was planned to by-pass the huge enemy bases at Truk and Rabaul. Saipan, located 1250 miles from Tokyo, was the headquarters of Japan's Central Pacific Fleet and was defended by 30,000 troops. Unlike flat Tarawa, the island of Saipan was 15 miles long, with mountains, cliffs, cities, beaches, and cane fields.

On 15 Jun 44, under the Command of Marine LTGEN H.M. SMITH, the 2nd and 4th Marine Divisions landed on the heavily defended beaches of Saipan, with the Army 27th Infantry Division in reserve.

The enemy had emplaced fixed guns, some as large as 8 inch in size, along with strategically placed blockhouses, pillboxes, and bunkers to defend the beaches. During the early phases of the assault the scene of sand, blood, and wreckage on the overcrowded beach resulted in much confusion. The effort by the troops to get off the beach was thwarted by seven anti-boat guns that continued to fire on each wave of Marines headed to the beach. Attacks and counter-attacks prevailed through out the first night. A Corpsman was killed D- night while manning a machine gun in his company.

Fierce fighting, often hand-to-hand, prevailed as the Marines headed inland to capture the high ground of the island. The Army 27th Division was ordered ashore on 16 Jun but did not complete the movement until 20 Jun.

AUTHOR: The following is the most detailed description of the activities of large medical units ashore with Marine amphibious forces that has come to light. I am indebted to the "History of the Hospital Corps" for this information.

During the height of the assault the Marines coming ashore, along with the equipment and the casualties caused total confusion. The shelling of the beaches by the enemy was continuous.

To add grimness to the environment the dead, both

Japanese and American, had been collected and laid out to await trucks for transportation to a burial ground. Into this melee, medical units were landed in LVT'S and LCT'S. The first groups to establish medical order were the medical sections of the beach parties. Composed of one medical officer and 8 hospital corpsmen from each troop carrier, they constituted the link between medical organizations afloat and ashore. Working in highly exposed positions for as long as 48 hours at a time without rest and subjected to the added hazard of strafing Japanese planes, they gave emergency medical treatment and set up casualty evacuation stations in the sand.

In the Fourth Marine Division, 161 medical officers and hospital corpsmen became battle casualties because they were unable to utilize protection or seek cover from enemy fire. Casualties to personnel during the first 5 days of the operation were enormous. One shore party evacuation station treated and evacuated 1,009 casualties during the period from D-Day to D-Day-plus-3 under the most difficult conditions.

Japanese LtGen Saito ordered evacuation of his Donnay field hospital on 30 June, with those ambulatory patients going to a nearby village. Those who couldn't walk were abandoned. The Chief medical officer advised the patients they should die an honorable death as Japanese soldiers; and hand grenades were handed out one for each 8 men, who were to gather in a tight circle with the man in the middle pulling the pin.

There is no record of whether the doctor followed his own advice, however Admiral Nagumo, the leader of the attack on Pearl Harbor, and Generals Saito and Igeta all committed hari kari.

Diseases accounted for about one-third of the admissions. In the 4th Marine Division there were 409 dengue patients, with 680 for dysentery, 26 fungus and 414 for combat fatigue.

Jeep ambulances with their loads of wounded were often hit by artillery fire. The landing of ammunition and gasoline near casualty evacuation centers on beaches that were subjected to continuous shelling did not lessen the difficulties of rendering first aid.

The presence of coral reefs and the loss of small boats during the assault made evacuation of casualties difficult. Unfortunately, the most effective evacuation ship, the LCVP, could not be beached because of the coral reef, but the DUKW was useful in the evacuation of casualties over the reefs. Rubber boats were also utilized to transport the injured.

As the battle for Saipan progressed, the segregation of slightly wounded patients from the more seriously wounded was extremely difficult on the beaches, where hundreds of wounded arrived at one time and mud vied with enemy fire to frustrate attempts at first aid and casualty evacuation.

Diseases accounted for about one-fourth of the admissions. In the Fourth Marine Division, there were 409 patients admitted for dengue fever, 680 for dysentery, 26 for fungus infection, and 414 for combat fatigue. Three or four days rest, a bath, and nourishing food resulted in complete recovery in from 75 to 80 percent of these patients.

One of the many problems confronting the Medical Department was how to make possible the speedy and effective burial of the dead, and the disposal of the decomposing bodies in block houses and bomb shelters. On Saipan thousands of our own and enemy dead lay on the beaches and the rugged inland terrain. Prior to the landing, careful plans were made for burial of the dead and details were trained and equipped for this work. Because of the intensity of battle, there was often a delay of several days before burial or disposal of the large numbers of enemy dead could be started.

Air evacuation was begun on D–day-plus-9 and 860 patients were evacuated, but because there were no flight surgeons to screen the patients and no medical attendants to accompany them, some died en route. At times, men wounded in combat had been without food for days.

American casualties were 6,713 Marines, 813 soldiers, and 245 sailors including 1,023 killed. Japanese deaths were estimated at 23,811.

Corpsman Stan Bowen continues his story following his experiences on Tarawa. (Thanks for the info Stan!)" I landed in the first wave this time. We had the new amphtracks and didn't have to jump over the sides. Our wave landed far to the left and as we headed inland into a cane field, the beach behind us was getting pounded as we dug in. There were few casualties that day, but the night made up for it. It was really hot that day and I had my first of several heat stroke victims.

We heard the Japs talking and moving around, but we kept quiet, as they couldn't see us. At night all hell broke loose and the call "Corpsman" came often and I would have to crawl over to treat another Marine knowing all the while that it wasn't a safe place to be.

Saipan had hundreds of caves to hide Japs and the poor civilian natives and the imported labor as well. It was very difficult to dig a foxhole in the mountains and it had flies by the millions. I remember batting them out of my eyes, from my ears, mouth and nose. When we ate, one hand would spoon the food while the other would beat off flies.

We moved inland with little resistance and I threw away my gas mask and filled it's pack with Jap socks. I had learned to change socks every day, more often if they got wet. Later on we had guys with fungus down to the bone and that was no excuse for you to be taken off the battle line.

I remember prior to our start over Mt, Tapotchau, we walked thru a grove of trees with no Japs, and ran into a company of Army guys of the 27th Division. We stopped and asked where they were going and they sheepishly said they were going to take that grove. We said "Hell, we just came thru there and there aren't any Japs." They sheepishly replied, "We know that, but orders are orders." It's the first time I saw how differen't the Army Infantry training was. Their Captain blew a whistle, actually blew a whistle, and every damn dogface started shooting at the banana trees. After a few minutes the Captain blew his whistle twice and the doggies all moved toward the grove still shooting. I swear they ran out of ammunition before they 'captured' the banana trees!

Later on we were able to sit on the side of the mountain and look down on the flat farmlands on the opposite side from where all the Marines were and watch Army units 'attack' a farm house in the same ridiculous manner. It got to the point that the whole Saipan operation was held up for days because of he Army's antiquated methods. Marines are taught not to fire until they have a target to hit and not waste ammunition, besides it's too heavy to carry.

Was it Tarawa or Saipan where our water tasted like gasoline? Can you believe our water cans had once been filled with gasoline? We used it only for drinking! By the time we got relieved off the line, my beard was caked with dirt, grime and sweat and my hair began to fall out in clumps as did everyone's. Twenty-one days on the line with no bath, no shave, no teeth brushed, no changed clothes and no hot food!

And so we went, day after day. Our platoon was always on the line, never fell back, and fought every inch up that damn mountain. We killed a lot of Japs, but most of them were pulled back in their caves by their buddies. One day we came upon at least a hundred or more wounded and dead Japs, all in a common area (were they the abandoned hospital patients given hand grenades?) The actual organized fighting lasted 25 days.

We were on the line 21 days, relieved for 1 day, then called back after a big banzai attack by the Japs. During the mop up operations I got real sick and my throat swelled up. I had come down with dengue fever, with the grandaddy of all headaches, and the awful pain in every joint. I was sent down the mountain to the 'hospital', which was nothing more than stretchers laying out on the ground. A few days later I said 'to hell with this' and just got up and left for my outfit.

The night before we were relieved the Japs made one final charge against our lines. More than 2,500 Japs full of saki made a banzai attack. Our machine guns stacked them up like cordwood, but they ran through the gap in the line left by the Army all the way back to the artillery before they were stopped.

White phosphorous grenades were horrible; they along with the flame-throwers, were the most horrible weapons we used. White phosphorous would explode like shrapnel and if it hit you would burrow deep into your skin and burn from the inside. Flame-throwers would shoot out a tongue of flame and engulf a person. One man fired the gun while the other manned the tank of fuel. Our flame throwing tanks were even worse.

The island was secured on 9 July, but not before the troops being witness to the grisly sights of hundreds of enemy soldiers and civilians, some mothers with children in their arms, some forced by Japanese soldiers, leaping from the high cliffs to their deaths on the rocks below. It is estimated over 22,000 civilians killed themselves after being told the Marines would kill them if they came over to our lines.

We were to rest for a few days before assaulting Tinian. During that time, the guys who had been overseas 32 and 36 months were being sent back home." (STANLEY BOWEN CPHM.)

One of the greatest tributes ever paid to a Marine came from an enemy. He was Col Yoshida, a Japanese Staff Officer captured at Saipan. He was the officer who wrote the plan for the final desperate Banzai attack on Saipan. AUTHOR: Ironically Col Yoshida was opposed to such a waste of men's lives, but he was overruled by his senior officers.

"The Japanese can never hope to defeat a nation that produces soldiers like your Marines," He told our intelligence officers. "In the Japanese army, we revere the spirit of Yamat Damashli, It means the Spirit of Old Japan, and our soldiers will die for it. We have learned that your Marines also revere the spirit of his country and is as willing to die as the Japanese soldier. Moreover, the Marine is a better soldier than the Japanese soldier.

He is individually stronger. His training and fighting technique is better.

The hard fought battle for Saipan was almost overshadowed by intra service rivalry resulting when Marine LTGEN H.M. SMITH removed Army Gen Ralph Smith of his Command of the Army 27th Infantry Division on Saipan. In an effort to assure a coordinated advance by the Army and Marine Divisions and to prevent even further loss of lives, Marine LTGEN H.M.SMITH was given permission by the Navy to relieve the 27th Army Division Commanding Officer Gen Ralph Smith. LtGen H.M.Smith, in his book Coral and Brass, explains how this came about: "After my previous experience with the 27th Div on Makin, I was uncomfortable using them again in battle but they were the only Army division available. Originally made up of NY National Guard Units they were one of only 2 National Guard Units that had not been broken up by the Army to receive further training.

The 1st day of Mount Topotchau attack the 2nd Marine Division advanced 1,000 yards, and the 4th Marine Division advanced 2,000 yards. The 27th were ordered to pass through and continue a coordinated attack. The 2nd and 4th jumped off on H Hour, Some elements of the 27th started 1 hour late with the 106th infantry over 3hrs late. This jeopardized the middle of the line and the lives of the attacking Marines. At nightfall a deep U was in the lines as a result of the 106th advancing very little since their starting point in the morning. The 105th Infantry (27th) ordered to advance on a position with less than 1,000 men, made a half hearted attack which failed to advance 200 yards. This allowed the remaining 500 Jap effectives to march in a column of two right through their lines forcing the Marines to contain them."

Gen H.M. SMITH went to Army Gen Jarman to ask him to talk with Army Gen Ralph Smith about his efforts. Gen Ralph Smith promised to do better the next day or "if I don't I should be relieved". He was himself troubled by the performance of some of his commanders.

Marine Gen H.M. Smith then discussed with Admiral Spruance the lack of aggressiveness on the part of Army Gen Ralph Smith and suggested putting Army Gen Jarman in command. Admiral Spruance authorized and ordered Smith to relieve Army Gen Smith of command of the 27th Div. And replace him with Army Gen Jarman. Understanding the problems he faced, one of Jarmans first acts was to relieve one of the Army's 3rd Regiment Commanders.

Gen Jarman's report to Army Lt General Robert C. Richardson Jr. (an implacable foe of the Marine Corps), read as follows:

"Frankly, 'Name Withheld', appeared to be muddled, the mountainous terrain and rough going was too much for him. I noticed certain things that give me some concern. Based upon my observation of the Division for a few days, there is first a lack of offensive spirit on the part of the troops, a battalion will run into one machine gun and be held up several hours. When they get any kind of minor resistance they immediately open up with anything that can fire in the general direction from which they are being fired upon.

Second, at night if a patrol comes around their bivouac area they immediately telephone in and state they are under counter attack and want to fall back to some other position.

Third, I found that troops would work all day to capture well-earned terrain and at night would fall back a distance varying from 400 to 800 yards and sometimes 1,000 yards to organize a perimeter defense. I had in the brief time I was in command of the Twenty seventh Division, to issue an order that ground gained would not be given up, that the perimeter of defense was to be formed on the ground captured, and troops in the rear should be brought up."

The Marines anticipated a final banzai attack and they correctly defined the area where it would most likely occur. The Army 27th Division was in this sector, but the 106th Infantry had a gap between the lines of two battalions through which an estimated 3000 Japs charged, some with bayonets tied to sticks for weapons. Thus another error by their officers resulted in the death of over 400 Army Infantrymen, at least some who could have been otherwise spared."

In spite of the confirmation by their own General Jarman, of the shortcomings of the 27th Div Units, the Army did not admit their officers were in any way incompetent. Instead they began a propaganda program to condemn GEN H.H. SMITH and the Marine Corps for battle plans costing needless lives of their men. Lost in the ensuing media battle was that delays in capturing an objective resulted in additional loss of Navy ships and the deaths of their crews as they had to stay on station until the enemy forces were defeated. Also left unsaid was that in the Pacific Theater of War Marines were used mostly as the initial assault force, with Army troops held in reserve or as an occupation force who would naturally have fewer casualties.

That a Marine General had the temerity to relieve an

Army General, sent shock waves throughout the Army, and earned SMITH the undying enmity of the Commanding Army General in the Pacific (Richardson), who had been lobbying for Smith's job prior to the invasion. In retaliation Gen MacArthur; who worked hard to remove the Marine Corps as the invasion forces in the Pacific, saw to it that Marine Gen Smith who had trained 7 of the Army's 17 amphibious divisions was the only Senior Marine Officer TO NOT be invited to the Japanese surrender ceremonies held aboard the USS Missouri in Tokyo Bay.

This was neither the first nor the last affront to the Corps by MacArthur. During the defense of Bataan and Corregidor, the 4th Marine Regiment fought valiantly before being ordered to lay down their arms, yet they were the ONLY fighting unit not awarded a unit commendation, and the American public had been kept totally in the dark about the 4th Marines valiant efforts. This lack of respect on MacArthur's part; was corrected by Army General Jonathan Wainwright after MacArthur was safely taken off the island prior to the Allied surrender, when he awarded the 4th Marines the unit commenadaion.

Again in his book Coral and Brass, GEN SMITH decries MacArthur's failure to give any recognition of the Marines part in the recapture of the Philippines. "You can search MacArthur's communique's describing the Philippines fighting and nowhere will you find a single reference to the Marines. I met one of our young Marines who was being flown back from Leyte. He was in great pain, but it was not the physical suffering that worried him," 'I don't mind losing a leg Sir, he said bitterly, but at least Doug might have mentioned the Marines were there!'

TINIAN, MARSHALL ISLANDS
25 Jul - 1 Aug 1944

RAIDERS KILLED IN ACTION ON TINIAN
PRATT, FRANK E.   WALLINGTON,LEN E.

2A RAIDER LT MELVIN J. SPOTTS WAS AWARDED THE NAVY CROSS FOR HEROISM IN COMBAT ON TINIAN

RAIDERS AWARDED THE SILVER STAR ON TINIAN
BARRON, STANLEY *   GLOEDE,RAYMOND PATRICK,CHARLES * Second Silver Star Awarded

Located just 3 miles off the coast of Saipan was Tinian. Approximately 12 miles long with a general flat terrain; Tinian was needed to construct an airfield with extra long runways. The top-secret need for the airfield, was of course to enable the Air Force planes to take off from the island with the atom bomb aboard while bound for Hiroshima.

3,612 of the 5,156 patients admitted to the medical companies on Saipan returned to duty in time for the invasion of Tinian by the 2nd and 4th Marine Division's on 24 Jul 44.
That day the 24th Marines reached the western edge of Airfield No 3, while on the 25th the 8th Marines took the Ushi Point Airfield and Mt Maga was seized by the 25th Marines

Mt. Lasso was captured unopposed by the 2nd and 4th Marine Divisions on 26 Jul and all resistance ended on 30 Jul 1944.

Japanese Admiral Kakuda defended the island with 9000 soldiers and sailors. Although declared secure on 1 Aug 44, the difficult job of destroying the remnants of the Japanese garrison lasted until the end of the year. Over 500 enemy soldiers were killed during that period while the Marines lost 38 killed and 125 wounded. The 2nd and 4th Marine Divisions lost 327 killed in action and 1,771 wounded in action.

Corpsman Stanley Bowens explains, " The only suitable beach for landing was near Tinian town. The pre-assault bombing and shelling took place for several days and many Marines were put in amphtracks to head toward the beach where the Japanese had rushed all their troops, only to turn around and head back to their transports. The most successful fake landing of the war had succeeded, while the 4th MarDiv landed on the northern part o the island. I was on the first wave second day and when Tinian was secured we were shipped back to Saipan. While there I received my Silver Star Medal."

13

Guam

Corpsmen treating wounded Marines on Guam
prior to evacuation after first wave of landings

INVASION OF GUAM
21 JULY 1944
FIRST PROVISIONAL MARINE BRIGADE
3rd MARINE DIVISION

Prior to this epic battle, the 1st Marine Raider Regiment was disbanded with most of the Raiders being given the honor of reforming the historic 4th Marine Regiment that had fallen in the early days of the war at Corregidor in the Philippine Islands.

On 20 Jul 1944, eight minutes after landing on Guam, two Marines raised the American flag and Raider MILTON A. FORD was there to take the original photo.

As 4th Marines, the former Raiders added to the glory of the Old Fourth again and again on Guam by distinguishing themselves in battle after battle. The reputation gained however was at a high cost as over 400 Raiders were killed in action (including 8 Combat Corpsmen) and over 1300 were wounded in action on Okinawa.

MARINE RAIDERS KILLED IN ACTION ON GUAM

ALFANO, DANIEL	ALLEN, PHILLIP E.
AUSTIN,HAROLD	BAGWELL, EARL
BAJKO, ALEX S.	BAKER, WESLEY
BALL, WALTER W.	BARKER, HARRY
BARNHART, RALPH	BARR, LEROY
BATTS, JAMES H.	BEANE, FRED E.
BEUDRY, LOUIS N.	BEHRENT,WILLIAM
BELKO, MAX	BENNETT,WILLIAM
BERGAMINI,JOHN	BERGFIELD, MAX
BERRY, JAMES B.	BOLIN, ROBERT G.
BOWLING,HERMAN	BRANCH,JAMES
BROWN, JAMES F.	BRUBAKER, R. W.
BULNES, S. E.	BUSBY, ALFRED E.
BYERLEY,WARREN	CAIL, ELDON H.
CALDERA,ROBERT	CAMPBELL,CLYDE
CAREY, LOUIS J.	CARLTON, RICHARD
CARTER, EUGENE	CASDORPH,JOHN
CASHMORE,GEORGE	CHAFFEE, ALLEN
CHRISTENSEN,F. F.	CHUDA, JACK R.
COLLINS, LEWIS	CUTHBERTSON, J.
DANIELS,NELSON	DICKSON, J.H
DOMANN, CARL P.	DOSS, JOHN M.*
DOSS LESTER K.	DOWNS, BILLY
DUFFY,DONALD	DURHAM,VICTOR
ENGEL, ROBERT	EVANS, MAX L.
FASNACHT, R. E.	FERRY,RAYMOND
FESHOH,WILLIAM *	FITTS, KENNETH
FLOWERS,HARLEY	FUQUAY, MARVIN
GADOMSKI, WALT	GARCIA, GEORGE
GILL, WARNER	GLASSEN, PAUL*
GLENN, ALTON	GOTTLEIB, MORT
GOVALETZ,JOHN	GRAVES, JAMES
HARMER, ERWIN	HARMON, FRANK
HARVEY, JAMES B.	HASSIG, DONALD
HAYNES, EUGENE	HELPINGSTINE, H.
HENDERSON, K. D.	HAROLD, FRED
HOFFMAN, C.	HOLLEY, JOHN W.
HONOHAN, WM. J.	HUBBARD, D. D.
HUNNIFORD, WM.	HUTCHINGS, KARL
ISAACSON, J. H.	IVEY, CLIFTON E.
JENDRASIAK, C.F.	JOHNSON, R. E.
JONES, BURTNETT	JONES, PHILIP W.
KATH, LLOYD E.	KELLEY, WILLIAM
KELLY, FRANCIS	KELLY, RAYMOND
KIRKPATRICK, J.H.	KLAUSE, OSCAR *
KOSTIC, GEORGE	KYZAR, ROBERT

LANSLEY, ROBERT	LATKOVICH, JOE
LEONARD, JULIAN	LEWIS, DALLAS O.
LEWIS, DAVID W.	LOWRY, HAROLD
LUEDTKE, EDWARD	LYONS, THEODORE
MALOUGHNEY,F.	MARZLOFF, H.P.
McALLISTER, C.R.	McCRACKEN, J.W.
McINTOSH, R. E.	McKELVEY, R. R.
MEYER, WALLACE	MINIER, LEE N.
MITCHELL, WM. E.	MITCHIE,CHARLES
MOCK, DONALD D.	MONTANO, LEO J.
MOORE, RALPH E.	MOORE, WILLIAM
MORGAN, JACK W.	MULLANEY, R. J.
MULLINS, PAUL L.	MURPHY, JAMES
MYSICKA, JOHN B.	NIELSEN, NEILS P.
NELLIGAN, JOHN *	NOWAKOWSKI, R.E.
ORIBILETTI, BRUNO	ORTON,CHARLES
OSTI, TONY	PARKS, STERLING
PAUL, GEORGE J.	PEARL, CORWIN
PERRY, CHARLES	PETERS, STANLEY
PHEMISTER, E.E.	PRIEST, THOMAS
PRYOR, ROLLAND	PUHALO, S.
PULLER, SAMUEL	REIBER, PAUL E.
RESER, HARRY	REVAK, MERTON
RICHARDSON, A.	RINGGOLD, C.F.
ROBERTS, FRANK	RODEITCHER,G.
ROGERS, DONALD	ROLETTE, ALLEN
ROSE, DANIEL H.	ROTH, ROBERT
ROUSE, HUGH E.	SALZMAN,EDWARD
SAMUELSON,JOE	SCHEFFER,FRAN
SCHULZ, WM. F.	SCHUSTER, K.O.
SELBY, ROBERT	SERGO, MIKE E.
SHANAHAN, E. J.	SHERIDAN, JOE
SIMMERS, CHAS.	SKELLY, JAMES
SLIVA, LEONARD	SMALL, GEORGE
SMITH, ROGER E.	STEWARD, GERALD
STOWE, MERLE	SUMMERS, WM.
SWANSON, R.E.	SWETLAND, FRANK
SWITCHENKO, F.	TOWNSEND, E. C.
VINSON, RAY	VITTORI, HARRY
WACHLIN, ALVIN	WALLIS, ROBERT
WARD, HERBERT	WATTENBARGER,W
WELLBAUM, D.E.	WHITE, MELVIN
WILLIAMS, ROY	WILSON, RAY
WOLFE, ROBERT	ZELINSKI, S.J.

* Corpsmen

13 Raiders remain missing in action on Guam

Various sources set the total 4th Marines WIA at more than 800.

The names shown are those confirmed from available records.

RAIDERS AWARDED MEDALS ON GUAM

NAVY CROSS

BARKER, HARRY   BRANCH, JAMES
CAIL, ELDEN   HERWIG,ROBERT
HUNNIFORD, W.J.   KINGSLEY, LUKE
MOORE, RALPH   ORBILETTI,BRUNO
ROBERTS, F.E.   ROGERS, NEIL L.
SALZMAN,EDWARD   SELBY, ROBERT
SERGO, MIKE E.   SHAPLEY, ALAN
SHAHEEN, A.J.   SHIVELY, ALLEN
SMITH, ROGER   STEA, ANTHONY
WIDDECKE, C.F.

SILVER STAR

BAILEY,BENNETT   JOHNSON,EDWIN
POLK, LEE R.   BATTERTON, R.J.
KARR, RAYMOND   PRUITT, WILBERT
BELLMAN, M.R.   KELLEY, WILLIAM
ROBERTS,CLAYTON   DALEY, LaVARRE
KOHNKE,WALTER   SCHUSTER, KEN
DODDS, TAD N.   LAMBERSON, G.B.
SEXTON,MARTIN   DUNBAR, MICHAEL
LANEVILLE,HOMER   SMITH,CHARLES
FOLEY, FRANCIS   LEONARD, JULIAN
STERLING, JOHN   GOHEEN, RICHARD
MACK, RICHARD   STEWART, WM. *
GREEN, BERNARD   MINIER, LEE N.
TOMAIKO,GEORGE   HOFER, WILLARD
MOORE, FLOYD E.   TOWNSEND, E.C.
HOYLER, H.M.   MURPHY, JOHN J.
WEHNER, WM.J.   HUFFSTUTTER,H.F
OSTEMEYER, O.W.   WELKY, JAMES
* Second Silver Star Award

RAIDER CORPSMEN AWARDED MEDALS ON GUAM

NAVY CROSS
METZGER,GEORGE

SILVER STAR
LAW, ROBERT D.   NELLIGAN, JOHN

7 CORPSMEN, 3 DOCTORS, AND FATHER REDMOND WERE ALSO AWARDED THE BRONZE STAR MEDAL ON GUAM

The terrain on Guam, which measured approximately 28 miles long and 4 to 8 miles wide, was similar to that of Saipan. There were about 19,000 fighting men on the island, who had the opportunity to construct additional formidable underwater defenses because of a five-week delay in launching the American invasion of the island. The defenders received concentrated bombardment from American air and naval forces, including a 13-day continuous naval bombardment, the most prolonged of the war to date.

D-DAY for Guam had been set for 18 June 1944. As the capture of Saipan was prolonged they had to serve as floating reserve, that resulted in a delay. After several weeks aboard LCI's the men of the 3rd Marine Division and the 1st Marine Brigade were allowed to leave their ships for a short period of time at Eniwetok Island. The 1st Provisional Marine Brigade's 4th Marine Regiment was made up of former Marine Raiders.

The invasion force's objective was to quickly take Apra Harbor on the West Coast and the Orote Peninsula bounding it to the south. The 3rd Division would go in to the north of the harbor, on what were called the Asan beaches. The 1st Provisional Brigade (4th and 24th Marine Regiments) would land about five miles to the south, just below the Orote Peninsula.

After beach reconnaissance and obstacle clearance by Navy "frogmen" (Underwater Demolition Teams), 20,000 3rd Division Marines landed July 21 on the Asan beaches.
The Japanese held the high ground overlooking the landing area, and the Marines took casualties as a result.

On July 21, the 1st Provisional Brigade faced Japanese fire in the form of mortar and artillery fire, beginning at the reef and continuing on the beaches. Unloading did not go smoothly, and ammunition and fuel were in short supply. Despite these difficulties, the Marines reached their initial objectives by afternoon, and were reinforced by GIs from the 77th Infantry Division.

On 22 Jul, LT Stormy SEXTON'S 3rd Battalion K Co (Raiders) 4th Marines faced continued enemy attacks on it's Hill 40 sector throughout the night, and engaged in hand to hand combat in foxholes with swords, knives and bayonets. The Raiders were well prepared for the banzai attacks with grenades on the ready.

The 1st Battalion (Raiders) 4th Marines repulsed a banzai attack by 5000 Japs that had penetrated their lines and gained the summit of Mount Alifan on 22 Jul. Japanese counter attacks against the lines of the 1st Provisional Marine Brigade (4th and 22nd Marines) were repulsed with heavy Japanese losses in the period of 25-27 Jul. As a result the 38th Japanese Infantry was destroyed.

With the air, Naval and artillery support the 4th and 22nd Marines captured Orote Peninsula and reached the old Marine Barracks on 29 Jul. Agana, capital of Guam fell on 31 Jul.

On 3 Aug the 4th Marines moved toward Toto in the north of the island where the 4th Marines were the first to reach both the southern and the northern ends of Guam during the campaign.

In the early days of the battle the hospital had been attacked with a large loss of life. Some of the wounded suffered additional wounds. Aid stations were hit by enemy shells and at least 20 Raider 4th Marine Corpsmen were wounded in action and 4 Corpsmen were killed in action.

Following their heroic efforts on Bougainville, the 1st and 2nd War Dog Platoons again proved their value in combat, as did the Navajo Code Talkers. Many Marines thanked the Lord for these dogs who allowed them to get a good nights sleep without the fear of being infiltrated by enemy troops.

From 21 to 31 Aug the 1st Provisional Brigade left the island for Guadalcanal to begin training for the capture of Okinawa.

Of the 30,214 Marine participants, 1,082 were killed, 125 were missing and 4,852 were wounded. Of the 17,958 men of the 77th Infantry Division, casualties were 193 killed, 20 missing and 704 wounded. More than 17,000 Japanese were killed.

The photo of the Guam flag raising was taken by one of the small band of our intrepid Raider photographers, 4HQ MILTON A.FORD, Kensington, MD. Who was later Associate Chief, Photographic Services National Geographic Society. Milt wrote, "The photo was widely used by newspapers and supplements. " Former Raiders were once again part of a truly historical event, the first American held territory prior to World War II, to be recaptured from the Japanese occupying forces.

Guam had been in Japanese hands for two years, seven months and ten days. To the Marines of 3rd Marine Division and. the 1st Marine Brigade, the recapture of Guam partially avenged the loss of 155 comrades, killed or captured when the Japanese over ran the small Marine attachment on 10 Dec 1941.

To Americans every where it meant we had won back our first piece of Jap occupied American territory.

Marine Raider, RUDOLPH G. ROSENQUIST 3K wrote "We were overrun on D-day night 21-22 Jul 44 by a Japanese Banzai attack. I was bayoneted in the left side, abdomen, and lower chest. Took a gun a shot wound in the right leg and suffered multiple shrapnel wounds of the right and left legs. 3 pieces are retained, in my right leg. I weighed 98 pound at that time.

PATCH EDITOR: GUAM BANZAI ATTACK 21-22 Jul 1944. While the 1st Marine Brigade's bridgehead was still tenuous, the Japanese attacked the 4th Marines on the right flank and near Hill 40. At 2330, they laid down an intense mortar barrage and charging enemy hurled demolition charges and small land mines like grenades. Six Marines were bayoneted in their foxholes. A platoon of Company K was dislodged from Hill 40 regrouped, and made 2 valiant, but unsuccessful attempts to drive the enemy off the Hill. Reinforcements (two squads) under LT MARVIN C. PLOCK arrived and the third assault recaptured and held the position. LT MARTIN J. SEXTON'S K Co 3rd BN men stopped the main enemy thrust but small groups of infiltrating Japanese were successful in reaching the rear where the Marine track howitzer positions; were located. They were eliminated at first light with 390 dead enemy littering the field and giving mute evidence of the effectiveness of the 3K Raider fire.

3HQ Corpsman Chester Malinowski, wrote of the beautiful day going ashore on Easter Day on Guam. "The first night I was in the last foxhole down the line. They called me when the LT was wounded. As I crawled from hole to hole trying to remember the password, I was having doubts about going out. We knew we had bypassed a lot of Nips and they were crawling around. I got to a tree across our line and he was in the second one from the tree, there was no one in the first hole as we were short of men. He was wounded in the butt with shrapnel and I patched him up but refused to go to the aid station in the rear. Later I saw a Jap sword on the ground and went for it, just as the Jap sprung up with it in his hand shouting 'Die Marine". The LT cut him down with his machine gun as well as the other Nips I thought were dead. The funniest thing on Guam was when Chaplain Boyd was wounded in the scrotum by shrapnel and we asked him if he was ever going to tell anyone or show them his scars? Another Raider Corpsman WILLIAM FRATUS was attending school to be a minister and had to bandage a Guamese woman who suffered a stab wound in her breast. He did it and no one knows how, as he Never Did LOOK to see what he was doing!"

1DB CHARLES M. THOMSON, Anaheim, CA wrote, "Mary Houseman, Grand Ledge. MI is trying to locate someone who knew her brother PFC GEORGE H. CASHMORE before he was KIA 2 Jul 44 at Guam. "I remember GEORGE, mostly in bits and pieces. We went overseas on the same ship MT VERNON, and we talked aboard ship because we both came from small towns in Michigan. GEORGE had a fish line sewed into the seam of his dungarees in case we were torpedoed. On arrival at New Caledonia I went into LT FRANK KEMP'S "D" Co, and GEORGE went into "B" Co 1st Raider Battalion. I was later transferred into "B" Co as the Company Clerk. When we arrived at Guam 21 July 1944 GYSGT RICHARD W. PRINGLE was acting 1st SGT. When he was shot through his tattoo on his arm it was then SGT MICKEY F. SPARKS (KIA 23 May 45 Okinawa until LT MAX BELKO was killed (21 Jul 44 Guam) then SPARKS went back to his Weapons Platoon and I handled the administrative duties. On the night PFC GEORGE CASHMORE was killed (2 Jul), I shared a foxhole with CPL JOHN U. DOSS (KIA 26 July 44 GUAM), who was our Company Commander's (CAPT ROGER C. FOLEY, KIA 27 May 45 Okinawa runner. We were at one end of the BAKER COMPANY perimeter next to the road. GEORGE was about half way around the perimeter near where the road exited our area again. This was the night and early morning when we were attacked by tank supported infantry. Our tanks came up and knocked.out the last of the Japanese tanks and as they were retreating George's area bore the brunt of the enemy attack and suffered heavily for it. I talked to a member of George's platoon in the morning and it might have been PALMER B. CANFIELD 1B, 51 Valencia St. Cuyahoga Falls, OH. He should remember GEORGE better than I do. In any case, I remember GEORGE'S smile it was big, friendly, lots of teeth. As I remember, GEORGE had almost no hair a real side wall haircut. A quiet, self sufficient sort of young man that everyone liked. I don't know if this helps Mary Houseman but I felt that I should write."

3L CHARLES J. BIDDLE, "I would like to ask COL 'STORMY' SEXTON if he remembers LT ALLEN P. HENSLEY. We were on a patrol on Guam when PFC DONALD P. MOCK 3ML was shot. He was up the hill between two rock cliffs. LT HENSELY said 'Let's go get him!' We ran up the hill and carried him out. We buried him on the beach. I was squad leader so I gave him last rites."

3MK HERMAN E. WOOTEN, wrote "I have been meaning

to add a little to the RUDY ROSENQUIST account of the Hill 4O fight that first night on GUAM 21 July 1944. CHARLES D. WHITMAN, WILLIAM R. SURA, CHARLES B. ROBINSON, LEONARD G. 'BONES' GORMAN and myself were manning a machine gun position to the left of Rudy's squad and on the left flank of our beach defense positions. It was a long night with Japs crawling all over the place. I don't think that ROSENQUIST and the other members of his squad ever knew that a ditch ran all the way from the front of their dug-in position to the mountains way off in the distance. Japanese crawled up this ditch all night, undetected by flares, and they were able to create a lot of confusion. Just about dawn, the enemy tried to set up a heavy machine gun facing our beach positions. We were the flank and looking right at them, so I'm proud to report that they never did get that gun set up. They were very determined and kept sending more men forward to do it. They ran into a steady stream of our fire and we piled them up. Later after it got light, we saw more Japs looking out of this ditch but we could not fire on them as we would be firing into our own positions. They were throwing grenades and carrying on a fight with CLARENCE R. 'SPADE' DE PAS, 3K, finallv Spade lumbered into the ditch and emptied a clip (20 rounds) of his BAR. As he came out the grenades kept coming. A tank came up and. fired a few. 'P5's into the ditch. It was like a MEAT MARKET with different cuts of meat flying around. Later we counted over 60 dead bodies in that ditch. I always thought Spade had received a decoration for his bravery but Spade reported that he never did."

1AD DONALD B. HEFFRON, Townsend, TN wrote "I don't have a picture of ROBERT W. BALL who was KIA on Guam 23 July 1944. He was the A Company runner for the first two days on that rock, he died a horrible death! He was found staked to the ground with a 2 x 2 stake driven through his chest and about 24 inches into the ground. His arms and legs were twisted grotesquely and his eye balls ware lying out on his cheeks. I can never forget the sight of it and I will continue to hate Japs. I will stop remembering now, as it hurts TOO MUCH!" AUTHOR:This letter is quoted from the Raider Patch.

2G31 WALTER T. DONALDSON, wrote "The 2nd Platoon of I Company, 3rd BN 4th Marines left their foxholes on Orote Peninsula, early in the morning to form a skirmish line with tanks supporting the attack. We advanced through thick vegetation and soon came upon heavy Japanese fortifications. The enemy opened fire on us from concrete pillboxes pinning us down. Our tanks advanced and began a barrage of flat trajectory fire that made shrapnel, trees and bushes fly in all directions. To escape the deadly fire, the enemy soldiers broke and ran in the direction of our lines. Several came directly at me and I dropped them with my BAR (Browning Automatic Rifle).

When I could see no more enemy and I found I had lost contact with GEORGE F. BEENEY, 3I, on my left flank and CLYDE SIZEMORE, 3I on my right. Suddenly I heard SIZEMORE yell for help. His carbine had jammed and he was bent over with his face pressed in the ground. A sword swinging Jap was flailing away on his head and back. ERNEST O. MANNING, 3L blasted the Jap from point blank range. Both MANNING AND BEENEY were later KIA on Okinawa.

After all the Japs were killed or cleared from the area our platoon reformed and we got a big laugh when we looked at CLYDE SIZEMORE. He was the demolition's man assigned to our platoon and had been carrying a pack of flame thrower Tetrol on his back when the Jap jumped him. His pack was chopped to shreds and his helmet gleamed like bright new steel where the Samurai sword had cut off the green camouflage paint. A bit shaken, SIZEMORE was unhurt."

Raider hero LUKE KINGSLEY was awarded the Silver Cross for his heroism on Guam on 21 July 1944. Upon review in 1950, however the Silver Star was recalled and the award was upgraded to the Navy Cross.

AUTHOR: This was one of the few times a Raider award was UPGRADED, usually it was the other way around.

1st Raider FRANK KEMP was first wounded in the arm near Enogai on New Georgia Island. Frank writes, "my second wound came in Okinawa, on the outskirts of Naha, while I was standing talking to Raider FRANK LAZETICH a fellow officer. A shell came over and killed several Marines and broke my right leg, The Corpsmen got me back to an aid station and then to a tent hospital before I was flown out to Mare Island Hospital and later to Bethesda Naval Hospital. The staff at both hospitals, were absolutely the finest in the world. Raider COL ALAN SHAPLEY, AND COL SAM GRIFFITH were two of the finest officers in the Marine Corps."

AUTHOR: FRANK KEMP received 2 Bronze Stars for heroism in combat in addition to his two Purple Hearts and the Soldiers Medal.

1st Raider VIC ANDERSON shared a hilarious, tongue in cheek reply that 1st Raider TOM BREEN wrote to the V.A. in 1947, after they tried to explain why his 110% disability, presently paying 100% disability, would under existing regulations of the

Veteran's Administration now be computed as 80% disability. This reduced his compensation from $180 to $152.40 monthly. And that included a special monthly pension of $42.00 for the loss of "only one foot." BREEN'S disabilities after being wounded 21 Jul 1944 on Guam were a total of 110% and included 40% for Amputation right leg, 20% Penetrating gunshot wound left leg. 10% Residuals of fracture to left leg. 10% Residuals of penetrating gunshot wound to right thigh. 10% Residuals of gunshot wound to muscles of right forearm.10% Fracture of the right collarbone, 10% Disfiguring scars to the right cheek.

AUTHOR: I will leave the fairness of the VA Determination of Disability to the judgement of the readers.

Cuppa Joe on Board Ship After Battle

Marine Firing Weapon Next to Dead Japanese Soldier

Death On Iwo Jima

14

Iwo Jima

Col. Justice M. Chambers, USMCR, Medal of Honor

OFFICIAL MEDAL OF HONOR CITATION

"For conspicuous gallantry and intrepidity at the risk of his life above and beyond the call of duty as Commanding Officer of the Third Assault Battalion Landing Team, Twenty-Fifth Marines, Fourth Marine Division, in action against enemy Japanese forces on Iwo Jima, Volcano Islands, from 19 to 22 February 1945. Under a furious barrage of enemy machine-gun and small-arms fire from the commanding cliffs on the right, Col. Chambers, then Lt. Col., landed immediately after the initial assault waves of his Battalion on D-Day to find the momentum of the assault threatened by heavy casualties from withering Japanese artillery, mortar, rocket, machine-gun and rifle fire. Exposed to relentless hostile fire, he coolly reorganized his battle-weary men, inspiring them to heroic efforts by his own valor and leading them in an attack on the critical, impregnable high ground from which the enemy was pouring an increasing volume of fire directly onto troops ashore as well as amphibious craft in succeeding waves. Col. Chambers led the 8-hour battle to carry the flanking ridge top and reduce the enemy's fields of aimed fire, thus protecting the vital foot-hold gained. In constant defiance of hostile fire, he maintained contact with adjacent units and forwarded vital information to the Regimental Commander. His zealous fighting spirit undiminished despite terrific casualties and the loss of most of his key officers, he again reorganized his troops for renewed attack against the enemy's main line of resistance and was directing the fire of the rocket platoon when he fell, critically wounded. Evacuated under heavy Japanese fire, Col. Chambers, by forceful leadership, courage and fortitude in the face of staggering odds, was directly instrumental in insuring the success of subsequent operations of the Fifth Amphibious Corps on Iwo Jima, thereby sustaining and enhancing the finest traditions of the United States Naval Service."

Iwo Jima

GySgt William G. Walsh, 3CL, Medal of Honor

OFFICIAL MEDAL OF HONOR CITATION

"For extraordinary gallantry and intrepidity at the risk of his life above and beyond the call of duty as Leader of an Assault Platoon, attached to Co. G., Third Battalion, Twenty-Seventh Marines, Fifth Marine Division, in action against enemy Japanese forces at Iwo Jima, Volcano Islands, on 27 February 1945. With the advance of his company toward Hill 362 disrupted by vicious machine-gun fire from a forward position which guarded approaches to this key enemy stronghold, Gunnery Sergeant Walsh fearlessly charged at the head of his platoon against the Japanese entrenched on the ridge above him, utterly oblivious to the unrelenting fury of hostile automatic weapons fire and hand grenades employed with fanatic desperation to smash his daring assault. Thrown back by the enemy's savage resistance, he once again led his men in a seemingly impossible attack up the steep, rocky slope, boldly defiant of the annihilating streams of bullets which saturated the area. Despite his own casualty losses and the overwhelming advantage held by the Japanese in superior numbers and dominant position, he gained the ridge's top only to be subjected to an intense barrage of hand grenades thrown by the remaining Japanese staging a suicidal last stand on the reverse slope. When one of the grenades fell in the midst of his surviving men, huddled together in a small trench, Gunnery Sergeant Walsh, in a final valiant act of complete self-sacrifice, instantly threw himself upon the deadly bomb, absorbing with his own body, the full and terrific force of the explosion. Through his extraordinary initiative and inspiring valor in the face of almost certain death, he saved his comrades from injury and possible loss of life and enabled his company to seize and hold this vital enemy position. He gallantly gave his life for his country."

Iwo Jima

First Flag-Raising

Marine Raiders were involved in both of the flag raisings on Mt. Suribachi, 23 February 1945 on the island of Iwo Jima.

The first flag raising (above) captured by Leatherneck photographer, Lou Lowery, shows Raider Cpl. Charles Lindberg, 2GHQ, standing at the right above Pfc. Michaels, on guard with his carbine.

Iwo Jima

After reaching the summit of Mt. Suribachi, the team notified their command post that they had been successful. They were ordered to go ahead and raise the flag.

A segment of broken water pipe made an ideal improvised pole.

Lt. Harold Schrier, PltSgt. Ernest Thomas, Sgt. Henry Hansen and Cpl. Charles Lindberg, (left to right) are shown attaching the flag to the pipe.

After Marine Pfc Gagnon reached the summit with the larger flag, Lt. Schrier chose the location for the second most historically famous flag. He then ordered the first flag to be lowered and the second flag to be raised simultaneously.

IWO JIMA BATTLE
19 Feb-26 Mar 45

Iwo Jima, a small pork chop shaped island just 330 miles from Tokyo was chosen as the next target in the allied war against the Japanese. Although heavy casualties were
expected; in the necessary frontal assault on the island, few thought such a tiny piece of land would play such an important part in the history of the Marine Corps, and in the lore of the Marine Raiders.

Army Air Force General "Hap " Arnold needed the island in American hands to shorten the flight time for his B-29 attacks on the Japanese mainland in order to save precious aviation fuel and as an emergency landing field for short of fuel or damaged planes. It was also important to the Marine Corps as it would be the first island of the sacred Japanese homeland to be occupied.

The 3rd, 4th and 5th Marine Divisions were chosen for the invasion of Iwo Jima, with D-Day set for 19 Feb 1945. Sprinkled among the 4th and 5th MarDiv's, were many battle hardened Raider and paratrooper Marines returning to active duty from hospitals after recovering from wounds or an illness. To those Marines fell the job of becoming the backbone of their units and providing leadership to those Marines who were new to combat.

Japanese General Kuribayashi was to defend Iwo Jima with 21,000 troops. His heavily fortified, defensive positions and firepower was the strongest in the Pacific Campaign. The 1500 caves, tunnels, gun emplacements, blockhouses and pillboxes stretched from the black sandy beach head to the heavily defended rocky approaches to the summit of heavily defended Mount Suribachi with it's volcanic crater and maze of tunnels and caves.

Kuribayashi also changed Japanese strategy from that of immediately attacking enemy assaults at the water line to one of preparing a coastal defense. He utilized 1500 caves, tunnels, gun emplacements, blockhouses, pillboxes bristling with artillery, rockets, heavy machine guns, mortars and even tanks buried up to their turrets in sand, with each zeroed in on the small area of the landings that stretched from the black sandy beach head to the heavily defended rocky approaches of Mount Suribachi with it's volcanic crater.

On D-Day the 23rd and 24th Regiments, 4th Marine Division and the 27th an 28th Regiments 5th Marine Division led the assault forces ashore. Puzzled by the largely unopposed landing the Marines, in attempting to rapidly move up the elevated shoreline to the airfield discovered they were unable to run fast enough in the ankle deep black sand to make room on the beach head for the second wave following right behind them.

The Jap troops had a clear view of the beach from their caves and tunnels on Mount Suribachi. When the beaches became crowded with trucks and jeeps stuck in the sand, men milling about and supplies being piled up, they opened up with artillery, rockets coastal guns, tank fire, mortars and machine guns that took a terrible toll among the men who had no place to go. Jap observers could direct 3-4 man suicide squads from their spider holes and trenches just beyond the beach to infiltrate the lines and use grenades to blow up ammunition and supply dumps during the night.

A sulphuric odor like that of rotten eggs permeated the air and it was difficult to dig a foxhole as the sides kept caving in. The volcanic sand was hot so the men fortunate enough to have a foxhole or crater for cover soon learned to line them with cardboard food ration boxes to keep from having their asses burned. Black stinging sand blew into their faces, landed on uniforms and stuck to and jammed weapons.

Enemy fire hit not only the beach but burst among the landing boats, as they were bringing in Marines and supplies and as they were carrying out the wounded. Boats were blasted out of the water, the dead were hanging over the sides, body parts were all about and bodies were floating in the water.

First aid stations set up on the crowded beach were subjected to continuous enemy fire. Wounded were lying all around. It was impossible to stand up on the beach so the wounded were dragged into any holes or depressions that could be found, given first aid and left there until they could be evacuated. Some were hit again two or three times, or even worse lost heir lives on the beach, or after being loaded on board the boats taking them to safety.

Amid all this confusion one Corpsman, new to battle, sutured up chest wounds of 4 Marines and undoubtedly saved their lives. A Marine blinded with both hands shot off, was wandering in the direction of the beach when a Corpsman dashed out and led him to safety. Another Corpsman went to the aid of his C.O. and buried the lower half of the officer's body to better protect him from snipers. Unfortunately the officer didn't survive. At the Battalion Aid Station bottles of blood plasma hanging from rifles thrust into the sand, and the wounded laying on stretchers became favorite targets for the Japanese.

Among those former Raiders in the assault force were LTCOL JUSTICE (Jumpin Joe) CHAMBERS Commanding Officer of the 3rd Bn 25th Marines of the 4th MarDiv, and GUNNERY SGT WILLIAM G. WALSH 3rd Bn 27th Marines, 5th MarDiv. Both Chambers and Walsh were to be awarded the Medal of Honor for heroism on Iwo Jima.

Before nightfall D-DAY, Chambers 3rd Bn K Co lost it's C.O., another company lost it's C.O. and two officers, and another company was missing two officers, while one of the rifle companies lost seven of it's officers. Nearly half of their enlisted men were lost on this day.

3 Bn surgeon Dr. William Hruza, LTJG USN went into battle with another doctor and 40 Corpsmen. By 1330 in the afternoon only Hruza and two Corpsmen were still on their feet. The rest were either dead or wounded. Col Chambers miraculously recovered from a sucking chest wound that was almost always resulted in death

Hruza was awarded the Silver Star for his heroics, but he said "they should have given a Navy Cross to every one of the 195 Corpsmen and 7 doctors who were killed on Iwo Jima." In one division, casualties among hospital corpsmen exceeded 50% in their 6 battalions. In 4 battalions, casualties exceeded 60%, and in 1 battalion, they were in excess of 68%. Battle casualties for all division medical personnel exceeded 25%. 529 Corpsman and 12 doctors were also wounded before the fighting ended.

A neurosurgeon, an opthalmologist and a neuropsychiatrist were included in the Corps medical battalion. The services of dental officers and technicians were invaluable as surgical operations went on despite mortar shells landing nearby. By D-day+30, 2,393 casualties had been evacuated by air to the Marianas. Air evacuation proved to be much more effective and tied up less personnel than the use of hospital ships.

COL HARRY "THE HORSE" LIVERSEDGE Commanding Officer of the 28th Marines of the 5th MarDiv and 1LT HAROLD SCHRIER who participated in both the first and the second flag raising on Mt Suribachi were among the twelve former Raiders to be awarded the Navy Cross.

Afloat as part of the 5th Fleet convoy aboard USS Missoula AT were the men of E Co 2nd BN 28th Marine Regiment. During training in Hawaii and while still on board ship, men of the 28th vied with each other as to who would be the first to reach the top of Mount Suribachi and plant the American flag there.

1Lt Greeley Wells the E CO 2nd BN adjutant, insisted it was his duty as adjutant to carry out that duty and while on board the Missoula, scrounged a small 54" X 28" flag for that purpose. Little did he or the men of Company E realized what an impact his decision would make upon their lives and upon the history of the Marine Corps.

The 1st and 2nd BN's of the 28th Marines landed just 400 yards from the base of 550' high Mount Suribachi. Continued shelling and a cold night allowed little rest to those clinging to their tiny foothold on the island.

The second day of frontal assaults yielded an advance of 200 yards for E Co 2nd BN, who suffered a 25% casualty rate. 1Lt Wells and four others were wounded, including the Corpsman who came to their aid. As he was being evacuated Wells turned his unit over to Plt Sgt Ernest "Boots" Thomas.

As the Platoon fought their way forward, CPL CHARLES LINDBERG (Raider) and Pvt. Robert Goode, directed streams of fire from their flame throwers into the peep holes of the bunkers in order to destroy them. By the end of the third day the 2nd and 3rd Bn's 28th Marines nearly surrounded the base of Mt Suribachi. In eight hours of fighting, 2nd Bn E Co 3rd Platoon of the 28th Marines had 17 men wounded, and earned one Medal of Honor, 3 Navy Crosses and one Silver Star Medal while surrounding the base of the mountain. Casualties for the first three days of fighting on the island reached 4,500.

That evening Marine General H.M. Smith ordered COL HARRY LIVERSEDGE (Raider) to "take Mount Suribachi" the next day. LtCol Chaney Johnson in turn received his orders from Liversedge "to Seize and Occupy Suribachi". CHANEY and Capt Dave Severance then gave Lt Wells' flag to (Raider) 1Lt HAROLD SCHRIER E Co Executive Officer and ordered him to take the 40 man assault patrol to the summit, secure the crater and raise the flag.

An earlier D Co 28th Marine patrol led by (Raider) JOHN J. WEILAND, including (Raiders) FRED FERENTZ and JAMES MULLIGAN volunteered to find routes of approach on Mt. Suribachi, on 23 Feb 44. They reached the summit without being fired upon so no problems were anticipated although they knew hundreds of Japs were still holed up in the crevices, tunnels and caves of the slopes. (There were 17 former Raiders in D Co.) WEILAND received the Silver Star for his bravery on Iwo Jima and one week later was wounded and became a parplegic for life.

Schriers patrol included a radioman, two teams of stretcher-bearers and Marine Staff Sgt Lou Lowery of Leatherneck Magazine bringing up the rear, photographing every step of the way. Marines below watched as the patrol moved forward in a difficult climb, slowly moving up the side of the mountain, sometimes crawling on hands and knees. Upon reaching the rim they crawled over the edge one man at a time.

Fanning out in the rim with minor enemy activity in the cave openings, a long piece of pipe was soon found and taken to a spot chosen by 1Lt SCHRIER. The flag was attached to the pole and Lowery snapped the picture of the first flag raising at 1010 A.M. on 23 Feb 45. The six men present as the flag pole was planted, were PltSgt "Boots" Thomas, Sgt Henry Hansen, Cpl CHARLES LINDBERG (Raider), 1Lt HAROLD SCHRIER (Raider), Pfc James Michaels and Pvt Louis Charlo. As it came into view the tired and dirty Marines below cheered loudly and a chorus of bells, whistles and foghorns emanated from the ships in the harbor.

At the same time all hell broke loose in the crater as the Japanese saw the flag flying. Enraged by the sight of the flag, grenades came flying and shots rang out from the caves with one shot just missing Lowery, who tumbled almost fifty feet down the side of the mountain before grabbing a bush to save himself and his camera. A Jap Officer carrying a sword then charged the group. The other members of the patrol quickly killed him and charged the caves firing machine guns and flame throwers while tossing demolition charges to seal them off. When the area was secured the platoon started back down the mountain only to meet another group coming up.

Gazing up at the small flag Col Johnson had a premonition that some S.O.B. would want that flag for a souvenir and immediately ordered that a larger flag be found to replace the smaller one. A much larger flag was obtained from LST 779 and given the 2Bn Runner PFC RENE GAGNON to take to the top. On the way he met several E Co men on their way down.

Photographer Joseph Rosenthal of the Associated Press was unaware of another flag being carried to the summit and wondered if there might be something to take a picture of at the top. Rosenthal, Marine Photographers Sgt William Genaust and Pvt Bob Campbell decided to follow Gagnon up the mountain and take a look anyway. When arriving Rosenthal saw that another flag was going to be raised and looked around for a good spot to take the picture from.

1Lt SCHRIER (Raider) ordered the first flag pole struck (lowered) at the same time the second flag pole was raised. The picture Rosenthal captured of Marines Cpl Harlon Block, PFC RENE GAGNON, Pfc Ira Hayes, Pfc Franklin Sousley, SGT MICHAEL STRANK (Raider) and Corpsman John Bradley raising the second flag caught the imagination of the American public and became the most famous photograph of the war. To the people back home starved for any good news in the long war against the Japanese, those Marines in the photo became heroes whether they wanted to be or not.

On 24 Feb, the 3rd MarDiv was committed and landed on Beach Black. The 9th Marines overran Hill Peter on 27 Feb and the 21st Marines captured Motoyama Village the following day.

Units of the 3rd and 5th MarDiv gained Hills 362A and 382 on 2 Mar and Airfield No 3 was cleared by the 3rd MarDiv on 3 Mar, as Hills 357 and 362B were captured by the 2nd BN, 21st Marines.

On 6 Mar the 3rd, 4th and 5th MarDiv attacked in an effort to roll over the final Japanese defense line. Co K, 9th Marines seized Hill 362C the next day.

The Japanese suffered heavy losses in a counterattack on 8-9 Mar. On 11 Mar the 3rd and 4th MarDiv began the final drive of the campaign. Regimental Combat Team 21 reached the north coast of the island ending all resistance in the 3rd MarDiv sector on 16 Mar. Regimental Combat Team 25 reached the Beach Road and the island was declared secure. Regimental Combat Team 28 eliminated the last area of Japanese resistance on 25 Mar 1945.

The battle for control of the eight square mile area was the bloodiest in Marine Corps history. Loss of life among the combat veterans meant that untried replacements were rushed into place early in the battle. Almost 90% of the Company Commanders were killed or wounded, and in the heat of battle platoons were sometimes led by Corporals, Pfc's, and in one case a Private. Many battalions made up of rifle companies with a complement of approximately 900 men were reduced to 150-350 effectives INCLUDING their replacements by the end of the campaign.

It seemed to the Marines, they fought the battles of Iwo Jima above ground while the Japs fought the battle underground in their spider holes, tank traps, ditches, tunnels and caves. Many Marines never saw a living Japanese soldier on the island.

Of the 24,200 casualties 6,140 were killed or died of

wounds. As with the Marine Raiders first assault on Tulagi, any thought that Jap troops had poor eyesight, was immediately erased by their accurate fire in hitting hundreds of attacking Marines with accurate head and chest shots.

Bravery was a given. Twenty-four Medals of Honor were awarded (two to Raiders), and four were presented to Corpsmen.

One Marine or Corpsman was a casualty for every three who landed on Iwo. Twenty-three Doctors and 827 Corpsmen were killed or wounded on Iwo. Thirty-six, of the forty man platoon that captured Mount Suribachi were killed or wounded before leaving the island.

Neither Lowery nor Rosenthal had any idea of the names of the men in their photo's, and the Marines had to search to identify them. Block, Sousely and Strank were later killed in action on Iwo. First flag raisers Charlo, Hansen and Thomas were also killed in action there while Lindberg and Michels were wounded in action.

RAIDERS KILLED IN ACTION ON IWO JIMA	
BARBER, DENZEL	BARNES, WILLIAM
BAULCH, LEVI C.	BEARD, ROY T.
BECKEL, DONALD	BISHOP, ROY JR.
BOWMAN, DAVID	BROWN,HUGHJR
BURNS,HAROLD	CAMPBELL,JAMES
CARNINE, H.L.	CONNORS JACK
CROSSON, C. S.	DEMELIA, WILLIAM
EVANS, ROBERT	FARMER,RUSSELL
FAVIA, VITO P.	FILLIPONI, N. P,
FITZGERALD,C. L.	FOLEY, GUY C.
FOSTER, JOHN	FOSTER, K.M.
FOWLER,THOMAS	HAAGA, MICHAEL
HAGEMEISTER,A.B	HALLMARK,FLOYD
HARRISON, Z.B.	HATHAWAY, W.C.
HAROLD, W.F.	HOMA, MICHAEL
HOUSE, JAMES JR	HUDSON,HOWARD
IZELL, WELDON L.	JOVANOVICH, G.E.
LIPPOLD, JACK E.	LUDFORD, PHILLIP
MARTIN, PERCY C.	MCMILLEN, ARVEL
MEARS, DWAYNE	MULLIGAN, JAMES
MURPHY, DANIEL	NOBLE, RAYMOND
PACE, CARL B.	PARKER, JOHN W.
PERCELL, WYATT	POARCHE,ROBERT
RIKK, JULIUS L.	ROBINSON, JACK R.

RUSSELL, WILLIAM SHERRY, ROBERT
SMITH, JAMES JR   SMITH, LEONARD J.
SNYDER, HOWARD   STRANK, MICHAEL
TANNER, KARL L.   THOSTENSON,T.M. *
TIDWELL, JASPER   VOLZ, CHARLES A.
WAGAMAN, LYLE E.   WALSH, WILLIAM G.
WANN, DANIEL M.   WHERRY, JOHN H.
WINSER, ROBERT   YOUNG,CHARLES
*Raider Corpsman

RAIDERS AWARDED MEDALS ON IWO JIMA

NAVY CROSS

ANTONELLI,JOHN   FALTYN, HUBERT
GARRETT, N.M.   JOVANOVICH,G.
LIVERSEDGE, H.B.   MEARS, DWAYNE
ROGERS, RAY D.   SCHRIER,HAROLD
TANNER, KARL   THOSTENSON,T.M.
TOWNE, HARRY   WHERRY, JOHN *
* Second Navy Cross Awarded.

SILVER STAR

ANTHONY, CLYDE   BEARD, ROY T.
BOYD, JACK Z. *   FAVIA, VITO P.
FERENTZ, FRED   GARY, ALBERT *
HALLMARK, F.V.   HARRIS,CHARLES
HEUMANN, W.J.   HOMA,MICHAEL
HORTON, ALBERT   JONES,EDWARD
KELLY,WALTER A.   KENT, JAMES E.
LEARY,JOHN J.*   LINDBERG,CHARLES
LIPSCOMB,NATHAN   McCLAIN,WILSON
McFADDEN,JOS T   MEAD, WILLIAM F.
MIDDLEBROOK, J.   PEEPLES, LARRY
PORTSCHELLER, E.   POTTER, JOHN W.
SALERNO, JAMES   SALMON, JOHN
SCHIER, HAROLD   SHIVERS, CLYDE
SMITH, LEONARD   SMOAK, TOLSON
WAGAMAN, LYLE   WAYNER, ROBERT
WIELAND, JOHN
* Second Silver Star Awarded

Most of the first flag raisers weren't aware of the second flag ceremony and when seeing Rosenthal's picture, Cpl

Lindberg said "that isn't the flag we raised." Neither group of flag raisers felt they did anything other than what they were ordered to do.

In the midst of all the adulation Bradley, Gagnon and Hayes were bothered by the total lack of interest in knowing the names of the men who raised the first flag. They were flown back home to participate in War Bond Tours, while the others were mostly forgotten. The first flag raisers were invited to the dedication of the Iwo Jima Memorial, but had no reserved seats. They were totally ignored as they sat unnoticed in the back of the crowd.

AUTHOR: In a 2003 telephone conversation with CHARLES LINDBERG the last surviving member of the first Iwo Jima flag raising, he confirmed the lack of respect and recognition given them both during and after the war.

(Raider) LT SCHRIER, while almost ignored in BOTH flag raisings, was recognized by Hollywood film directors and chosen to play himself in the movie Sands of Iwo Jima, starring John Wayne. (Raider) Captain, later General, Leonard Fribourg, acted as technical director of the film. Marine enlistments still increase to this day after each re-run of the film.

Volcanic Heat Warms Coffee on Iwo Jima

Iwo Jima
Assaulting Pill Box

Corpsmen Treating Wounded on Iwo Jima Beach
Alongside Dead Comrades

Preparing to Assault Caves on Iwo Jima

Higgins Boat Nearing Iwo Jima

Iwo Jima - Stretcher Case

Near Summit of Mt. Suribachi - Iwo Jima

15

Okinawa

Cpl. Richard E. Bush, USMCR, Medal of Honor

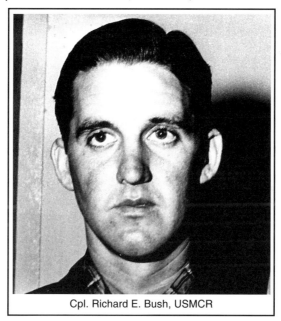

Cpl. Richard E. Bush, USMCR

OFFICIAL MEDAL OF HONOR CITATION

"For conspicuous gallantry and intrepidity at the risk of his life above and beyond the call of duty as a Squad Leader serving with the First Battalion, Fourth Marines, Sixth Marine Division, in action against enemy Japanese forces during the final assault against Mt. Yaetake on Okinawa, Ryukyu Islands, 16 April 1945. Rallying his men forward with indomitable determination, Cpl. Bush boldly defied the slashing fury of concentrated Japanese artillery fire pouring down from the gun-studded mountain fortress to lead his squad up the face of the rocky precipice, sweep over the ridge and drive the defending troops from their deeply entrenched position. With his unit, the first to break through to the inner defense of Mt. yaetake, he fought relentlessly until seriously wounded and evacuated with others under protecting rocks. Although prostrate under medical treatment when a Japanese hand grenade landed in the midst of the group, Cpl. Bush, alert and courageous in extremity as in battle, unhesitatingly pulled the deadly missile to himself and absorbed the shattering violence of the exploding charge in his own body, thereby saving his fellow Marines from severe injury or death despite certain peril to his own life. By his valiant leadership and aggressive tactics in the face of savage opposition, Cpl. Bush contributed materially to the success of the sustained drive toward the conquest of this fiercely defended outpost of the Japanese Empire and his constant concern for the welfare of his men, his resolute spirit of self-sacrifice and his unwavering devotion to duty throughout the bitter conflict enhance and sustain the highest traditions of the United States Naval Service."

THE BATTLE FOR OKINAWA

THE BATTLE OF OKINAWA
4th MARINE REGIMENT, 6th MARINE DIVISION
1 APRIL - 21 JUN 1945

223 MARINE RAIDERS WERE KILLED IN ACTION ON OKINAWA

AHLGRIM, ALVIN	ALFORD,LEONARD
ALLEN, THOMAS J.	ANDERSON, JOHN
ARNOLD,CLIFFORD	BANKER, ROBERT
BARTCZAK, L.D,	BEENEY GEORGE
BLODGETT, LYLE	BOCK, WM. G. JR.
BOONE,CHARLES *	BOWLAND,KENNETH
BRASWELL, JACK	BROOKS, JACK
BOWN, JAMES F.	BROWN,MARSHALL
BURLEIGH, PHILIP	CAMPBELL,DARYL
CARLSON, WM. H.	CARPIAUX, RICHARD
CARR, GEORGE	CARRILLO,STEPHEN
CHICK, ROY C.	CLEARY, PIERCE
COLE, KENNETH A.	CONANT, JUDSON
CONNELL, ROBERT	CONNER, EUGENE
CONROY, THOMAS	COWHERD,REGINAL
CREMIN, PATRICK	CROSBY, GEORGE
CURTIN, PAUL D.	DALE, NELSON C.
DEBERRY, ROBERT	DICKEY, RICHARD
DODDS, THAD N.	DOTSON, DONALD
DOYLE, PHILLIP D.	DUGAN, JAMES JR.
DUNHAM, ED H.	EDER, CARL F. JR.
EHLEN, WM. H. JR.	ELA, WENDELL P.
FAULKNER, JACK	FEELER, WOODROW
FENNELLY, EDWARD	FISCHER, LEONARD
FLANERY, CHARLES	FLECK,LAURENCE
FLOWERS, S.JR.	FOLEY, ROGER C.
FORD, RICHARD E.	FORNOF, BILLY B.
FRAILEY, ROBERT	FRANK, HILLARY
FROST WILLIAM G.	GAINES, FRANK A.
GOLDEN, JAMES	GONZALES, F.E.
GRANT, ROBERT	GRASSI, EVERETT
GRAVES, ROBERT	GREEN, BERNARD
HAMILTON,DOUGLAS	HARLIN, BERNARD
HARRINGTON, R. J.	HARRIS, CHARLES

HART, JAMES JR.	HASH, CHESTER
HAYS, RICHARD A.	HEALY, FRANCIS
HEATH, CLAYTON	HERKO, ALEX
HINDE, HUBBARD	HIGGINS, JOHN J.
HILL, RAYMOND	HOJNACKI, JOHN
HOLMES, JOHN B.	JABLONICKY, J. A.
JACOBSON, KIB A.	JASPERS, W.M.
JERNIGAN, CLAUDE	JOHANNES, R. J.
JOHNSON, CAM	JOHNSON, CARL
JOHNSON, RALPH	JONES, HAROLD
KARR, GEORGE J.	KELCHNER, EVAN
KERBY, JOHN P.	KETTERER, F. C.
KILGORE, WM.G.	KING, GEORGE H.
KLONOWSKI,B.L.	KRAEMER,THOMAS
LACKEY, BLAINE	LAUGHTER, WM.
LAWSON, E.A.	LEVET, CHARLES
LEWIS, EARL J.	LEWIS, EDWARD I.
LIEBERMAN,D.B.	LORANGER, L .I. *
LORD, WILLIAM F.	LUCAS,EUGENE
MALLOY, JOHN L.	MANNING, AL R.
MANNING, ERNIE	MANSFIELD, MAX
MANWARING,H.E.	MASON, DONALD
McAULIFFE, JOHN	McCABE, ED. W.
McCASKILL, OL	McDONALD, DALE
McLAUGHLIN, T.	McNEELY, BILLIE
MEYERS, H. C.	MEZA, RAYMOND
MICKLAS, R. F.	MIKULA, THAD
MILLER, ARTHUR	MILLER, IRA D.
MILLER, STANLEY	MIODUSKI, J.F.
MORRIS, SIMS JR.	MUNDELL,S.E.
MURPHY, JAMES	MYERS, LEO
MYERS, PETER *	NEBESH, PETER
NEWMAN, C. L.	NICKEL, EUGENE
NOLAN, JOHN R.	NORTH, HUGH D.
NYMAN, ROBERT	O'BRIEN, WALTER
O'BRYHIM, ERNIE	OKUNEVICH, C.K.
OLSON, IRVING A.	O'NEILL, JOHN A.
OWEN, EUGENE	OWENS, GILES W.
OWENS, "J" "E"	PANETTA, DOM
PARKER, VIRGIL	PARRISH, WM.
PEAVY, LEON L.	PROBST,DONALD
RAYNES,WILLIAM	REES, DANIEL T.
REILLY, J.M.	RHINOW, WILLIAM
RICHARDS, J. Z.	RIOS, CHARLES

ROBBINS, ART G.
ROBERTSON, J. D.
RODZINKA, A. J.
RUDKIN, B. W.
SANDERS, D. L.
SCHAFALE, JACK
SCHILDT, R.D.
SEALY, JOHNNIE
SHAW, ARNOLD
SILAKOWSKI,LEO
SKURA, WILLIAM
SMITH, THOMAS
SODERBERG,L. E.
SPACKMAN, R. D.
SPELLMAN, GEO.
STEVENSON, L.
STINE, JACK D.
STOUT, GLENN
SUDRO, JOHN F.
SUMMERS, F.J.
SUTTLE, DALE
THOMAS, VERN
THURMOND,KEN
USHER, WILLIAM
VANNATTER, L.J.
WAGNER, RAY
WALCK, JOHN W.
WARNER, C. L.
WILLARD, JACK
WILLIAMSON,WM
WOOD, ALBERT
WOOD, JOHN R.
YOAKUM, MA
*Corpsmen

ROBERTSON,C. L.
RODRIGUEZ, S. D.
ROMO, ROBERT
RUTHERFORD, T.
CALES, SIDNEY
SCHELLENBERG,J.
SCHNELLE, G
SELIG,LAWRENCE
SIEKKINEN, PAUL
SIMS, BYRON K.
SMITH, CHESTER
SMITH, WM. M.
SORENSON R. S.
SPARKS, MICKEY
STAHLECKER,D.
STEWART, JOHN
TOSKOF, O.J.
STUBBY, MAYO
SULLIVAN, A. F.
SUMMO, DANIEL
TAYLOR, C. J.
THORNTON, A,F.
TOUSIGNANT,P.L.
AN CAMP, L. J.
VAUGHN, NOEL
WAGNON,JOSEPH
WARDEN, D. R.
WHITE, JAMES T.
WILLIAMS, JOHN
WINDOM,HOMER
WOOD,FRANK
WRIGHT,BILLY

RAIDERS AWARDED MEDALS ON OKINAWA

NAVY CROSS

ALLEN, THOMAS
GRASSI, E.B.
JOHNSON, C.E.
McAULIFFE, JAS.
VOGEL, HUGH A.

DUNHAM, E. H.
GOHEEN,R.R.P.
LAQUINTANO, J.
RUIZ, EDWARD J.

SILVER STAR	
ALFORD, LEN*	HILLS, CLIFFORD
RANNELS, M.C	ANDREWS, G.A.
HINES, DENNIS	ROBERTSON, J.D.
BEANS, FRED D.	ISLER,JOSEPH
RODRIQUEZ, S. D.	BATTERTON, R.J.
JAMES,CHARLES	ROMO, ROBERT
BROWN,JAMES F.	JOHNSON, C.E.
SARACINO, J.E	BURTMAN, VERN
JOHNSON, R.W.	SILVERTHORNE,S
CAMPBELL, D.D.	KELCHNER, EVAN
SKURA, WM.S.	CARPIAUX, R.J.
MANNING, A.R.	SMITH, CHESTER
CARR, WM. J.	MANWARING,H.E.
SNELSON, FRANK	COOK, DELL M.
McDONALD, J.L.	THOMAS, RALPH
CROSS, WAYNE	McMASTER, R.G.
THOMAS, VERN	DOYLE, PHILLIP
MILLER, F. H.	THOMPSON,DUEY
FINNELLY, ED A.	MILLER, IRA D.
THORPE,ROBERT	FISCHER, W.F.
MINDELL, S.E.	WALKER,ANTHONY
GAINES, HOUSTON	PERSKIE,MARVIN
WRIGHT, BILLY R.	GOEGLEIN, R.M
PETERSON, D.J.	YOAKUM, MARK
HASSELL, HAL D.	PLOCK, MARVIN
HERWIG, R.J.	POWERS, D.H.

*Second Award

The Oruku Peninsula on the Island of Okinawa had once been one of the main links in the chain of airplane bases connecting Japan with her far flung empire to the south. Its high ground commanded Naha Harbor, and while the Japanese held the island it remained a threat to the flank and rear of American forces driving toward the south in the central part of the island.

On 1 April 45 the Easter dawn was hailed by the crash of guns from some 1,200 ships, the largest war fleet that ever sailed, with the heavy artillery of battleships and cruisers concentrating on the sloping ground from the beach to Yontan airfield that was 1,200 yards inland.

Yontan airfield was secured by the 6th Marine Division's 4th Marines (Raiders). After being relieved of the responsibility for the Yontan airstrip on 4 April the 6th Marine Division attacked north up the West Coast road.

In the thick mud ashore troops were encountering more mines than at any other time during the operation, so many, in fact that the disposal squads were swamped with work. Mine removal men attached to the tanks often had to get out in front of the vehicles to probe suspected areas with their knives, while demolition's personnel were busy sealing the numerous cave entrances. In this type of measured progress the lines reached, by dusk, a point 1,500 yards in from the beach and including part of Naha airfield, at a cost of about fifty casualties.

During the rainy night the enemy kept the front under fire from mortars and artillery fire. On the morning of 14 Apr the 4th Marines and the 29th Marines launched an amphibious assault against the Motobu Peninsula. The attack moved slowly forward against stubborn resistance until about noon, when the advance of the 3rd Battalion, 4th, on the extreme right of the lines, was stopped by an enemy strong point near the village of Toma.

Tank support was called for, and despite the difficulty of operating over terrain muddy from the heaviest storm the Marines had seen on the island, Company C of the tank battalion reached the front lines. They found the infantry pinned down by shell fire and automatic weapons. Coordinating their actions with the infantry the tanks gave prompt help, knocking out machine guns and shelling caves. Soon the infantry was able to move on again.

The next morning's operations confirmed the fact that the heaviest enemy defenses were concentrated along a ridge running northwest and southeast, parallel to the Kokuba Estuary. The 29th Marines, in whose zone the backbone of the ridge lay, made little progress, while the 4th was able to advance only its right flank. Throughout the day troops assaulting the cave-studded approaches to the key ridge came under heavy fire from automatic weapons, mortars and rockets. Later, when General Clement, the veteran of Bataan, examined the emplacements along this line, he remarked that Oroku was "stronger than Corregidor."

In the 29th Marines zone a typical cave position was discovered, and the men moved in cautiously, expecting to find a crudely fashioned rifle or machine-gun position. A hundred and fifty yards inside the hill a Jap soldier suddenly stepped out of a recess, bellowing something and reaching in his pocket. A Marine fired three quick shots and the Jap fell dead, his hand gripping a grenade. Beyond him the two Marines came upon an intricate system of winding corridors, with sleeping quarters for enlisted men, more elaborate quarters for officers and enough equipment to supply a battalion, the whole on three floors, connected by sturdy ladders. The corridors were from two hundred to three hundred yards long and had been well lighted; their power lines stretched to a central station in Naha City.

All were lined with the straw mats on which the Japs had slept and in the clay beside each mat was a niche for the man's personal belongings. Along similar corridors the officers' quarters were spaced out fifty yards apart, their walls covered with quilting and their entrances draped with cloth material. One of them was described as an ideal living compartment, with two fine overstuffed chairs, a desk, writing equipment and a good-sized bed.

On the deepest level were storage spaces for everything from gasoline drums to bags of flour. One room contained medical supplies and cots, another was a well stocked galley. A third had been the communications center, with a switchboard and radio equipment. There were even pigeon roosts for carrier pigeons, and all through the place, mortars, and ammunition boxes of all kinds, light cannon and repair shops for ordnance and communications equipment. When hills like these were manned, they made very formidable obstacles.

The 6th Divisions 4th Marines found progress least difficult on their right, where the flat ground around Naha airfield offered the enemy little opportunity for entrenchment.

Early the next day the 4th Marines moved its 1st Battalion into positions on the right flank under cover of a smoke screen. The battalion then attacked the high ground immediately south of Uibaru. It was an all-day battle of the most intense character, but it ended with the Marines in possession of the ground they had sought.   During the early part of the day the remainder of the 4th did not fare so well. Hill 38 stood across the path, northeast of Takamiya, and every attempt to advance around the flanks of

Finally the 2nd Battalion turned the Japs' own ingenuity against them by moving assault elements through the extensive tunnel system the enemy had dug into the hill. The covered approaches made the attack a surprise, a strong force was swiftly built up on the reverse slope and the hill was taken. This maneuver was repeated several times during the day and was successful each day. By 20 Apr the 4th and 29th Marines had eliminated all organized resistance on the peninsula.

On 8 May the first elements of the 6th Marine Division entered the lines on the islands southern front and captured the Sugar Loaf position.

In the early morning hours 4 Jun, the 4th Marines

embarked in their LVTs near Machinato airfield for an amphibious attack on the Oroko Peninsula and began a two-hour approach, moving southward along the reef. Overhead they were supported with intensive Naval and artillery shelling. The assault troops reached the beach, closely followed by the tanks, where there was little opposition and the 2nd Battalion promptly pushed forward against scattered machine-gun fire. They seized the nose of the high ridge to the left of the landing area, while the 1st Battalion drove directly inland to capture the ridge at the seaward flank of the beach. The Oroku landing was clearly one of those complete successes that are born of surprise. Long before the enemy could redistribute his forces, the 4th Regiment had a firm foothold and was driving steadily inland.

The final sweep of the remaining areas was completed June 13, when the 29th Marines engaged a stubborn force of estimated company strength, firmly entrenched in Easy Hill, immediately south of Oroku Town. As the determined attack developed, the breaking morale of the enemy was clear from the confusion and indecision in their ranks. Some resisted to the end and were killed where they stood; some offered no resistance whatever; others killed themselves, and a small group surrendered. Similar conditions were encountered by the 4th and 22nd Regiments, and during the day as 861 Japanese were killed, while seventy-two prisoners were taken.

The ten-day fight had been a hard one, against an enemy that had made the utmost use of ground peculiarly well adapted to a defense in depth. General Clement's remark that it was stronger than Corregidor was no overstatement; the Japanese had obviously worked for a long time at converting the ragged coral outcroppings and the many small precipitous hills into a strong and intelligently planned defensive system.

In one of the cave networks near Tomigusuki was found the headquarters of Admiral Minoro Ota, who had commanded New Georgia and Kavieng before being placed in charge of the Okinawa Naval Base Forces defending valuable Oroku Peninsula. This cave was discovered and investigated by a patrol of Marines led by Lieutenant Colonel Williams, the Division Intelligence Officer. LTColonel Williams was looking for the bodies of the Admiral and his staff, who reportedly had committed suicide in the cave. Lieutenant Frederick Van Brunt one of the party, has described the cave as a labyrinth of corridors, operations rooms, barracks and storage chambers." The headquarters was completely equipped down to electricity and a system of hot and cold running water. In the last days of the battle it had been used as a hospital, and when the patrol entered they found themselves walking on a carpet of dead and dying Japanese.

The search for the Admiral's body continued for two days; it was finally found, with the bodies of several other high-ranking Naval officers, who had composed the admiral's staff. In accordance with the code of honor of a Japanese officer faced with defeat, Admiral Ota and his staff had died in the traditional manner.

There was an ironic note; in that the same Admiral who had been outmaneuvered and defeated by the Marine Raiders on New Georgia, would suffer his second and final defeat, at the hands of the Division that included a number of the same Marine Raiders he had encountered in the Solomons.

"The indomitable spirit and professional skill displayed by the Sixth Marine Division will be a source of pride and gratification to all Marines." General Shepherd said: "The more than four thousand Japs killed during the ten day period are not alone the measure of the Division's accomplishment, nor are the successes realized in the bitter battles for Hill 53, Hill 58, Hill 62 and other well organized defensive positions."

"The workmanlike execution of a complex amphibious operation—planned, prepared and executed aver a 36-hour period is an impressive tribute to the tactical and logistical ability of all hands.

Okinawa was a brilliant victory, but at a price few would forget. On a hillside looking out across the East China Sea, the Sixth Division cemetery was dedicated on Independence Day, just ninety-five days after the Division's first units set foot on the beaches below. By truck, by jeep and on foot thousands of men who had survived one of the Pacific's most arduous campaigns came to the brief and impressive ceremony. Long before the program started they gathered around the rows of crosses and Stars of David that marked the graves of 1,697 who fell in battle.

On 13 Jun, Marine MajGen Lemuel Shepherd announced that all organized resistance on Oroku Peninsula had ceased. But as in all such declarations, the enemy didn't know they were defeated and the mop up continued.

Some Japanese wanted to surrender. They were waving white flags out on the flat in groups of threes and fours. Some were so well camouflaged in little ditches that Marines walked to within three or four yards of one group before seeing them.

A group of thirteen Japanese surrendered in one day. Another platoon found that most of the Japs were opposed to surrender, preferring the suicide way out, one entire group of ten blowing themselves up with an explosive charge as the Marines closed in.

Not all Japanese gave up or surrendered during the battles on the island; To the end these enemies showed the old Jap trickery so often employed in the Pacific war, and thirteen Marines were caught in a trap when three of the enemy waved a white flag. "The three were spotted on a small rock fifty yards offshore near the southern tip of the island,"

Corporal John H. Pearson tells the story. "They waved a white flag, so we went over to get them." The way led through a cane brake at the edge of the water. At the beach Pearson, serving as interpreter, told the three Japs to undress. While he was talking to them another squad of enemy soldiers slipped around behind the cane brake and opened fire. "By then we had the three soldiers," said Pearson. "We hit the deck and fired back. Four of our men were hit, one killed. A platoon of Marines about five hundred yards away saw what was happening and came to our rescue. Then we retreated. I think the three prisoners were part of the ruse, but we took them back anyway."

For many years the Japanese had realized the dominating position of the peninsula so they had spent much effort and material in organizing the whole place as a self sufficient fortress. Admiral Minoro Ota, who commanded the forces on the peninsula disposed the bulk of his troops along the ridge line that guarded the base of the peninsula and sited most of his mobile weapons to fire in that direction.

The percentage of surrenders was comparatively high and one of the men most responsible was Pfc. Harry M. Tuttle, an interpreter who worked with the assistance of a captured Japanese warrant officer. He succeeded in convincing more than twenty of the enemy that being a prisoner was better than being dead. "Their greatest fear," he said, was of maltreatment at the hands of their captors

The most successful of all the efforts at taking prisoners was that of (Raider) LT SILVERTHORNE, a veteran language officer, who had served with the Raiders on Bougainville, Emirau and Guam. Working through the paddy land with a native he succeeded in inducing no less than fifty-six Japs to come in.

On one occasion during the busy day when he made this haul, Silverthorne glanced around in time to see that a Jap lying prone had a Browning automatic rifle trained on him. The 225-pound former Williams College football star walked directly up to the muzzle of the rifle, telling its operator in Japanese that he had nothing to worry about; then pushed the weapon to one side and took the Jap prisoner. "The muzzle kept looking bigger and bigger to me as I approached it," Silverthorne said later. "By the time I got within three feet of it, I would have sworn that I was walking up on a 155 howitzer." At this time the number of military prisoners taken by the Division had already passed the two thousand mark and was still climbing steadily.

On June 20, the 4th and 29th Marines resumed their attack to drive the enemy off Kiyamu Ridge and pin him against the sea. On the front of the 4th the resistance was soon over, but it was necessary for units of the Division to comb the whole area for groups of the enemy still determined to kill a few Americans. Suicides, singly and in groups, occurred all along the cliffs and beaches of the southern end of the island, while quite unprecedented numbers of Japanese continued to surrender. At one time those in the compound near the Division command post far outnumbered the Marines in the vicinity.

One of the more intriguing stories of the war was that of Lieutenant George Thompson, a platoon leader in the 29th Marines. In hot pursuit of ten Japs when he and four men with him rounded a turn in the trail to find themselves confronted by no less than 350 armed enemy soldiers. This was more than he had bargained for, but the lieutenant kept his head. Standing on a natural platform offered by an outcrop of rock, he bowed, smiled and waved to the surrounding laps, keeping up a running description of the scene over a walkie-talkie to his company command post. He pushed his pistol into his rear pocket and motioned for the men with him to sling their rifles over their shoulders. The Japs around him looked flabbergasted, but there was not much fight left in them. Some killed themselves with grenades as little as ten yards from Thompson, and he noted that many of the enemy officers had women companions, whom they shot before destroying themselves.

Those who were not ready for suicide crowded around. Shouting "Tobako! Tobako! Tobako!" Thompson responded by shouting "tobaco, and as several of the enemy soldiers extended their hands, he distributed the contents of four packages passed to him by his companions. Not for a moment did he cease smiling and chattering words apparently addressed to the Japanese, but really his running account of the event. He begged no one at the other end to interrupt him with questions. "I have an idea that if I did stop talking or smiling the Japs will kill us," he said.

A Japanese officer killed a woman, walked toward Pfc Rufus E. Randall, snapped to attention, saluted and handed the surprised Leatherneck two sabers and a wrist watch. Then he stepped back ten yards and blew his head off with a grenade. This touched off a wave of suicides, with the enemy officers continuing to surrender their sabers, watches and flags to the amazed Marines.

In the midst of this extraordinary scene four grenade-laden Japs approached the group menacingly. "Here it comes," said Thompson. One of them grunted: "Tobacco." "They want cigarettes and we've run out," said Thompson. When he shook his head some of the Japs angrily hurled their helmets to the ground. Thompson had an inspiration. With the widest possible grin he pointed up the cliffs toward the American lines, shouting: "Lots of tobacco up there!"

By this time patrols sent out by battalion were on the scene. Thompson warned them to keep their weapons out of sight. "That way we won't have to fight and maybe some of the Japs will surrender." Thompson's tactics were successful; 150 enemy soldiers followed our troops to the rear with astounding meekness and a few minutes later no less than 350 Okinawan civilians streamed out of nearby caves from which they had been watching the whole performance.

On another occasion Marines in an LCI were broadcasting via loudspeaker to a group of several hundred Japanese soldiers and Okinawan civilians wandering aimlessly along a beach. The broadcasters directed them along the beach to the west where they would pass through the Sixth Division lines, but only a little way along they ran into a fire-fight between Marines and a group of entrenched Japs. Several of the wanderers were hit and for a few moments pandemonium reigned along the beach.

Then someone in the LCI noticed a man who appeared to be an officer among the Jap soldiers. "Fall them in! Fall them in!" cried a voice over the loudspeaker in Japanese. The Jap officer obeyed, ordering the civilians to form a column and marching them briskly back along the beach until they reached the 7th Infantry Division lines, where they were surrendered.

Amongst all this a group approached. In the center of the circle three Marines and a Navy corpsman marched toward a small mound. They were veterans of the entire campaign. Platoon Sergeant S. S. Semetsis; Sergeant Narolian H. West; Pfc. Daniel Dereschuo; and Hospital Apprentice 2d class Joseph M. Bangart. They carried a roughly hewn pole and an American flag. It was the same flag these same men had unfurled over the island's northern most point only a month before.

The Marines stood in quiet reverence as the quartet

placed the mast on the mound. Our men stepped back a pace. A bugler came forward, raised a battered instrument to his lips and blew the first stirring notes of "Colors." The men who had fought eighty two bloody days to reach this point. On the outer edge of the circle, grim and battered Marines faced outward, rifles at the ready.

The Okinawan campaign was officially declared over on 2 Jul 45. Marine KIA and MIA totaled 3,443, while the Navy lost 4,824 men, 34 ships and 763 aircraft. There were 107,539 killed and 23,764 sealed in caves or buried by the Japanese themselves. 10,755 Jap troops were captured or surrendered.

In keeping with their efforts to evacuate casualties to rear areas as soon as possible, 11,771 casualties were evacuated by air, 11,731 by hospital ships and only 1,405 by APA, APH surface vessels. Japanese aircraft attacked the hospital ships USS Relief on 2 Apr, and the USS Solace on 20 Apr with no damage done. On 28 Apr the USS Solace was hit amidships by a kamikazi suicide plane amidships, with 29 killed,1i missing and 33 wounded, as was the USS Pinkney APH2, with 22 killed, 11 wounded and 19 missing.

Examples of heroism by Fleet Marine Force Corpsmen, Doctors and Chaplains were commonplace on Okinawa. PHM2 Victor MacSorley amputated a Marines foot at night with only his combat knife while a mortar barrage was taking place, and only occasional star shells providing light for the surgery. MacSorley attended 18 wounded Marines that night and returned to his aid station at dawn carrying a sergeant, his last patient, across his shoulders.

PhM3 Robert Martin was in the front lines dug in on the side of a ridge when a Jap banzai attack started. A Marine was hit and when Martin jumped up to go to his aid, three Japs came at him. He lashed out with his fists at the one closest to him kicked at the second, and knocked down the third in order to reach the wounded Marine and treat him. With repeated cries of "Corpsmen, Corpsmen", the Corpsman broke cover time after time while Japanese small arms fire continued all over the area.

Dr. Herbert Valentine and two PhM2 Corpsmen left their command post to go to the aid of several Marines whose artillery gun and ammunition had suffered a direct hit by a Japanese shell. Although 4 of the crew were killed, they were able to treat 3 others.

A large pool of replacements for Corpsmen were needed on Okinawa. There were for instance, 478 casualties among Corpsmen of the 1st Marine Division during the campaign in southern Okinawa. 49 of those were killed in action, 226 wounded in action, 17 injured and 186 sick.

Former Raider JIM WOOD wrote, " I don't know any Marine from WW II that was not impressed by our Corpsmen. As a rifle squad leader who lost two squads on Okinawa, I saw great deeds performed by our Corpsmen. With about a month to go on Okinawa, our company clerk BILLIE McNEELY (Raider), was following the company in a jeep when he was hit by Japanese firing from about 100 yards away. The driver jumped out and ran for cover, but McNEELY could not make it out. I ran about 50 yards and started pulling him out with the help of our platoon Corpsman who also ran up to us. The Japs were still shooting and McNEELY was hit again before we got him to safety. There were at least 10 Marines closer to him than the Corpsman and myself. I was awarded a Letter of Commendation, presented by General Lemuel Shepherd while in Japan. The Corpsman, whose name I don't remember, was later hit real bad and sent back to the states. I also saw our Corpsmen risk their lives many times on Guam and Bougainville."

AUTHOR: BILLIE R. McNEELY died of wounds received on 20 JUN 45!

1st Raider VIC ANDERSON awoke on Okinawa after being wounded, only to hear a Doctor saying, "we will have to amputate that arm." Vic who attended pre-med school before becoming a Raider, used his medical knowledge to convince doctors to try a new experimental procedure that ultimately saved his arm.

Navy Lieutenant Commander PAUL J. REDMOND (Raider) Chaplain of the Fleet Marine Force spoke: "This is not a bivouac of the dead. It is a corner of heaven. And some part of us all is buried here."

In his dedicatory address General Shepherd said the men buried here, "the heroes of the war." gave the last thing they could give—their lives. "

But not all the heroes were in that cemetery. Some went through the mortar bursts, the rain of shellfire and the driving machine-gun bullets, displaying that extra something, and came out alive. Their deeds were an inspiration, and it is both pleasing and proper to record those who were recognized. Among them were:

Lieutenant SPENCER V. SILVERTHORNE, (Raider) a language officer with the division intelligence section. First Lieutenant Silverthorne continually volunteered to lead patrols on dangerous missions that furnished information of great value.

On numerous occasions he exposed himself to intense enemy fire, entering many caves not previously reconnoitered, thereby risking his life in order to obtain the information. On June 13 he voluntarily exposed himself to enemy fire for a period of five hours in an effort to induce a strong enemy group to surrender. With complete disregard for his own safety, he moved ahead of the advancing troops in an attempt to persuade the enemy to surrender their arms and themselves. Despite innumerable difficulties, he accomplished unprecedented results that expedited the completion of the operation and undoubtedly saved the lives of many Marines.

Corporal DUEY C. THOMPSON, (Raider) a fire team leader with Company A, 1st Battalion, 4th Marines. Upon moving onto Hill 58 on Oroku Peninsula with his platoon, Corporal Thompson observed an enemy mortar firing on adjacent friendly troops from a small cave on the forward slope of the hill. Despite the enemy fire he made five trips down the forward slope and threw a grenade into the cave each time. Failing to destroy the enemy mortar with his grenades, he quickly prepared a demolition charge, ran down the forward slope to the very lip of the cave and dropped the charge into the entrance. The resulting explosion sealed the cave, thereby destroying the enemy.

3L MARVIN PERSKIE was one of high spirit, wit and at times wild originality. His love for food was such that if he could not acquire it, he would pick a foxhole bunky that would. He meant different things to different people. To me, he is the best remembered by two events, both on Okinawa. ON 2 Apr 45 (Landing plus 2) "L" Co, 3rd Bn was attacking in the Sampa Misaki area, north of Yontan Airfield. 1Lt Perskie became C.O. of L3 upon news that Capt Nelson C. Dale, KIA 2 Apr 45, had been severely wounded with Lt DANIEL B. BREWSTER'S 2nd Platoon, which was out ahead in a deep draw and being attacked from all sides. Perskie's 1st Platoon tried relief to Brewster's left but was pinned down. LT EVERET A. HEDAHL'S 3rd Platoon tried to attack Brewster's right flank but came under heavy machine gun fire. Hedahl was WIA and evacuated. The evening was dropping fast, Perskie stated, "We will not leave them alone this night!! Everything else has failed now we go frontal assault!" L3 Banzaied it and it worked as we carried the enemy positions. Again on 21 May 45 (Landing plus 51) Company L had fought over the top of Sugar Loaf Hill, down the valley and up on Horse Shoe Ridge. Casualties were high. We had moved down to the right flank of the 3rd Battalion and prepared to attack the Asato River. 3L had been reduced to 2 short squads per platoon. I came upon LT MARVIN PERSKIE sitting near a burning, bombed-out structure. I noted his much needed eye glasses were missing, I remarked "Damn!! Lieutenant, you are half blind without your glasses." He answered, "There are some things here I would just as soon not see." The next day with rejuvenated spirits we attacked again. These seemingly two insignificant events told me: Here was a man who would not let you down, no matter what the odds! At the same time, here was a man with a deep, strong, compassionate feeling for those who fought with him. LTCOL MARVIN D. PERSKI was a Damn Good Marine Raider."

LIEUTENANT COLONEL FRED D. BEANS, (Raider) Executive Officer of the 4th Marines. While serving as regimental executive officer, Lieutenant Colonel Beans was called upon to take the place of a battalion commander killed in action while the battalion was engaged in a fierce fire fight for Mount Yaetake. Heavy artillery, mortar and small arms fire had inflicted heavy casualties. Lieutenant Colonel Beans, with an indomitable fighting spirit, took command of the badly shaken battalion and through his own example of coolness and courage under fire led the battalion to the brilliant accomplishment of the mission of capturing the enemy bastion of Mount Yaetake. His keen tactical ability and faithful devotion to duty aided materially in the rapid destruction of the fanatical enemy forces on Motobu Peninsula.

The 6th Marine Division then returned to Guam on 2 Jul for rest and further training, where the 4th Marines were designated to spearhead the Marine invasion of the Japanese mainland. The unconditional surrender by the Japanese government to end the war, instead made the 4th Marines the first contingent to step ashore in Japan on 30 August 1945, three days prior to the signing of the peace treaty, as part of the Allied forces to occupy Japan.

HQ III AMPHIBIOUS CORPS PHOTO SECTION, FRANK CANNISTRACI (Raider) our intrepid photographer relates the following story, " In June after being with the advancing units of the 4th Marine Regiment I was sick and walking down down this dusty road on the way back to my outfit. A carryall skidded to a halt with several fellow photographers aboard. We were all talking about how we could score some food as the Marines are always last in the food chain after the Army, Navy, Seabees and any other damn outfit they can think of. It was common practice for the Marines to beg, borrow, trade or steal any food we could lay our hands on. Our section clerk told us he brought along all our negatives from Guadalcanal including all the nudes and sexually explicit ones.

The following day I gathered some Jap souvenirs and with a box of 8 X 10 photos I was driven to the beach where I caught a DUKW going out to the USS Panamint, this was the command ship with Admirals and Generals and who eats better than those fellas? I bribed the coxswain with a few photos to be sure he would bring me back ashore. Saluting the Flag and Officer of the deck, I was sweating because here I was on this clean ship with mud covered boots and dirty dungarees. I hadn't shaved or bathed in over 5 weeks and my putrid odor was unmistakable. I requested permission to see the commissary steward, aware that my ass could be in a sling if anything went wrong.

The commissary steward stopped about 4 feet away and asked, ' do you want to see me?' I said 'yeah', and asked if we could talk in private. 'There are 15 starving Marines who want you to have these gifts'. I proceeded to hand him the Jap rifle, flags, money, and when I was sure nobody was looking I opened the box of photo's that had a nude shot of an exquisite body with the head of Ginger Rogers transposed upon it. I silently handed him photo after photo and when I got to the sexually explicit I thought he lost his power to breathe. He started to sway and I caught him to keep him from falling down. He stammered, Wha', wha', what do you want from me? My original thought was to ask for some minor items, but seeing his condition I altered my thinking. 'I want a side of beef, half a crate of fresh eggs, and a five gallon tin of coffee. He said I can't do that, but give me a few minutes to show some of these to a couple of guys and I think we can do something. I was gripped with fear and disappointment and was going to get the hell off this ship. I looked for my DUKW and he's nowhere around. I keep telling myself not to panic. When I saw the DUKW approaching the ship I started packing up in a hurry. Then I heard the Officer of the Deck yelling and I turned and there was the commissary steward pointing up to the next deck where a cargo net was suspended over the ship. I saw the load drop into the DUKW and handed everything over saying, 'it better be what I wanted or I will come back and blow your brains out!' About 50 yards away from the ship I opened the poncho cover and everything was there. The next morning it was steak and eggs for all hands."

AUTHOR: Frank has the pictures to prove his story. He also told me, "When I got back to my campsite, I immediately took a bath and shaved out of my helmet. Someone gave me a clean pair of khaki pants. NO ONE would give me a clean pair of socks. I don't blame them. In combat any Marine will tell you good food is the #1 priority, clean socks is #2."

4CP FRANCIS HEPBURN wrote, "I stayed in the same company to the end of the war. 4CP Raider Company became G Company, 2nd BN 6th Marines. The Japs devastated us on the Motobu peninsula on Okinawa. Our officer staff suffered so many casualties that a CPL RAYMOND H. "WHITEY" KARR 4CP, inherited, the 2nd Platoon. Captain Archie Norford was KIA right off the bat, MALCOLM McCARTHY was wounded and tough old LEO J. "GUS" GOTTSPONER, 4E, headed up the company by nightfall. I was holding a bottle of plasma over (Raider) ROY C. GRENIER's wounded body when a bullet shattered the bottle. I could have crapped my pants! We didn't get much to eat in those days. Priority for front line Marines was shoes and ammunition. Food and other goodies were gobbled up along the system as the supplies moved from ship to shore to the front. Over half of the company had been wiped out and the half that were left were sore, real sore! COL ALAN SHAPLEY, 2HQ retired our company for a few days to recuperate. I have a picture of him talking to us back in the rear area. He got replacements guys with only 3 or 4 months in the Corps, a bunch of lonely young draftees soon to die north of Naha.

Odd things happened to our G Company men. Demolition CPL KIB JACOBSON 4HQ, while blasting Jap caves with six pound packs of Composition C was blown up when his buddy, PFC DONALD B. LIEBERMAN, 4Hq, accidentally touched a cigarette to the fuse of the charge. GOTTSPONER took JAKE'S death real hard. I had to get a detail under LT GEORGE B. LAMBERSON'S 4O, and fill two stretchers with body parts to send to Graves Registration, otherwise the two would have been declared missing in action. The 1STSGT who replaced 1STSGT CHESTER D.HASH, 4CP, (KIA Okinawa), was killed in an unbelievable accident. The fighting was over, mopping up was in progress and we were awaiting a ship to take us back to Guam. This guy walked to the company mailbox in front of my shelter and I watched him drop a letter in the box and then fall to the ground dead. He was hit in the head by a stray bullet. Raider Corpsman THOMAS G. KRAEMER died trying get to a wounded Marine. A Japanese mortar round exploded on his helmet.
AUTHOR: Fran Hepburn was the Editor of the Raider Patch for many years. The Raider Patch has been a gold mine for military historians including myself. Thanks for all your hard work Fran!

4P FRANKLIN L. FERGUSON wrote, "I joined the 4th Raider Battalion as a replacement right after the New Georgia battles and when we became the 4th Marines, I was in G Company. Served at Emirau, Guam and Okinawa. I read the FRANCIS HEPBURN story and remember what a brave man CPL WHITEY CARR was. He made 2LT in the field. CAPT ARCHIE NORFORD died in my arms and we lost two other Captains. The company ended up in GUS GOTTSPONERS hands for the rest of the campaign. I was his Company Runner and I know how tough he was. Even shrapnel in his butt hardly slowed him down. Now for the rest of the story! Later when we landed South of Naha one night a Jap jumped into my foxhole right on top of me and bit me on the finger during our struggle. FRANCIS HEPBURN remembers me yelling my head off while my buddies brought me a knife to finish him off." I received the Purple Heart for that Jap finger bite, on Okinawa.

4P JOHN BARGER said, "I was wounded at Yonton, Okinawa on 19 May 1945, and taken to a first aid station with 2 rows of cots. Placed on a table to have shell fragments removed from my shoulder, I for some reason refused to take any morphine. As luck would have it, as the two doctors began to operate, the Japs chose to launch an air raid on the airfield with a plane landing and disgorging suicide troops in an effort to destroy as many planes as they could. When the air raid alarm sounded the two doctors rushed to their air raid shelters leaving me alone on the table. Had I taken morphine I would have been unable to get up and go back to the area where the Corpsman had treated me initially before taking me to the first aid station. My corpsman saved my life by applying several compresses to stop the flow of blood. I will be forever grateful to that unknown Corpsman and only wish I could find him to express my thanks." AUTHOR: It isn't unusual for a wounded Marine not to know or remember the name of the combat Corpsman who treated him, especially many years after it happened.

4 DQ REX G. GUYMAN, Price, UT sent the following information and on some of his former buddies. LLOYD KATH was my squad leader. He was shot in the liver on the last New Georgia patrol and evacuated to a hospital ship. He died two days later. I sent his personal effects to his parents. ALLEN D. HASKELL was from Gardiner, ME. As we were landing on Guam in the first wave, he was our PLSGT, and about 1,000 yards inland he was hit by gunfire. I helped evacuate him but never saw or heard of him again. RAYMOND C. WALLACE was a hard rock miner from Butte, MT. On Okinawa he was shot in the neck from behind the lines and evacuated. I did not hear of him again. CAIL A. PHILLIPS JR was a good friend of mine in the Raiders.

For a short time he was a runner for FATHER REDMOND. He later became 'BUM' PHILLIPS, Head Football Coach of the Houston Oilers." Patch 78.

NEIL P. STILES wrote, "in writing several buddies of the passing of WADE REAGAN, I remembered, THOMAS A. MOORE 4CP, fondly known as 'OLD TOM' as he was the youngest member of 1st Platoon. Our trails crossed again in Okinawa when we were both serving as Company GYSGTS in 3rd Bn 3rd Marines, 3rd MarDiv where OLD TOM was wounded. At the instant TOM got hit he was yelling to a squad member, 'GET YOUR ASS DOWN' and was shot clean through the mouth from left to right. NO bones or teeth were touched." Patch 78

2HQ&I. JAMES C. ALSOBROOK, "ran into an old Raider buddy EDWARD E. POWARZYNSKI 2BE. When Hq CO 2 BN broke up, I transferred to Hq Co, 1st BN. 4th Marines. On Okinawa, April 14, 1945 our Commanding Officer, MAJOR BERNARD W. GREEN and Father O'Neil were both KIA. I was a CPL Squad Leader at the time. My squad went back up the hill and recovered the bodies. We brought them back to the C.P. for FATHER REDMOND.

4 DQ JOHN H. McCORMICK (PhD) wrote "I clearly recall KENNETH E. BUSHYHEAD, Sand Springs, OK, he was pretty skillful and emphatic with both lefts and rights, when I called him a bad name. The old Bushmaster put a little crease in the bridge of my nose, which I still see when look in the mirror. JAMES F. BROWN was our SGT on Oknawa when he was KIA halfway up one of those miserable little ridges, Half Moon Ridge. We were held up for about an hour when JIM "COON ASS" BROWN said "We will, give it one more try'. He led the attack. He had taken about 30 steps when a Jap in a spider trap shot him under the chin. PAT W. ALMOND, Baton Rouge, LA, a BAR man poured 20 rounds into the Jap but it was too late for JIM.

FRANK A. ANDERSON. Portland, OR was our squad leader and I remember one night when BERNARD 'BEN' COLE and I got drunk while standing guard on the beer dump. ANDY was called on the carpet next day to explain all the midnight hilarity. One night on Okinawa, Motobu Peninsula, at sundown, we needed ammo, food and water. ANDY and I and dozen volunteers went back down that miserable hill about 2 miles where supply jeeps couldn't climb. When we started up once more, each man carried a case of .30 caliber ammo, and two five gallon cans of water or two cases of C-rations. We were exhausted when we staggered into our defense area.

ANDY and I shared the same foxhole and I took the first

watch. We alternated each hour. Sometime after midnight ANDY began to snore. Have you ever heard a jack-ass bray? A fog horn bellow on a lost ship? That was ANDY'S snore.

The Japs were close and. I was nervous and I woke him twice and he promised to stop but went immediately back to sleep and snored louder than ever. When I shook him awake again he grabbed his .45 stuck the barrel under my chin. It was not a gentle act. 'Goddamn you MOE', he emphasized with a jab. 'If you wake me one more time about this snoring crap, I'll blow your nose off. Just let me sleep he said.' I crawled out of our foxhole and slid under a bush a few yards away. In 30 seconds ANDY was snoring again. Suddenly there was a pop in front, a hand grendade blasted off, dark figures rushed through our line, as I let go with the BAR. From a hundred yards' behind us came the explosion of grenades, shots, a long burst of automatic rifle fire.

The firing spread up and down the line. Star shells popped overhead. Our 81mm mortars came to life and salvo of 105 shells hit several hundred yards ahead of us. IT WAS ONE MAGNIFICENT HULLABALOO. A half dozen infiltrating Japanese tried to reach our mortars and were blasted as they reached the defensive perimeter of the mortar platoon a hundred yards or so to our rear. I crawled over to see about ANDY. He was still asleep and snoring loudly. It was almost daybreak and I didn't disturb him."78 Patch

Corporal HUGH A. VOGEL, (Raider) was a reconnaissance non-commissioned officer of a 37-millimeter antitank platoon with Weapons Company, 4th Marines. Corporal Vogel was assigned the mission of observing enemy fire so that he might direct the fire of his platoon. In order to gain better observation, he coolly and unhesitatingly advanced beyond the front lines, heedless of personal danger from enemy heavy machine gun and mortar fire. While advancing he came upon an enemy dual purpose 13-millimeter weapon. He quickly killed the crew, captured the gun and turned it upon the enemy, destroying a mortar position and killing all members of the mortar crew. After the successful completion of this mission, he proceeded to attack two enemy held caves during the hours of darkness. Exhibiting superior skill and personal courage, he destroyed these caves with demolition charges, killing all enemy occupants.

PAUL J. REDMOND, Carmel, CA wrote, "I am sending you a picture on the death of Lt General Simon B. Buckner. Commanding General of the 10th Army on Okinawa. He was killed by shell fire while observing in the front lines. I was near the General when he was hit, and his Chief of Staff, BGen Elwyn D. Post, put me in charge of the burial detail. By jeep and 3 Cub planes the body escort detail flew back to the 1st Marine Division Chapel where the body was placed on a make shift catalfalque overnight. The next day when the Army claimed the body, I continued as escort and accompanied the body. The movie actor Bill Lundigan, the General's Aide and an Army Colonel and I flew the body to the Army Cemetery. Lt General Simon B. Buckner was the only American serviceman buried in a casket. The photo shows me helping to move the body from a jeep to one of the planes."

1AHQ EDWARD F. McCALL wrote, "I served at Emirau, Guam Okinawa & Occupation of Japan. I was WIA on Guam and hit with shrapnel in my wallet in my left hip pocket on Okinawa. I served with FATHER REDMOND in his burial detail. JOHN D. LEONETTI and I drove one of the trucks that picked up our dead comrades and took them to the burial site. We tried to bury each Marine individually but so many bodies came in so fast and the coral was too hard to break thru. Finally a bulldozer was called in to the burial site to speed up the operation. There were so many flies we had to get the dead underground to stop the spread of disease. The flies tried to eat us alive!

Hon Raider 6th Marine Division, Wiliiam C. Council, wrote, " I recently bumped into CPHM Frank Strickland who served as Corpsman in F4, 6th Division on Okinawa. Together we vividly recalled that midnight in Naha when a mine expoloded in the midst of a platoon of Marines killing two and resulting in Corpsman LYLE BRANDT and another Marine to suddenly become double amputees. Strickland worked in the darkness with skill and haste, then escorted the wounded to the beach where they were taken aboard a hospital ship. Those Corpsmen deserve so much credit for their great service."

4DQ PAT ALMOND, WIA on Okinawa, recalled, "Doctor Tessman rigged a foot pedalled dental drill on Epiritu Santo. That was the talk of the island."

AUTHOR: Our Raider Dentists were always busy.

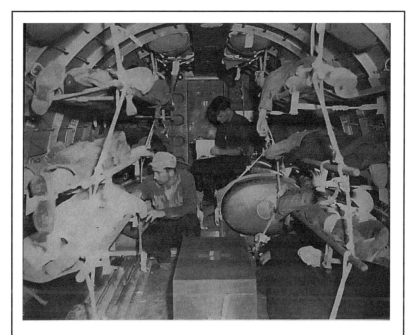

Air Evacuation of Wounded from Okinawa

Wounded Being Evacuated in a Higgins Boat from Okinawa

Japanese Suicide Boat Loaded With Explosives

Japanese Schoolgirls With Rifles

16

Landing On Japan's Shore

4th Regimental Combat Team Wades Ashore on Japan

OCCUPATION OF JAPAN

On 10 Aug 45 the Fleet Marine Force, Pacific, directed the 6th Marine Division to furnish a Regimental Combat Team to the 3rd Fleet for possible early occupation duty in Japan.

Japan accepted the Allies unconditional surrender terms on 14 Aug 45 and Admiral Halsey planned to begin the occupation of Yokosuka, Japan on 25 Aug. However, a threatening typhoon forced a postponement until 28 Aug.

The 4th Marine Regimental Combat team, (former Raider Battalions) assigned to occupation duty in Japan arrived at Guam on 20 Aug 45.

Following a delay ordered by General MacArthur, the first landing craft carrying elements of the 2nd Bn 4th Marine Regimental Combat team, (4th Raider Battalion), landed at Futtsu Saki to determine that the coastal guns and mortars had been rendered useless and re-embarked.

They were led by 4CP Raider Sgt Roger C. Spaulding who became the first Marine, and the first man in history to set foot in Occupied Japan.

OCCUPATION OF YOKUSUKA, JAPAN

Speculation was rife about a possible Japanese surrender following the second atomic bomb attack on Nagasaki. When surrender became a reality the momentous task of switching from an attack mode to that of an occupying force; presented enormous challenges to all forces, but in particular to the 4th Marines who had been training to spearhead the invasion of Japan.

Instead, they became the core group of Task Force A, in the preliminary plans for the landing force, drawn up by the III Amphibious Corps, on 11 August 1945.

Quartermaster officers were told that the force must be prepared to embark within forty-eight hours. This called for the complete re-outfitting of six thousand men, the correction of all equipment shortages (of which there were still many) and the preparation of plans for combat loading the seven ships that were to carry the force.

Operations officers had little opportunity to make advance plans; as the task force was organized only twenty-four hours before its headquarters left Guam. In those twenty-four hours intelligence officers hastily assembled maps and reports, while personnel officers filtered replacements received from the Transient Center, Marianas Area, to fill out the 4th with the six hundred men needed to come up to full strength.

Marine General Clement and the Headquarters unit of eleven officers and forty-two enlisted men left Guam on August 13 aboard USS Ozark to report to the commander of the Third Fleet.

Behind them aboard the transports there was nervous discussion of whether the Japanese surrender offer might not be one more trick. There was plenty of precedent for the idea that this was the case, and during the two weeks between the end of hostilities and the beginning of the occupation, there were brief flurries of fighting here and there across the Pacific.

This concern was well founded as Japanese documents described the total mobilization of the entire Japanese population. All students were assigned jobs in war plants or were preparing to become the future defenders of their homeland. Even the youngest grade school children were enrolled in programs in learning how to fight with sharpened bamboo sticks, swordsmanship, marksmanship and judo. There has never been any doubt in a Raiders mind; the entire population would have fought to the last man, woman and child if asked to do so by Emperor Hirohito.

There were thousands of caves located on hillsides surrounding the bay with guns pointed toward the water. Japan had over 6000 kamikazi airplanes remaining, many "human torpedoes rigged" and hundreds of suicide boats with their bows filled with dynamite.

Japanese officials asked for a delay because not all field commanders had received the cease-fire order. This allowed additional time for occupation force planning however, combat units were well aware of fake surrender tricks used by the Japanese in past battles. And there were isolated instances of local commanders ordering the killing of any prisoners under their control.

On August 16, twenty-four hours after the orders arrived ordering the end to the offensive against the Japanese, an escort ship reported sighting a torpedo wake across the bow of the Ozark at one thousand yards.

The battleships Iowa, Missouri and Wisconsin, with an array of carriers that included the Yorktown, Saratoga and Bon Homme Richard was far more reassuring to the landing troops than any number of apologies from the Japanese Emperor.

On August 18 Marine General Clement had already reported to Admiral Halsey aboard the Missouri where he discovered that the task force was to be built up almost to division strength by the addition of a provisional regiment of sea-going Marines.

The assembly and operations of the landing force presented some problems unique even in Marine experience. Only the 4th Marines and its reinforcing elements, with the Royal Marine Commando had been combat trained as units; supplies had been embarked for no more than the elements provided by the Sixth Division, and the diverse units had had no opportunity to work together. In fact, the units from the Fleet were not even formed into companies and battalions until after the breeches buoy transfer had taken place. They had no field radios

The transfer of the landing forces from their warships to eight transports took place at sea. Each transport had a warship on either side, steaming slowly ahead, while the 3,500 men were moved across by breeches buoy, the whole task was accomplished in just two days.

Modified orders were then given to the 4th Marines for their landing at Futtsu Saki, that included a landing by the reserve battalion of the 4th Marines; as soon as possible after daylight, three days prior to the formal surrender by the Japanese. As soon as this mission was completed the battalion was to re-embark in its landing craft and act as reserve for the main 4th Marines landing at Yokosuka Navy Yard.

Two underwater demolition teams were assigned to the mission. One to the British units for their island landings and the other to the 2nd Battalion of the 4th Marines for Futtsu Saki. The 2nd Bn was also was furnished a team of ten Navy gunners' mates to demilitarize the heavy coast defense guns on the peninsula.

The main landing was scheduled for August 30. On the 28th, General Clement and Admiral Badger aboard the USS San Diego proceeded into Tokyo Bay where they gave instructions to the commander of the Yokosuka Naval Base area and other officials.

The Japanese were directed to clear the landing areas of all personnel except skeleton maintenance crews. To demilitarize and mark all coast defenses and antiaircraft installations with white flags visible four miles at sea, to have Japanese officers and guides at the beach to meet the landing force, and to provide motor transport and other facilities to aid the landing troops.

On the morning of August 30, Task Force 31 entered Tokyo Bay through the pre-dawn darkness and the men on the decks wondered about the extensive fortifications that were said to saturate this area of Japan.

"Land the landing force", came the order at 0410 that morning, and the troops began scrambling down the sides of their transports into the landing craft. As the brightening day revealed details on Futtsu Saki 1,500 yards away, they could see the massive forts, with white flags flying over them as prescribed.

"I hope they mean it," remarked one Marine, as he surveyed the scene over the ramp of his LCVP. At 0550, the first American troops to set foot on Japanese soil, and the first foreign invaders ever to touch the Japanese mainland, reached shore. They were men of the 2nd Battalion, 4th Marines (4th Raider Bn) commanded by Major Frank Carney and led by SGT ROGER SPAULDING (4th Raider Bn, who first stepped ashore.

4CP ROGER C. SPAULDING wrote, "I, a Marine Raider first set foot in Japan, on 30 Sep 45, 3 days prior to the formal surrender on 2 Sep 45. The Marine Raiders both started the action against Japan and finished the action."

While two companies were seizing the main fort and

armory at the center of Futtsu Saki, the third company landed on the extreme tip of the peninsula and occupied the second fort. At both places caches of arms and ammunition were taken and Nipponese soldiers surendered meekly.

4CP FRANCIS HEPBURN wrote, "We landed in Japan in August 1945 where a Japanese Coastal artillery unit surrendered to us. They had stacked guns, ammo, grenades and knives as they had been ordered to, only their C.O. was still wearing his Samurai sword. GOTTSPONER using the muzzle of his carbine tapped the sword and motioned for it to be thrown in with the other swords on the ground. The face of that Jap turned as red as the bulls eye in the center of the rising sun flag. Boy was that Japanese mad!"

This seemed to be the answer to the question everyone on the transports had been asking. Whether the Japanese would fight or not, no one could yet be sure, and the Marines went energetically about their task of demolishing the powerful fortifications that would imperil shipping if the Japanese should change their minds.

Meanwhile at 0930 the 3rd Battalion (3rd Raider Bn) 4th Marines, commanded by Major Wilson B. Hunt, landed and occupied Yokosuka Naval Base without incident. Simultaneously the 1st Battalion (1st Raider Bn) under Lieutenant Colonel George B. Bell, seized Yokosuka Airfield and began demilitarizing the installations there.

As the Marines moved inland there was no resistance and no violence. Only a few Japanese were present, all wearing white armbands as instructed, to indicate they were essential to the maintenance and operation of public utilities. Guards were left at the warehouses and other installations, and the troops moved on through the Navy yard and across the airfield, checking guns to see that the breech-blocks had been removed and herding non-essential Japanese before them. The initial phase of the occupation was completed when the British forces seized three island forts in Surago Channel and landed on Azuma Peninsula.

General Clement and his staff came ashore at 1000 and established the landing force command post on the beach. They were met by a Japanese Navy captain, a Kempetai colonel, and a party of other officers who formally surrendered the area and received instructions as to what forms of cooperation were expected of them, with the warning that failure to cooperate would be severely dealt with.

The General then proceeded on to the old Headquarters

Building, where the U.S. flag was raised over the Naval base at 1015 with appropriate ceremony. The flag used was the same that had been raised by the First Provisional Brigade on Guam and by the Sixth Division on Okinawa. Following this occasion, Vice Admiral Totsuka, commandant of the naval base, was instructed to be present at 1030 to formally surrender the Tokyo Bay area to Rear Admiral Carney, Chief of Staffl to Admiral Halsey.

The actual ceremony took place at 1045 and it marked a memorable moment in Marine Corps history, the climax of the four years of Pacific fighting that began with the black days of Bataan and continued on and on through the horror filled days, months and years that followed.

On 6 September, the 4th Marines took over the entire naval base area and the sailors, sea-going Marines and British forces returned to their ships. It had become apparent by this time that the Japanese civilian authorities were sincere in their effort to cooperate.

English speaking Japanese (some of them former soldiers) accompanied the Marine patrols as interpreters as they penetrated inland, where many Japanese gazed at them in wonderment, not having heard of the surrender.

The liberation of the Allied prisoners provided many pleasant and stirring episodes. Among the famous Marines released by the occupation forces was Lieutenant Colonel James Devereux, who had commanded the Wake Island detachment that took so heavy a toll of Japanese before the island fell.

At Yokosuka 120 liberated members of the "Old 4th" Marines were brought down from Yokohama to meet the men of the "New 4th", who were mostly Raiders. The regimental band played while the liberated heroes of the Philippines sat down to a steak dinner, with the men who had carried on the name of their organization and General Clement shook hands with men he had last seen on Corregidor.

Tales of the horrors of Japanese imprisonment were exchanged for those of victories across the Pacific, and there was even Japanese beer to seal old and new friendships. Two half-brothers, one in the old regiment, one in the new, were joyously reunited after never expecting to see each other again. At the close of the dinner the New 4th held a formal guard mount and presented their regimental colors to the men of the Old 4th.

The 6th Marine Division, including a small contingent of the 4th Marines, (4th Raider Battalion) began landing at Tsingtao, China on 11 November 1945, and secured Tsaangkouas Airport as part of the occupying force in that area.

On 25 October 1945, the Japanese formally surrendered the Tsingtao garrison in Shantung to Major General Lemuel C. Shepherd.

798 MARINE RAIDERS WERE KILLED IN WW II

THE RAIDERS WERE IN THE MIDST OF THE FIGHTING FROM THE BEGINNING TO THE END OF THE WAR IN THE PACIFIC

THEY HAD BEEN BOTH THE FIRST TO ATTACK JAPANESE OCCUPYING FORCES IN STRENGTH ON TULAGI, THE LAST TO FIGHT THEM ON THE KILLING FIELDS OF OKINAWA, AND THE FIRST CONQUEROR'S IN THE HISTORY OF THE JAPANESE EMPIRE TO SET FOOT ON THE SACRED SOIL OF THEIR HOMELAND WHAT A FITTING TRIBUTE TO THE ELITE OF THE ELITE!

Marines Praying on Iwo Jima
Notice Buddies Standing Guard

Rescued Old China 4th Marine Regiment POW's

Destroying Japansese Weapons

17

Korea

Cpl. Mitchell Red Cloud, Medal of Honor
Former Raider Gave His Life in Korea

OFFICIAL MEDAL OF HONOR CITATION

Rank & Organization: Corporal, US Army, Co. E, 19th Inf Reg., 24th Inf Div. Near Chonghyon, Korea 5 November 1950. "Cpl. Red Cloud distinguished himself by conspicuous gallantry and intrepidity above and beyond the call of duty in action against the enemy. From his position on the point of a ridge immediately in front of the company command post he was the first to detect the approach of the Chinese Communist forces and give the alarm as the enemy charged from a brush-covered area less than 100 feet from him. Springing up he delivered a devastating point-blank automatic rifle fire into the advancing enemy. His accurate and intense fire checked this assault and gained time for the company to consolidate its defense. With utter fearlessness he maintained his firing position until severely wounded by enemy fire. Refusing assistance he pulled himself to his feet and wrapping his arm around a tree continued his deadly fire again, until he was fatally wounded. This heroic act stopped the enemy from overrunning his company's position and gained time for reorganization and evacuation of the wounded. Cpl. Red Cloud's dauntless courage and gallant self-sacrifice reflects the highest credit upon himself and upholds the esteemed traditions of the U. S. Army."

Red Cloud became the 8th Marine Raider to receive the Medal of Honor and the 28th Raider (26 Marine Raiders, 1 Raider Combat Corpsman and 1 Raider Doctor) to have a U.S. Navy Ship named after him.

Semper Fi Mitch, all Raiders were proud of you!

Many former Raiders distinguished themselves in Korea, where their combat experience in WW II proved helpful in training and leading troops with less experience into battle.

The deep cuts in Marine personnel following the war limited advancement in the Corps, so the Army and Air Corps proved attractive to many veterans. The Army of course was extremely happy to obtain the services of any available former Raider.

RAIDERS WHO LOST THEIR LIVES IN KOREA

CARROLL, DANIEL J.	EVANS, WILLIAM S.
HARRIS, RICHARD G.	LUSHER, LLOYD R.
NOURIE, RAYMOND L. *	RED CLOUD, MITCHELL
THOMAS, ROBERT H.	

* Raider Doctor

**FORMER RAIDERS AWARDED THE
NAVY CROSS IN KOREA**

YANCY, JOHN*
* Second Navy Cross Awarded

For the Raiders and their Corpsmen who fought together in the Pacific in WW II it is difficult to imagine the horrors faced by Allied troops fighting in North Korea and the Chosin Reservoir in 1950 with temperatures 30 and 40 degrees below zero. At that altitude the wind chill factor was two or three times the recorded temperature.

American and South Korean Forces Under U.N. Supreme Commander-In-Chief General MacArthur repulsed the North Korean invading force and captured the North Korean capital of Pyongang with other U.N. forces racing to the Yalu River. MacArthur ignored orders not to cross the Yalu and the Chinese Communists rushed nearly one half million troops into the assault.

Following the ambush of 7000 U.S. Army 2nd Division troops, they cut off the 1st Marine Division near the Choisin Reservoir.

In one of the most courageous actions in Marine Corps history the Marines fought out of the encirclement reaching Hungnam and were safely evacuated. They brought back all their dead, wounded and ill men, while suffering 7,500 casualties of which 50% were frostbite. It is believed they inflicted 40,000 casualties on the Chinese.

The troops, mostly Marines, fought 120,000 Chinese. 678 Fleet Marine Force Corpsmen lost their lives. 4 Corpsmen were awarded the Medal of Honor. Corpsmen and Doctors not only faced the daunting task of keeping the men on the line, but were also forced to take up arms in an effort to save their own lives.

They had to struggle with blood plasma that coagulated and froze causing many unnecessary deaths. Corpsmen had to place morphine syrettes in their mouths and under their arms so they remained useable.

Complete information on those killed and those receiving medals may never be known as the Marine Command destroyed all records when surrounded by wave upon wave of attacking Chinese. Many men deserving of medals never received them because of the lost records.

Reminiscent of Washington's troops at Valley Forge the Marines valiantly fought their way out of the encircling Chinese at Chosin. The half-frozen Marines walking or riding watched over their wounded and tied or loaded aboard the dead bodies of their buddies to trucks, jeeps, artillery or any piece of equipment that moved.

Those unfortunates who were overrun and captured faced cruel treatment from both the Chinese and North Koreans who failed to honor the Geneva Convention.

One such story is that of Billy Rivers Penn, MD. Billy is a neighbor of Raider Pat Almond who served with the Raider 4th Battalion. Pat convinced Dr. Penn to permit your author to excerpt portions of his manuscript written in 1995 at the request of General Barrow a former Commandant of the Marine Corps. His story shows why Marine Raider and Fleet Marine Force Combat Corpsmen were armed when going into combat with Japanese troops that failed to recognize the Geneva Conventions relating to unarmed non-combatants during WW II and continued throughout the Korean War.

I wish to thank Dr. Penn for providing a first hand account of his experience as a Fleet Marine Force (FMF) Combat Corpsman in Korea and his subsequent capture by the Chinese.

"I arrived in Korea on Friday the 13th in February 1953. During a mortar attack on our way forward, we were told to get away from our truck and we ran everywhere. When the attack was over, our driver discovered I was in the middle of a mine field and called the engineers to get me out of it.

We replaced a line company that had suffered 90% casualties when they attacked a Hilltop called Oongot. Being the only Corpsman, I had to go on both patrols that night. During another patrol I had a bad casualty I was trying to drag back when I ran into some Chinese so we both laid in the ditch that night for a long time. Finally Roscoe Woodward of Lucedale, MS came back for us. "Woody" had been wounded twice, but chose to stay in Korea rather that to go stateside.

Shortly after I was transferred to the 5th Marines 3rd Battalion H Company. One afternoon we got word they needed a Corpsman on outpost Vegas and I volunteered. I knew that Woody was already out there as a machine gunner. I went straight to the bunker and while inside I could hear someone calling for a Corpsman. While I was taking care of him two Chinese jumped me in the trench. The Chinese were all over us like ants.

One struck a bayonet through my left leg and when he couldn't get it out I saw his finger on the trigger and it clicked. We had been taught that if you ever bayoneted anyone and couldn't get it out to pull the trigger, so I knew I was about to lose a foot. Luckily I was an expert with a .45 Calibre pistol so I got it and shot him in the head. The Chinese ran up the hill while their artillery was still firing. Finally I was able to remove the bayonet from my foot and started pulling the Marine toward the command bunker.

I was then hit in the knee superficially with shrapnel, took a burp gun shot in the right shoulder, a through and through wound. I didn't really know about the shoulder until later when I saw how much blood I had lost. A bayonet glanced off my flak jacket and when I turned my elbow hit my enemy in the throat, he fell and I jumped on him hitting him until he no longer moved.

We were outnumbered by the Chinese troops and I picked up an entrenchment tool and started swinging. The way his body shook I thought I had decapitated him. Another of the enemy and I were in hand to hand combat on the ground with his bayonet over his head driving it toward me. I reached up and gouged out both of his eyes and remember seeing him running around screaming. When I got back to the bunker with another wounded Marine one of his eyes was still in my hand. I still have nightmares to this day, mostly of eyes staring at me!

Dead Chinese were all over and our machine gunners had really done a good job on the first wave. I was told the first wave attacked with weapons while the second wave was supposed to get theirs from the fallen first wave.

Everyone was in hand to hand combat. I saw Woody standing outside his bunker swinging his M2 like a baseball bat. I was going down the trench dragging a wounded Marine with my left hand and my medical bag in the right. A Chinese soldier jumped into the trench in front of me screaming loudly and charged me with his rifle and bayonet attached. I dropped my medical bag, reached for my .45 but couldn't get it out of the holster. He was almost on top of me when I grabbed my K Bar knife, got inside the thrust of his bayonet, and buried the knife in his stomach. His body fell off to the side and I grabbed the Marine and my medical bag and returned to the command bunker.

When I bent down to start out of the bunker again a rifle butt struck my helmet. Instinctively I raised my .45 and when it went off it was at the tip of my attackers nose. Backing into the bunker a satchel charge came in the door and all I remember was a big flash of white light.

I don't remember how long we were buried before the Chinese dug us out. When they did get me out of the bunker they put a bandage around my eyes and started pushing and shoving me for perhaps 300 yards into a tunnel. I realized they had tunneled up inside our outwire. When we came out into a large trench they put me in a truck with four or five wounded Marines or GI's and we were driven to a small area with several huts. We remained there for two to three days without food or water.

One Marine, Sammy Armstrong had a bad arm wound and I thought he was bleeding one night. I couldn't see but when I checked him I could smell gangrene. I tried to rouse the guards and they pushed me away, but took him away. I saw him later in a prisoner exchange without an arm.

We then were forced to walk for a day to an old abandoned mine and came across a wounded Army man. He couldn't walk and I couldn't see so we made a good pair. The Navy emblem on my Marine shirt really confused the Chinese. They thought I was a forward observer for the artillery or the big ships out there so I was in isolation for a long time. My isolation domain was a hole in the ground 5 1/2' long, 3' wide and 4' deep with several 2" x 12" boards about 1" apart covering the opening.

This turned out to be the camp head. I had received no medical treatment for my wounds and wore only a T-shirt, and fatigue pants with no shoes or socks. It was cold. My feet, toes, and fingers were black. My food ration was a very small handful of rice daily.

The brain washing started for me then. I was accused of germ warfare. After a few rifle butts to the head and body I told them I was from Mississippi and had a father, mother, and two brothers. After about four days of no sleep, being hit and kicked with rifles you learn to fake unconsciousness after the first rifle butt to your head or ribs.

Then started the 15 to 16 straight days of fake firing squads. They would take me out, go through "READY, AIM, FIRE, THEN CLICK". At the time I was hoping they would kill us. Once or twice they'd send a live round close to my head into the rock wall behind me in order to catch my attention.

We had a Chinese interrogator who graduated from the University of Illinois who we called "blood on hands" because he kept telling us we had Chinese blood on our hands. He informed us we had killed 5,000 Chinese. This was the first we knew of how well we had done. One time after a firing squad he informed me my father, brother, and brother were killed in a car wreck. I asked about my sister and he said she was killed also. I was angry and told him he was a liar as I had no sister. He called in some guards who held me down and pulled the nail from my right finger with a pair of pliers.

The wounds on my leg, knee and shoulder were healing. There were two Australians in our hut. One was a cook that supplied me with boiling water to pour on my wounds to remove the exudate. By the grace of God I had a tube of opthalmic ointment in my top pocket that I kept putting in my eye and my eyesight was returning, ·

There was a young Marine with a bad wound in our camp that had a tattoo of the American flag on his biceps. There was a tear in his shirt that he would pull away to unveil the flag to everyone - a beautiful sight - we even said the Pledge of Allegiance to our flag. We were beat every time they caught us doing it. Finally they took him and me to the firing squad routine, tied his hands behind him, put a gun to the base of his skull and executed him 3 feet away from me. God Rest His Soul!

One day we were placed in trucks and transported to Kaesong where we were held in an old Buddhist temple. We met other POW's there and were given clean bandages and clean clothing, none of which fit. We were told we were to be part of an exchange of sick and wounded POW's.

My name was finally called and we were taken to Panmunjon and Freedom Village. The first nurse I saw was an Army Lieutenant and boy was she pretty! She took the bandage from my right eye and I almost passed out. It was then I realized it must have been in pretty bad shape. I ran into another Corpsman who filled me in. Woody and most of the others were killed and they already had a memorial service for me.

My experience with the Marine Corps makes me very proud. Even today if they called me I would go back. Thank you General Barrow for encouraging me to do this. Maybe my feelings have been selfish in the past in not wanting to talk about what happened to me, but now I feel I can't let my comrades down by keeping silent. I pray for them all and hold them in my heart". B.R. Penn.

Former Raider 3K COL MARTIN J. "STORMY" SEXTON, served as Aide-de-Camp to the Commanding General in the initial year of the Korean War. In a letter to your author, COL SEXTON said, " The duty performed by Corpsmen and Doctors at the Chosin Reservoir in Korea was unbelievable!"

JOE BIBBY, 2nd Bn was one of many Raiders who later became Marine Pilots after serving with the Raiders. Bibby recalled being picked up after being shot down at Koto Ri, Korea, by a jeep that went down the road a piece and knocked over Lt. Col. Olin L. Beall, a former Raider, what a small world!

Another flyer was Raider Corpsman HAROLD McFANN JR. 1st Raider Bn who was also the first enlisted Corpsman awarded the Silver Star in the Solomon's during WW II. McFann returned to the U.S. and went on to earn his wings and became a Marine pilot. He was killed in a plane crash in 1943.)

4th Bn Raider JACK SHAFFER, became a fighter pilot after leaving the Raiders. He and I were friendly rivals in New Zealand, after having " fallen" for a lovely blonde lady on our one liberty in Auckland in 1943. Upon leaving the Marines Jack became a successful dentist in Tampa, FL where we both still attend the Raider Lunch Bunch meetings on a regular basis.

. 1LT JOHN YANCEY and SSGT DANIEL M. MURPHY, on 27 Nov 1950 in Korea tried desperately to hold the line against the advancing enemy troops. YANCEY'S E Co. was reduced o a platoon and the 2 A Co. platoons in this action had 40 KIA and WIA. Yancey was awarded a Navy Cross for a second time for his leadership and bravery in this attack.

1C CARL WILLIAM CLARK wrote, "I made it through WW II with a little shrapnel wound, but the North Koreans tried to take my head off. They only got one eye and most of my teeth, but what the hell, look at all I have left!"

2C Col Ross R. Miner wrote, " I participated as a CPL with the 2nd Raider Bn at Midway and Guadalcanal. Then I was commissioned and participated at Leyte, Luzon, Borneo, Consolidations of the Southern Philippines, Manila Bay, 3rd Fleet operation against Japan, four campaigns in Korea and four campaigns in Vietnam.

4HQ LTCOL ROY BATTERTON related the story of Hospitalman John E. Kilmer in Korea. Kilmer, though wounded, continued to treat his patients and was killed by a mortar shell while shielding a fellow Marine. For his heroism, he became the first of 4 Corpsmen to receive the Medal of Honor during the Korean War.

Patrol Moving up Mt. Suribachi

18

MARINE RAIDER ASSOCIATION EDUCATIONAL FUND

Honoring SgtMaj Sir Jacob Vouza

SgtMaj Sir Jacob Vouza

U.S. MARINE RAIDER ASSOCIATION EDUCATIONAL FUND FOR SOLOMON ISLAND NATIVE CHILDREN

For more than 30 years the Marine Raiders have continued to befriend the Solomon Island natives, in gratitude for their invaluable assistance during the Solomon Island campaigns. They fought beside us, carried our sick and wounded to safety, rescued hundreds of downed flyers and ship wrecked sailors, and generally helped us to survive in the war of attrition with the enemy.

The UNITED STATES MARINE RAIDER ASSOCIATION established the SGTMAJ JACOB VOUZA SCHOLARSHIP FUND in 1972. The Fund is believed to be the only fund established by any American military unit for such a purpose. The goal was to help with the secondary education of qualified SOLOMON

ISLAND children and to honor our many wartime native allies by establishing a Living Memorial in honor of all the brave SOLOMON ISLANDERS.

The fund was named after our old ally SgtMaj Vouza. He was a retired Native policeman who offered to serve under Coastwatcher Martin Clemens and was with him when their small band of natives marched down the beach to greet General Vandegrift and the Marines when they landed on Guadalcanal in August 1942.

While on a scouting mission Vouza was stopped and searched by Japanese troops. They found a small American flag he had hidden and tied him to a tree trunk and became torturing him for information. He was badly beaten and repeatedly bayoneted to the point they believed he was dead and left him still tied to the tree. He managed to free himself and somehow was able to crawl over 2 miles through the jungle to reach the Marine perimeter. Not expected to live this tough old islander confounded everyone and was back to work within several weeks time.

The Japanese were to pay dearly for their mistake. He quickly became a legend among his own people and the Marines as well. He helped train the Natives as scouts and as soldiers and recruited others as bearers for the allies.

As part of Carlson's 2nd Raider 30 day patrol behind the Japanese lines on Guadalcanal he performed bravely. The Raiders never forgot him nor did he forget them.

Vouza was awarded the British George Medal and the American Silver Star and lived to see his beloved Solomon Islands win their independence from Great Britain on 7 Jul 1978. He was Knighted, by the Queen of England on the Queen's birthday 8 Jun 1979. In his own words Sir Jacob Vouza said, "After I was discharged from hospital after bayoneted by Japs, I was do my fighting with the Japs and paid back all what they have done to me."

Except for one government High School and five government elementary schools, the education of Solomon Island's children has been left in the hands of the Churches. These dedicated groups have gone into the remote areas to set up small village schools capable of giving a basic education to the 1st Primary (Grades 1-4). The 2nd Primary (Grades 5—7) schools are fewer in number but together the Missions have about 400 of the Primary schools established. Two Mission High Schools now exist. About one student in a hundred receives the chance to go to High School.

Through competitive examinations, children that complete their primary education and desire a secondary education are helped by this fund if chosen.

Six Church Mission groups, and one school that inter-cooperates on education in New Georgia are the schools participating.

A worthy student has a choice of three High Schools. The families of many bright and talented children simply cannot raise the necessary money to pay for the tuition and room and board for a student.

In this manner, the Raiders continue to honor our many wartime native allies by establishing a Living Memorial in honor of all the brave SOLOMON ISLANDERS.

Since it's inception over 2,000 Solomon Island native children have been able to attend school because of the continued generosity of the Raider Association and their caring members. Over the same period the Raiders have shipped over 42 tons of school items, including books, furniture, school supplies and even bicycles that were shipped to Honiara, the Capitol City.

The continued assistance to the sons and daughters, grandchildren, great grandchildren and now great-great grandchildren of the native islanders who fought alongside the Raiders, enable them to see the strong bonds of friendship and love forged between their forefathers and the Raiders over those 60 long ago years!

In 1992 the Raider Association placed $52,000 in restricted funds in the Vouza Educational Fund; while continuing to donate another $2000 annually in memory of our gallant Solomon Island comrades. SgtMaj Vouza and the loyal Solomon Island Natives were there to help us when we needed it the most!

An indication of how deep that common bond between the native islanders and the Raider's, can be no more poignantly illustrated than what took place on Butaritari (Makin) Island, in early 1999.

The Army
Laboratory Hawaii (CILHI) recovery unit would have failed to discover the grave site of our nineteen 2nd Battalion Raiders killed in action at Makin Island, during the famous raid on the island from submarines on 17 Aug 1942, without the help of Mr. Tokarei Bureimoa.

Prior to boarding the submarines COL CARLSON had given the island Chief some gold coins to see that the Raiders who were killed in action had a decent burial. Mr. Bureimoa a native islander, a youngster of 16, was forced by the Japanese to help bury the Raiders following the raid. He was instrumental in pointing out the location of the mass grave to CILHI members, in their 1999 search for the remains.

The most astonishing thing concerning Mr. Bureimoa was that during the official ceremony to place the remains aboard planes for a flight to Hawaii, he was able to "sing the entire MARINE HYMN" while standing at attention. How he had learned the words, nobody seemed to know!

Mr. Bureimoa has since died and the U.S. Marine Raider Association has honored him by placing a plaque with his name at the burial site.

"May we one day meet this loyal Friend once again in Heavens Gates"!

Young Vouza at Guadalcanal

19

Raider Museums
Located at Richmond, VA and MCRD San Diego

Raider Museum in Richmond, Virginia
From left: Robert Buerlein, George MacRae, 3K, Curator

The two museums are dedicated to the United States Marine Raiders of World War II and offer a fascinating look at the two-year existence of the four Raider battalions. Both are testaments to the devotion, courage and patriotism of the members of all four battalions.

The museum in Richmond, Virginia was the first. It is filled with memorabilia, artifacts, weapons, equipment, photos and history of teh Raider Battalions of World War II. It is privately endowed and supported by the United States Marine Raider Association.

The second museum established to honor those brave and tenacious warriors of 1942-1944 is located in San Diego, California. It is appropriately called "The Raider Room" and is within the confines of the Command Museum, Marine Corps Recruit Depot, San Diego. It is part of the Marine Corps history and museum system.

Both museums contain thousands of unique and rare historical items donated by former Raiders. New items are continually arriving for future display.

The U. S. Marine Raider Association is vigorously pursuing two other major sites for additional exhibits to provide maximum exposure to the American people, of the Marine Raiders, especially to the younger generations and future Marines.

The Raider Room at MCRD, San Diego is part of each recruits training. They spend a specific amount of time at the museum, including the Raider Room. Under the guidance of local retired Marines, they listen intently and are encouraged to ask questions about these Marine warriors of long ago. It is a tremendous addition to their already detailed and rigorous training program.

At these two Raider museums, the heritage, legacy and history of these magnificent warriors of World War II live on.

Raider Museums

Located at Richmond, VA and MCRD San Diego

Raider Museum, MCRD San Diego
From left: Harry Reynolds, 2BHQ, John McCarthy,
and Howard "Buck" Stidham, 2AG

The photo on the previous page shows Robert Buerlein, President of the American Historical Foundation and Honorary Raider and, at right, George MacRae, 3K, Assistant Curator of the Richmond, Virginia Raider Museum. They are shown posing with the museum's most unique tribute. The Honor Doors behind them contain the names of all known Raiders who served in one or more of the four Raider Battalions.

In the photo above, three hard workers who helped put together the Raider Room at MCRD, San Diego are shown. From left are Harry Reynolds, 2BHQ, John McCarthy, Raider Patch Editor and Howard "Buck" Stidham, 2AG. The hand-carved Raider logos between them are impressive. This Raider tribute was entirely put together by Raider veterans with the guidance of the Command Museum officials.

RAIDER PATCH AND RAIDER WEB SITES

Marine Raiders are justifiably proud of the their history. Their official publication, the Raider Patch has told the story of their exploits for over 50 years. The Raiders have also established two Web Pages that may be accessed by those who wish to learn more of this Elite Marine unit, who pioneered the military tactics used in modern combat to this day.

The Official U.S. Marine Raider Web Site (Home Page shown below), may be accessed at:
http://www.usmarineraiders.org/index2.html

Special Edition for the 21st Century
RAIDER PATCH
Official Publication of the United States Marine Raider Association

ACCEPT OUR INVITATION TO LEARN THE HISTORY, LEGEND AND LEGACY OF THE WORLD WAR II
UNITED STATES MARINE RAIDERS
Who Successfully Engaged the Japanese in the Following Battles:
Midway Island, Tulagi Island, Makin Island
Guadalcanal: Tasimboko Raid, Edson's Ridge,
First Matanikau River, Second Matanikau River,
Asamana, Mount Austen, Russell Islands, Wickham
Anchorage (Vangunu), New Georgia: Segi Point, Viru
Harbor, Enogai Inlet, Bairoko Harbor, Bougainville: Empress
Augusta Bay, Puruata Island, Piva Trail, Koiari Raid.
Sponsored by the:
U.S. MARINE RAIDER ASSOCIATION
A National non-profit organization supporting scholarships in the United States and Solomon Islands, the Raider Museum in Richmond, Virginia and the Raider Room in the Command Museum, Marine Corps Recruit Depot, San Diego, California.

Our Official Publication was initially named the U.S. Marine Raider Bulletin in April 1953. The first Raider Patch in color was, published in October 1956.

The Raider Patch has been most fortunate in having

many hard working Editors over the last 50 years. Their goal of helping to keep the Raider legacy alive while providing a forum to help all Raiders remain close friends throughout their lifetimes, has proven eminently successful.

The Official Raider website is the brainchild of Raider Ervin Kaplan MD. Dr.Kaplan initiated the planning for the project, and enlisted the support of Andrew and Luciana Young, The Youngs, are contributing their web design skills in honor of Andrew's father, the late James L. Young Jr. of Houston, Texas, who served with the Marine Raiders, and the 6th Marine Division.

There is also an independent Raider website, set up by 4th Marine Raider Dan Marsh in February 1998, and located at: http://www.usmcraiders.com/index.html

Dan's son Louie Marsh, the webmaster, was recently appointed to the Raider "shadow" Board of Director's.

This group of Honorary and Associate Raider Members are making preparations to assume leadership of the Marine Raider Association; at an appropriate time in the near future.

Thank you Patch Editors, past and present, Dan Marsh, Louie Marsh, Dr. Kaplan, Luciana Young, Andrew Young, John McCarthy, the Members, Officers and Directors of the Raider Association!

Because of your hard work and support, the Raider children, grandchildren and Associates, have the Raider Patch and two Raider web sites to draw support from, in their goal to preserve the legacy of the U.S. Marine Raiders of World War II.

BIBLIOGRAPHY

The War With Japan Parts 1, 2 and 3. (Restricted)
U. S. Military Academy

Solomon Islands Campaign, Restricted
Office of Naval Intelligence

War Crime Trial Admiral Abe, et al
U.S.Navy

Chicago Daily Tribune
Gowran, Clay

Chronology U.S. Marine Corps
HQ USMC

History USMC Operations in WWII
HQ USMC

History Medical Dept,USN WWII
U.S. GPO

Those Who Served
Beau, Jerome J.C.MajUSMC

Marine Raider Historical Handbook
Sexton, Martin Col. USMC

Raider Patch
Bulger,Hepburn,Sexton,et al

Bless 'em all
Peatross,Oscar F. MajGenUSMC

Marine Raiders
Turner Publishing

Our Kind of War
Rosenquist,Buerlein,Sexton

Edson's Raiders
Alexander,JosephCol USMC

A Special Valor
Wheeler, Richard

Marines in WWII,Commorative Ser
USMC Historical Center

From Makin to Bougainville
Hoffman, JohnT. USMCR

History of 4th Marines
HQ USMC

History of 6th Marine Division
HQ USMC

Manuscript
MacCrae. George

Manuscript
Bowen, Stanley

Manuscript
Penn, Billy Rivers , MD

Lonely Vigil
Lord,Walter

The Coast Watchers
Feldt, Eric A

US Naval Operations in WW II
Morison,Samuel E.

The Battle for Guadalcanal
Griffith,S.B.,II.BGen.USM

Marines in the Central Solomons
HQ USMC

History of Chaplain Corps USN
Drury, Clifford M.

Special Marine Corps Units WW II
HQ USMC

Navajo Code Talkers
Aaseng, Nathan

Marines in the Central Pacific
Rentz

Handbook of the Hospital Corps
        USN Hospital Corps

Manual of the Medical Department
        USN

Tennozan
        Feifer, George

Tarawa
        Weinstein, Irving

Marine Combat Correspondent
        Stavisky, Samuel E.

Development USN Amphib Tactics
        Smith,H.M.General USMC

USMC Web Sites
        USMC Historical Center

USMC Official Photographs WW II
        USMC Historical Center

Department of Defense Photographs WW II, Korea
        US Department of DefenseHQ, USMC

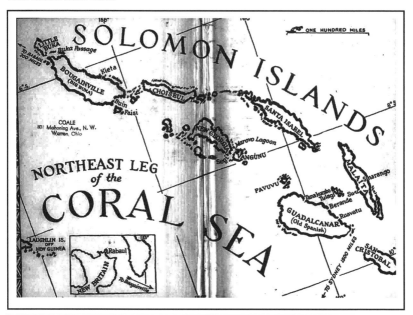

Demolition Charge Being Lowered
To Destroy Japanese in Cave

Index

Symbols

A

I

J

K